C000172133

RUSSIA
IN THE
NINETEENTH CENTURY

The New Russian History

Series Editor: Donald J. Raleigh,
University of North Carolina, Chapel Hill

This series makes examples of the finest work of the most eminent
historians in Russia today available to English-language readers. Each
volume has been specially prepared with an international audience in
mind, and each is introduced by an outstanding Western scholar in
the same field.

RUSSIA
IN THE
NINETEENTH CENTURY

AUTOCRACY, REFORM, AND SOCIAL CHANGE, 1814-1914

Alexander Polunov

Edited by **Thomas C. Owen**
and **Larissa G. Zakharova**

Translated by **Marshall S. Shatz**

Routledge
Taylor & Francis Group

LONDON AND NEW YORK

First published 2005 by M.E. Sharpe

Published 2015 by Routledge
2 Park Square, Milton Park, Abingdon, Oxon OX14 4RN
711 Third Avenue, New York, NY 10017, USA

Routledge is an imprint of the Taylor & Francis Group, an informa business

Copyright © 2005 Taylor & Francis. All rights reserved.

No part of this book may be reprinted or reproduced or utilised in any form or by
any electronic, mechanical, or other means, now known or hereafter invented,
including photocopying and recording, or in any information storage or retrieval
system, without permission in writing from the publishers.

Notices
No responsibility is assumed by the publisher for any injury and/or damage to
persons or property as a matter of products liability, negligence or otherwise,
or from any use of operation of any methods, products, instructions or ideas
contained in the material herein.

Practitioners and researchers must always rely on their own experience and
knowledge in evaluating and using any information, methods, compounds, or
experiments described herein. In using such information or methods they should
be mindful of their own safety and the safety of others, including parties for
whom they have a professional responsibility.

Product or corporate names may be trademarks or registered trademarks, and
are used only for identification and explanation without intent to infringe.

Library of Congress Cataloging-in-Publication Data

Polunov, A. Iu. (Aleksandr Iur'evich), 1966–
   Russia in the nineteenth century : autocracy, reform, and social change, 1814–1914 / by
Alexander Polunov ; [translated by Marshall S. Shatz].
       p. cm. — (The new Russian history)
   Includes bibliographical references and index.
   ISBN 0–7656–0671–2 (cloth : alk. paper) — ISBN 0-7656-0672-0 (pbk.   )
      1. Russia—History—1801–1917. I. Title. II. Series.

DK189.P64 2005
947.'07--dc22   2005007919

ISBN 13: 9780765606723 (pbk)
ISBN 13: 9780765606716 (hbk)

Contents

List of Illustrations

Except where noted, the illustrations herein are reprinted from *Tri veka* (Three Centuries), a multi-volume illustrated collection published in Moscow by I.D. Sytin in 1912 to commemorate the tercentenary of the Romanov dynasty. The first of the three Gorshield engravings that appear in Chapter 3 are reprinted from *Russkii arkhiv*, 1869, no. 4 ("The Surrender of Shamil") and from *Russkii khudozhestvennyi listok Vilgelma Timma*, 1860, no. 9 ("The Murids") and 1859, no. 33 (Prince Aleksandr Ivanovich Bariatinsky). The portraits of Alexander II in Chapter 4, Count Loris-Melikov in Chapter 7, and General Skobelev in Chapter 8 are from the State Archive of the Russian Federation (GARF) while the portraits of Nicholas Miliutin in Chapter 4 and Dmitry A. Miliutin in Chapter 8 are from the Manuscript Division, Russian State Library.

Foreword

Larissa Zakharova

The author of this book, Alexander Polunov, is a young Russian historian whom I know well. He was my student both as an undergraduate and in graduate school, and we have continued to work together without interruption. Polunov received his professional training in the late 1980s and the early 1990s. These were critical years in which the Soviet Union disintegrated and the Soviet system and the Communist regime collapsed. Three years after graduating from Moscow State University in 1989, Polunov completed his graduate studies and defended his candidate's dissertation. It formed the basis of his book *Under the Rule of the Supreme Procurator: Church and State in the Era of Alexander III*, published in 1996.

Polunov carries on the tradition of Professor Petr Zaionchkovsky in Soviet historiography and rightly considers himself a member of Zaionchkovsky's school. He has also been able to take advantage of the new opportunities in research and teaching that became available to his generation. Fluent in English and with a reading knowledge of French and German, he has kept abreast of new research and approaches to history and is well-versed in contemporary Russian and world historiography. He has held visiting appointments in the United States at the Harriman Institute of Columbia University and the Kennan Institute for Advanced Russian Studies, and at the Maison des Sciences de l'Homme in Paris. He has participated in international conferences and received grants and prizes from international scholarly organizations.

The idea of writing this book grew out of Polunov's teaching and scholarly interests. At Moscow State University he has taught comprehensive survey courses on Russian history from ancient times to the present, while focusing his research on the imperial period. The book covers one century of

Russian history, the hundred years that elapsed between two wars with far-reaching consequences for Russia, the Patriotic War of 1812 and World War I. The author addresses one of the fundamental questions of Russian history: what caused the social and political upheaval that destroyed the age-old foundations of tsarist Russia and led to its collapse?

The major event of the twentieth century, the revolution of 1917, initiated the formation of the Soviet regime; its fall ushered in the current era of Russian history. Unless we examine the history of the last century of Imperial Russia, it is difficult to understand the Russian Federation's complex, contentious, and painful development since the collapse of the USSR. Many aspects of contemporary Russian life bear obvious similarities to problems that faced the country in the nineteenth and early twentieth centuries. Those similarities impel us to take a new look at Russia's past so as to understand the events of the present. As the historian Vasily Kliuchevsky succinctly put it, "We must study the past not because it is receding but because, as it recedes, it leaves its consequences behind."

Polunov regards the abolition of serfdom in 1861 and the reforms that followed it as the determining events of nineteenth-century Russia. Although the Great Reforms of the 1860s and the 1870s did not bring about a sharp break with the past in all areas of public life, they laid the foundations for such a break and precluded a return to pre-reform practices. The reforms undermined a basic principle of Russian life, that progress was linked with serfdom. Russia's modernization proceeded on a new basis of free labor, private initiative, and the emergence of a civil society. In this respect, 1861 marks the turning point from which "a new history, a new era begins in Russia," as many contemporaries interpreted the abolition of serfdom and as many historians have agreed. Polunov makes clear the organic connection between the Great Reforms and Russian socio-economic and political developments in the first half of the nineteenth century, as well as their similarity to liberal reforms in the European countries, from which they sometimes borrowed.

Polunov points out the shortcomings of Alexander II's later reforms, especially in the agricultural sphere, financial policy, and the creation of a new court system. He demonstrates, however, that the reforms were by no means unsuccessful. The foundations of a state based on the rule of law began to arise, industrialization grew rapidly, and by the end of the nineteenth century the financial system was strong enough to permit convertibility of the ruble. The author argues convincingly that the "old regime" at the beginning of the twentieth century was not doomed. Contending forces pulling in different directions, and the conflict between the government and society, determined its fate. Russia's participation in World War I precipitated the revolutionary outcome.

Polunov's attention to socio-economic developments does not mean that he neglects other areas of history. The book covers the basic trends in Russian foreign policy, the organization of the imperial state, the emergence of ethnic issues, and the rise of the liberal and revolutionary movements. The author provides a full picture of the country's life in the last century of the tsarist regime and shows how the various elements of the historical process interacted.

A virtue of the book is its introduction, which provides an overview of Russian history from ninth-century Kievan Rus to the war against Napoleon. Its conclusion is also valuable, culminating in a description of the challenges that face post-Soviet Russia.

Polunov's book successfully synthesizes Russian and Western scholarship on Imperial Russia and supplements existing knowledge with his own archival research. It will interest anyone who wishes to learn about Russia's past and to understand the historical context from which present-day Russia has emerged.

Foreword

Thomas C. Owen

To inform English-speaking audiences of current trends in Soviet scholar-ship, M.E. Sharpe, Inc., publishes several quarterly journals of translations, among them *Soviet Studies in History*, begun in 1962 and renamed *Russian Studies in History* in 1992. During the late 1980s, in the era of perestroika (restructuring of the Soviet system) and glasnost (open discussion), Donald J. Raleigh, an American historian of the early Soviet period who edited the journal from 1979 to 1994, recognized the need to produce a series of books in English by Russian experts on Russian and Soviet history.

Ten such books appeared between 1993 and 2002 in the New Russian History series, published by M.E. Sharpe and edited by Raleigh. Drawing information from documents in newly opened archives and writing freely, unhindered by Soviet censorship, the authors offered fresh interpretations of neglected aspects of Russian and Soviet history from the reign of Peter the Great (d. 1725) to the mid-1950s. The subjects included the status of women, the personalities of the most important Romanov emperors and empresses, the career of one of Joseph Stalin's closest economic advisers, the chronic shortage of consumer goods under the five-year plans, relations between the Soviet state and the Russian Orthodox Church, and the functioning of the prison system (Gulag). Alexander Polunov's book on the Russian Empire between 1814 and 1914, in Marshall S. Shatz's precise and elegant transla-tion, completes the New Russian History series.

Polunov not only demonstrates a mastery of current trends in Russian and American scholarship but also examines the legacy of the tsarist and the Soviet autocracies in our time. His interpretation of the last century of impe-rial rule marks a sharp break with Soviet-era histories of the late Russian

Empire. Rather than view the events from the Napoleonic Wars to World War I as the prehistory of the allegedly socialist revolution of 1917, he examines the decay of the two major institutions of the empire—serfdom and autocracy—from an essential liberal and democratic standpoint. An undercurrent of tragedy pervades Polunov's analysis of the social psychology of the major social groups in Russian society under the last emperors, from serfs and priests to merchants, landowners, and bureaucrats. His account helps to explain why the tsarist government successfully resisted fundamental change at crucial moments in the nineteenth century and why a reformist, evolutionary path did not become an alternative to the Bolshevik Revolution. The moral and political dramas described by Polunov have lost none of their relevance. The struggle between militarism and authoritarian rule on the one hand and humanitarianism and the rule of law on the other persists in the post-Soviet era as well.

Readers interested in the recent work of Russian historians of Russia and the Soviet Union will find more fascinating material in the journal *Russian Studies in History* and in *After the Fall: Essays in Russian and Soviet Historiography,* edited by Michael David-Fox, Peter Holquist, and Marshall Poe (Bloomington: Slavica, 2004).

Preface and Acknowledgments

During the twentieth century Russia endured shock waves rarely equaled in world history. The collapse of the monarchy and the coming to power of the Bolsheviks, the formation and consolidation of the Soviet regime, and that regime's fall at the end of the century were not only milestones of Russian history but profoundly affected the world as a whole. We cannot understand these events without analyzing their origins, above all in the nineteenth and early twentieth centuries.

In historical perspective, the question of origins presents us with a peculiar paradox. The nineteenth century differed from the twentieth both in its character and in its orientation. What made Russia's historical experience so distinctive? The establishment of local self-government and an independent judiciary, the development of a market economy, and the inception of a multi-party parliamentary system hardly seemed to foreshadow the events that would take place in the following decades. How did the movement toward a civil society and a state based on the rule of law even become possible in a country that lacked firm democratic traditions? What were the roots of the government's successful reforms "from above" in the nineteenth century, and why were they unable, in the last analysis, to prevent the fall of the monarchy? Was the revolution at the beginning of the twentieth century inevitable?

To answer these questions, I focus on the economic and social spheres, including the abolition of serfdom, the development of private property, the establishment of market relations, and the role of the state. Other aspects of Russian history, such as ideological conflict, cultural affairs, and relations among ethnic groups, also deserve attention, of course. They are reflected here, but I believe that the success or failure of the fundamental social reforms enacted at the center of the Russian state determined events in these other spheres.

The main purposes of this book are to trace developments in society and the governmental apparatus that gave rise to the reforms; to assess the significance of the various factors that influenced the way the reforms were implemented, such as foreign affairs and individual personalities; and to analyze the far-reaching impact of the reforms on the economy, society, and relations among ethnic groups. To do this, I present the work that has been done on the reforms in Russian historiography since the collapse of the USSR and synthesize it with Western scholarship and with my own research.

Acknowledgments

I would like to express my thanks to all those whose help I received in the preparation of this book. The book would not have been possible without the careful editorial assistance, advice, and support of my teacher, Larissa Georgievna Zakharova. My participation in Professor Zakharova's seminar, the defense of my dissertation, which she supervised, and our subsequent collaboration over the years have been major milestones in my development as a professional historian. The conception and thematic content of the book took shape in large part under the influence of Professor Zakharova's work. I have drawn particularly on her research on the abolition of serfdom. I am grateful also to my colleague Dr. Valery L. Stepanov, on whose work I relied in the chapter on the socio-economic development of post-reform Russia. Andrei V. Mamonov gave me invaluable assistance in selecting the illustrations.

As the book is intended for an international audience, I could not have written it without the help of colleagues in the United States. In planning the book and through all the stages of its composition I received the unfailing support of Professor Donald J. Raleigh, the editor of the New Russian History series. Don was attentive and tactful in dealing with the problems that inevitably arise in writing a work on a broad topic, especially under the difficult circumstances of present-day Russia. The thoughtful and scrupulous advice of Professor Thomas Owen helped me to formulate many of the book's concepts and conclusions more precisely and to make it more accessible to non-Russian readers. Professor Marshall Shatz's translation conveys not just the letter but the spirit of the text. I hope that the publication of this book, which is devoted to one of the most important periods in the history of Russia, will draw Russian and Western historical scholarship closer together and thereby contribute to greater understanding between our two nations.

RUSSIA
IN THE
NINETEENTH CENTURY

Introduction

At the end of the eighteenth century and in the first decades of the nineteenth, Russia confronted the need to change the institutions that lay at the very foundation of its way of life: autocracy and serfdom. Similar changes were taking place at this time in Central Europe, particularly in Austria and Prussia. The Napoleonic Wars had dealt these countries a heavy blow, and they realized that they had to adjust to a world that was rapidly changing in the aftermath of the Great French Revolution. Its similarity to Europe notwithstanding, however, the development of the Russian Empire was marked by a significant difference: the abolition of serfdom took place only in the middle of the nineteenth century, and the revolutions of 1830 and 1848 completely passed Russia by, helping to turn it into a bulwark of European conservatism. These distinctive features, which profoundly affected the country's future, were in turn determined by its past.

Russian history abounded in radical changes. As a result, by the beginning of the nineteenth century the Russian political and social system was riddled with deep contradictions. Russia combined enormous military power with social and economic backwardness, and its backwardness frequently served as the basis for its power. "A country of facades," was the scathing comment of the Marquis de Custine, a Frenchman who visited Russia in 1839. Fifteen years later, future Minister of Internal Affairs Petr Valuev drew the following conclusion from Russia's defeat in the Crimean War: "Take a look at some piece of government business, examine it closely, separate its essence from the paper that encases it . . . and rarely will you find any solid benefit. All is splendid on the surface but rotten underneath."[1]

To be sure, we may not want to trust the critical opinions of a foreigner or to believe a high official who was rising to the pinnacle of his career by criticizing the previous regime's failures. But we also have the opinion of a man whom it would be hard to suspect of harboring an excessively critical attitude: Russia "can be compared to a harlequin's costume, the many-colored pieces of which have been sewn with a single thread and hold together splendidly. That thread is autocracy. Pull it out, and the costume will fall apart."[2] That was the view of Leonty Dubelt, a high-ranking secret-police official in the reign of Nicholas I (1825–55). What was the origin of that "thread," autocracy? Why would the entire Russian political and social system inevitably collapse without it?

The roots of Russia's distinctive historical character go back to the early Middle Ages, when tribes of Eastern Slavs began to colonize the vast expanses of the East European plain. Features of the land and climate—severe winters, a short summer growing season, poor soil, and distance from the seas—left a deep imprint on the country's development. "Historically, of course, Russia is not Asia," wrote the eminent Russian historian Vasily Kliuchevsky, "but geographically it is not Europe, either . . . Its culture has joined it inseparably to Europe, but nature has imposed characteristics and influences on it that have always attracted it to Asia, or attracted Asia to it."[3]

The "attraction of Asia to Russia" led to attacks by nomadic peoples of the steppe region, which adjoins the East European plain in the southeast and links it directly to the expanses of Central Asia. The pressure exerted by the nomads became one of the causes of the disintegration of Kievan Rus, the Eastern Slav state that existed from the middle of the ninth century to the middle of the thirteenth. The decline and collapse of this state, which encompassed the territory from the Baltic Sea to the Black Sea, created a political vacuum that facilitated the expansion of the Eastern Slavs' neighbors, both from the east and from the west. In the first half of the thirteenth century the knights of the Teutonic and Livonian orders seized the Baltic coast, impeding Rus's access to the sea and intensifying its religious alienation from the West. The knights advanced under the rallying cry of spreading the influence of the Catholic Church, posing a threat to Orthodox Christianity, which Rus had adopted from Byzantium in 988. The struggle for access to the sea—not only with the Livonian Order but also with Sweden, which posed a menace from the north—would become one of the leitmotifs of Russian foreign policy for many centuries.

The "struggle for the land" was as vital for Russia as the "struggle for the sea." When Kievan Rus disintegrated, a considerable portion of its lands in the thirteenth, fourteenth, and fifteenth centuries fell under the rule of a dynamic young state, the Grand Duchy of Lithuania. This distinctive Slavic–Baltic federation, in which the population of the former Kievan Rus formed an absolute majority, preserved many of the practices of the Kievan state.

The nobility enjoyed significant political privileges in relation to the ruler, the upper strata of society participated in the legislative process, the separate parts of the state had autonomy, and there were elements of municipal self-government.[4] Distinctive Ukrainian and Belorussian cultural and ethnic traditions developed among the Eastern Slavs in the lands of the Grand Duchy of Lithuania. After the unification of Lithuania and Poland into a single commonwealth in the mid-sixteenth century, those traditions came under the strong influence of Western culture. A sizable part of the local nobility converted to Catholicism, while the common people continued to profess Orthodoxy. Although a strengthened Russian state seized the eastern part of Ukraine from the Commonwealth in the middle of the seventeenth century, the Ukrainian lands long remained an alien body within Russia and a constant source of internal problems.

The situation in the seventeenth and eighteenth centuries was complicated still further by the difficulty of confining Russian expansion to the Ukrainian and Belorussian lands. In the open spaces of the East European plain it was practically impossible to stay within any natural boundaries, and conflict between states often led to mutual annihilation. Russia annexed Belorussia, Lithuania, and the western part of Ukraine in the second half of the eighteenth century, and central Poland at the beginning of the nineteenth. As a result, the ethnic diversity of the Russian state grew steadily. Russians (that is, Great Russians) constituted about 90 percent of the country's population at the end of the sixteenth century, but their share had fallen to less than 50 percent by the beginning of the nineteenth century.[5]

What took place in the Middle Ages in the northeastern lands, the part of Kievan Rus that became the cradle of the Russian state? What factors influenced the formation of the Russian (Great Russian) nationality? The most important was the Tatar–Mongol invasion of Rus in the mid-thirteenth century, followed by more than two centuries of rule by the Golden Horde, the state that the Mongols founded in the steppes of Eurasia.

The role of the Mongol invasion in Russian history has always been a subject of sharp debate, particularly in those periods when Russia faced a choice between West and East. At the beginning of the 1920s a group of émigré historians, journalists, and sociologists formed a movement called "Eurasianism." The Eurasianists saw Russian national character as a product of the Mongol invasion. The sociologist Nikolai Trubetskoi claimed that the Mongols brought with them to Rus a "Turanian personality type," characterized by a spirit of self-sacrifice, scorn for material possessions, a striving for the common good over that of the individual, and a readiness to subordinate oneself to a single strong authority.[6] Those qualities, the Eurasianists maintained, had allowed Russia to stand its ground in historical combat with its enemies, while the Ukrainians and Belorussians had lost their historical distinctiveness by submitting to the influence of Western culture.

Were the Eurasianists right or wrong in their assessments of Russia's history and its interactions with other parts of the Slavic world and Western culture? Certainly, there is a good deal in their doctrines that merits attention. The domination of the Horde actually fostered the consolidation of princely power in northeastern Rus; and in some regions, such as Novgorod, it did not have a destructive impact. The ability of the nomadic Mongols to exert influence on heavily forested Rus was limited. Nevertheless, on the whole the invasion of the Horde was a disaster for Rus. This was reflected in the numerous eyewitness accounts by contemporaries: church writings, chronicles, popular songs and tales. "What punishments have we not received from God!" exclaimed Serapion, the bishop of Vladimir and a prominent religious figure of medieval Rus, in one of his sermons. "Has our land not been taken captive? Have our fathers and brothers not strewn the land with their corpses? Have our wives and children not been led away into captivity? And have those who were left not been enslaved to do bitter work for the foreigners? Our grandeur has been humbled, our beauty destroyed. Our riches, our labor, our land—all is the property of the foreigners!"[7]

The Mongols did not mold Russian national consciousness. Instead, they shattered existing conceptions associated (at least in the upper ranks of the aristocracy) with a recognition of personal independence, the honor of the clan, and inalienable privileges in relation to the ruler. For example, when the Mongols dealt with disobedient Russian princes, they subjected them to humiliating punishments and forced them to perform pagan religious rituals they knew were unacceptable to them. They sought in this way to achieve the princes' unconditional psychological abasement before the all-encompassing power of the khan.[8]

It was not only the consciousness of the upper classes of Rus that changed. To a considerable degree their membership also changed as a result of the invasion. According to the calculations of Vladimir Kobrin and Andrei Iurganov, up to two-thirds of the representatives of the local princely clans were killed in the lands that were invaded. There were comparable losses among the higher aristocracy (the boyars), who formed the prince's own military retinue. The new members of the prince's retinue consisted largely of military servitors of lower rank, the "gentry," who had no memories of ancient traditions of equality with the prince and were much more inclined to submit to his authority.[9]

The invasion dealt a heavy blow not only to the aristocracy but to the towns, the focal points of power and wealth and the most developed part of the Rus economy. Of the seventy-four towns of Rus, forty-nine were destroyed in the invasion, fourteen of them ceased to exist, and fifteen turned into villages. Urban development in Rus declined markedly, and the majority of towns became military and administrative centers rather than centers of commerce and handicrafts. Stone construction in most of the Rus lands ceased for a century after the invasion, the secrets of many complex crafts were lost, and a considerable number of skilled craftsmen were killed or led off into slavery.

The tribute the Mongols imposed on Rus drained off significant economic resources to the Horde. Moreover, the tribute had to be paid in precious metals, so that in the East, Rus was then called "the land of silver mines." Lack of precious metals led to an economy based largely on barter, to which the harsh natural environment also contributed. It also had an impact on the extremely slow growth of the towns and the insignificant proportion of townspeople in the population of Rus.[10]

Despite the crippling blow that the invasion inflicted on the economy and the population, by the end of the fifteenth and the beginning of the sixteenth centuries a "Russian miracle" had been achieved on the slender economic base of the northeast as the ravaged lands and principalities came together in a unified state with its center in Moscow. This occurred at almost the same time as the creation of unified states in the most developed countries of the West: England, France, and Spain. In Russia the impetus for unification came from the necessity of defending against attacks by the Horde and the effort to throw off its domination, but compared to the West the social and economic bases for such unification were weak. In the West the vestiges of fragmentation died out by themselves, as it were, with the growth of towns and the development of commercial and financial networks. In Russia they had to be eradicated by force. This contributed to the broad application of violence and coercion in Russian life, and to the curtailment of legal limitations and restrictions on the arbitrary exercise of princely power.

The methods of rule customary in the Golden Horde served as a model in many respects for the methods employed in the unification of the Russian lands. Many historians believe that, in the course of consolidating their power, the princes of Moscow borrowed extensively from the Horde's administrative structures and practices.[11] In the struggle for supremacy in the Russian lands the antagonists were not inhibited in their choice of means: treachery, the breaking of agreements, and assistance from the Horde in quarrels with rivals. In the end, Moscow emerged the victor by employing all of those means to the greatest effect.

Was there any alternative to Muscovite centralization given the conditions of the fourteenth and fifteenth centuries? A number of nineteenth-century historians, as well as some contemporary scholars, have argued that there were other possibilities: unification of the Russian lands by Tver, Moscow's chief rival, and a union of Russia and Lithuania. The process of unification would then allegedly have been "softer," preserving the social rights and freedoms inherited from Kievan Rus. While such a view is plausible, it has to be said that in the actual circumstances of the fourteenth and fifteenth centuries—the pressure of the Horde and the weak economy—"soft" alternatives to Muscovite centralization were unlikely to succeed. Alexander Herzen, the outstanding Russian thinker and political journalist, perceived this tragic feature of Russian history: "Moscow saved Russia by stifling everything that was free in Russian life."[12]

By the end of the fifteenth century Moscow had become the spiritual and religious as well as the political center of the Russian lands. The seizure of Constantinople by the Turks in 1453 contributed to this development. In 1480, soon after the fall of Constantinople, Moscow freed itself from the domination of the Golden Horde and became the world's only independent Orthodox state. That led to an enormous growth of Moscow's importance in Russian religious thought. The belief arose within the Muscovite state that it was historically unique. Moscow came to be seen as the "Third Rome," the last center of true Christianity, which it would remain until the Day of Judgment.

While Moscow may have "saved Russia," the methods of Muscovite centralization left a deep imprint on all of Russia's subsequent development, on the psychology of the masses and the political consciousness of the upper classes. The grand prince of Moscow expanded his prerogatives ever more insistently and encountered ever fewer obstacles. His growing power caught the attention of contemporaries as the unification of the Russian lands proceeded. Sigismund von Herberstein, the ambassador of the Holy Roman Empire who visited the Muscovite state at the beginning of the sixteenth century, wrote of Grand Prince Vasily III: "In the power which he has over his subjects he far exceeds all the monarchs of the entire world . . . He oppresses everyone in equal measure with a brutal slavery . . . All [his subjects] call themselves bondsmen, that is, slaves of the sovereign."[13]

The question of the role of state power in society, and of the relations between the sovereign and his subjects, arose with special force in the reign of Ivan IV (1533–84), the first Russian ruler to take the title of "tsar." Many historians have tried to interpret the events of Ivan's reign—the division of the country into two parts, the *oprichnina* territories made directly subject to the tsar and the *zemshchina* lands remaining under the boyars (big landowners), and the terror against various segments of the population—in sociological terms. A number of pre-revolutionary scholars, including two of the most prominent, Sergei Soloviev and Sergei Platonov, argued that the tsar was contending with the opponents of state centralization, the boyars and the Church, while relying for support on the lower stratum of servicemen, the gentry. The contemporary historian Vladimir Kobrin believes that in sixteenth-century Russia there were no opponents of centralization. At issue was the nature of the government in a unified state, whether it would respect the rights and interests of its subjects or take the form of naked despotism.[14]

Ivan himself, known for his cruelty as "the Terrible," pursued the second alternative. He scornfully condemned the parliamentary systems that had evolved in the states of Western Europe. In 1570 he wrote to Queen Elizabeth of England: "We believed that you were the queen of your state and attended to the honor and interests of your state . . . It appears, however, that in your country other persons around you wield power, including men of commerce, and that they attend not to the chief officials of your state or the honor and interests of the country but seek their own commercial profit, while you remain in your virgin rank, like any simple maiden." In addition to this insult, Ivan announced the cancellation of the commercial privileges that he had previously granted to English merchants, stating that "the Muscovite state was not poor when it had no English wares." In a letter to the Polish king, Stephen Bathory, in 1581, Ivan claimed divine right for his absolute power, calling himself "the bearer of the crusading banner and cross of Christ" who ruled the Russian lands "according to God's will, not the rebellious wishes of mortal men."[15]

The *oprichnina* terror not only confirmed the absolute nature of tsarist power but also eradicated conceptions of private property that the Muscovite state had inherited from Kievan Rus. Ivan ordered mass deportations and confiscations of large landholdings. In 1570 he devastated Novgorod, the most highly developed town in Russia, which had maintained close economic ties to the West and a system of republican self-government until its annexation by Moscow in 1478. Continuing and expanding the policy of his predecessors, Ivan divided the confiscated lands into parcels called *pomestie* estates, which the gentry received on the condition that they perform state service. Numerous historians believe that Ivan was following the practices of the Golden Horde, where the khan was deemed the supreme owner of all the lands in the state.

Ivan's attempt to secure unlimited power for the tsar ultimately proved self-defeating. The terror ravaged the country, Russia's international position was undermined, and in the end the *oprichniki* (agents of the *oprichnina*) surrounding Ivan fell victim to the violence themselves. Nevertheless, Ivan's campaign of terror left a lasting mark. It contributed to the brutalization of the government, and it broadened the prerogatives of the tsar, though not to the degree Ivan had intended. Most of all, it accelerated the rise of serfdom, which, along with autocracy, would become the most important feature of Russia's social and political system.

Like the establishment of autocracy, the emergence of serfdom was closely related to the country's geography and the features of its land and climate. After the overthrow of Mongol rule at the end of the fifteenth century, Russia found itself in a peculiar geopolitical trap. Its main adversary, the Golden Horde, had ceased to exist, but the vast frontiers of the Muscovite state were now subject to raids by the heirs of the Horde: the khanates of Kazan and the Crimea. Russian forces succeeded in subjugating Kazan in 1552, but the Crimea remained beyond their reach for many centuries. To protect against Crimean raids it was essential to construct and fortify lines of defense and maintain a sizable army, which imposed a severe burden on the population.

That burden weighed the more heavily because the population of Russia's core territory over the centuries remained small and sparse. Wars and raids took their toll, and in the sixteenth century new opportunities arose for migration to the borderlands. After the annexation of the Kazan khanate in 1552, Russian forces subdued the khanates of Astrakhan (1556) and Siberia (1580s–90s). Those conquests in turn made colonization beyond the Urals possible. By the end of the seventeenth century Russian settlers had reached the shores of the Pacific Ocean and appeared on the Amur River, in Chukotka, and in Kamchatka. In the next century they began to colonize the Aleutian Islands and Alaska in North America. These territories remained under Russian rule until 1867. There was a reverse side to these successes, however. As a result of the continual outflow of colonists, the population density of central Russia remained extremely low: 1–5 persons per square kilometer at the end of the seventeenth century, compared to 10–35 persons per square kilometer in most European countries at the time.

The total population of Russia at the end of the seventeenth century (10 million) just slightly exceeded that of Spain (9.2 million), and it was considerably lower than the population of France (25 million) and the Austrian Empire (14 million). Only in the mid-eighteenth century would Russia's population begin to grow steadily, reaching 36 million by the end of the century.[16] By that time Russia had surpassed all the countries of Europe in population size, but it still had a lower population density. The standard of living remained low for the vast majority of the population because of traditional agricultural technology and the onerous taxes and mandatory service by which the Muscovite state maintained its relatively large and costly military institutions.

Faced with open frontiers, constant military threats, and low population density, the authorities found that the only way to secure a military force was through "payment in kind," that is, by providing its servicemen (the gentry or nobility) with *pomestie* estates and by binding the peasants to the estates to work. Thus serfdom began to develop. Sergei Soloviev called it "a cry of despair uttered by a state that found itself in a hopeless economic situation."[17]

Serfdom appeared just as a unified state was taking shape. In 1497 the government limited the right of peasants to leave their landlord by setting a specific time of year after the harvest season for such a move: the two-week period around St. George's Day (November 26), when the harsh weather discouraged peasants from leaving their villages in search of a new landlord. In 1550 the payments the peasants made to the landowners for the use of their land were raised, curtailing still further the peasants' ability to move. The chaos and destruction of the *oprichnina* terror significantly hastened the process of enserfment. In the 1580s the government began to decree "forbidden years," during which the movement of peasants was entirely prohibited, and in 1592 it introduced "registration books," a census of the peasant population indicating who belonged to a specific proprietor. Some historians believe that at the time the registration books were compiled the government issued a decree formally binding the peasants to the land, but the text of that decree has not been found.

Not surprisingly, the measures to enserf the peasants provoked acute discontent. The growing strains within the society, which coincided with the extinction of the old Muscovite dynasty, led to a full-scale social and political upheaval, the Time of Troubles (1598–1613). The events of the Troubles demonstrated that Russia "lacked the right to a civil war," as Sweden and Poland immediately exploited the country's internal conflicts by seizing significant parts of Russia's borderlands, thereby reducing the country's territory and draining it of human and material resources it could ill afford to lose. Under these conditions the separate groups within Russian society laid their claims aside and rallied around the new Romanov dynasty, which was elected to the throne in 1613.

As Russia faced economic ruin and foreign threats, the great bulk of the population was forced to submit to the inexorably tightening grip of serfdom. A code of laws that applied to all of Russia, the Law Code of the Assembly of the Land (*Sobornoe ulozhenie*, 1649), definitively tied the peasants to the land. At the same time, townspeople were bound to their parts of the towns (the *posads*, or trading quarters) to ensure the regular payment of taxes and the fulfillment of their other obligations. The resulting system gave the government a reliable instrument for mobilizing the country's resources to carry out national tasks, but it weighed heavily on the economy by preventing it from developing freely and by stifling initiative.

It was not just the lower classes, the serfs and townspeople, who bore the burdens of this system. The requirements of state service (especially military service) proved as oppressive for the boyars and gentry as taxes and dues were for the common people. All were bound to the sovereign by their duties, while the head of state, the tsar, was in turn constrained by religious principles and traditional concepts that permeated the entire social fabric of the Muscovite realm. A "service state" emerged, different in principle from the state based on law that developed in the West in these years. Even the wealthiest merchants needed the tsar's permission to engage in foreign trade and to sell salt, furs, and other valuable commodities. In return for their privileges, these merchants served the state as unsalaried collectors of taxes and import duties. Such devices of the autocratic state naturally hindered the development of towns in Russia. Unlike the monarchs of medieval Europe, who granted charters to cities and allowed them a significant degree of self-government, the rulers of Muscovy denied merchants and artisans the right to accumulate wealth under the protection of royal laws. The German expression "town air makes one free after a year and a day" *(Stadtluft macht frei nach Jahr und Tag)* had no analogue in medieval Russia. "There were commanders, soldiers, and workers," Vasily Kliuchevsky wrote, "but there were no citizens; that is, the citizen had been turned into a soldier or a worker to defend the fatherland or to work for it under the direction of a commander."[18]

The extent to which Russia had fallen behind the West became particularly evident in the second half of the seventeenth century after a series of Russian defeats in its efforts to secure outlets to the Baltic and Black seas. The rapid advancement of West European science, technology, industry, and trade demanded ever more insistently that Russia reform its social and political structure to close the gap with the West. The fourth tsar of the Romanov dynasty, Peter I ("Peter the Great"), who reigned from 1689 to 1725, in large part carried out that task. Peter's reforms introduced many of the principles of European culture into Russia, but the foundations on which the reforms were based remained profoundly traditional. This contradiction greatly intensified social, political, and spiritual tensions in Russia.

Through the extensive use of serf labor and various forms of state compulsion, Peter rapidly created a manufacturing industry that was advanced for its day. (This process resembled Stalin's industrialization drive in the 1930s.) Peter paid particular attention to the branches of industry that supplied military needs, such as armaments, metallurgy, woolen cloth (for army uniforms), and sailcloth. Some two hundred factories were in operation at the end of Peter's reign, and by the end of the eighteenth century their number had grown to twelve hundred. In the mid-eighteenth century Russia led the world in the production of pig iron and continued to do so until the beginning of the industrial revolution in the West. Western countries, including England, eagerly purchased the products of Russian industry, particularly ironware, pig iron, and sailcloth.[19]

As in the West, many factories in Russia were privately owned—established by private individuals or given to them by the state. The similarity was largely superficial, however, because the prosperity of a private entrepreneur depended greatly on receiving government orders, subsidies, and credits and on the duties that the state imposed on imports. If a government order fell through or economic conditions changed, an enterprise could be confiscated. The factories that Peter created used the forced labor of peasants attached to them by the state. This dependence on serf labor condemned Petrine industry to backwardness in relation to Western industry. During his reign, Peter issued corporate charters to only nine enterprises. Property rights remained so fragile under his arbitrary rule that Russians ignored his call to create trading companies to rival those of the Dutch, the English, and the French.

Nevertheless, the immediate effect of Peter's reforms was significant. Relying on his powerful navy and re-equipped army, Peter resolved Russia's most important foreign-policy problems. As a result of the prolonged war with Sweden (1700–21), Peter "cut a window onto Europe." He conquered the Baltic littoral, proclaimed Russia an empire, and built a new capital on the shores of the Baltic Sea. St. Petersburg, founded in 1703, served as the capital from 1710 to 1918. Peter's successors continued his policies. The reign of Catherine II ("Catherine the Great," 1762–96) saw advances in the west and in the south. Russia conquered the Crimean Khanate, wrested the northern Black Sea coast from Turkey, and extended its borders far to the west with the partitions of Poland (1772, 1793, and 1795). By the end of the eighteenth century Russia had become one of the mightiest world powers. "I do not know how things will turn out in your day," Prince Aleksandr Bezborodko, Catherine II's chancellor, told his young colleagues, "but in our day not a single cannon in Europe dared fire without our permission."[20]

To reiterate, most of Peter's innovations required the harsh application of coercive methods. The victorious Petrine army was brought up to strength by recruitment levies in which military service was assigned to a certain proportion of peasant households, and the basic form of taxation became the "soul tax," paid by all the taxpayers in an urban or rural commune. Both measures contributed to a significant tightening of traditional mechanisms of social control (the commune and collective responsibility), which were supplemented by new ones: regular censuses, called "revisions," and an internal passport system. The population was sharply divided into two categories, taxpaying and non-taxpaying, and the gulf between them grew rapidly.

Was Peter a tyrant or the wise enlightener of Russia? Did his reforms draw Russia and Europe closer together or drive them farther apart? The answer to these questions is complex, and it still provokes a multitude of arguments. On the one hand, Peter believed unconditionally in the absolute power of the monarch and rejected anything that might limit the prerogatives of the state. "Foreigners say that I rule over unwilling slaves," he

Empress Catherine II. Portrait by Dmitri G. Levitsky.

declared to his close associates. "I rule over subjects who obey my decrees. Those decrees are good for the state, not harmful. English freedom has no place here; it would be like beating your head against a wall. You have to know a people and how to govern them . . . That man is free who does no evil and obeys the good."[21]

Under Peter the principle that the tsar possessed unlimited power, which had previously existed at the level of traditional concepts, was officially embodied in law. "His Majesty," one of Peter's laws stated, "is an autocratic monarch who need answer to no one on earth for his deeds but holds power and authority, his states and lands, as a most Christian monarch, to govern by his own will and good judgment."[22] A bureaucratic apparatus based on European models began to take shape in Peter's reign. He also eliminated the independence of the Church by abolishing the post of patriarch (head of the Church) and replacing it with the Most Holy Synod, completely subordinate to the will of the emperor.

Peter believed that it was harmful to grant rights and freedoms to any particular section of society, for such privileges would threaten the interests of the state as a whole. At the same time, he proclaimed the principle of the "common good," which derived from European political theories, and thereby introduced a new concept into Russian social thought. Because everyone now had to serve the "common good," including even the monarch, the monarchy itself was open to the judgment of society and could be criticized from the standpoint of the "public interest."

In the course of the eighteenth century, this new concept began to take root in the educated segment of the nobility, the main representative of Europeanization and modernization in Russia. Its importance had grown as Russia was drawn into European cultural and political life. Russia's need to comprehend and assimilate the foundations of European culture, to master European technology, and to apply European methods of diplomacy and government made crude coercion—in which the Petrine era had been abundant—inappropriate. After Peter's death the service obligations of the nobility were gradually reduced, while its rights at the expense of the other segments of society were broadened. In 1762 Peter III issued the Manifesto on the Freedom of the Nobility, which emancipated the nobles from mandatory state service. In 1775 Catherine II's Statute on the Administration of the Provinces gave the nobility a large share of local administrative, police, and judicial power.[23] In 1785 the Charter to the Nobility confirmed the nobles' freedom from corporal punishment, their right to "trial by peers," and the inviolability of their landed property. It also gave them institutions of self-government in the form of noble assemblies in the provinces and districts. In essence, it is only from this time onward that we can speak of the affirmation of the principle of private property in Russia, albeit limited to the sphere of landholding and associated with the ownership of serfs. These gains remained restricted to the nobility, however. The failure of Peter I and Catherine II to stimulate entrepreneurship by autocratic decree was clearly reflected in the limited individual initiative displayed by merchants and artisans throughout the eighteenth century. Although a few favored individuals grew immensely wealthy as purveyors of military supplies to the state, towns remained small and without meaningful self-government.

Besides enjoying broad social rights, guarantees of personal inviolability, and a certain independence in relation to the sovereign, the nobility also became the main recipient of education, the most important innovation connected with the Petrine reforms. Under Peter I, education had been mainly utilitarian, of a military and technical character, but in the mid-eighteenth century general education began to receive more attention. Moscow University, the first in Russia, was founded in 1755. In 1786, by order of Catherine II, the creation of a nationwide system of elementary and secondary schools began. (However, elementary education was still not universal when the empire came to an end.) As well-to-do nobles hired teachers and tutors from Europe, the country estates of aristocrats became centers of culture in a synthesis of the achievements of architecture, painting, sculpture, and landscape art. Patrons and connoisseurs of art began to arise in the aristocracy, and they initiated the custom of prolonged journeys to Europe, both at their own expense and at that of the state.[24]

Familiarity with European culture, of course, inevitably brought Russia into contact with European ideas, including ideas that were profoundly hostile to the foundations of Russian life. The result was a clash between part of the nobility and the reality that surrounded it, as well as the government that supported that reality. At first, such frictions were relatively mild. Catherine II strove to create an image of herself in Europe as an "enlightened monarch." She therefore allowed independent journals to engage in debates with the semi-official journals that were published under her patronage. Soon, however, the idyll came to an end. The government increasingly began to regard society with suspicion, while radical tendencies, particularly under the influence of the French Enlightenment, grew within society. The conflict burst into the open in 1790, when a well-to-do nobleman and government official, Aleksandr Radishchev, published a book entitled *A Journey from St. Petersburg to Moscow*, in which he warned of a revolutionary overthrow of the autocracy and abolition of serfdom if the imperial government refused to eradicate those twin evils by peaceful means.[25]

"Oh, if the slaves weighted down with fetters, raging in their despair, would, with the iron that bars their freedom, crush our heads, the heads of their inhuman masters, and redden their fields with our blood! What would the country lose by that?" Radishchev exclaimed.[26] His compassion for the serfs was well founded. As the rights of the nobles expanded in the course of the eighteenth century, the position of the serfs steadily worsened. By the middle of the century it truly approximated slavery. The serfs' increasing oppression stemmed in part from the nobles' demands for political power at the local level, but to a large extent it reflected objective circumstances. The Europeanization of the nobility's lifestyle that the government demanded proved so expensive under Russian conditions that it inevitably led to intensified exploitation of the serfs.[27]

Intensified exploitation, in turn, required that the landowner obtain greater powers over the peasants. In the 1740s and the 1750s, landowners had been given the duty of collecting the soul tax from their peasants; they were granted the right to sell peasants at retail (that is, without land); and nobles received a monopoly on the ownership of land inhabited by peasants. In the course of her reign, Catherine II distributed about 800,000 state peasants to private individuals. A landowner could exile a serf to Siberia (1760) or even send him to hard labor (1765). In 1763 the serfs themselves were required to pay the costs of troops sent to suppress their uprisings, and in 1767 they were deprived of the right to lodge complaints against their masters. The existence of all these measures fully justified Radishchev's declaration: "In the law the peasant is dead."

The most oppressive measures regarding serfdom came in the reign of the "enlightened monarch" Catherine II, whom many historians have accused of hypocrisy. This accusation is mostly unjust. Catherine was no admirer of serfdom, but she understood perfectly well that at the slightest attempt to encroach on the nobility's chief privilege she would immediately be "stoned to death." Therefore the actions that she took against serfdom remained mostly in the realm of ideas. In 1767 she convened the Legislative Commission. The commission's immediate task was to prepare a new code of laws, but it had a larger purpose: to work out a compromise among the various estates through free discussion of basic social problems. In the end, Catherine's plan failed. When the commission met, noble deputies stubbornly defended their right to serf labor, while some representatives of the non-noble estates advanced proposals for resolving the peasant question that frightened Catherine with their radicalism. As a result, she dismissed the commission after a year and a half of work.[28]

A few years later, the peasants gave their own response to the intensification of serfdom in the form of the vast uprising led by Emelian Pugachev, termed a "peasant war" in Soviet historiography. In 1773–74 the insurgents seized huge stretches of territory along the Volga River and in the Urals region, burning thousands of landed estates and murdering tens of thousands of nobles, priests, and officials. The uprising revealed the extent to which the

Emelian I. Pugachev. Eighteenth-century engraving.

majestic edifice of the Russian Empire rested on shaky foundations; it exposed the weakness of the state administration in outlying areas and the intense hatred of the masses for the upper classes. In one of his manifestos Pugachev called on the peasants to deal mercilessly with the nobles: "all nobles . . . who have opposed our rule, who have rebelled against the empire, and who have ruined the peasantry should be seized, arrested, and hanged, that is, treated in the same manner as they have treated you, the peasantry, without the slightest Christianity."[29]

While attacking the nobility, Pugachev did not, however, call for the abolition of the power of the tsar. On the contrary, he proclaimed himself to be the tsar, the miraculously saved Peter III (Catherine II's husband, who had been overthrown and in fact killed in a palace coup d'état). In the eyes of the peasants the tsar remained their supreme defender, the arbiter of justice who could restrain the boundless appetites and selfish intentions of the upper classes. A key phrase in Pugachev's manifesto perhaps expresses most vividly the cherished desires of the peasants: "we grant to everyone who formerly was in serfdom or in any other obligation to the nobility . . . to be faithful personal subjects of our crown."[30]

Paradoxically, an individual who differed in every respect from Pugachev tried to make use of a similar idea: Paul I (ruled 1796–1801), the son and heir of Catherine II. Because his mother had kept him out of power during the long years of her reign, Paul dreamed of revenge. Upon coming to the throne he set out to overturn Catherine's initiatives. He rescinded the Charter to the Nobility, restricted the activity of the noble assemblies, and gradually replaced nobles in the local administration with crown officials. At the same time, he attempted to improve the position of the peasants. In 1797 he issued a Manifesto on Three-Day Labor Service, which limited the serfs' obligatory labor for their masters to three days a week.

Paul's eccentric and inconsistent behavior gave contemporaries grounds for considering him mad. His actions had their own logic, however. He was trying to equalize all classes of society before the sovereign and to strengthen order and discipline in the state administration. But the equality that Paul was striving for was "equality in the lack of rights." He continued the distribution of state peasants. During his brief reign, he gave away approximately 600,000 of them to private owners. The Manifesto on Three-Day Labor Service for the most part remained a proclamation that made no practical improvement in the situation of the serfs. The emperor did not have a sufficiently well-developed bureaucratic apparatus to exert pressure on the landowners. Paul's attempt to change political course ended tragically for him. On March 11, 1801, he was killed in the last palace coup d'état in Russian history, which brought his son, Alexander I, to the throne.[31]

Emperor Alexander I. Portrait by V.L. Borovikovskii

The failure of Paul's efforts to establish "equality in the lack of rights" showed that elements of a civil society—even if limited entirely to the highest estate—had successfully taken root in Russia. The concepts of personal dignity and independence in relation to the sovereign had made their appearance. That made it impossible to return to the "service state" of Petrine and pre-Petrine times and underscored the necessity of extending society's rights and freedoms. Another powerful factor drew the policies of the Russian government in the same direction: the influence of the French Revolution, which made itself felt both by the impact of its ideas and in direct clashes between Russia and revolutionary and Napoleonic France. In 1798–99 Russian troops undertook campaigns in the Aegean Islands, the Adriatic, and northern Italy as part of an anti-French coalition. In 1805–7, in alliance with Austria and Prussia, Russia conducted a struggle with Napoleon in Central Europe. The last of these wars ended unsuccessfully for Russia, which was forced to conclude the disadvantageous Peace of Tilsit, but contemporaries clearly perceived the provisional and fragile nature of this agreement.

The rapid spread of the ideas of the French Revolution throughout Europe aroused debates in the highest circles in Russia. Some (like Paul) felt that Russia had to be protected as much as possible from Western influence, while others thought that it was better to anticipate inevitable change and introduce needed reforms through governmental action. Alexander I, who ruled from 1801 to 1825, shared the latter view. Catherine II's favorite grandson, Alexander had been educated by the Swiss republican Frédéric-César La Harpe in the spirit of the French Enlightenment. Alexander's education instilled in him a respect for the ideas of equality and legality and the need to broaden social freedoms and limit autocratic arbitrariness. "He confessed to me," the Polish aristocrat Prince Adam Czartoryski, a friend of Alexander's youth, recalled, "that he hated despotism everywhere, in whatever form it took, that he loved freedom, which in his opinion must belong equally to all men, and that he was extremely interested in the French Revolution; that without approving of its terrible mistakes he still wished the Republic success and rejoiced in it."[32]

Having come to the throne as a result of the conspiracy that led to his father's death, Alexander seems to have felt a sincere revulsion against autocratic power and a desire to limit it by means of a constitution. But how was constitutional reform to be implemented? On this issue Alexander and his intimate circle—the so-called "young friends": Czartoryski, Count Pavel Stroganov, Count Viktor Kochubei, and Nikolai Novosiltsev—found themselves enmeshed in difficulties. The introduction of a constitution presupposed the convening of a parliament, but that would be hard to reconcile with the existence of serfdom, as shown by the history of Poland before

22

Europe, 1801–1855, During the Reigns of Alexander I and Nicholas I

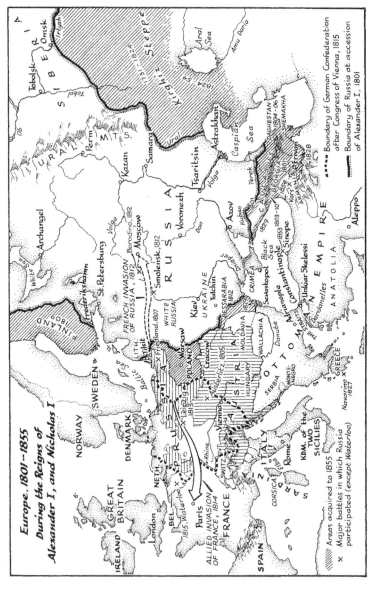

Europe, 1801–1855
During the Reigns of
Alexander I, and Nicholas I

Source: A History of Russia, Seventh Edition, Nicholas V. Riasanovsky and Mark Steinberg p.295. Copyright © 1963, 1969, 1977, 1984, 1993, 2000, 2004 by Oxford University Press, Inc. Used by permission of Oxford University Press, Inc.

1795. In the first years of his reign, Alexander took a series of steps aimed at curbing serfdom. He ended the practice of distributing state peasants to private owners, prohibited newspapers from advertising the retail sale of serfs, and allowed non-nobles to buy land without peasants. None of these measures affected the institution of serf-holding itself, however.

A more serious innovation was the Decree on Free Cultivators of 1803, but its meager practical accomplishments demonstrated the true complexity of the peasant question in Russia. This reform had several features that would reappear in the government's efforts to resolve the issue of serfdom. It was intended to stimulate the development of market relations in Russia by allowing the peasants to receive land through a redemption process upon emancipation, but it was voluntary on the part of the landowners. Immediately after issuing the decree, the government initiated a peasant reform in the Baltic region (1804–6) with a long-range plan in mind: to make this western borderland of the empire a "test case" for the introduction of reforms and to "stimulate" Russian landowners by showing them an example of successful change. In the Baltic region the reform on the whole was successful, though in the form of a landless emancipation, but in central Russia it proved a failure. In the entire reign of Alexander I, only 160 redemption agreements were concluded and some 47,000 peasants (about 1.5 percent of the serfs) became free.[33] Commercial and financial relations in Russia remained so poorly developed that it was unprofitable for the landowners to relinquish unpaid peasant labor, and the peasants lacked the economic means to redeem their freedom.

The principle that reform would be voluntary on the part of the landowners doomed the government's plans to failure, but Alexander, with his father's sad fate in mind, could not resort to compulsion. These considerations led to a new stage of reform that was to be broader in character and deal initially with the country's political structure. This time Alexander chose as his collaborator not a circle of young aristocrats but a man of modest origins: Mikhail Speransky, who had made a brilliant career thanks to his personal abilities and hard work. Speransky owed his elevation to a position of enormous power solely to the favor of the tsar. Alexander's choice was dictated by his immediate needs, but at the same time it reflected a broader historical trend: the formation of a stratum of professional bureaucrats capable at some point in the future of acting as a restraint on the nobility.[34]

By 1809 Speransky had drawn up a plan for political reform entitled "Introduction to a Code of State Laws." It proposed the separation of powers within the government, the introduction of jury trials, and the formation of an elected legislature, to be called a national State Duma. "The legislative estate [that is, institution] should be structured in such a way," Speransky emphasized, "that it cannot carry out its decisions without the autocratic

Mikhail M. Speransky. Nineteenth-century engraving.

power, but so that its opinions are free and express the opinions of the people."[35] Speransky intended that the sovereign would retain the prerogatives necessary to implement reforms while at the same time achieving a broader social base for the monarchy and strengthening legality.

Alexander and Speransky had had the unhappy experience of clashes with the gentry and court aristocracy, so they decided to introduce their reforms gradually. First came the creation in 1810 of a consultative State Council, which was to serve as the connecting link between the emperor and the State Duma. The emperor appointed the State Council's members from the ranks of the higher officials. Reorganization of the ministries, which had been introduced in 1802 as the central departments of the administration, followed in 1811. To make sure that these new institutions would be staffed by professional bureaucrats, Speransky insisted on two decrees. One, issued in 1809, made ranks at court purely honorary and deprived them of any state service rights; the other made a university diploma a requirement for advancement in the service.

The university system, which was to provide support for Speransky's reform plans, represented another major innovation of Alexander's reign. Speransky considered education the necessary link between the two fundamental sets of reforms, the introduction of a constitution and the elimination of serfdom. It would serve as the mechanism for making the transition from almost universal slavery to political freedom. For nearly fifty years, Moscow University had been the only university in Russia, but five new ones were added at the beginning of the nineteenth century, in Kharkov, Kazan, St. Petersburg, Vilna (Vilnius), and Derpt (Tartu). In 1804 the universities were granted autonomy, and each became the center of an educational district comprising a network of elementary and secondary schools. The government established a series of special high schools (*litsei*, from the French *lycée*) for privileged young men, notably the Tsarskoe Selo School, which trained students for careers as officials in the upper ranks of the bureaucracy. Wealthy individuals created high schools, such as the Demidov School in Yaroslavl and the Prince Bezborodko School in Nezhin. In addition, the government maintained high schools with a classical Greek and Latin curriculum (*gymnazii*), essential for entrance to a university. Liberal censorship regulations adopted in 1803 enabled journalism and book publishing to flourish. The government also provided significant support in the form of subsidies to writers and publishers and awarded decorations to literary figures.[36] The vigorous growth of writing on public affairs, the open discussion of current social and political issues, and the strengthening of cultural ties with Europe reflected the successful expansion of the civil society that had begun to take shape in the time of Catherine II.

The formation of a civil society, however, brought with it consequences that the reformers had not anticipated. The free expression of ideas permitted the emergence of conservative sentiments opposed to Speransky's policies. The growth of national consciousness in the first years of the nineteenth century lent support to these sentiments. Even as Russia drifted toward war with Napoleon, Speransky was using many of the institutions and laws of Napoleonic France as the model for his reforms. That made his policies seem a kind of "national betrayal."

The writer and historian Nikolai Karamzin became the spokesman for the conservatives in the discussions of public affairs at the beginning of the nineteenth century.[37] In his *Memoir on Ancient and Modern Russia* (1811), which was addressed to the tsar, he asked indignantly: "Is this why we have toiled for one hundred years or so to produce our own comprehensive code, in order now to confess solemnly to all Europe that we are fools, and bow our grey heads to a book pasted together in Paris by six or seven ex-lawyers and ex-Jacobins?" Karamzin was particularly critical of the central point of Speransky's plan: the attempt to combine autocracy with a representative system and constitutional limitations on the monarch. "Two political authorities in one state," he maintained, "are like two dreadful lions in one cage, ready to tear each other apart; and yet law without authority is nothing."[38]

Karamzin considered the abolition of serfdom impossible in the near future. By violating the gentry's property rights, it threatened to undermine Russia's social and political stability. A formal limitation of autocracy was equally impossible. Over time, "salutary customs, principles, and public opinions . . . will keep future sovereigns within the bounds of legitimate authority far more efficiently than all the ephemeral forms." Everything would run properly in Russia, Karamzin proposed, if Alexander were to find "fifty wise and conscientious individuals" and appoint them provincial governors.[39] Karamzin's views in fact anticipated elements of the political program of Alexander's successor, Nicholas I, as well as some elements of Slavophile doctrines.

Karamzin's undisputed moral authority reinforced the pressure that court circles were exerting on the tsar, and in the end he was forced to withdraw his support from Speransky. In March 1812 he removed Speransky from all his posts and sent him into exile. Alexander had no intention of renouncing reform, however; he made no secret of the fact that he had parted with Speransky only because of the opposition at court. The ruling circles now waited to see which of the contending directions in governmental policy the tsar would choose. Meanwhile, tension was steadily building in international relations, above all in relations with France. It was in these circumstances that Russia confronted one of the greatest challenges in its history, Napoleon's invasion, followed by the Russian army's advance into Western Europe.

Chapter 1

On the Path to Reform

At what point does the story of the abolition of serfdom in Russia begin? Historians have answered this question in various ways. Some consider the starting point to be the era of Catherine II, when serfdom reached its apogee but, at the same time, open protests against it rang out at the Legislative Commission. Others cite Aleksandr Radishchev's revolutionary call to destroy autocracy and serfdom. Still others focus on the first practical steps toward emancipation taken under Alexander I. To be sure, all these events played an important part in Russia's history. For the movement to eliminate serfdom to become irreversible, however, a major shock was required, one that affected every segment of society and clearly pointed to the inevitability of change. That shock was provided by the War of 1812.

The war affected Russian society so strongly that Alexander Herzen called it "the beginning of real Russian history (until then we had only prehistory)."[1] The invasion of Russian territory by enemy forces—for the first time since the Time of Troubles at the beginning of the seventeenth century—called forth an outburst of patriotism that united all segments of the population. Popular resistance began the moment Napoleon crossed the Russian frontier. Peasants withdrew from the path of the Grande Armée, destroyed supplies, burned houses, and attacked separate detachments of French troops. Patriotic demonstrations took place in the towns, thousands of men enrolled in the militia, and vast sums were donated to the defense of the country. The voice of public opinion grew louder and was not afraid to make demands on the tsar. In the threatening atmosphere of the war, the concepts of "tsar" and "fatherland" did not always coincide. The popular general Mikhail Kutuzov, whom the tsar reluctantly had to appoint commander-in-chief, became the national hero, not Alexander.

The two outstanding events of the war were the Battle of Borodino on

"The Burning of Moscow" (1812). Nineteenth-century watercolor.

August 26/September 7, 1812, in which the Russian army withstood the attack of Napoleon's main force, and the burning of Moscow, Russia's ancient capital, which the population had abandoned before the French troops entered it. In effect, Napoleon was shut up in Moscow, deprived of reinforcements and provisions, and forced to begin retreating from Russia. The retreat gradually turned into flight. The European campaigns of the Russian army in 1813–14 led to the creation of a new anti-Napoleonic coalition consisting of Russia, England, Austria, and Prussia, which completed the rout of the French emperor. On March 18/30, 1814, a Russian colonel, Mikhail Orlov, accepted the surrender of Paris.[2]

The brilliant victory over Napoleon significantly elevated Russia's international authority and for a long time secured for it a preeminent position in Europe. The contrast between the country's power in foreign affairs and the backwardness of its internal structure became all the more striking, however. The free ancestors of the Russians "would look with horror upon the contemptible position of their descendants," exclaimed Major Vasily Raevsky, a participant in the War of 1812. "They would tremble in amazement, not daring to believe that Russians had become slaves, and that we whose name and power extend from the inaccessible North Pole to the shores of the Danube, from the Baltic Sea to the Caspian, and give laws and rights to innumerable tribes and peoples, in all our grandeur fail to see our own abasement in the slavery of the peasants."[3]

As many contemporaries recognized, the victory over Napoleon could not have been achieved without the active participation of the peasants, who returned to floggings and the chains of serfdom. "The war was still going on," Aleksandr Bestuzhev-Marlinsky, an officer and writer, recalled, "when the soldiers, upon their return home, began to spread murmurs of discontent among the people. 'We shed our blood,' they said, 'and they are forcing us again to toil at labor service. We saved the country from a tyrant, and the lords are again tyrannizing over us.' "[4] These contradictions seemed so sharp and glaring that immediately after the army's return from its foreign campaigns a revolutionary movement arose within the officer corps. The conspiracy later came to be called the "Decembrist movement," after the attempt by its participants to carry out an uprising in December 1825.

The Decembrist uprising resembled the revolutions of the 1820s in Spain, Portugal, Italy, and Greece, but it differed in one significant respect. Unlike southern Europe, Russia was not subject to foreign rule or threatened by a powerful neighbor. Therefore the Decembrists, who regarded their protest against social oppression as a continuation of their patriotic mission, had to invent "foreign" oppressors. The Decembrists accused the emperor of "patronizing Germans" and denounced the "foreign origins" of

"Blessing the Militia." Nineteenth-century painting.

the ruling dynasty. It was characteristic that they protested the introduction of a constitution in the Polish lands that Russia acquired in 1815. As the Decembrist Dmitry Zavalishin wrote, "Russians were offended at the granting of a constitution to defeated and conquered Poland before one was given to Russia, which had vanquished it."[5] Indignation arose not over constitutional principles themselves, which fully corresponded to the Decembrists' views, but over Alexander's imprudent effort to begin reform in the western borderlands. This was taken as evidence of the emperor's contempt for "native Russians."

A heightened sense of patriotism permeated every aspect of the Decembrists' outlook. It found various forms of expression, such as searching for models of "sacred freedom" in the national past, attempting to counteract the "influx of Germans" into the Russian service, substituting "immemorially Russian" words for European political terms, and proposing that the emperor be killed for supposedly planning to "cede Russian lands to Poland." In its most extreme form the Decembrists' patriotism could take on features of aggressive nationalism, as in the program of Pavel Pestel [see page 36].

The Decembrists, of course, recognized the similarity of their movement to the revolutions of southern Europe and were inspired by their example. They tried to take as their model the Greek *Hetairia* and the Italian Carbonari.[6] They found it extremely difficult, however, to transfer the European experience to Russia. The revolutionary movements in Europe, though they arose within secret societies, had broad support within the bourgeoisie and intelligentsia. In Russia, the revolutionary movement at the beginning of the nineteenth century remained confined almost entirely to the nobility. The Decembrists recognized that because of the distinctive features of Russian history their social base was very narrow, and therefore they adopted the tactic of military revolution as their chief method of action. They understood that European slogans of constitutional liberties meant nothing to the common people, and that the fury of a mass uprising would fall upon all the nobles, including the Decembrists themselves. These considerations prompted the Decembrist officers, while sincerely devoted to the welfare of the masses, to keep them as far from the insurrection as possible, and to be very cautious about disclosing the true aims of their movement even to their soldiers.

How did the Decembrist movement develop? The first secret society, the Union of Salvation, arose in 1816. This extremely small organization of just thirty officers employed conspiratorial methods. In 1818, signs of a more liberal turn in the government's policies encouraged them to form a new society, the Union of Welfare, with a membership of about 200. The members of the Union of Welfare attempted to disseminate enlightened views. They spoke out in salons against serfdom and the brutal treatment of soldiers, gave help to starving peasants, created mutual-instruction schools in the army (a system in which the more advanced pupils helped teach the others), purchased the freedom of talented self-taught serfs, and served in the courts and administrative institutions. Educational work did not satisfy the revolutionary zeal of the majority of the Decembrists, however. The government's definitive turn to reaction at the beginning of the 1820s impelled them to disband the Union of Welfare and to create two secret organizations, the Northern and Southern societies, which resolved to prepare a military revolution.

The sentiments of the young officers, and perhaps even the very existence of the secret societies, became known to Alexander I. He himself shared many of the ideas that inspired them. He was speaking of the Decembrists when, at a late stage in the development of their movement, he said, "it is not for me to punish them." From the time when he was still the heir to the throne, Alexander had dreamed of limiting autocracy and abolishing serfdom, but he intended, of course, to pursue the path of peaceful reforms from above. He believed that the end of the Napoleonic wars had created the best conditions to carry out those reforms. The calamities of war and revolution would incline governments and peoples to compromise and accustom them to mutual concessions. At Alexander's insistence, after the defeat of Napoleon a constitutional structure was preserved in Switzerland and introduced in France and a number of the German states. Even within the Russian Empire, Finland, which had been conquered from Sweden, received a constitution in 1809. To guarantee the postwar structure of Europe, Alexander insisted on the conclusion of the Holy Alliance, in which the monarchs of Europe promised to treat their subjects "like the fathers of families" and each other "in a spirit of brotherhood."[7]

The heart of Alexander's postwar policy was the annexation of central Poland (the "Kingdom of Poland") to Russia, and the granting to it of a constitution. Alexander hoped that this measure would simultaneously eliminate a hotbed of tension in the center of Europe and advance constitutional reforms in Russia. A reform project entitled The Constitutional Charter of the Russian Empire was drawn up in the office of Alexander's old friend Nikolai Novosiltsev, whom he had appointed imperial commissioner of the Kingdom of Poland. The charter proposed the creation in Russia of a two-chamber parliament to be called a Sejm; elections on the basis of a property qualification; fundamental civil freedoms of speech, conscience, and the press; inviolability of person and private property; and equality of all subjects before the law. The most important innovation was to be the transformation of Russia into a federation. According to the charter, the country would be divided into twelve autonomous "lieutenancies," or regions, each with its own parliament.[8]

Although usually cautious and secretive, Alexander felt it necessary in this instance to make a public announcement of his intention to extend "the salutary influence of free and legally defined institutions. . . . to all the countries that Providence has entrusted to my care." At the opening session of the Polish parliament (Sejm) on March 15, 1818, the Russian emperor gave a speech that became the last and most complete exposition of his liberal convictions. Alexander said to the Poles:

> Show your contemporaries that free and legally defined institutions [*les institutions libérales*], the sacred principles of which they confuse with the destructive doctrines that have threatened the social order with a disastrous collapse in our times, are not a dangerous dream, but that, on the contrary, when such institutions are implemented with a righteous heart and are directed with pure intentions to the attainment of an objective that is useful and salutary for mankind, they are fully in accord with order and general tranquillity and establish the true prosperity of nations.[9]

While making plans for constitutional reform, the government prepared the reorganization of Russia on the federal principle.[10] Alexander also ordered discussions within the government to investigate different ways to eliminate serfdom, such as a gradual redemption of the landowners' serfs by the state and the introduction of various forms of private property in land. In 1816–19, a peasant reform was carried out in the Baltic region, giving the peasants freedom without land. One can scarcely call the basic principles of the peasant reform in the Baltic progressive. Nevertheless, as the historian Sergei Mironenko has observed, it was "the first act in several centuries by which the autocracy neither deepened nor expanded serfdom, but, on the contrary, terminated it, if only in part of the territory of the enormous Russian Empire."[11] The so-called "Baltic version" of serf emancipation now became part of the autocracy's arsenal of social policies and a possible model for resolving the peasant question in Russia. The abolition of serfdom in the Baltic region increased the chances for constitutional reform in Russia. Yet, despite the emperor's forthright declarations and the great number of preparatory measures, he did not implement any of the reforms. How can we explain such a paradoxical result?

Above all, the good intentions of the tsar-reformer and his government came up against the insuperable opposition of most Russian landowners. The unpaid labor of the serfs suited most of the gentry very nicely, they lacked a long-term perspective, and the country's international position seemed unshakable after the victory over Napoleon. "Our blessed fatherland has always been and will always be tranquil," declared State Secretary

Aleksandr Shishkov, an eminent dignitary, during the discussion of the peasant question in the State Council in 1820. "It is more successful and more
prosperous than any other nation . . . Under such circumstances, it would
appear that if it really were necessary to make some changes, this is not the
time to consider them. We clearly see the grace of God upon us. The right
hand of the All-High is protecting us. What more could we want?"[12] The
resistance of the nobility prevented the implementation not only of peasant
reform but of constitutional reform as well. It was clear that political freedom would inevitably entail the abolition of serfdom. Mindful of his father's
sad fate, Alexander decided not to oppose the wishes of the nobility.

As time went on, Alexander himself began to lose interest in the idea of
reform, and particularly in the prospect of limiting his own power. The principle of compromise, which the emperor strove to follow in every situation,
in this instance presupposed the combination of the incompatible: West European constitutionalism and traditional Russian autocracy. Prince Adam
Czartoryski wrote: "The emperor loved the external forms of liberty as people
are captivated by theatrical spectacles. He liked the phantom of a free government, and he boasted of it, but he sought only the forms and the external
appearance, without allowing them to become a reality. In a word, he would
gladly have granted liberty to the entire world on the condition that everyone
voluntarily submit exclusively to his will."[13]

International events contributed to the reactionary turn in Alexander's
policies. It became clear that the peoples of Europe were not inclined to
settle for the moderate liberties granted them after the Napoleonic wars. At
the beginning of the 1820s a series of upheavals rocked Europe and once
and for all undermined Alexander's faith in the salutary power of liberal
principles. As already mentioned, revolutions broke out in Spain and Portugal in 1820, and uprisings occurred in Naples in 1820 and Piedmont in
1821. Against the background of a steadily rising wave of revolutions, the
Holy Alliance began to turn into "a conspiracy of monarchs against the
peoples." Thanks to its efforts, counter-revolutionary interventions took
place in Spain, Naples, and Piedmont. Inside Russia's borders, tension increased in constitutional Poland, whose rights the Russian government was
consistently curtailing. In 1830–31 this conflict would lead to open insurrection. In deference to his conservative principles, Alexander even refused
to support the uprising of the Greeks against Turkey in 1821. This decision, which clearly contradicted Russia's national interests and long-standing traditions of Russian foreign policy, drew a sharply negative response
from the most varied circles of Russian society.

Within Russia, political reaction found expression in the increasing sever-
ity of censorship and the repression that was imposed on the recently founded

universities of Petersburg and Kazan. The government expelled the most talented professors, subjected the students to strict discipline, and monitored the content of lectures. In an effort to reinforce conservative principles within society, Alexander turned to religion, but he did so in an unfortunate manner, by using outright administrative coercion to instill religious ideas. In 1817 he created a special Ministry of Religious Affairs and Public Education, which lumped together the administration of educational institutions and all the religions in Russia, from Orthodoxy to Lamaism and the paganism of the Siberian tribes. With the government's backing the Bible Society, which cultivated a kind of "non-denominational" Christianity and mysticism, expanded its activities.[14] These policies drew protests from both liberal-minded contemporaries and defenders of the paramount role of Orthodoxy. Alexander's popularity continued to decline.

Still more protests arose over another of Alexander's initiatives, the introduction of military colonies in 1816. Russia faced a difficult situation after the Napoleonic wars: the combination of enormous financial losses and the need to maintain a large army. In the military colonies, the state peasants in some provinces became subject to military command and were required to maintain the soldiers settled among them. Military discipline regulated the routines of work and everyday life. Conceived as a way of alleviating the burden of taxes and military service, the colonies turned into the worst form of serfdom. Alexander placed at the head of the colonies his trusted subordinate Aleksei Arakcheev, a crude, merciless, and brutal administrator who elicited universal hatred.[15] "Arakcheev destroyed the whole of Russia, he made good people weep," went a folk song. The introduction of the military colonies provoked numerous uprisings, but Alexander remained adamant. He declared: "The colonies will stay, even if corpses have to line the road from Petersburg to Chudov" (the beginning of the first line of colonies, a distance of more than 100 kilometers).[16] At such moments those archetypes of autocracy Peter I and Paul, with their fanatical faith that they could bestow good on the people from above, came to life in the person of the crowned reformer.

By the last years of his reign, Alexander's political role was played out. He spent more and more time traveling around the country and left administrative affairs to Arakcheev. In November 1825, on one of his journeys, Alexander died at the age of forty-eight in the small southern town of Taganrog. His failure to leave clear instructions regarding the succession to the throne added to the confused political situation in the country.[17] The sudden demise of the emperor gave rise to the legend that he had staged his own death, secretly renounced the throne, and in the guise of "elder Fyodor Kuzmich" set out to wander through Russia, atoning for his sins before the people. In any event, Alexander's death and the interregnum that it created spurred the Decembrists to open rebellion.

How had the Decembrists' political program evolved by the middle of the 1820s? Nikita Muraviev, a colonel on the General Staff and the leader of the Northern Society, drew up a moderate version of the program. (He was the son of Mikhail Muraviev, who had been Alexander I's tutor and subsequently the curator of Moscow University.) For his project, which he called a "constitution," Muraviev drew on the liberal constitutions of European countries, such as the French constitution of 1791 and the Spanish constitution of 1812, as well as elements of the political experience of England and the United States. Some historians believe that Novosiltsev's proposed Constitutional Charter of the Russian Empire, with which Muraviev was familiar, also influenced him.[18] In Muraviev's project the powers of the tsar were limited by parliament, like those of the U.S. president. For example, he would have the right to conclude international treaties and to appoint supreme court judges and senior government officials with the consent of parliament. As a guarantee of democracy, the new Russia would be reorganized on a federal basis, with the country divided into thirteen autonomous "states." The parliament (the National *Veche*) was to consist of two chambers. The members of the upper chamber (the Supreme *Duma*) would be elected by the separate "states," like the U.S. Senate. (The terms *veche,* which means assembly, and *duma,* which means council, were borrowed from institutions that had existed in Russia's past.) Russian landowners would become something like the English gentry: landlords exercising dominance in the country's social and political life. The right to elect parliamentary representatives would be restricted by a high property qualification. Serfdom would be abolished, but the peasants would be emancipated with practically no land: a minimum allotment of two desiatinas (5.4 acres).

Muraviev's project, which presupposed the preservation of the monarchy and a virtually landless emancipation of the serfs, evoked numerous protests among the Decembrists. Pavel Pestel, a colonel and the leader of the Southern Society, reflected those objections in his program, called "Russkaia Pravda" (a reference to the first Russian law code, which can be translated into English as "Russian Justice" or "Russian Truth"). Pestel advocated the emancipation of the serfs with land and universal suffrage in a republic to be governed by a single-chamber parliament. "All newspapers and political works," Pestel later explained, "so greatly glorified the growth of prosperity in the North American United States, attributing it to their political system, that it seemed to me clear proof of the superiority of a republican government."[19] At first glance, Pestel's project seems more democratic than Muraviev's, but in fact the thinking of the Southern

Society's leader was quite complex. Although he gave a prominent place to outwardly democratic principles, Pestel actually planned to introduce a profoundly authoritarian system, the only kind he believed capable of maintaining social stability in Russia.

Pestel argued for the establishment of a republic mainly in order to forestall the restoration of a monarchy, which he termed "a rabid reign of evil." "Any government," he emphasized, "in which the head of state is a single individual, especially if that office is hereditary, will inevitably end up as a despotism."[20] He planned the complete extermination of the imperial family and even designated for this purpose a special "lost detachment" (*garde perdue,* or *cohorte perdue*), which would itself be publicly executed after the revolution, as though to avenge the regicide. In contrast to Muraviev, who planned to convene a Constituent Assembly, Pestel intended to give power to a military dictatorship during a ten-year transition period to a republic. Even after the transition period, Pestel's republic was to have a very distinctive character: it would ban private education and social organizations independent of the government, and it would implement strict administrative centralization, including the Russification of all the non-Russian peoples of the empire. Pestel considered it essential to assimilate the non-Russian peoples, Christianize the eastern borderlands, deport the "wild" elements of the Caucasian mountaineers to interior regions of Russia, and exile the Jews to Asia Minor.[21]

Pestel's views were certainly notable for their pronounced democratic features, but their essence lay in what he meant by "democracy." Above all, Pestel sought to guarantee the equality and well-being of the people, but for the sake of that objective he was prepared to sacrifice political freedom. He stressed that an "aristocracy of wealth" was much more harmful than a "feudal aristocracy." Therefore not only was it essential to "disallow" such social groups but even "to destroy them wherever they exist." While permitting and even encouraging the existence of a bourgeoisie, Pestel strongly opposed granting it any political influence on the grounds that it posed a threat to political stability. "The so-called common people," he declared, "create disturbances only when they are oppressed or when the rich bribe them or incite them. Left to themselves, they always remain tranquil."[22]

To guarantee the "tranquillity of the common people," Pestel put forward a special plan to resolve the agrarian question. All the land in the country would be divided into two parts, one of which was to serve as a "necessary reserve," the other as a "surplus reserve." Land in the second part could be bought and sold, forming the basis for the development of a commercial economy. Land in the first category would be withdrawn forever from the market, to be distributed to whoever wanted it, so as to prevent proletarianization and destitution. A partial confiscation of the gentry's landed property would create the public land fund. Many historians have seen in Pestel's agrarian project an anticipation of the reform of 1861, which legitimized the communal landholding of the peasants side by side with private landholding. The desire to secure the material well-being of the people, to create an authoritarian political system, and thus to disregard social freedoms also accorded on the whole with Russian traditions.

Pestel anticipated not only the concrete steps that governmental reformers would later take but also certain currents in the Russian radical movement. Thus the project to create a public land fund led Alexander Herzen to call Pestel "a socialist before socialism." However prophetic Pestel's ideas may have been, they all related to the distant future. How was land to be allocated to the private and public funds? Would the lands confiscated from the gentry suffice to create the public fund? What forces could be relied on to suppress the opposition of the landowners, who would doubtless resist the confiscation of their property? Pestel had no answers to any of these questions. "Throughout 1825," he admitted later, "my [revolutionary] way of thinking began to diminish, and I started to see things somewhat differently, but it was already too late to reverse course . . . The possibility of civil strife and dissension worried me greatly, and that prospect made me grow much cooler to our objective."[23] Arrested at the end of 1825, Pestel did not take part in the open rebellion.

Although arrests had already begun and plans for the revolt were not clearly thought out, the Decembrists decided to take advantage of the interregnum following the death of Alexander I and carry out an uprising. On December 14, 1825, the members of the Northern Society led some three thousand soldiers and sailors onto Senate Square in Petersburg and tried to voice their political demands. They were dispersed by government artillery fire. The uprising of the Chernigov Regiment in Ukraine organized by the Southern Society also ended in defeat. About 120 Decembrists were exiled to hard labor or forced settlement in Siberia, or were demoted to the ranks. Pestel was executed, along with four of the other most active participants in the movement: Mikhail Bestuzhev-Riumin and Sergei Muraviev-Apostol, the leaders of the uprising in Ukraine; the poet Kondraty Ryleev, one of the leaders of the Northern Society; and Petr Kakhovsky, who had shot the governor-general of Petersburg, Mikhail Miloradovich, during the uprising on Senate Square. In the wake of the rebellion the government's policies grew considerably harsher. The authorities tightened their control over society and created a special secret-police department, the Third Section of His Majesty's Own Imperial Chancellery. From now on, discussion of basic political changes would take place in strict secrecy. The "parting of the ways" between government and society, a characteristic feature of Russia's political development in the nineteenth and early twentieth centuries, had begun.

Nicholas I, who ascended to the imperial throne after Alexander's death, was one of those most profoundly affected by the Decembrist uprising. Nicholas exposed himself to mortal danger during the uprising and personally directed its suppression. A military man by profession, by education, and by his entire life experience, he regarded the insurrection as further evidence of the need for strict army discipline over society. Each year for many years he celebrated the fourteenth of December with his closest advisers and the heir to the throne as a day of great victory over the enemies of the autocracy. Suppression of any attacks on the monarchical order, both within the country and abroad, would now become his most important task. "Revolution is on Russia's doorstep," he declared soon after he came to the throne, "but I vow that it will not cross her threshold as long as I still have the breath of life, as long as I am emperor by God's grace!"[24]

Liberal and revolutionary contemporaries heaped criticism on the emperor. Friedrich Engels, for example, called him a "tsar-despot," "a limited individual with the outlook of a platoon commander." It would be a mistake, however, to think that his policies consisted solely of authoritarian and repressive measures. A pragmatist and realist by nature, Nicholas understood perfectly well the depth of Russia's problems. The investigation of the Decembrist affair revealed a glaring picture of disarray that demanded urgent intervention by the government. Nicholas ordered a summary of the Decembrists' testimony to be compiled, and he made extensive use of it in administrative matters. At the beginning of his reign he repeatedly declared that he did not oppose reforms as such but would not permit attacks on the existing political order. In the Manifesto of July 13, 1826, on the execution of the Decembrists, Nicholas stated: "Not by daring and rash dreams, which are always destructive, but gradually, and from above, laws will be issued, defects remedied, and abuses corrected. In this manner all modest hopes for improvement, all hopes for strengthening the rule of law . . . will be gradually fulfilled. The legitimate path, open for all, will always be taken by Us with satisfaction."[25] To strengthen autocracy as much as possible and to introduce gradual reforms under its sponsorship, to prepare Russia in an unhurried fashion for a transition to a new course of development—that was Nicholas I's political program.

In this context, administrative centralization, a salient feature of Nicholas's regime, represented an element of reform. Nicholas believed that the strengthening of control over society would guarantee stability in the country and create the basis for solid improvements. Even the militarization of the governmental apparatus, long regarded as evidence of the

Emperor Nicholas I.

emperor's "limited" nature, should not be interpreted in a one-sided manner. To be sure, the military men who for many years occupied high positions in Nicholas's secret police, Aleksandr Benkendorf and Leonty Dubelt,
vividly personified the repressive side of the government. However, Pavel
Kiselev, a hero of the War of 1812 who had commanded large military
forces, became the most outstanding reformer of Nicholas's reign. It should

Aleksandr Kh. Benkendorf. Nineteenth-century portrait by
Petr Fedorovich Sokolov.

not be forgotten that during the Napoleonic Wars the army attracted many
brilliant and talented men.

Militarization of the government under Nicholas implied not only the
appointment of military commanders to administrative posts. It also meant
the application of military practices to various spheres of social life and
civil administration and the assignment of important tasks to officers in the
emperor's retinue. The growing significance of the retinue and the imperial
chancellery reflected Nicholas's desire to create a system of personal administration that would bring the most important spheres of public life under his direct control.[26] From a long-range political perspective, however,

Count Pavel D. Kiselev

another tendency in Nicholas's reign had a greater significance: the continued strengthening of the ministerial system created at the beginning of the
nineteenth century, coupled with the formation of a professional bureaucracy. Between 1800 and 1860 the number of officials grew sixfold, from
15,000–16,000 to 100,000.[27] Both the social composition and the social
status of the bureaucracy changed. Many sons of ruined or impoverished

noble families joined its ranks. These "new" bureaucrats, whose salary some-times constituted their chief means of support, regarded state service as their basic occupation, as their profession. In their minds, the interests of the state took precedence over the interests of particular elements of soci-ety, including the nobility.

The new generation of officials—the "enlightened bureaucrats"—shared a common ethos, which included the demand for strict observance of the law, a worship of science, and a desire to understand the changes taking place in the West and to prepare Russia to absorb them. Much of this ethical system came from the education these officials received in the universities and privileged academies. The enlightened bureaucrats were relatively few in number, but they had a considerable amount of corporate solidarity. The system of promotion that prevailed in the 1830s and the 1840s enabled them to advance rapidly in the service and occupy high positions. Although products of Nicholas's regime, they developed a hostile attitude to its foundations, and they gradually realized that it needed comprehensive reform.[28]

The reforms that Nicholas introduced along with his repressive measures consolidated the position of the enlightened bureaucracy within the govern-mental apparatus. The most important reform was the codification of Russia's laws by Mikhail Speransky, head of the Second Section of His Majesty's Chancellery, in the late 1820s and the early 1830s. Speransky had been brought back to Petersburg by Alexander I, and under Nicholas he returned to gov-ernmental activity. It was not by chance that the autocrat turned to a dis-graced dignitary whose constitutional projects of the 1810s had ruined his reputation. While trying in every way to strengthen his autocratic power, the emperor at the same time sought to remove the stigma of arbitrariness and despotism from his rule and provide it with a legal basis. Russia's lack of a code of laws was a serious obstacle to achieving that objective. It created a purely practical problem as well. The confused state of the laws severely hampered procedures in the administration and the courts, opening the way for unscrupulous officials to manipulate contradictory legal norms.

In carrying out the codification, Speransky had to follow Nicholas's strict order "to compose no new laws" but "first of all to base the old ones on new principles," that is, to limit himself to regularizing existing legal norms. Within just a few years, Speransky and his assistants completed their enormous task: to collect 36,000 legislative acts passed since the Law Code of 1649 and to arrange them in general categories. By 1833 they had drawn up two basic legislative collections: the *Complete Collec-tion of Laws of the Russian Empire*, which included all published legisla-tion, to be supplemented as new laws were issued; and the *Digest of the*

Laws of the Russian Empire in fifteen volumes, which included only those laws still in effect.[29] The successful codification was the crowning achievement of Speransky's career. At a session of the State Council a few months before Speransky's death, Nicholas solemnly conferred Russia's highest decoration, the Order of Saint Andrew, on the once disgraced official and granted him the title of count.

For all its significance in bringing order to Russia's laws, Nicholas's codification contained major defects. The unlimited nature of the emperor's power blatantly contradicted the principle of supremacy of the law. Article 1 of the *Digest* solemnly proclaimed: "The Emperor of Russia is an autocratic and unlimited monarch. God Himself enjoins submission to his supreme power not only out of fear but also out of conscience."[30] Nevertheless, the importance of the codification should not be underestimated. Work on the *Digest* fostered the improvement of legislative techniques, and its publication strengthened society's understanding of the law. The *Digest* curtailed arbitrariness in the courts and the administration, thereby undermining the foundations of serfdom. Finally, the codification project gave rise to a cohort of jurist-officials in the Second Section and the Ministry of Justice who would play an important part in implementing the judicial reform of the 1860s.[31]

Another aspect of Nicholas's policies, his attempts to introduce social reforms, touched directly on serfdom. Nicholas could not ignore the demands for reform of the archaic system of social estates that the Decembrists' programs had voiced. Certain practical problems after the Napoleonic Wars demanded resolution, such as the ongoing ruin of the landowners, whom Nicholas regarded as the most important pillar of the autocracy. In addition, Russia's backwardness in relation to the West, which was experiencing the rapid growth of cities and the expansion of industry, grew more pronounced in the 1830s and the 1840s.[32]

To be sure, Nicholas's government, lulled by the victory over Napoleon, did not pay enough attention to developments in the West. Nevertheless, it did not simply ignore them. Along with typical "old regime" measures to shore up the gentry, the government made some efforts to stimulate the development of the towns and to raise the status of urban dwellers. In 1832 it introduced a new estate category of "honorary citizens" for urban commercial and professional elites and gave them a number of privileges. In 1846 a system of municipal self-government began operation in St. Petersburg, aimed at drawing together the social groups living in the city and encouraging their active participation in urban life. This reform marked the growing role of the Ministry of Internal Affairs in the resolution of social problems. Nikolai Miliutin, an official in the ministry and the nephew of Pavel Kiselev, drafted this reform. He rapidly became one of the leaders of the enlightened bureaucracy.[33]

Along with measures affecting the urban population, the government took steps to resolve the crucial peasant question. Nicholas understood the connection between serfdom and the country's slow economic development as well as the threat that serfdom posed to social stability. (In one of its reports, the Third Section bluntly termed serfdom "the powder magazine beneath the state.") During Nicholas's reign, ten secret committees worked on solutions to the peasant question. The most important measure his government carried out was the reform of the state peasantry in 1837–41, which affected the lives of 20,050,000 peasants, or 34 percent of the population of European Russia. (Privately owned serfs numbered 21,164,000, only 1 million more.)[34] In 1842 the government issued the Law on Obligated Peasants, which gave landowners a new way to emancipate their serfs, by giving them land not as their property, as Alexander I's Decree on Free Cultivators had required, but only for their use. In the end, however, the practical results of all the measures on the peasant question proved no greater under Nicholas than they had under Alexander. Why was this the case?

Above all, from the very beginning Nicholas imposed strict limits on reform. Emancipation had to proceed gradually and, as much as possible, without the serfs themselves being aware of it. In no case must it infringe on the gentry's landownership. The gentry's land "is something holy, and no one may touch it," he declared in 1848.[35] Those words could serve as an epigraph for all his activity. Soviet historians regarded this approach as proof of the "pro-gentry class character" of the autocracy. Another explanation is possible, however. Nicholas did not want to disturb the delicate balance of forces in society by undermining the principle of the inviolability of private property, which had been applied to the gentry's estates since the time of Catherine II. There were other reasons as well. The ruin of the bulk of the gentry threatened to paralyze the system of administration, which in fact had no other agents outside the major towns. Nicholas's government was simply unable to carry out the intricate task of separating the gentry's power over their serfs from their prerogatives as landowners.

The reforms also had meager results because they were debated in socalled secret committees, whose work remained secret not only from society but from most members of the government. Often the highly placed reformers simply could not imagine how the country would receive a particular measure. Moreover, because they were secret, the committees remained immune to any influence from public opinion. Most dignitaries of the time stood for the preservation of serfdom. Therefore the reformers, even when they enjoyed the support of the emperor, had no way of inducing the committees to take practical decisions in regard to the peasant question. This determined the fate of the Law on Obligated Peasants, which Kiselev proposed. In their discussions of the project, the members of the secret committee of 1839 step by step rejected its main provisions. In the end, they made the law voluntary for the landowners rather than mandatory, as Kiselev had planned. Faced with the stubborn opposition of the highly placed dignitaries, Nicholas decided not to support his closest collaborator.[36]

The fate of Kiselev, the most outstanding reformer of Nicholas's era, merits detailed examination. Kiselev belonged to the generation of administrators and military men who rose to prominence in the patriotic upsurge of 1812. A hero of the war with Napoleon, he commanded the Southern Army and was closely acquainted with many of the Decembrists. His military career continued under Nicholas. From 1829 to 1834 he headed the administrative apparatus in the Danubian principalities of Moldavia and Wallachia, which had come under Russian administration after a war with Turkey. In his new post, Kiselev devised and implemented a series of reforms that dealt especially with regulating relations between landowners and peasants. His ability to combine the qualities of a military commander and a reformer assured him of the emperor's confidence. Nicholas called him his "chief of staff for peasant affairs."[37]

The extent of Kiselev's ties to the Decembrists and the degree to which he was aware of their plans remain unclear to historians. He certainly did not share their ideas for a revolutionary restructuring of Russian society. At the same time, however, he did not endorse conservative views. In Kiselev's opinion, Russia urgently needed timely reforms from above if it were to avert a social explosion from below. "The more I see," he wrote in 1852 of his governmental activity, "the more I fear a peasant uprising that would threaten the tranquillity of Russia and the existence of the gentry. It would be more sensible, of course, to ward off this evil than to let it develop and await its deplorable consequences with folded hands."[38] Reforms aimed at warding off a social explosion presupposed a broad application of the principle of compromise among the social estates.

On this principle Kiselev based his pet project, the Law on Obligated Peasants. He opposed giving the peasants land as their private property on the grounds that the peasants "by the force of an unbridled majority would upset the balance between the parts of the state organism."[39] At the same time, he rejected any thought of a landless emancipation of the serfs. He saw the solution as a compromise: giving the peasants land not as their property but for their use, while precisely spelling out in law the peasants' personal rights. The landowner would remain the owner of the land, but he would lose his power over the person of the peasant and could neither reduce the latter's allotment nor increase his obligations. Their personal freedom secured, the peasants would continue to fulfill their obligations to the landowners.

Kiselev understood, of course, that even under the most favorable conditions the landowners would not begin emancipating their serfs without a powerful outside stimulus. That was to be provided by the force of example, with the state peasants as the model to be copied. Thus reform of the state peasants, along with the Law on Obligated Peasants, became the most important part of Kiselev's program. In Kiselev's thinking, changes in the position of the state peasants, such as expanding their personal freedoms and strengthening their property rights, would inspire the landowners to change their relationship with their serfs.

As already mentioned, the transformation of the state-peasant village affected the daily lives of millions of people and became one of the autocracy's first experiences in large-scale social reform. Kiselev recognized the complexity of the task he faced, and he drew many young enlightened bureaucrats into the Ministry of State Domains, which had been created under his direction in 1837. In turn these officials, in 1837–41, helped to prepare and implement a series of reforms that were unprecedented in the history of the autocracy. The government put peasant landholding on an orderly footing by surveying allotments and resettling peasants from thickly populated to sparsely populated districts. It eased the burden of army recruitment. It shifted taxation from the "soul tax," on the person of the peasant, to landholding and handicraft production, that is, to the peasants' actual economic resources. The reforms included measures to prevent epidemics and fires, the creation of small-scale credit institutions and food warehouses in the event of famine, and the establishment of hospitals as well as veterinary and agronomy centers.[40] Between 1837 and 1856, the number of schools in state-peasant villages rose from 60 to 2,551, and the number of pupils from 1,800 to 110,994.[41] Kiselev also took steps to reorganize and strengthen the institutions of peasant self-government. Village and canton assemblies (a *volost,* or canton, was an administrative unit consisting of several communes) elected elders and other village officials, had charge of petty judicial cases, maintained order, and apportioned and collected taxes.

Although the government refrained from infringing on the rights of landowners in central Russia, it proceeded to do so in regard to the Polish gentry in the Western Region, who had actively participated in the Polish insurrection of 1830–31. In 1847 the government began to introduce "inventories," that is, regulations on the size of peasant allotments and the extent of their obligations. This reform improved the status of the peasants in the Western

Region—Lithuania, Belorussia, and the western part of Ukraine, which had once been part of Poland. These inventories formed the essence of Kiselev's original project on "obligated peasants." Many Russian dignitaries opposed the inventory reform, viewing it as a blow to the interests of the nobility as a whole and fearing the prospect of peasant reform throughout the territory of Russia. The inventory reform affected the southwestern provinces of Kiev, Volynia, and Podolia. Although suspended in the Northwestern Region (Vilna, Kovno, and Grodno provinces), it continued to hang like a sword of Damocles over the local gentry. It was no accident that the Northwestern Region would be the focus of reform in the next period of Russian history, the second half of the 1850s.

For all their accomplishments, Kiselev's reforms also had a negative side. In the course of their implementation, the number of bureaucratic officials grew considerably, imposing a heavy burden on the peasants for their maintenance. Zealous officials often treated the peasants in a high-handed fashion and interfered in their traditional economic practices. For example, the so-called "potato riots" of 1841–43, which involved some 300,000 peasants in European Russia, broke out when officials ordered peasants to set aside part of the land for the compulsory planting of potatoes.

Kiselev's reforms, for better or worse, clearly exposed the limits of the traditional system of all-embracing bureaucratic tutelage and demonstrated the necessity of finding new ways to implement governmental policy. In a report to Nicholas on the census in some of the provinces, one of his adjutant-generals wrote: "Out of one department in the Ministry of Finance there suddenly grew three departments, several chancelleries, fifty chambers, and hundreds of district boards, so that instead of 120 local boards there were now more than 1,500. Such an increase in the number of officials would be harmful in any country, but in Russia it has been and is ruinous to the empire."[42] The enlightened bureaucrats who followed in Kiselev's footsteps would retain their patron's belief that the state had to take the initiative in social reforms. They would adopt less direct methods of governmental intervention, however, in an effort to relieve the administrative apparatus of matters of secondary importance.

The contradictory course of the state-peasant reform in large part prevented Kiselev from holding his own in the discussions of the Law on Obligated Peasants and weakened his position in the committee of 1839. The practical results of the voluntary law were negligible. In fact, by the mid-1840s the government's plans to resolve the peasant question had failed, as the tone of Nicholas's speeches regarding serfdom clearly demonstrated. Even in the discussion of the Decree on Obligated Peasants in the State Council, Nicholas declared: "There is no doubt that serfdom in its present form is a palpable evil that is obvious to everyone, but to touch it now would be even more destructive."[43] The European revolutions in 1848 further reinforced the emperor's conservatism. Henceforth, deliberations on the peasant question—and on all other reforms—came to a halt, and the regime was left without a clear political program in the face of its inexorably growing contradictions.

The over-centralization and bureaucratization of Nicholas's system of administration underscored the impasse in the social sphere. Petty police controls failed to guarantee the observance of the laws and bred abuses and arbitrariness. The attempt to supervise nearly every aspect of social life from above led to an enormous growth of bureaucratic paperwork, which frequently hid the country's real problems from the authorities. The vastly increased number of officials gave rise to corruption and red tape. Formal reports, which often represented no real activity, became the chief criterion for evaluating the work of the bureaucracy. The higher echelons of the administration were overwhelmed by the flood of documents that rained down on them, and real administrative decisions fell in large part to middle-ranking officials. "I am not the one who governs Russia," the emperor himself declared in a fit of temper, "ten thousand department heads govern Russia."[44]

The administrative crisis of the early 1850s was also a personal crisis for Nicholas, for it represented the collapse of the principles on which his view of the world was based. In the words of Anna Tiutcheva, a maid of honor at court who knew Nicholas well, the emperor

> sincerely believed that he was in a position to see everything with his own eyes, hear everything with his own ears, regulate everything according to his own understanding, and transform everything by his own will. As a result, he merely surrounded his unchecked power with a heap of colossal abuses, all the more pernicious in that they took shelter from the outside behind official legality, and neither public opinion nor private initiative had the right to point them out or the possibility of combatting them.[45]

Nevertheless, the activity of Nicholas's government in regard to the problems facing Russia was not entirely fruitless. First of all, the legislative work on the peasant question generated a mass of material that would be used in the reform efforts of the second half of the 1850s. The enlightened bureaucrats in the Ministry of State Domains gained practical experience in the preparation of large-scale social reforms. They participated in the organization of economic and statistical research, collected and analyzed information, and learned to separate the kernel of truth from the mass of "official lies" that Nicholas's bureaucratic machine generated. The focal point of this type of work within the Ministry of State Domains was the Economic Department, "with its scholarly and progressive character," under the leadership of the eminent statistician and economist Andrei Zablotsky-Desiatovsky. Officials in the Ministry of State Domains cooperated with those in the Ministry of Internal Affairs. They exchanged opinions, ideas, and experiences. By the mid-1850s, at the middle level of the administration in central departments of the government, a cohesive group of officials had emerged who were ready to take part in the reforms that were now imminent.

Chapter 2

"A Time of External Slavery and Internal Freedom"

While reformers drew up plans in the government's chancelleries, the preconditions for reform were developing in Russian society, which seemed to have been cut off from all participation in politics. Nicholas I's strict police measures did not prevent the development of intellectual life in Russia. It became particularly active in the 1830s and the 1840s, attaining maturity and distinctiveness and forming clearly defined trends of thought. In trying to comprehend the surprisingly intense intellectual life under a strict police regime, Alexander Herzen called these decades "a time of external slavery and internal freedom."

How did this phenomenon come about? First, an "infrastructure," the external framework for the development of intellectual and cultural activity, took shape. Although suspicious of any manifestation of freethinking, Nicholas could not oppose education and learning as a whole, nor did he wish to do so. The educational and cultural institutions established under Alexander I continued to develop. In the first fifteen years of Nicholas's reign, the number of high schools increased from forty-eight to sixty-four, and in the course of his reign the number of students enrolled in those schools increased from seven thousand to eighteen thousand. Between 1836 and 1848 the number of university students more than doubled, from 2,002 to 4,016.[1] In the era of Nicholas I, state schools supplanted forms of education that had been popular earlier among the nobility: home schooling, boarding schools, and the use of private tutors.[2]

The growth of periodicals and book publishing supplemented the influence of the schools. By the end of the 1850s some two thousand books appeared each year, and the circulation of journals reached six thousand. The number of newspapers and journals issued in Russia in the first half of the century nearly quadrupled, from 64 to 230.[3] The size of the "reading public" also grew. This public then demanded books or journals to satisfy its thirst for knowledge of events in Russia and abroad. In the periodical literature of the 1830s and the 1840s, the literary almanac gave way to the "thick journal," a publication supported by subscribers and devoted to literary and public affairs. Frequently a thick journal became the outlet for a particular tendency in public opinion that could not set forth its program openly under the conditions of the time. The government, of course, vigilantly tracked attempts to broach political questions in the journals and quickly put a stop to them. Nevertheless, opportunities remained for the growth of intellectual life and the discussion, in veiled form, of current political and social problems. In large part, that was a result of governmental policy, and particularly of the activity of Sergei Uvarov, the minister of public education.

Under Nicholas I, Uvarov played the same role in the development of education and culture that Speransky had played in the legislative sphere and Kiselev in the area of peasant reforms.[4] A brilliantly educated man, with expertise in ancient history and philology, he became president of the Petersburg Academy of Sciences in 1811. Uvarov began his career in the reign of Alexander I as a staunch liberal, but the events of 1825–35—the Decembrist uprising, the Polish insurrection of 1830–31, and the wave of revolutions in the West—profoundly altered his worldview. Although he retained his faith in the great importance of culture and education, Uvarov concluded that they had to be conservative in nature and linked to Russia's historical traditions. He formulated a new governmental ideology—the theory of "Official Nationality"—to replace the rationalist ideas of the eighteenth-century Enlightenment.[5]

In a report on his ten years of activity as minister of public education in 1843, Uvarov wrote:

> In considering the task that had to be carried out without delay, . . . reason involuntarily almost gave way to despondency and vacillated in its conclusions with regard to the social storm then rocking Europe, the echo of which, more faintly or more strongly, reached us and threatened us with danger. Amid the rapid decline of religious and civil institutions in Europe, the universal spread of destructive ideas, and the grievous events that surrounded us on all sides, it was essential to place the fatherland on firm foundations that would serve as the basis for its prosperity, strength, and national life. It was necessary to find the principles that constitute the dis-

tinctive character of Russia, . . . to gather the sacred relics of its nationality into a single whole, and to fasten the anchor of our salvation to them.[6]

Those "firm foundations" became the three elements of Uvarov's formula: "Orthodoxy, Autocracy, Nationality."

Historians differ as to the sources and exact meaning of Uvarov's ideology. The three-part structure of his formula, which gave his ideas the appearance of a doctrine, reflected the thinking of the times. German philosophy, in which the principle of the triad figured prominently, was beginning to influence Russia in these years. The principle of "nationality" paid tribute to Romanticism and nationalism, widespread in Europe in the Napoleonic and post-Napoleonic period.[7] That was the most innovative, dynamic, and complex principle of Uvarov's ideology. In his formula, Uvarov sought to underscore the devotion of the common people to the tsar and to explain the defeat of the Decembrists as well as Russia's social and political tranquillity in a time of European revolutions. His interpretation emphasized that autocracy provided the best defense of the people's interests. His concept of "nationality" had another side to it, however. It included the idea that Russia's unique path of development would allow it to avoid Europe's upheavals.

Defining that path was a difficult task. Uvarov himself failed to give a precise description of it. He wrote in his report on the Ministry of Public Education:

> The question of nationality does not have the same unity as the two that precede it [Orthodoxy and autocracy]; but all three emanate from a single source and are linked on every page of the history of the Russian realm. With regard to nationality, the difficulty consisted of harmonizing ancient and modern notions; but nationality does not force us to go backward or to stand still; its ideas do not require immobility. The structure of the state, like the human body, changes its external appearance as it grows; its features alter over the years, but its physiognomy does not. It would be inappropriate to oppose this process; it is enough for us to preserve inviolate the sanctuary of our national concepts.[8]

Apparently Uvarov assumed that the principle of "nationality" would acquire substantive content in the course of the free development of intellectual and cultural life. Hence he adopted complex and contradictory policies in the area of education. On the one hand, following the general pattern of Nicholas's rule, Uvarov embraced strict measures "to increase, wherever possible, the number of intellectual dikes." He encouraged the closing of

"Public Fair in Moscow, Early Nineteenth Century." Engraving.

several journals, participated in the drafting of the harsh censorship statute of 1828 and the school statute of the same year, and intensified educational restrictions based on social status. The statute of 1835 significantly limited university autonomy. At the same time, even under the harsh statute, the censorship was quite flexible, and well-known scholars and literary figures served as censors. A number of journals enjoyed Uvarov's patronage, and the Academy of Sciences carried out an extensive program of scientific research.[9] Of particular significance was a program that sent young scholars abroad to study, thus guaranteeing Russia's universities a supply of native instructors and considerably raising the level of Russian higher education.

It must be emphasized that for all the strictness of his policies Uvarov in no way opposed education as such. He constantly stressed to the emperor the need to develop "the sound education that our era requires," to "make public education correspond to our order of things but not be alien to the European spirit," and to be attentive to "European ideas, which we can no longer do without."[10] Uvarov's disciples, however, adopted his slogans to further their careers, inevitably coarsened and vulgarized his ideas, and often reduced them to a primitive kind of self-glorification and advocacy of isolationism. "Of course, there is no country in Europe that can pride itself on such a harmonious political existence as our Fatherland," proclaimed Stepan Shevyrev, a professor at Moscow University. "That is the treasure . . . upon which Europe, divided within itself, gazes with particular envy."[11] The government's ideology also found reflection in the rather crude novels of Mikhail Zagoskin, the plays of Nestor Kukolnik, and the journalism of Faddei Bulgarin and Nikolai Grech.[12]

It is not surprising that such sentiments aroused protest in the most educated and thoughtful segment of society, including young professors who had been sent to Germany "for learning." Uvarov's policies failed to achieve their objective. He stimulated debate over Russia's national distinctiveness, but that debate went far beyond the limits acceptable to the government. Instead of creating the consensus within society that he had anticipated, the discussions grew inflamed. Protest—social and political as well as intellectual—continued.

Secret societies, mainly in the form of student circles that sprang up within the walls of Moscow University, had given rise to political protest at the beginning of Nicholas's reign. Some of them sought to prepare an immediate armed uprising, such as the circles of the brothers Petr, Mikhail, and Vasily Kritsky and Nikolai Sungurov, while others discussed urgent social and political problems in a spirit of opposition to the government, like Vissarion Belinsky's "Room Eleven Society" and the circle of Alexander Herzen and Nikolai Ogarev. The severe conditions of Nicholas's regime doomed such societies to destruction. The police quickly discovered the circles and broke them up; and their participants suffered various kinds of punishment, ranging from many years of hard labor to governmental service in provincial exile. The failure of these attempts at political protest led to a change in the forms of public activity. University lecture halls, the editorial offices of journals, fashionable salons, and groups of friends who met to discuss philosophy and literature replaced revolutionary organizations. The salons and philosophical circles became particularly prominent in the intellectual life of Russia in the 1830s and the 1840s. The authorities did not regard them with great suspicion, and they created the opportunity for people of diverse views to come together in an informal setting.[13]

Even before the Decembrist uprising, a circle called the Lovers of Wisdom, formed in Moscow to study the philosophy of Friedrich Schelling, included Dmitry Venevitinov, Vladimir Odoevsky, Stepan Shevyrev, Ivan and Petr Kireevsky, and Aleksandr Koshelev. The Lovers of Wisdom turned to philosophy in reaction to the exclusively political interests of the "men of December 14." Schelling's doctrine that every nation has its own mission challenged the naive Eurocentrism of the Decembrists. Interest in philosophical questions intensified with the defeat of the Decembrists. The catastrophic failure of the "Russian Robespierres" in 1825 and the government's refusal to allow the emergence of a liberal movement that might have been led by a Russian of the stature of the Marquis de Lafayette or Benjamin Constant demonstrated that before anyone undertook to remake Russia it was essential to understand what Russia was, what place it occupied in the world, and what basic forces determined the direction of its future development. The ideas of the German philosophers, particularly Georg Wilhelm Friedrich Hegel, provided an excellent tool for reflections of this kind. Hegel's ideas enabled the Russians to construct grandiose theories of world history, to generalize and systematize the facts of historical development, and to find logic and consistency in the chaos of past events.[14] Hegel's philosophy was the principal object of study in Nikolai Stankevich's circle of 1831–39, which included Konstantin Aksakov, Mikhail Bakunin, Vasily Botkin, Timofei Granovsky, Mikhail Katkov, and Vissarion Belinsky. The most important stimulus of Russia's intellectual life, however, was the publication in 1836 of Petr Chaadaev's "Philosophical Letter."

Although Chaadaev played an enormous role in the intellectual life of the 1830s and the 1840s, by birth, education, and ties of friendship he belonged to a different generation, that of the Decembrists. A brilliant guards officer and an aristocrat by origin, he was educated in the spirit of the Enlightenment. Even before the Decembrist uprising, however, he underwent a spiritual crisis, withdrew from society, and immersed himself in the study of mystical religious literature. He expounded the results of his reflections in a series of "Philosophical Letters," the first and most important of which appeared in 1836 in the journal *The Telescope*. (The other seven letters remained unpublished in his lifetime.) In Herzen's words, it was "a pistol shot in the night."[15] Chaadaev's "Letter" was a mirror image of the government's ideology. In response to the official glorification of Russia's differences from Europe, Chaadaev, while fully acknowledging and even emphasizing those differences, cast them in a starkly negative light. This interpretation came as a genuine shock to Russian society.

"We are alone in the world, we have given nothing to the world, we have taught it nothing," Chaadaev wrote. "We have not added a single idea to the sum total of human ideas; we have not contributed to the progress of the human spirit, and what we have borrowed of this progress we have distorted." Chaadaev took an extremely negative view of Russia's past: "There are no delightful recollections or charming images in our national memory, no powerful lessons in our national tradition." In fact, he considered Russia incapable of independent historical development. The source of this cheerless state of affairs went very deep. It originated with the baptism of Rus, which chose the Eastern, or Orthodox, variant of Christianity, thus binding Russia, he maintained, to the stagnant and decadent civilization of Byzantium. The Russians, deprived of the influence of the Catholic Church, with its dynamism and universalism, had no history of their own and were doomed to imitation.

> We must deliberately hammer into our heads things which have become habit and instinct with other peoples . . . We move so oddly in time that, as we advance, the immediate past is irretrievably lost to us . . . We are one of those nations which do not appear to be an integral part of the human race, but exist only in order to teach some great lesson to the world . . . We do not belong to any of the great families of the human race; we are neither of the West nor of the East, and we have not the traditions of either. Placed, as it were, outside of time, we have not been touched by the universal education of the human race.[16]

The reaction of the authorities to the appearance of such opinions in the press was not hard to predict. The government closed down *The Telescope* and exiled its editor, Nikolai Nadezhdin, to Ust-Sysolsk, a town on the Vychegda River in the northern forest. The censor who had approved the publication of the article, Mikhail Boldyrev, lost his position as rector of Moscow University. Chaadaev himself was officially declared insane and placed under medical and police supervision. The impact of the "Letter," however, was irreversible. Chaadaev's views offended literally everyone, something he may have counted on when he took the risky step of publishing them. Those who placed a high value on Western institutions shared Chaadaev's criticism of Russia but disagreed with his unconditional separation of Russia from Europe. Those who believed in Russia's distinctiveness without adhering to the government's ideology also felt offended. The "Letter" thus became the catalyst for a detailed formulation of the intellectual currents that were gradually emerging in Russian society.

The period from the end of the 1830s to the end of the 1840s, a time of intense spiritual and intellectual life and passionate discussions, has become known as the "remarkable decade." It should be noted that Chaadaev himself participated in these discussions, and his intellectual development continued. Following the publication of the "Letter," he wrote the "Apology of a Madman," in which he repudiated his negative views. The "Apology," unpublished in his lifetime, was widely discussed in the philosophical circles and salons. In the "Apology," Chaadaev interpreted Russia's lack of rich historical traditions as an advantage that would enable the country to make a "great leap" into the future without the hindrance of old prejudices. "I am thoroughly convinced," he wrote, "that we are called upon to resolve a large share of the problems of social life, to complete a large share of the ideas that have arisen in the old societies, and to answer the most important questions that occupy mankind . . . By the very nature of things, so to speak, we are destined to be the real arbitrators of many of the disputes that will come before the great tribunal of the human spirit and human society."

Chaadaev claimed that as a "young country" standing "on the edge" of the civilized world, Russia possessed all the advantages of a detached observer "free of unbridled passions and contemptible self-interest." He wrote: "I believe that we have come later than others so as to do better than they have, so as not to fall into their errors, delusions, and superstitions. It would be a profound misunderstanding of our destiny to assert that we are somehow doomed to repeat the whole long series of mad deeds committed by nations that found themselves in a less favorable position than ours, and to endure all the misfortunes that they have experienced."[17] Chaadaev's paradoxical position, which recognized that Russia was backward but interpreted that backwardness as an advantage, would become the axis on which ideological debates would turn in the rest of the nineteenth and the early twentieth centuries.

"Russia is not part of the West, but it absolutely must have close relations with the West and is perfectly capable of establishing them." That was the basic idea of the Westernizers, one of the intellectual currents that emerged in the 1830s and the 1840s. Employing Hegel's doctrines, the

Westernizers argued that all mankind follows a single path of develop-ment, that every country must assimilate the achievements of West Euro-pean civilization in one way or another, and that it is impossible and dangerously utopian to oppose inevitable change. Timofei Granovsky, a professor at Moscow University and the founder of the Westernizers, drew on the history of Western Europe to argue that the replacement of some social forms by others was inevitable, so that feudal relations everywhere must die out, the system of social estates must collapse, and hired labor must replace the compulsory labor of the serfs.[18] Granovsky's audience did not find it difficult to draw analogies with contemporary Russia. Granovsky's teaching, based on the philosophy of Hegel, strongly implied that social development followed regular laws. In Herzen's words, Granovsky "thought with the use of history, taught with the use of history, and then made propaganda with the use of history."

Granovsky's scholarly works and teaching activity created an intellectual atmosphere that contributed to the formation of the reform program. During his tenure as a professor, many future public figures and reformers of the 1860s and the 1870s studied at Moscow University. At the end of the 1840s, he established close contacts with the brothers Dmitry and Nikolai Miliutin, prominent representatives of the enlightened bureaucracy who belonged to the Petersburg circle of Westernizers.[19] His public lectures in the 1840s en-joyed enormous popularity, which governmental pressure and the official ideology were powerless to combat. The attempt by Professor Shevyrev to give public lectures of his own in the spirit of "Official Nationality" as a counterweight to Granovsky ended in failure.[20]

The essence of historical progress, in Granovsky's view, lay in the lib-eration of the individual and the triumph of a rational worldview: "man becomes more and more conscious, and the essence of his being becomes clearer and better defined." Vissarion Belinsky, the leading critic of the journals *Notes of the Fatherland* and *The Contemporary*, held the same views as Granovsky and asserted them even more staunchly. "Reason now seeks itself in everything," he proclaimed, "and recognizes as real only that in which it finds itself. In this respect, our times are sharply distinguished from all previous historical eras. Reason has subjugated everything and prevailed over everything . . . Everything must derive from it the confirma-tion of its own independence and reality."[21] Critical analysis must extend to every sphere of life and become a powerful stimulus for drawing Russia and Europe together: "What is truly great will always withstand doubt and will never decline, be diminished, or suffer eclipse; it will only be strength-ened, exalted, and enlightened by doubt and negation . . . Doubt and nega-tion are the true signs of the moral death of whole peoples, but of which peoples? Those that have grown antiquated and exist only mechanically, like living corpses, such as the Byzantine and the Chinese." That did not apply to the Russian people, who are "so youthful, fresh, and virginal." "We . . . not only will be but are already becoming European Russians and Russian Europeans. We have been since the reign of Catherine II, and are now succeeding day by day."[22]

The Westernizers, of course, admitted that Russia's historical traditions and the general tenor of Russian life hardly favored the triumph of the principles that they were proclaiming: individualism, rationalism, and Western education. They placed little hope on the common people, who, in Granovsky's words, resembled "nature or the Scandinavian god Thor—senselessly cruel and senselessly indifferent"; they "grow inert under the weight of their historical and immediate circumstances."[23] Progress depended on the heroic deeds of a strong individual, specifically an individual standing at the helm of the state. It is not surprising that the Westernizers idolized Peter the Great. Belinsky wrote: "Peter is my philosophy, my religion, my revelation in everything that concerns Russia. He is an example for the great and the small who want to do something positive and be useful in some way."[24] The Westernizers deemed Peter's reforms so significant that they accepted the coercion, mass suffering, and expansion of the principles of compulsion associated with the achievements of the tsar-reformer.

The "younger generation" of Westernizers, consisting of the Moscow University professors Konstantin Kavelin, Sergei Soloviev, and Boris Chicherin, developed the general ideas of the Westernizers, made them more concrete, and applied them to Russian history.[25] Kavelin elaborated the theory of the dying out of "clan life," from which the autonomous individual emerged in the course of historical progress. He believed that Peter's reforms marked the most important stage in this process. Soloviev viewed Russian history as a struggle between the pro-state and anti-state tendencies, with the former ultimately triumphant. The state, which Soloviev viewed positively, eventually triumphed in this context. He included among the anti-state tendencies the remnants of clan life in the government of medieval Rus and popular uprisings during the seventeenth and eighteenth centuries. Chicherin propounded the idea of the "enslavement" and "emancipation" of the social estates. He argued that the Russian state, in the unfavorable economic and geopolitical circumstances of the fifteenth to the seventeenth centuries, found it necessary to "enslave" the various estates, that is, to limit their freedom and subject them to the fulfillment of tasks specified by the state. Subsequently, as conditions improved, the state "emancipated" the estates. In 1762 the nobility won its freedom from obligatory service, and by the middle of the nineteenth century the time had come to emancipate the peasants from serfdom. Thus the Westernizers' interpretation of Russian history served as a theoretical foundation for future reforms.

The historical concepts of the Westernizers in the 1830s and the 1840s blurred the dividing line between educated society and state officials. They provided a theoretical justification for the existence of an all-powerful Russian state and validated its allegedly creative role in future reforms. Fruitful contacts became possible between representatives of educated society and progressive officials, particularly the enlightened bureaucrats.[26] The Westernizers' position also had a weak spot, however. The cult of the all-powerful state threatened to justify a scornful attitude toward the interests of society. Likewise, the emphasis on individualism relegated the "dark masses" of the people to the background. Not everyone regarded the path taken by the West as a cloudless vista in an era that witnessed revolutions, the rise of an industrial proletariat, ruthless competition, unemployment, and other "evils" of industrial capitalism. Within educated society, therefore, the arguments of the Westernizers provoked protests, one of the most striking of which came from the Slavophiles.

In contrast to the Westernizers, the Slavophiles—Aleksei Khomiakov, Ivan and Petr Kireevsky, Ivan and Konstantin Aksakov, Iury Samarin, and Aleksandr Koshelev—clung to the Romantic idea that every nation has a special historical mission; Russia's mission was higher than the West's. They repeated much of Chaadaev's logic, interpreting as advantages those features of Russian history that had traditionally been considered defects. Yes, the Slavophiles declared, the principle of the individual scarcely existed in Rus, but that fact allowed it to smooth over the sharp edges of individualism that were manifesting themselves destructively in the West's revolutions. According to Ivan Kireevsky,

> A man belonged to his commune, and the commune to him. Landed property, the source of individual rights in the West, belonged to society in Russia . . . The uniqueness of the private individual, the foundation of Western development, was as little known in Russia as social despotism . . . Society was not despotic and could not organize itself or invent laws for itself, because it was not divided from other, similar societies that were governed by unchanging custom.

The lack of legal principles in Rus merely reflected the rule of unwritten customs, which exerted a more powerful influence than formal laws. "The very word 'law' was unknown to us in its Western sense and signified only fairness, or justice."[27]

Finally, the Orthodox Church, which had not created a rationalistic philosophy of its own, preserved a more important intellectual foundation: "en-lightenment is not brilliant but profound; it is not a matter of luxury, of mate-rial well-being, that has as its objective the comforts of external life, but it is something internal and spiritual." On the whole, as Aleksei Khomiakov wrote, "it would be shameful for us not to surpass the West . . . Westerners must set aside their entire past as something vile and create all that is good within themselves. For us, it is enough to resurrect and clarify the old, to bring it into consciousness and life. Our hopes for the future are great."[28]

At first glance, the Slavophiles' doctrines may seem to be self-glorify-ing and to bear a close resemblance to the theory of "Official Nationality." In fact, an unbridgeable gulf existed between these ideological systems. To be sure, the Slavophiles published in the journal *The Muscovite*, which was edited by Mikhail Pogodin, one of the pillars of "Official Nationality," and they approved of some of the initiatives of Pogodin, Shevyrev, and their associates.[29] The most radical, intransigent Westernizers, particularly Belinsky, exacerbated the ideological conflict by consciously and system-atically lumping the Slavophiles together with the proponents of "Official Nationality." Nevertheless, the two cannot be fully equated. The Slavophiles consistently criticized the government, which viewed them with even greater suspicion than it viewed the Westernizers.[30] The Aksakovs, Khomiakov, and their friends sharply attacked the defects of Russian reality, including serfdom, the estate system, and Nicholas I's method of rule by police and bureaucracy. They had no intention of eliminating them by following Eu-ropean models, however. In fact, the Slavophiles believed that those de-fects stemmed directly from the Petrine reforms. They were inseparable from the coercion, compulsion, and destruction of popular customs cre-ated by the individualistic outlook of a tiny noble elite. The continued ex-istence of Peter I's system, and especially any attempt to repeat its methods in the nineteenth century, raised the threat of revolution. Salvation required a return to pre-Petrine patterns of development.

What were those patterns? In the opinion of the Slavophiles, state and society (the "land") in pre-Petrine Russia enjoyed a special relationship, based on trust, unknown in the West. The state concentrated all political activity in its own hands, while society exercised complete freedom outside of politics: in the family, the economy, and spiritual life. This demarcation of spheres began literally with the first stage of Russian history. (According to the Pri-mary Chronicle, the Russian state originated when the Slavs called in for-eign rulers, the Varangians, or Normans.) Konstantin Aksakov wrote: "The Slavs do not form states themselves, they invite them in . . . They do not confuse the 'land' with the state, and they resort to the latter as a necessary means of preserving the former. The state, the political structure, was not the object of their desire, for they separated themselves, or the life of the 'land,' from the state, and they called in the latter to preserve the former."[31]

The Slavophiles argued that Peter's bureaucratic empire had destroyed the harmonious interaction between the state and the "land." Peter had sought to change the age-old customs of the people and to bring all areas of social life under his control. The pre-Petrine harmony must now be restored, leaving the political sphere to the state and granting "spiritual" freedoms to the people: freedom of speech, freedom of the press, freedom of conscience. The Slavophiles decisively rejected Western constitutionalism. "No guarantee is necessary!" Konstantin Aksakov exclaimed. "A guarantee is evil. Where it is necessary, good is absent; it would be better for a life from which good is absent to be destroyed than to exist with the help of evil. Strength resides in the ideal. What is the meaning of conditions and agreements if there is no inner strength?"[32] The most precise formulation of the Slavophiles' demands in the political sphere appeared in Konstantin Aksakov's memorandum to Alexander II in 1855: "Let *the government have the right to action* and consequently the power of the law; let *the people have the right of opinion* and consequently freedom of speech."[33]

The doctrines of the Slavophiles are harder to interpret than those of the Westernizers, and more difficult to place on the spectrum of political ideas. On the one hand, in drawing a clear distinction between the "state" and the "land" and placing a firm limit on the government's interference in the "land's" affairs, the Slavophiles formulated a more complex, dynamic, and in some respects more profound conception of social development than that of the Westernizers. According to Andrzej Walicki, Konstantin Aksakov "subconsciously accepted and applied to Russia's past one of the chief assumptions of Western-European liberal doctrine—the principle of the total separation of the political and social spheres."[34] On the other hand, the Slavophiles' contempt for legal principles and their suspicion of individualism mean that they cannot unconditionally be ranked as liberals. The historian Nikolai Tsimbaev has proposed the term "untraditional liberalism" to define the Slavophiles' outlook.[35]

Likewise, the Westernizers' outlook was so distinctive that it is equally difficult to identify it wholly with liberalism.[36] For all their contradictions and disagreements, the Westernizers and the Slavophiles had many views in common. They could agree in their protest against bureaucratism, serfdom, and the estate structure, their realization that reform was essential, and their anxiety over Russia's increasing backwardness in relation to the West. There is a good deal of evidence that they maintained respect for each other. Alexander Herzen, a prominent Westernizer, wrote: "Yes, we were their opponents, but very strange ones. We had the same love, but not the same way of loving. From our early years, the same powerful, unaccountable, physiologically passionate feeling burned in both of us. They took it for a memory and we for a prophecy: a feeling of limitless, all-embracing love for the Russian people, Russian life, the Russian cast of mind. Like Janus, or the double-headed eagle, we looked in different directions, but one heart beat within us."[37]

The Westernizers and Slavophiles gave the discussions of the 1830s and the 1840s depth and substance, allowing important issues of social development to be examined from different angles. In the words of Pavel Annenkov, a Westernizer, "The parties had to contend the way they did, in the public eye, in order to elucidate the full importance of the ideas they were presenting."[38] Their "cross-examination" of Russia's key problems enabled them to elaborate theoretical principles for the future reform of Russia's economic, social, and administrative system. Reformist ideas aimed at gradual improvement were not the only product of the intellectual ferment of the "remarkable decade," however. Most important was the emergence of a revolutionary ideology calling for the total reconstruction of the existing order.

Vissarion Belinsky played a special role in this respect. Ivan Turgenev called him the "driving force" in the intellectual life of the 1830s and the 1840s. Extremely gifted and receptive to new ideas, Belinsky also exhibited a characteristic feature of the intellectuals of his time: a predilection for abstract debate and for conclusions that he could not verify in practice. A thirst for absolute truth and a tendency to maximalism drove Belinsky from one theory to another, taking each one to its extreme.

At the end of the 1830s, under the influence of a poorly understood formula of Hegel—"everything real is rational, and everything rational is real"—Belinsky went through a brief period of "reconciliation with reality." Believing in the "rationality" of autocracy, he published a series of articles, close in spirit to the official ideology, that extolled the existing order. The patent incongruity between Russian reality and the ideals of the Westernizers, however, and the absence of real reforms in Russian life, prevented the period of "reconciliation" from lasting very long. By the beginning of the 1840s, Belinsky was angrily cursing his "vile desire to reconcile with vile reality." "My Lord, how many loathsome abominations I uttered in print, in all sincerity, with all the fanaticism of wild conviction!" Belinsky wrote to his friend Vasily Botkin, a Westernizer. "The thought of what came over me—a fever, or madness—is frightening. I feel like a convalescent."[39]

Disillusioned with his previous idol, Belinsky began to reexamine the contemporary order with redoubled energy and concluded that it could be forcibly overthrown. This position created a gulf between Belinsky and most of the Westernizers (except for Herzen), for whom revolution was unacceptable. On the whole, Belinsky retained his hopes for reform and did not approve of a revolutionary course in every respect. Under the influence of his hatred for the existing order, however, sentences burst from his pen that a Granovsky or a Chicherin could not accept. He wrote, for example, "People are so stupid that they must be led forcibly to happiness," and declared: "The thousand-year kingdom of God will be established on earth not by the sugary and enthusiastic phrases of idealistic and starry-eyed Girondists [liberals during the French Revolution], but by terrorists—by the double-edged sword of the words and deeds of Robespierres and Saint-Justs."[40]

Views of this sort, of course, could not appear in the censored press. Instead, Belinsky expressed them in an open letter of 1847 to Nikolai Gogol, which at once achieved immense popularity in Russian society and circulated in thousands of copies. Gogol, the great Russian writer and Belinsky's idol, had undergone a severe moral and spiritual crisis and in the late 1840s condemned his earlier work. He now called for spiritual self-perfection and the complete acceptance of the existing order. To Belinsky, such a position seemed not just absurd but a desecration of his most cherished ideals. The pages of his letter to Gogol painted a dismal picture of Nicholas's Russia, "the dreadful spectacle of a country in which men trade in men, . . . a country where people refer to themselves not by their proper names but by degrading nicknames such as Van'ka, Steshka, Vas'ka, Palashka; a country, finally, which not only affords no guarantee for personal safety, honor, and property but which cannot even maintain internal order and has nothing to show but vast corporations of office-holding thieves and robbers." The solution, in Belinsky's opinion, lay in radical social and political transformation: "Russia sees her salvation not in mysticism, not in asceticism, not in pietism, but in the achievements of civilization, enlightenment, and humanitarianism."[41]

With the "Letter to Gogol," Belinsky finally burned his bridges to the government. In the last years of his life, the authorities were preparing a "nice warm cell" for him in the Peter and Paul Fortress, and after his death in 1848 the secret-police official Leonty Dubelt said with regret: "He departed too soon. We would have let him rot in the fortress." Mention of Belinsky in the press was forbidden until the death of Nicholas I in 1855, and publication of his "Letter to Gogol" was banned until 1905. Nevertheless, despite the government's repression, Belinsky's letter and his other works continued to enjoy great popularity. Their circulation in manuscript form attested to the failure of the official ideology.

Who were the men seeking answers in Belinsky's works to the questions that troubled them? They were the so-called "men of diverse ranks," whose entry into the historical arena reflected social displacements in Nicholas's Russia and foreshadowed greater ideological changes in the second half of the nineteenth century. Despite the efforts of the authorities in Nicholas's reign to increase the number of university students who were of noble origin, the nobles still preferred to send their sons into military or civil service. The proportion of sons of nobles and officials enrolled in the universities fell from 67 percent to 61.2 percent between 1836 and 1844.[42] The vacant places went to students from lower social strata: impoverished gentry, clergy, lower officials, and some townspeople, merchants, and peasants. These individuals brought a particular worldview to the ranks of educated society, one that differed appreciably from that of the nobility. Because the "men of diverse ranks" had broken their ties with the customs and traditions of the social estates from which they came, they were prepared to adopt the most extreme theories for reconstructing the world around them, and their bitter sense of social inferiority goaded them into opposition to the authorities. It is not surprising, therefore, that in the 1840s they sought inspiration not only in Belinsky's writings, which were permeated with a spirit of rejection of the existing order, but also in Western social and political theories, including the most radical of them, socialism.

Mikhail Butashevich-Petrashevsky's circle, a literary and political society active in Petersburg from 1845 to 1849, discussed the works of Charles Fourier, Claude-Henri de Saint-Simon, and other West European socialists, as well as Belinsky's "Letter to Gogol." The circle included writers, high-school teachers, university students, lower officials, and junior officers. Most of its members limited themselves to discussions of political and social theories and news of political life in the West. Some of the "Petrashevists," however, led by Nikolai Speshnev, went on to discuss the possibility of preparing a peasant uprising. At the same time, the Cyril and Methodius Society, whose members included Taras Shevchenko and Nikolai Kostomarov, attempted to combine theories of social and ethnic emancipation in Ukraine and began drawing up plans for the creation of a federated socialist republic of all the Slavic peoples. When the European revolutions of 1848 broke out, the government dealt extremely harshly with the secret societies. The Petrashevists received particularly severe punishment. The members of the circle were sentenced to various terms of imprisonment, hard labor, and military service, and the most active participants, twenty-one in all, received the death penalty. Just as a firing squad prepared to execute these men, their sentences were commuted to long terms at hard labor. One of the condemned, Fyodor Dostoevsky, spent four years at hard labor in Omsk, Siberia, and another five years as a private in the army.

The events of 1848 revealed the failure of Uvarov's system. Social thought was moving in a direction unacceptable to the government, and Uvarov's policy of alternating between leniency and repression had inexorably reached a dead end. After Uvarov himself retired in 1849, the government reverted to open repression. As a supplement to preliminary censorship, a secret committee under the direction of Dmitry Buturlin meted out punitive censorship. Society lost nearly all opportunity to express its views in the press. The government restricted the number of university students and abolished the remnants of university autonomy. The content of professors' lectures was now subject to review by university authorities, and the teaching of certain topics was forbidden, including political economy, foreign law, and the history of philosophy. The government virtually prohibited the travel of foreigners to Russia and of Russians to the West. In essence, these measures represented the death throes of the regime, and it could not pursue them consistently for any length of time.

The repressions of the "seven dismal years," from 1848 to Nicholas's death in 1855, affected all currents of Russian social thought. While the police were planning Belinsky's arrest and breaking up the Petrashevsky Circle and the Cyril and Methodius Society, the Slavophiles Iury Samarin and Ivan Aksakov were also arrested for brief periods. (The police charged Samarin with criticizing the government's nationality policy in the Baltic region, and Aksakov with expressing sympathy for Samarin in a private letter.) In 1852, after an unsuccessful attempt to publish *Moscow Miscellany*, a journal that expounded Slavophile doctrines, Aksakov was prohibited forever from serving as an editor. All the representatives of educated society took an extremely negative view of the government's policies in the "seven dismal years." Aksakov wrote, "It is vile and depressing . . . every honest thought is labeled Jacobinism, and the triumph of the old order of things in Europe allows our rotten society to triumph as well." Granovsky wrote to Herzen, "My heart aches when I think of what we were before and what we have become now."[43] At the same time, Russian society had matured considerably by the end of the 1840s. It was no longer willing to submit to government repression, and it now had opportunities for resistance. Herzen, who had emigrated from Russia in 1847, in 1853 founded the Free Russian Press in London, which became the rostrum of uncensored Russian thought. His press would play a special role in the late 1850s, when the peasant reform was being planned.

In emigration Herzen also developed a new theory of revolution that Russian radicals would adopt in the second half of the nineteenth century. Representatives of the radical and revolutionary wing of Russian social thought felt an acute need for such a theory at the beginning of the 1850s. European socialist ideas held out the attractive prospect of a decisive transformation, but they had little to offer Russia specifically. They suggested that Russia would once again trail behind Western Europe, even on the road to a socialist society. Herzen tried to work past this difficulty. He had the advantage of observing the revolution of 1848 in France, when the bourgeoisie brutally suppressed a proletarian uprising that took place under the banner of socialism.

In evaluating the revolution of 1848, Herzen concluded that Europe was incapable of achieving socialism because it was too thoroughly steeped in bourgeois values. Russia, where bourgeois relationships were practically unknown, would be the first to reach socialism. In effect, Herzen repeated Chaadaev's thesis of the advantages of backwardness: "On some issues, we are freer and more advanced than Europe because we are so much more backward . . . The liberals are afraid of losing their freedom, but we do not have any freedom; they are afraid that the government will interfere in industrial matters, but our government interferes in everything; they are afraid of losing their individual rights, but we have yet to acquire them." Herzen asserted that "our natural, half-savage way of life corresponds more fully to the ideal that Europe has dreamt about than the tenor of life of the Romano-German world. What is only a hope for the West, toward which all its efforts are directed, is already an accomplished fact for us, from which we are beginning. Though we are oppressed by the imperial autocracy, we are halfway to socialism, just as the ancient Germans, while worshiping Thor or Odin, were halfway to Christianity."[44]

Herzen, of course, did not regard Russia as a "blank slate" on which one could simply inscribe "socialist characters" to make the transition to a new society. He believed that the precondition for the establishment of socialism in Russia was the peasant commune, in which individual ownership of land did not exist and the common good took precedence over private interests. By placing the commune at the center of his theory, Herzen tried to eliminate a weakness of the Westernizers' doctrines: their scornful attitude toward the common people, their customs, and their traditions. (Most Westernizers were decidedly hostile to the commune.) Recognition of the commune did not bring Herzen closer to the Slavophiles, however. They regarded the commune as an instrument for reconciliation and the smoothing over of contradictions, while Herzen viewed it as the basis for a decisive social and political transformation. During the preparation of the peasant reform in the coming years, the Slavophiles would act in concert with the moderate Westernizers, and Herzen's appeal to the Slavophiles—the notion that socialism was "a bridge on which we can shake each other's hand"—would meet with no response.[45]

On the whole, the theoretical discussions of Russia's future in the "remarkable decade" came to an end in the early 1850s. A transition to practical action began that would divide the participants in those discussions in new ways: the Westernizers and Slavophiles together would form the moderate camp, opposed on the left by the radicals and revolutionaries. As for the conservative proponents of "Official Nationality," they would suffer intense disappointment and the bankruptcy of their former views in the mid-1850s as a result of Russia's defeat in the Crimean War of 1853–56.

Chapter 3

A Colossus with Feet of Clay

After expelling Napoleon from its territory in 1812 and playing the leading role in his defeat, Russia became one of the most influential participants in the Concert of Europe. In the words of Professor Mikhail Pogodin, "Having victoriously repulsed such an attack, liberated Europe from such an enemy, and deposed him from such a height, does Russia have anything to fear? Given the resources that it possesses, it needs no one, and everyone needs it. Who would dare dispute its primacy, who would prevent it from determining the fate of Europe and the fate of all humanity if it wished to do so?"The journalist Nikolai Polevoi wrote, "How can a European boast of his puny little fist? Only the Russian has a real fist, a fist *comme il faut*, the ideal of a fist. Indeed, there is nothing reprehensible in that fist, nothing base, nothing barbaric. On the contrary, it possesses a great deal of significance, power, and poetry."A resolution of the Secret Committee on Peasant Affairs of 1846 declared: "As long as an unforeseen fate does not deprive Russia of its unity and might, the other powers cannot serve as an example for it. This colossus requires a different foundation for liberty and different concepts of liberty, with regard not only to the peasantry but to all the social estates. Russia's foundation has been and must remain autocracy. Without it, [the Empire] will not be able to exist in its present grandeur."[1]

These statements reflect the attitude of Russia's ruling circles in an era when nothing seemed to threaten the country's power. Neither before nor after that time, however, was tsarist Russia destined to exert such influence. The defeat in the Crimean War of 1853–56, which brought an end to the period of Russia's power, came as a great shock. The impotence of Russia's huge army against a relatively small allied expeditionary force, the country's international isolation, and the hostility of European public opinion jolted

Russian society and prepared it for the reforms of the 1860s and the 1870s. These reforms marked the beginning of a new era in Russian history.

Russia's predominance in European affairs—"we were Europe's chief of police," as Ivan Aksakov put it—led contemporaries to question Russia's future intentions. How would the empire use its enormous potential? Many observers were convinced that Russia's principal aim was to extend its influence as far as possible. The Marquis de Custine, the French traveler, wrote:

> the Russian people must have become unsuited for anything except the conquest of the world . . . one cannot explain the sacrifices imposed here on the individual by society in any other way. If excessive ambition parches the heart of a man, it may also dry up thought and pervert the judgement of a nation to the point where it will sacrifice its freedom for victory. Without this deep motive, whether admitted or not, which many men perhaps unknowingly obey, the history of Russia seems to me an inexplicable enigma.[2]

The belief in Russia's inherent aggressiveness was widespread in European society. The reality, however, was more complex. As a conservative in matters relating to the country's internal order, Nicholas I did not seek to expand its frontiers. He understood that ambitious attempts at conquest would undermine Russia's social and political stability. Nicholas left a will in which he urged his son and heir Alexander II not to enlarge the empire but to concentrate on its internal well-being. The government instructed Russian diplomats and secret agents of the Third Section abroad to emphasize constantly that aggression and territorial expansion were not Russia's objectives.[3]

Nonetheless, Custine's suspicions had some basis. Although Nicholas did not harbor any aggressive plans, he stood firmly for the preservation of the status quo in Europe as the essential condition for maintaining stability in Russia and was prepared to support it with all his might. In opposing revolution, Nicholas constantly spoke of "the common enemies of peace and order" who threatened all the European states. In addition, Nicholas assumed on the basis of the experience of 1789 that any revolution would be a prologue to a great European war. These considerations impelled him to revive the Holy Alliance, though with limited objectives and devoid of the ideological fervor of his predecessor, Alexander I. In 1833 Russia, Austria, and Prussia concluded the Berlin Convention, under which the government of each country, in the event of internal disorders, could request assistance from the others to suppress revolution.

In Russia's foreign policy, the personal influence of the emperor was particularly pronounced. Nicholas's minister of foreign affairs, Count Karl Nesselrode, served for the most part as just a highly placed assistant to the emperor. Nicholas paid close attention to foreign affairs in order to preserve Russia's status as a powerful participant in the Concert of Europe and as a great military power. It was no accident that the military element became a prominent feature of the "image of autocracy" in the era of Nicholas I.[4] The "soldierly" conduct of the emperor himself, the appointment of generals to high government posts, the ceremonial parades, and the "empire" style of official architecture, were all intended to convince his subjects of Russia's inexhaustible military might and invincibility. This approach impressed many contemporaries, but it was fraught with serious danger. In tying the success of his policy to diplomatic and military victories, Nicholas imposed a heavy burden on his regime. Not just a clear defeat but even an equivocal outcome of an international conflict threatened to deal it a heavy blow. Outwardly, Nicholas's system seemed highly formidable, but in reality it remained a fragile structure.

How did Russia's foreign policy develop? At the beginning of his reign, Nicholas broke with Alexander I's ambivalent policy in the Middle East and decisively supported the Greek uprising. "Unless all my allies unanimously and conscientiously seek the same goal, a speedy end to this affair, they will force me to take it in hand and complete it alone," Nicholas declared to the French ambassador.[5] His threat was effective. Britain and France acted in concert with Russia. In October 1827, a joint British, French, and Russian squadron destroyed a Turkish fleet in Navarino Bay. A Russo-Turkish War followed in 1828–29, as a result of which Greece won autonomy and subsequent independence. Turkey ceded to Russia the strategically important territories of the Danube delta and the Black Sea coast of the Caucasus.

The conquered territories were important, but they were insignificant in comparison with what Russia might have received, with its army poised outside of Constantinople itself. Nicholas's moderate demands surprised contemporaries, for he seemed to hold the fate of the Turkish Empire in his hands. He had explicitly limited the losses Turkey was to incur. "We do not want Constantinople," he wrote to Nesselrode. "That would be the most dangerous conquest we could make."[6] Nicholas assumed that preserving Turkey as a weak neighbor served Russia's interests better than destroying it. A logical extension of this policy was his direct support for the sultan when the pasha of Egypt rebelled at the beginning of the 1830s. In 1833, a Russian expeditionary corps landed on the shores of the Bosporus and saved the sultan from the Egyptian forces threatening him. Nicholas declared that he "would always remain an enemy of revolt and a true friend of the sultan."[7]

That policy paid large dividends. The sultan, now essentially under Russia's protection, was forced to conclude the Treaty of Unkiar-Skelessi in 1833, a great success for Nicholas's Middle Eastern policy. Under its terms, Turkey opened the Black Sea Straits to Russian warships but closed them to the warships of all other powers. This success had a dark side, however: it was achieved at the price of keeping numerous Slavic and Orthodox peoples under the rule of the Turkish Empire. At the time, Nicholas regarded this state of affairs as unavoidable. In international relations he gave first priority not to ethnic or religious considerations but to geopolitical calculations and the desire to maintain the existing order in Europe. Nicholas's government, despite its assertion of Russian uniqueness in the ideology of "Official Nationality," regarded the doctrines of the Slavophiles with great scorn. Official documents emphasized that "Slavism is nothing but a mask concealing the revolutionary propaganda of the French and the Poles, who seek to incite the Slavic subjects of the Austrian Empire and the sultan," and that Russian patriotism should proceed "not from the Slavic principle, which has been created by the play of fantasy, but from the Russian principle, with no admixture of political ideas."[8]

Nicholas reexamined this policy, however, when the Crimean War began. The manifesto on the declaration of war proclaimed that "Russia is fighting for Christian truth and the defense of its co-religionist brothers who are being oppressed by savage enemies." During the war, the Russian command made plans to provoke an uprising of Austrian and Turkish Slavs. By this time, however, Nicholas's policies had considerably undermined Russia's reputation and the government made no efforts to gain the support of the Balkan Slavs.[9]

Nicholas's suspicion of the principle of national self-determination arose also from the threat that nationalist movements were beginning to pose to the integrity of the Russian Empire itself. At the end of 1830 the long-simmering discontent in Poland broke out into open insurrection. The rebellion had two causes: Petersburg's numerous violations of the Polish Constitution, and the desire of the Polish upper classes to restore the old boundaries of Poland, which had included Lithuania, Belorussia, and part of Ukraine. After some vacillation, the insurgents "dethroned" the Romanovs, that is, declared them divested of their rights to the Polish throne. The Western powers, contrary to the expectations of the insurgents, offered them no appreciable support, and Russian military forces dealt the insurrection a crushing defeat. The Russian government replaced the Constitution of 1815 with the Organic Statute, which abolished Poland's political independence while retaining some elements of administrative autonomy.

Different segments of Russian society reacted to the Polish insurrection and its suppression in different ways. Proponents of liberal and especially revolutionary ideas sympathized with the insurgents and condemned the emperor's actions. Nicholas, however, took an extremely harsh position in regard to the insurrection. "I would have ceased to be a Russian in my own eyes if I had taken it into my head to believe it possible to detach Lithuania from Russia," he wrote to his brother Konstantin, who was in effect the viceroy of the Kingdom of Poland. "Which of the two should perish, Russia or Poland, since it is evident that one of them must? Decide for yourself."[10] The belief that the conflict between Russia and Poland was one of mutual annihilation was widespread in educated Russian society. Eminent Russian cultural figures such as Aleksandr Pushkin and Vasily Zhukovsky, the tutor of the future Alexander II, supported the suppression of the uprising. Many scholars believe that the upsurge of nationalist and patriotic sentiments was an important source of the theory of "Official Nationality." The suppression of the uprising, however, turned the western borderlands into a source of constant tension, requiring that Russia station an army in the region and undermining the country's reputation in European public opinion.

At the beginning of the 1830s, after the war with Turkey, the Treaty of Unkiar-Skelessi, and the defeat of the Polish insurrection, Nicholas's regime stood at the pinnacle of its success. Behind the majestic facade of the empire, however, the foundations of its power were inexorably eroding.

The most serious problems lay in the economic and fiscal realm, the Achilles' heel of Imperial Russia. On the whole, the country still had a natural economy, which limited the government's financial resources. Any extraordinary expenditure brought the state budget to the verge of bankruptcy. During the reign of Alexander I, Napoleon's invasion of Russia and the foreign campaigns of the Russian army had required very large expenditures. Only the considerable subsidies that England provided made the campaigns themselves possible. At the conclusion of the Napoleonic Wars, the Russian economy and the government's finances were in an extremely grave condition. Alexander's experiment with military colonies stemmed not just from political reaction but also from fiscal pressures. His attempts to resolve the peasant question and to introduce military colonies brought little economic return. He was forced to resort to the tried and true methods of raising taxes and issuing paper money, called assignats. Between 1811 to 1817, the number of assignats in circulation rose from 581 million to 836 million rubles. The value of the paper ruble fell to 20 silver kopecks.[11] The gentry's exemption from taxation exacerbated the government's fiscal problems.

The energetic efforts of Egor Kankrin, who served as minister of finance from 1823 to 1844, succeeded in rescuing the government's budget for a time. Kankrin was one of the most capable statesmen whom Nicholas inherited from his predecessor. Many historians find his achievements highly impressive, given the limitations of Russia's serf economy. By exercising strict fiscal discipline, Kankrin was able to build up a supply of silver, and by the end of the 1830s he had succeeded in raising the value of the assignats. To increase revenue, he applied measures that were somewhat dubious from an economic standpoint. In particular, in 1827 he introduced tax farming in the sale of alcohol, which fostered corruption in the state administration. He also increased tariffs on the importation of foreign goods. As a result, he enhanced Russia's reputation in international financial markets and secured sizable foreign credits. The government was able to begin redeeming the assignats, and in 1843 it declared the paper ruble, now firmly backed by silver, the basic unit of currency.

Kankrin understood that fiscal measures alone could not provide the regime with a sound economic basis. Besides strengthening the currency, he took steps to stimulate economic expansion and especially industrial development. He organized industrial exhibitions, established new technical institutes, and improved existing ones. His efforts contributed to vigorous industrial growth in the 1830s and the 1840s. New mills and factories arose, the number of hired workers grew, and the extensive mechanization of industrial production began.[12] Growth, however, was confined almost exclusively to light industry, located mainly in the central and northern regions of Russia. The land there was not very valuable, and the landowners allowed their serfs to seek wage work in mills and factories. Heavy industry, located predominantly in remote regions of the Urals, remained dependent on compulsory labor, almost untouched by the latest advances of the industrial revolution. As a result, the gap between the level of economic development in Russia and in Western Europe widened. By the 1850s it had reached menacing proportions. At the end of the eighteenth century, Russia and England had smelted roughly the same amount of pig iron, but by the middle of the nineteenth century England produced sixteen times as much as Russia. Russia also lagged far behind Western Europe in railroad construction. Like many tsarist bureaucrats, Kankrin opposed building railroads. He feared that "all the returns would go to foreigners," while railroads "would injure the peasants engaged in transporting goods, and the steam engines would destroy the forests for lack of coal."[13]

Deterioration occurred even in fiscal matters, especially after Kankrin's death in 1844. It gradually became clear that Russia's backward economy, based on serfdom, could not sustain the level of financial stability Kankrin had achieved. The state budget was kept secret, thereby preventing timely recognition of the impending danger. Expenditures frequently exceeded the budget, and foreign loans covered the deficits. The average annual budget was 200 million rubles, but the deficit amounted to 38 million rubles in 1850. Funds were lacking to modernize the army and navy, just when the Western powers were rearming their military forces. In an attempt to ward off catastrophe, the government again resorted to issuing unsecured paper rubles. Inflation grew, and when the Crimean War began in 1853 the paper ruble finally collapsed.[14]

While facing steadily worsening economic and fiscal conditions, Russia had to confront increasingly complex military and foreign-policy challenges. In the course of its advance toward the Black Sea at the end of the eighteenth century, the Russian Empire had taken Georgia, a Christian state in Transcaucasia under threat from Muslim Turkey and Iran, under its protection. In 1801–4 Russia annexed Georgia.[15] Wars with Iran and Turkey followed. As a result, the Russian Empire in the 1810s and the 1820s acquired northern Azerbaijan, eastern Armenia, and the Black Sea coast of the Caucasus.[16]

Although the acquisition of Transcaucasia went relatively smoothly, it created serious difficulties for the future. For many decades, the northern Caucasus posed a major problem for the Russian government. At the beginning of the nineteenth century, several dozen tribes and ethnic groups inhabited the region. The economic and social makeup of the mountaineers was highly diverse. Some of them had states, such as the Avar Khanate in Dagestan, but numerous clan associations also existed, "free societies" that did not recognize any governmental authority. The natural environment of the mountains was too poor to feed the entire population, and raids on territories in the plains were an integral part of the mountaineers' way of life.

The raids, as well as the anarchy of the mountaineers, worried the Russian authorities, who were trying to establish stable communications with their newly acquired Transcaucasian territories. Aleksei Ermolov, the eminent military commander and hero of the War of 1812, wrote to Alexander I, "The mountain peoples, by their example of independence, arouse a mutinous spirit and love of independence in Your Imperial Majesty's own subjects." In 1817 Ermolov became commander of a Special Caucasian Corps and commander-in-chief of Georgia. His systematic offensive against the mountaineers of the northern Caucasus helped to provoke a larger Caucasian war. "I cannot tolerate disorder," Ermolov wrote in 1818, "and much less do I like to see rabble like these mountain peoples daring to resist the authority of the sovereign."[17] In an effort to end the raids, Ermolov systematically drove the mountaineers from the plains, placing them in a desperate position. Their discontent generated religious movements, including Muridism. This radical Islamic doctrine demanded the unquestioned obedience of fighters for the faith, or *murids*, to their spiritual leader, the imam.

The Russian authorities had not anticipated the rise of Muridism in the northern Caucasus, and they were long unable to devise a policy for dealing with it. When Russia had annexed Muslim areas in the past, such as the

"The Murids." Engraving by Theodore Gorshield.

Volga region and the Crimea, Petersburg had formed an alliance with local elites and supported traditional Islam, granting considerable privileges to its clergy. The authorities tried to implement a similar policy in the northern Caucasus.[18] Meanwhile, developments among the mountaineers in the first half of the nineteenth century were destroying the foundations of the old aristocracy's authority and giving rise to new elites drawn from the "free societies." The new aristocracy sought to establish uniform ideological and legal norms based on a "pure" Islam, that is, purged of the remnants of paganism. Under these circumstances, the mountaineers were extremely sensitive to Russia's efforts to transplant Russian institutions and the imperial system of administration to the northern Caucasus. Their resistance developed under the banner of Muridism.

Muridism's combination of secular and spiritual motives gave it exceptional power and made it a crucial force in the northern Caucasus in the 1830s and the 1840s. The first imams of mountaineer origin appeared in these years, Kazi-Mullah in 1828 and Gamzat-Bek in 1832. Then Shamil, who became the third imam in 1834, succeeded in creating a stable theocratic state consisting of northern Dagestan and southern Chechnya. An outstanding administrator and a talented military commander, Shamil brilliantly exploited the terrain of the northern Caucasus to draw Russia into a long and exhausting war. He created an army of 20,000 men, which resisted a Russian force of 60,000–100,000. He formed a state administration and supplied his army with provisions and skillfully devised weapons, including artillery. Shamil divided his state into viceregencies headed by his closest lieutenants, called *naibs*, and based his administration on Islamic law, the *Sharia*. Foreign states, particularly England and Turkey, rendered Shamil considerable assistance in the form of money, armaments, and military supplies.

Shamil used his army and his strong political structure to inflict a series of painful defeats on the Russian army in the 1840s. His resources were not equal to those of the Russians, however, and the despotic methods of government he employed began to repel the mountaineers. In the eyes of the populace, the new aristocracy that came to power with Shamil was little better than the old one, and many of the mountaineers went over to the Russian side. In the 1850s Shamil's position began to deteriorate. In 1856 Prince Aleksandr Bariatinsky, a gifted military commander, was appointed viceroy of the Caucasus. In 1859 he captured the village (*aul*) of Gunib, Shamil's last refuge, and took the imam himself prisoner.[19]

At the same time, the mountain peoples in the western part of the northern Caucasus, the Cherkess and Adyge, conducted a struggle against Russian forces independently of Shamil. Fighting in this area, immediately adjacent to the Black Sea, posed a particular danger in the eyes of the Russian military

"The Surrender of Shamil to Prince Aleksandr Ivanovich Bariatinsky." Engraving by Theodore Gorshield.

Prince Aleksandr Ivanovich Bariatinsky. Engraving by Theodore Gorshield.

because it might become a landing stage for an enemy attack. Therefore, after the Crimean War and the defeat of Shamil, the Russians directed their main efforts at "pacifying" the western region of the northern Caucasus. In 1864 Russian troops took the mountaineers' last stronghold, Kbaada. A considerable number of mountaineers, about 300,000 people who were unwilling to remain under Russian rule, migrated to Turkey after the war.[20]

What was the impact of the Caucasus War on the lives of the mountain peoples and on the history of Russia? The war was indisputably one of the most painful and contradictory episodes in the history of both sides. On the one hand, Russian annexation brought an end to raids, civil wars, and slave trading in the northern Caucasus and introduced more advanced economic and cultural practices. Secular schools, libraries, theaters, museums, railroads, and factories began to appear in the region. On the other hand, the annexation had required the use of violent means, and both the mountaineers and the Russians suffered heavy losses. Historians calculate that in the course of the war about seventy-seven thousand officers and soldiers of the Caucasian Corps were killed, captured, or missing. The Caucasus War consumed vast resources—10–15 million rubles a year in the 1840s and the 1850s—and contributed to the destabilization of the Russian budget.[21] The protracted nature of the war tarnished Russia's prestige as a military power of the first rank and spurred its opponents to greater activity.

Nicholas's efforts to play the role of "gendarme of Europe" by opposing revolutionary and nationalist movements added to the hostility of Russia's adversaries and the decline of its international authority. The emperor himself sincerely believed that his actions maintained the stability of Europe. In 1831 he demanded that Belgium remain part of the Kingdom of the Netherlands, declaring that he was "not opposed to Belgium but to the universal revolution that is approaching." He justified even his intervention in Turkish affairs on the grounds that if the Egyptian pasha conquered Constantinople, "we would have as our neighbor a nest of all the individuals, homeless and without a fatherland, who have been expelled from all the well-ordered societies." "This entire war," Nicholas emphasized before dispatching an expeditionary force to the Bosporus, "is nothing but a consequence of the seditious spirit that has now seized Europe, and especially France."[22] At this time the governments of the West had adopted the principle of noninterference in each other's internal affairs. According to a recent history, "the threat to the empire scarcely corresponded to the measures the tsarist government took to ward it off. Nicholas I obviously preferred active measures of defense. As a result, tsarist policy increasingly began to resemble ordinary aggression, and for a time it seemed that what Nicholas intended to protect against the 'threat from the West' was not his own empire but the West itself."[23]

In the end, Nicholas failed in his attempt to act as the "gendarme of Europe." Not only European liberals and radicals but European governments opposed him out of fear that Russia's influence would increase. Moreover, as parliamentary institutions and democratic principles developed in Europe, the dividing line between society and government began to blur. Prussia, for example, rejected Nicholas's proposal in 1830 for counter-revolutionary intervention in France. "We cannot risk a war with France, for such a war would not become a national cause," one Prussian minister declared. "We would not dare to undertake it unless public opinion supported it."[24] Nicholas was forced to make concessions, further undermining Russia's authority. He had to accept Louis Philippe as the "official substitute" for Charles X in France and to recognize Belgium when the Dutch king did so.

Just as Nicholas's policies undermined Russia's position in Europe, they also damaged Russian interests in the Balkans. In the name of conservative and legitimist principles, Nicholas felt it necessary to curtail national-liberation movements and to keep the Balkan Slavs subordinate to the Turkish sultan. At times, this policy amounted to outright dictation. The Russian government instructed its envoy in Serbia to tell the local authorities that "all the benefits they have been granted are nothing but the fruits of Russian arms, that their preservation depends solely on Russia and on no other, and, finally, that their prosperity is based on their unconditional fulfillment of the [Russian emperor's] orders, which are that the government and people of Serbia make use of the favor they have been shown and not be enticed by dreams of making new claims against their sovereign,"[25] the sultan. It is not surprising that the new Balkan states increasingly sought Western protectors. Serbia looked to Austria and Greece to England for support. Even Moldavia and Wallachia, where Petr Kiselev had introduced reforms in the late 1820s and the early 1830s, rejected Russia's influence and found a new patron in France.

The Western countries' growing economic penetration of the Balkans and the Middle East aggravated Russia's problems. In the 1830s and the 1840s, Turkey's imports from Britain and France grew by 500 to 700 percent.[26] Hampered by its backward economy based on serfdom, Russia was unable to counter this threat to its commercial interests. Adversaries, especially England, took advantage of the changing circumstances to go on the offensive. English diplomacy's greatest success was the revision of the Treaty of Unkiar-Skelessi. The London Conventions of 1841 placed navigation in the Black Sea Straits under international control and closed the Straits in peacetime to warships of all nations. These provisions confined Russia's navy to the Black Sea and exposed the southern borders of the empire to attack, for if Turkey declared war on Russia it could open the Straits to foreign military vessels.

Nicholas agreed to the London Conventions in the hope that his concessions would achieve a rapprochement with England, detach England from its alliance with France, and consolidate France's international isolation. Nicholas regarded France as a dangerous breeding ground of "revolutionary infection" and the source of political instability in Europe. To a considerable degree, his fears were justified. In 1848 a new revolution broke out in France and quickly spread to other states, engulfing even the lands of Russia's allies, Austria and Prussia. "The solemn moment that I have been predicting for eighteen years has come," Nicholas wrote to the Prussian king, Frederick William IV. "Revolution has risen from the ashes . . . An unavoidable danger threatens our common existence."[27]

Immediately after the February revolution in France, Nicholas began to mass troops on the western borders of the Russian Empire. In March he issued a manifesto declaring that Russia stood ready, fully armed, to confront the onslaught of revolution. The manifesto ended with a bellicose exclamation: "God is with us! Understand this, peoples, and submit: for God is with us!"[28] No one directly threatened Russia at that moment, however. Western public opinion interpreted the manifesto as blatant evidence of Russia's aggressiveness. Nor did Nicholas's new attempt to organize a counter-revolutionary intervention succeed. England registered a determined protest, while Austria and Prussia refused to allow Russian troops to pass through their territory. The Prussian king did not turn to Nicholas for assistance, even when disturbances broke out in his realm. He even tried to appropriate the revolutionaries' slogans by calling for the unification of the German lands.

The one instance in which Nicholas managed to fulfill his counter-revolutionary plans was the suppression of the Hungarian insurrection in 1849. Nationalist movements represented a mortal danger for the Austrian Empire, whose ruler, Francis Joseph, asked Nicholas for help when the insurrection began. On Nicholas's order, a Russian army of 100,000 men entered Austrian territory and defeated the insurgents. The suppression of the Hungarian uprising angered Russian liberals, who believed that Nicholas had sacrificed Russia's national interests for the sake of dynastic and legitimist principles. "Conservative blindness may prove useful to the decrepit Austrian government," Boris Chicherin wrote, "but to apply it to youthful Russia, which is just beginning to display its strength, can only be called the height of folly."[29]

Deep down, Nicholas himself doubted the necessity of intervening in Austrian affairs. He justified his action on the grounds of concern for the stability of the Russian Empire, claiming that "I would not have intervened had I not been looking out for my own skin." Count Nesselrode provided a detailed argument for this position: "The emperor was not making a choice. He was involuntarily obeying not a personal preference but the demands of self-preservation . . . The sovereign was not voluntarily serving Austria and

Prussia. In no way did he sacrifice Russia for the benefit of Austria and Prussia. He was merely defending his own house by extinguishing a fire in his neighbor's house."[30] In Nicholas's view, the Hungarian insurrection might have stirred up unrest in the Polish lands of the Russian Empire. To both Russians and Westerners, however, this justification sounded unconvincing. European public opinion and governmental circles took Nicholas's intervention as final proof of Russia's aggressive intentions and of the need to put an end to its predominance in Europe.

On the surface, the suppression of the Hungarian uprising seemed to enhance Russia's influence. "Do people not see," a Prussian diplomat exclaimed in 1850, "that there, in the north, the present-day Napoleon of the world holds sway?" Another German observer wrote that the Russian emperor "in a few years, at the least, will be prescribing laws for Europe."[31] Indeed, Nicholas energetically sought to influence European affairs. He induced the king of Prussia to renounce plans for the unification of Germany and the annexation of Danish provinces inhabited by Germans. Nicholas also demanded that the king deal resolutely with German revolutionaries. In Germany, the power of the Russian tsar was deemed so awesome that mothers used his name to frighten their children.

In fact, however, that power was about to undergo a steep decline because of a new aggravation of the Eastern Question. In the early 1850s a quarrel broke out between Orthodox and Catholic clergy in Palestine over possession of the keys to a church in Bethlehem. The sultan, with French support, resolved the issue in favor of the Catholics. Under the terms of the Treaty of Kuchuk-Kainardji of 1774, however, Russia had received a vague right to protect Christian churches in the Holy Land. Nicholas treated the clashes over "the issue of the keys" as an opportunity to resolve the Eastern Question to Russia's benefit once and for all. He felt that the time had come to renounce the policy of supporting Turkey as a weak neighbor and to begin dismembering it. Confident of Russia's military power, the emperor deliberately sought a rupture with Turkey. When Turkey refused to accept a Russian ultimatum, Nicholas sent troops into Moldavia and Wallachia in April 1853 and precipitated a Russo-Turkish war.

Nicholas assumed that international circumstances at the start of the war were particularly favorable for Russia. France, weakened by internal discord, would be unable to intervene in an international conflict. Austria would feel grateful to Russia for its help in suppressing the Hungarian insurrection. Nicholas counted on coming to an agreement with England by promising it a share of Turkey's possessions.

Virtually all of Nicholas's calculations proved groundless. Napoleon III, who had come to power in France, needed a victorious war to consolidate his authority. Austria had its own economic and political interests in the Balkans. Moreover, the growth of Russian influence in the region made the Austrians fear for their Slavic possessions. These considerations made Austria an adversary of Russia. "We shall astound the world with our ingratitude," Prince Felix zu Schwarzenberg, the Austrian prime minister, remarked in 1850.[32]

Nicholas's failure to understand the new system of international relations displayed itself most of all in his relations with England. The country on whose support Nicholas had counted most heavily adopted a sharply hostile attitude toward Russia. The ruling circles in England were developing far-reaching plans in regard to Russia. They hoped to restore Poland's independence, to give Finland back to Sweden, to return Georgia and the Crimea to Turkey, and to create an independent state of "Circassia" in the northern Caucasus under the protection of England.[33] Nicholas did not understand that his personal friendship with conservative English aristocrats such as the Duke of Wellington and Lord Aberdeen, the British prime minister, would not guarantee England's friendly behavior as a state. In the words of the German historian Theodor Schiemann, Nicholas lived in a world of "dynastic mythology" and placed excessive reliance on personal contacts and ties of blood and friendship within the European elite.[34]

Nicholas's plans began to unravel at the very start. Instead of a single weak enemy, Turkey, he now confronted two powerful adversaries, England and France, as well as an unfriendly or indifferent attitude on the part of the other European states. Austria reacted in a hostile fashion to Russia's declaration of war on Turkey and concentrated large forces on the Russian frontier. Nicholas was forced to withdraw his troops from Moldavia and Wallachia. When, at the end of 1853, a Russian squadron under the command of Admiral Pavel Nakhimov annihilated a Turkish fleet in the Bay of Sinope, England and France considered this an act of aggression and sent their warships into the Black Sea. Russia's war with Turkey had become a war against an international coalition.

European public opinion as a whole opposed Russia. In a speech in parliament, Lord Clarendon, the British foreign secretary, called the war a struggle for "the independence of Europe," for "civilization" against "barbarism."[35] Of all the Western countries, only the United States adopted a friendly attitude toward Russia. An American warning of an impending attack by an Anglo-French fleet in the Far East permitted Russian commanders to take timely measures for the defense of Petropavlovsk-Kamchatsky. American volunteer doctors took part in the defense of Sevastopol.[36]

The allied attack on the Crimea immediately altered the situation to Russia's detriment. Unlike Napoleon in 1812, the allies did not try to invade. Instead, they struck at a key outpost on the empire's frontier: Sevastopol, the principal base of the Black Sea fleet. Under these circumstances, Russia's vast expanse worked against it. The country's extensive borders forced the Russian commanders to disperse their forces, so that the million-man army ceased to be a decisive advantage. In an effort to make Russia's position even more difficult, the allies made forays on all the empire's ocean frontiers, at Petersburg, the Solovetsky Islands in the White Sea, and Kamchatka on the Pacific. The poor condition of the country's dirt roads and the utter lack of a railroad network prevented the Russians from transferring troops quickly to the theater of military operations.

Russia's economic, military, and technological backwardness became apparent immediately after the attack on the Crimea. The archaic system of military recruitment prevented a rapid expansion of the army in wartime. Russia's fleet of sailing ships was impotent against the steamships of England and France, and a large part of it had to be sunk in Sevastopol Bay. Russia's sluggish military industry, based on serf labor, failed to supply the army with sufficient gunpowder and shells. The troops, marching into battle in close-order columns with smoothbore muskets, were literally mowed down by the allies' long-range artillery fire. The highly centralized, inflexible system of administration stifled the initiative of officials and military commanders, but at the same time it could not prevent colossal abuses in the supply system. Despite the heroic resistance of the Sevastopol garrison, the outcome was inevitable. In August 1855, after an eleven-month siege, the allies took Malakhov Hill, which dominated Sevastopol, and forced the Russian troops to abandon the city. A few months before the fall of Sevastopol, when Russia's impending defeat had become obvious, Nicholas died suddenly.[37]

The Peace of Paris in 1856, which concluded the Crimean War, put an end to Russia's predominance in European affairs. Russia lost strategically important territory at the mouth of the Danube River. The Black Sea was demilitarized, so that both Russia and Turkey lost the right to keep a navy in the Black Sea and maintain fortresses and arsenals there. This stipulation actually left Russia defenseless against external aggression, for Turkey could move its fleet from the Aegean Sea as well as allow the warships of foreign powers to enter the Black Sea through the Straits. In 1870, taking advantage of the outbreak of the Franco-Prussian War, Russia unilaterally abrogated this provision of the Treaty of Paris, but the demilitarization of the Black Sea prevented Russia for some time from pursuing an active policy in the Balkans and the Middle East. The Peace of Paris also demonstrated the growing influence of France. At the insistence of Napoleon III, the signing of the peace took place on March 18, the day the allies had taken Paris in 1814. Prince Aleksei Orlov, who signed the treaty for the Russian side, was the brother of

Colonel Mikhail Orlov, who had accepted the surrender of Paris in 1814. History had completed a cycle.

How did Russian society regard the Crimean War and its consequences? The Slavophiles had hoped at the beginning of the war for a "rebirth of the Slavic world" under Russia's protection: Turkey would finally be crushed and an Orthodox empire, with its center in Constantinople, would be restored. The poet Fyodor Tiutchev foresaw the restoration of a Christian altar in the Cathedral of Hagia Sophia. "Fall down before it, o tsar of Russia, and arise as tsar of all the Slavs," he wrote, addressing Nicholas. The Russian defeat forced the Slavophiles to turn their attention to the negative sides of Nicholas's regime: the absence of intellectual freedom, particularly freedom of speech, the alienation between the government and the people, and bureaucratism. "Sevastopol did not fall by accident," Ivan Aksakov wrote to relatives. "Its fall was an act of God to expose the true rottenness of the governmental system and all the consequences of repression."[38]

As for the Westernizers, they had been skeptical of Russia's prospects in the Crimean War from the beginning. "How have we prepared ourselves for a struggle against civilization, which is sending its forces against us?" exclaimed Timofei Granovsky.[39] As the war ended, opposition-minded Westernizers and Slavophiles were not alone in denouncing the regime that had held sway in Russia for thirty years. Even highly placed dignitaries, such as the future Minister of Internal Affairs Petr Valuev, and profoundly conservative individuals like the historian Mikhail Pogodin, the proponent of "Official Nationality," gave voice to such criticism. The most diverse circles joined in repudiating Nicholas's system of government. When the new emperor, Alexander II, ascended the throne on February 19, 1855, society was ready for the introduction of reforms. The immediate impetus for initiating them was the conclusion of the Crimean War.

Chapter 4

The End of Serfdom

Russia's defeat in the Crimean War not only underscored the need for reforms but largely determined their direction and character. Stability at any price ceased to be an absolute priority. "Internal discord and revolts have shaken Europe for several years, while we have enjoyed uninterrupted tranquillity. Nevertheless, where have internal and external forces developed more rapidly and consistently during this time?" asked Petr Valuev, the future minister of internal affairs. He had Western Europe in mind as the answer to his question.[1]

Representatives of the ruling circles in Russia now referred more frequently to the experience of Europe. Even Mikhail Pogodin, one of the official ideologists of Nicholas's reign and a staunch proponent of Russia's uniqueness, spoke positively of Western Europe. During the Crimean War he wrote, "One cannot live in Europe without participating in its common progress, without following its inventions and discoveries . . . The current war is Russia's crusade. Its purpose in European history is to rouse Russia, which has been keeping its strength under wraps, to take an active part in the common advance of the progeny of Japheth toward civil and human perfection."[2] Everyone realized that social, economic, administrative, and educational problems demanded more attention than grand diplomacy and military power. "We have to examine ourselves," wrote the Slavophile Iury Samarin, "to investigate the root causes of our weakness, to hear a truthful expression of our domestic needs, and to devote all our attention and all our resources to satisfying them."[3] In this atmosphere the abolition of serfdom finally appeared essential, and preparation for it began.

In undertaking the peasant reform—the watershed event of the nineteenth century—the imperial government made one of the most important attempts in the whole of Russian history to break with the traditions of the "service

Emperor Nicholas I with his brothers, Grand Dukes Konstantin Pavlovich and Mikhail Pavlovich, and his son, Grand Duke Alexander Nikolaevich. Nineteenth-century *lubok* (popular print).

state" and the "police state." In the words of the American historian Bruce Lincoln, "Russia thus began her evolution from a nation of servitors into a nation of free men and women obliged to assume increasing responsibility for their destinies and those of their neighbors . . . This heralded the beginning of the greatest era of social and economic renovation to occur in Russia's history since the death of Peter the Great."[4] In an effort to join the mainstream of European civilization, Russia implemented major reforms based on the principles of hired labor, free competition, political democracy, and ideological pluralism. Although the "service state" ultimately proved stronger and reemerged triumphant after 1917, the period from 1861 to 1917, and the peasant reform with which it began, merit the closest attention.

The reform of 1861, a major turning point in Russian history, was paradoxical in many respects. The transformation of the system of social relations that it entailed occurred relatively peacefully, under the control of the state. The authors of the peasant reform, confident of the autocracy's ability to carry out change, even made it their proud task "to postpone revolution in Russia for five hundred years," in the words of Konstantin Kavelin.[5] Their expectations proved unrealistic. Nevertheless, the revolutionary upheavals at the beginning of the twentieth century that shattered the old order were not predetermined or inevitable. They stemmed primarily from the suspension of the government's reform activities at the end of the nineteenth century and the wars of the early twentieth century, developments that the authors of the abolition of serfdom could not have foreseen. Many historians justifiably believe that the principles that underlay the reform of 1861 gave Russia a real opportunity to develop in a peaceful, evolutionary fashion. Thus there is good reason to examine in detail the planning and implementation of the reform.

Why did serfdom come to an end in the mid-nineteenth century? The answer to this question has always provoked heated disputes because it reflected divergent ideological and political views. Soviet historiography treated the peasant reform in the Marxist framework of "the replacement of feudalism by capitalism," which permitted it to represent the Soviet order, socialism, as the culmination of historical development. This approach impelled Soviet historians to look for elements in the life of pre-reform Russia that corresponded to Marxist doctrine, such as highly developed capitalist relations, mass peasant disturbances, and the activities of an organized revolutionary underground. Vladimir Lenin regarded the peasant reform as "a by-product of the revolutionary struggle." As a result, interest in the mechanics of the reform was negligible. The end of serfdom supposedly occurred "by itself," in the course of a popular revolution, and the autocracy's actions merely corrupted and distorted the natural course of history.[6]

The Soviet view of the peasant reform stood in sharp conflict with pre-revolutionary, mainly liberal, historiography, and bore distinct traces of that opposition. Liberal historiography attributed the decisive role in the abolition of serfdom to the autocracy. A symbolic expression of that interpretation was the cover of the fiftieth-anniversary volume *The Great Reform*, published in 1911, which depicted the quill pen Alexander II used to sign the manifesto abolishing serfdom. As historians examined the historical sources more closely, the contrast between these two views diminished. Petr Zaionchkovsky elaborated a distinctive "middle way" in the study of the peasant reform. He stressed the role of the state in carrying out the reform while recognizing the importance of objective social and economic factors. Larissa Zakharova, who focused particularly on the political history of the abolition, has continued this line of research.[7]

The views of Terence Emmons and Daniel Field, American historians who have studied the peasant reform, parallel those of Zaionchkovsky and Zakharova.[8] Both were students of Zaionchkovsky. Emmons focused his analysis on long-term social and cultural factors: the feelings of shame over the preservation of serfdom that had arisen within Russian educated society after a century and a half of exposure to Western ideas, and the influence of economic theories that associated a country's development with the adoption of hired labor, the accumulation of capital, and the free play of market forces. While recognizing the importance of the "peasant factor," Emmons emphasized that peasant uprisings as such did not influence the introduction of the reform. Rather, the government acted out of fear that they might increase if serfdom were retained.

Field developed Emmons's arguments, showing that an upsurge in peasant disturbances occurred after the abolition of serfdom, not as a precondition of the reform but as a result of it. In Field's view, the political and ideological foundations of serfdom had already crumbled by the 1850s. As soon as the state, with some reservations, withdrew its support from the institution of serfdom, it collapsed. The end of serfdom resulted not from a personal decision by the tsar and his advisors but from a complex process that lasted some seven years.

What were the components of that process? The personal qualities of the autocrat played a significant role. Alexander II, who has gone down in history as the "Tsar-Liberator," was the son of Nicholas I. Although not a reformer by nature, inclination, or vocation, he became one largely because of objective circumstances, which forced him to overcome within himself the legacy of Nicholas I.

In contrast to his father, Alexander Nikolaevich was proclaimed the heir to the throne in his childhood and from an early age began to receive the

Emperor Alexander II. Photograph.

education of a future autocrat. His tutor, the poet Vasily Zhukovsky, drew up an extensive Plan of Study, in which humanistic subjects—history, economics, law, and foreign languages—figured prominently. Alexander's teachers included eminent scholars and statesmen, such as Mikhail Speransky, who gave him a course in jurisprudence. By Nicholas's special permission, the heir to the throne even studied the history of the French Revolution, a subject strictly forbidden in Russia.

Zhukovsky realized the primary importance of maintaining the country's internal well-being. In the Plan of Study he urged Alexander "to examine with respect the true needs of the people, the laws, education, and morality," pointing out that "armies do not constitute the power of the state." Zhukovsky, however, was not the only influence on the heir's education. Nicholas insisted that his son "must be a military man at heart, otherwise he will be lost in our era." The result was a contradiction in Alexander II's outlook and policies. In certain periods of his reign, Zhukovsky's humanistic precepts would rise to the surface and he would turn his attention mainly to the country's domestic needs. At other times his father's military education would incite him to undertake territorial acquisitions and pursue an imperialistic policy.[9]

Alexander's ingrained lack of will and persistence also exerted a negative influence on his reform policy. In the words of one of his tutors, "upon encountering the least difficulty" he would fall into "a kind of sleep-like state of inactivity."[10] Nevertheless, in Russia's critical circumstances after its defeat in the Crimean War Alexander recognized the need for reforms. In his manifesto of February 19/March 3, 1856, on the conclusion of the Peace of Paris, he hinted at the prospect of reform: "Let [Russia's] internal well-being be confirmed and perfected; let justice and mercy reign in her courts; let the striving for enlightenment and every sort of useful activity be developed everywhere and with new vigor; and let everyone, under the protection of laws that give equal justice and protection to all, enjoy in peace the fruits of his honest labor."[11] A few days later, in a speech to the Moscow nobility and in response to widespread rumors of impending reforms, Alexander openly proclaimed the inevitability of the abolition of serfdom: "It would be much better for it to take place from above than from below."[12]

What role did the "peasant factor," the favorite subject of Soviet historiography, play in the decision to eliminate serfdom? As mentioned previously, Russia in the second half of the 1850s was in no immediate danger of a mass peasant revolt. Nevertheless, the influence of the peasantry on the plans for reform should not be underestimated. The ruling circles feared a spontaneous peasant uprising, a new Pugachev Rebellion, and they made every effort to prevent its occurrence.

The government's apprehensions increased considerably in the late 1850s, when the number of peasant movements grew alarmingly and became better organized than before. The unpredictability of the peasants frightened the authorities, who found their behavior and the mentality underlying it incomprehensible. When the government appealed for the creation of army and navy militia units at the end of the Crimean War, thousands of serfs sought to gain their freedom by enrolling. With the conclusion of the Peace of Paris, masses of serfs set out for the Crimea, hoping that the tsar would accept them there. Finally, in 1859, the so-called "sobriety movement" developed in protest against the abuses of tax farmers. (Tax farmers obtained from the government an exclusive right to sell alcoholic beverages in a certain territory and then grew rich on the sale of adulterated spirits by bribing government officials.) Although these demonstrations remained peaceful, and the "sobriety movement" did not even touch on the question of serfdom, they heightened tensions within the government and forced it to accelerate the introduction of reform. Iury Samarin, an active participant in the preparation of the peasant reform, wrote: "Given the current mood of the serf estate, any incident that attracts attention, such as a fugitive soldier's drunken speech, a misunderstood decree, the appearance of an unprecedented disease, the tsar's arrival in Moscow . . . can produce alarm somewhere and in an instant arouse the thought of freedom. An insignificant disturbance can just as easily turn into a riot and the riot develop into a general insurrection."[13]

The impact of the economic factor on the peasant reform was equally complex. On the one hand, the Russian economy did not experience a comprehensive economic crisis in the mid-1850s. In agriculture, the sown area continued to grow, 1856 was a good crop year, and the country exported grain. On the other hand, the government was particularly sensitive to other signs of insolvency. In monetary and fiscal affairs, the consequences of the Crimean War were truly catastrophic. The total budget deficit for 1853–56 rose from 52 million rubles to 307 million, the ruble's gold backing fell by more than half, and the government was forced to end the exchange of paper currency for gold and silver. By 1862 state debt stood at 2.5 billion rubles and state bankruptcy became a real possibility. Because of the decline of public confidence in state banking institutions, total savings in 1857–59 fell from 150 million rubles to 13 million. A wave of bankruptcies of joint-stock companies founded during the war swept the country.[14]

The government's dire fiscal straits impelled it to speed up the transformation of the archaic serf economy. It sought to put the economy on a commercial basis, which would be more progressive as well as more promising in terms of balancing the state budget.[15] In the pursuit of its own interests, the government in fact "rushed" the historical process, fostering changes in a still largely natural economy that was not entirely ready for them. The state's interests clearly took precedence over society's interests, and consequently the reforms imposed painful consequences on various segments of the population.

The state's interests predominated even in the early stages of planning for the reform, although at first the process of renovation was quite timid. The government rescinded only the most odious of Nicholas I's regulations. It removed the restrictions that had been imposed on the universities after 1848, resumed the granting of passports for travel abroad, finally eliminated the military colonies, forgave tax arrears, and reduced the size of the army. Even these steps were enough to raise society's spirits, however. Nicholas's system had degenerated into a brutal system of rule by the mid-1850s, and the public took any changes in it as a sign that the government was reversing course. The amnesty for political prisoners that Alexander II announced at his coronation in August 1856 was of particular significance. Nine thousand men, including surviving Decembrists, Petrashevists, and participants in the Polish insurrection of 1830–31, were released from administrative and police supervision. Many of those amnestied, including the former Decembrists Ivan Pushchin and Evgeny Obolensky, took an active part in the country's social and political life and participated in the preparation of the peasant reform.

Society displayed its excitement in a flood of so-called "underground literature"—memoranda, circulating in manuscript form, on various social, economic, and foreign policy problems. Mikhail Pogodin, Petr Valuev, Konstantin Kavelin, Iury Samarin, and Boris Chicherin were among those who composed memoranda. The government, having lost its former authority in the Crimean defeat, lacked reliable information on society's mood. It was forced to reconcile itself to a discussion of social and political issues that was not only free but often sharply critical of the authorities. The relaxation of censorship prohibitions soon after Alexander's accession allowed new periodicals to spring up one after another, "like mushrooms after rain," as one contemporary put it. Articles that could not be published in Russia found a place in Alexander Herzen's publications abroad. Sensing a change in the political situation, Herzen began to publish the almanac *Northern Star* in 1855, the collection *Voices from Russia* in 1856, and the newspaper *The Bell* in 1857. Smuggled into Russia, these publications became widely known to the reading public, including the tsar and the tsarina. The government even made use of them in drafting the peasant reform.

The government's relatively tolerant attitude to the circulation of Herzen's publications in Russia reflected another important change, the realization that the country had to emerge from its international isolation and restore its tarnished prestige. In pursuit of this objective, the government founded a semi-official Russian newspaper, *Le Nord,* in Belgium in 1855, "to acquaint Europe with the real situation in Russia" and "to strive to eliminate false and unfounded conceptions about our Fatherland." A similar motivation underlay the lifting of prohibitions on travel abroad. The government acknowledged the need "to consolidate our commercial ties with foreign states and to borrow from them the scientific advances that have recently been made in Europe."[16] These measures contradicted the arrogant theory of Official Nationality and served as further recognition by the government that Nicholas's system had failed. Under these conditions, the authorities urgently needed to regain the political initiative and keep the process of renovating the country on course.

Preparation for the reform began in an entirely traditional manner. In January 1857 Alexander created yet another secret committee on the peasant question and at the same time encouraged the gentry to take the initiative in introducing reform. At first, neither step produced results. The gentry stubbornly remained silent, and the committee tried in every way to draw out its work. Delay was impossible, however. Several influential individuals in the tsar's entourage came out in favor of reform, including Petr Kiselev, the former minister of state domains; Grand Duke Konstantin Nikolaevich, the tsar's brother; and Grand Duchess Elena Pavlovna, the tsar's aunt. Elena Pavlovna's salon and the Naval Ministry, headed by Konstantin Nikolaevich, became meeting places for many of the future reformers: enlightened bureaucrats, scholars, and public figures, both Westernizers and Slavophiles. The Ministry of Internal Affairs, under Count Sergei Lanskoi, was also a major focal point of reform.

The pressure exerted by these circles helped move the reform process forward. At the end of 1857 Vladimir Nazimov, the governor-general of the Lithuanian provinces of Vilna, Kovno, and Grodno and a personal friend of Alexander, extracted a petition to the tsar from the local gentry concerning the emancipation of their serfs. (Nazimov pressured the nobles by threatening to apply the "inventory" regulations, discussed in chapter 1, to the Lithuanian provinces.) Alexander in reply instructed the nobles to establish local committees to discuss the conditions for reform. At the insistence of the minister of internal affairs, Alexander's rescript, or instruction, to Nazimov was published, and preparation of the reform became irreversible. The secret committee, now no longer secret, was renamed the Main Committee on Peasant Affairs. Alexander Herzen, an implacable enemy of autocracy, hailed Alexander as "the Liberator." The gentry in all the provinces were forced to address petitions to the tsar similar to that of the Lithuanian provinces.

In the course of 1858 and early 1859, gentry committees formed in the provinces throughout Russia. In all, there were forty-six committees and

Grand Duke Konstantin Nikolaevich. Engraving.

two commissions, in Vilna and Kovno. About forty-four thousand noble serfowners, 40 percent of the total, took part in electing members of the committees and in drawing up addresses to Alexander II. The gentry committees greatly enlivened social life in the Russian provinces, an important step in the creation of a civil society. Men of diverse political views served on the committees: amnestied Decembrists and Petrashevists, Slavophiles and Westernizers, liberals and conservatives. The committees formed ties with one another, and their meetings were open and well publicized. The work of the gentry committees influenced the actions of other social estates. The philanthropic endeavors of the merchants and the social activities of the clergy displayed new vigor. Public figures of different generations established contacts. In 1858 the Decembrist Ivan Pushchin, who had returned from Siberia, sent the leader of the liberal gentry of Tver Province, Aleksei Unkovsky, a copy of Nikita Muraviev's constitution to use in the work of his provincial committee.[17] The complex nature of the peasant question led the provincial committees to issue a variety of proposals for abolishing serfdom, which in turn stimulated public discussion and the clash of contending viewpoints.

The reform proposals of the provincial committees fell into two basic categories: landless emancipation of the serfs, and emancipation with land by means of redemption. The second variant did not enjoy broad support among the gentry. Most of the provincial committees opposed it, except for the Tver committee, where, under the leadership of Aleksei Unkovsky, proponents of giving the peasants ownership of land in return for redemption payments predominated. Nor did it have firm support in the ruling circles. Highly placed magnates, who had a vested interest in serfdom, wanted to retain possession of all the land after the emancipation of the serfs, like the Baltic barons and English landlords. The tsar himself initially inclined to this point of view. It is indicative that Konstantin Kavelin, a prominent public figure and tutor of the heir to the throne, lost his position and fell into disgrace in April 1858 for publishing an article in the journal *The Contemporary* that considered the possibility of redemption of the peasants' allotments. Within a few months, however, a contrary opinion began to gather strength and then prevailed within the government. By the end of 1858, the government had accepted the basic principle of emancipating the serfs with land in a redemption process. What caused this reversal?

Outside pressures on the government certainly played a role. At the end of April 1858, a peasant insurrection occurred in Estland (Estonia), not far from Petersburg. Forty years earlier, the peasants of Estland had been emancipated without land. The insurrection was suppressed, but it seriously diminished the attractiveness of the "Baltic experience" in the eyes of the authorities. In central Russia in the same year, the appanage peasants, who belonged to the imperial family, refused to accept a landless emancipation. Herzen's *The Bell* and the journal *The Contemporary,* which enjoyed great popularity in Russia, consistently opposed emancipation without land. Within the government, the presence of a cohesive group of enlightened bureaucrats who defended the idea of a landed emancipation also influenced the government's reversal of policy. The most outstanding of these enlightened bureaucrats was Nikolai Miliutin, an official in the Ministry of Internal Affairs.

In the summer of 1858 Adjutant-General Iakov Rostovtsev, Alexander's personal friend and an influential member of the Committee on Peasant Affairs, also came around to the enlightened bureaucracy's viewpoint. Personal factors played a significant role in Rostovtsev's change of position. In his youth, Rostovtsev had been friendly with many of the Decembrists, although he did not share their political views and refused to join a secret society. On the eve of the insurrection in Petersburg, without concealing his intention from his friends, he informed Nicholas I of the conspiracy and then participated in the suppression of the uprising. During Nicholas's reign, Rostovtsev made a brilliant career in the military and at court. Russia's defeat in the Crimean War, the collapse of Nicholas's regime, and the return of the amnestied Decembrists from Siberia impelled Rostovtsev to reexamine his views. He established ties with his former friends and corresponded regularly with one of them, Evgeny Obolensky, from whom he sought advice on the peasant question. Particularly important in Rostovtsev's change of heart was the dying plea of his younger son, in the summer of 1858, "to assist the cause of emancipation of the peasants" and thereby erase the stain from the family's name.

The tsar's confidence in the enlightened bureaucrats rose, and their position became the basis of the government's program. Why did the enlightened bureaucrats insist on a landed emancipation despite the wishes of the majority of the nobility? They particularly wanted to avoid the creation in Russia of a huge landless rural proletariat and a repetition of the revolutions in Western Europe. This motive runs like a red thread through the arguments of the enlightened bureaucrats and their highly placed patrons: "if we cut off the peasants from the land, we will set Russia ablaze"; we must not "give the peasants grounds for dissatisfaction, so as to avoid riots"; we have to "maintain social tranquillity by creating a strong conservative element within the numerous agricultural population."[18]

Prince Vladimir Cherkassky, a public figure who had close ties to the enlightened bureaucracy, articulated its position in a memorandum "On the Status of the Peasant Issue," which he submitted to the Ministry of Internal Affairs in September 1859. "All the German states in turn," he wrote, "recognized the peasants' need to obtain ownership of land . . . Even in France, amid the general fluctuation of morals and institutions, only the wide dispersal of landownership and its peasant proprietors represent some element of stability. A considerable share of the poverty and anxiety of contemporary Europe must be attributed to the fact that the European governments realized these sensible principles too late, and consequently a rural proletariat developed too rapidly in the states of the West."[19] Confi-

Nikolai Miliutin. Painting ca 1830–40.

dence in Russia's ability as a "backward" country to take into account the negative experience of the West and to avoid repeating it had become part of the intellectual arsenal of Russian society at least since the time of Chaadaev. This outlook had penetrated the bureaucracy as well and influenced its mode of thought and its actions.

The enlightened bureaucracy also wanted to emancipate the serfs with land in order to counterbalance the predominance of the noble landowners. That would strengthen the political position of the autocracy and enhance its role as arbiter of conflicts among the various segments of society. Referring in his memorandum to the impending establishment of the Editing Commission, the special governmental body charged with creating the framework of the peasant reform, Cherkassky defined its role as follows: "It must intercede for the peasants, whose voice goes almost unheard in the provincial committees, and it must determine the just measure of the nobility's sacrifices, which the provincial committees, by their very nature, have been unable and unwilling to do." According to Larissa Zakharova, "the image of the state as a judge standing above the classes and regulating the discordant interests of the various estates and groups was an illusion characteristic of many currents of social and political thought at this time."[20]

Finally, a landed emancipation promised the government immediate financial reimbursement. The enlightened bureaucracy's plan for the peasant reform called for a protracted redemption operation in which the state would have to serve as creditor and intermediary.

In the opinion of the enlightened bureaucracy, the personal emancipation of the serfs would represent the initial stage of the reform, and their transformation into petty proprietors the final stage. The intention was to combine the experience of France, which had created masses of landowners, and Prussia, which had carried out its reform mainly from above and with a minimum of social upheaval. The decision to emancipate the serfs with land inevitably entailed a series of additional reforms. The most important was the judicial reform, which created a court system with jurisdiction over all the social estates and independent of the governmental administration, and the introduction of local institutions of self-government in which all the estates participated.

The enlightened bureaucracy had great faith in the possibility of "social engineering," that is, its own ability to channel the country's development in certain directions. "In this respect, Russia is more fortunate [than the West]," an explanatory note of 1860 to the enlightened bureaucracy's peasant reform plan stated. "Our country has been given the opportunity of utilizing the experience of other lands . . . to comprehend all at once the path that lies ahead, from the beginning of this endeavor to the termination of obligatory relations [between masters and serfs] through redemption of the land."[21] This approach presupposed strict regulation, from above, of relations among the different segments of society and vigilant state supervision of the country's social development.

The government made clear just how strict its supervision would be as soon as it accepted the new program for resolving the peasant question at the end of 1858. As indicated earlier, most members of the provincial committees favored a landless emancipation. In pursuit of "good results," the government resorted to authoritarian methods to support the minority favoring a landed emancipation. The Ministry of Internal Affairs limited the degree to which sessions of the provincial committees could be publicized and prohibited discussion of the peasant question in the noble assemblies, the nobility's institutions of corporate self-government. Special "members from the government" were appointed to the committees in order to give the minority viewpoint an artificial preponderance.[22] "Progress through coercion," the introduction of a new, more progressive course of development by means of compulsion from above, was a frequent contradiction in Russian history, and now it made its appearance once again.[23]

A sizable proportion of the great lords in the upper ranks of the government still opposed emancipation with land. To overcome their opposition, the enlightened bureaucrats had to resort to behind-the-scenes manipulation and bureaucratic infighting, typical features of an absolute monarchy. One device was the creation in 1859 of a special institution, the Editing Commission, to draw up the basic principles of the reform. Formally, the Commission served merely as the executive body of the Main Committee, but in fact it reported directly to the tsar. Alexander personally ordered the appointment of Rostovtsev as chairman of the Commission, underscoring its distinctive status. In the words of a contemporary, the Commission represented "a separate temporary institution within the state." Alexander himself considered it a "governmental body."

The Editing Commission occupied an exceptional place in the autocratic monarchy's system of government. The dominant figure in the Commission was Nikolai Miliutin. When he established the Commission, Alexander appointed Miliutin deputy minister of internal affairs (but added "temporarily carrying out his duties"). Rostovtsev, the chairman of the Commission, gave Miliutin sweeping authority to select the members of the new institution, most of whom shared his views. They included seventeen representatives of ministries and departments and twenty-one experts drawn from local landowners or specialists on the peasant question, such as scholars and journalists. The majority were men of the same generation, between thirty-five and forty-five years of age. Many of them knew each other from their previous activities and meetings in discussion circles, salons, and scientific societies. Konstantin Kavelin, though not a member of the Commission, stayed in constant contact with it. The Commission's members included Petr Kiselev's closest associate, Andrei Zablotsky-Desiatovsky, and the future ministers of finance Mikhail Reutern and Nikolai Bunge. Along with Miliutin, the Slavophiles Iury Samarin and Vladimir Cherkassky played leading roles in the Commission.

The Editing Commission operated in a decidedly untraditional manner. It worked swiftly, sought to publicize its conclusions as widely as possible and provide them with scientific backing, and maintained an informal atmosphere in its meetings. Whereas the secret committee had met eleven times in the course of a year and the Main Committee twenty-eight times in 1858, the Editing Commission held 409 sessions, each lasting from three to six hours, in the year and seven months of its existence. Its members refrained from wearing official uniforms at its sessions, and they held their meetings in apartments and dachas belonging to Rostovtsev or other colleagues, or over a glass of tea or a bottle of champagne on festive occasions such as birthdays. In the summer they met in tents put up by peasants who were aware of the nature of the Commission's work. Within a few days of each session, three thousand copies of its minutes appeared in print. The Commission drew on statistical surveys of landed property and on economic data. It created a library of all recent books and articles on the peasant question in Russia and Europe, even including, by permission of the tsar, Alexander Herzen's publications.[24]

The Editing Commission played a complex and contradictory role in the preparation of the peasant reform. On the one hand, this body of energetic, well-educated, and professionally trained individuals greatly accelerated the preparation of the reform and gave it a more purposeful character. Because of the shared outlook of its members, the Editing Commission for a short time served as the surrogate for a ministerial cabinet, an institution that actually appeared in Russia only in 1905–6.[25] On the other hand, the like-mindedness of the Commission's members was to a considerable degree an artificial creation. The opponents of the enlightened bureaucrats, some of whom had to be appointed to the Commission, remained a minority, unable to influence its decisions on matters of principle. Minority opinions expressed at meetings were not included in the minutes and were therefore not publicized. Petr Valuev, the future minister of internal affairs and an opponent of the enlightened bureaucrats, had every reason to say of the Commission: "It was constituted in such a way that no one could oppose the majority's views."[26]

The authoritarianism inherent in the planning of the peasant reform manifested itself particularly in the relations between the government and the deputies of the gentry committees who came to Petersburg in the summer of 1859. In the course of his journey through Russia in 1858, Alexander had promised the nobles that their representatives would participate in the discussions of the final draft of the reform. However, upon their arrival in the capital the members of the provincial committees were told that they could not consider themselves authoritative representatives of the nobility and did not have the right to meet together or even call themselves "deputies." Their sole function was to provide answers to questions that the Editing Commission had drawn up in advance. "You are no more than walking reference books," Iury Samarin commented sarcastically. Not surprisingly, the deputies reacted with great anger to the curtailment of their rights. In their "addresses" to Alexander II they condemned "bureaucratic arbitrariness" and the "despotism of the officials," and they insisted on a revision of the Editing Commission's draft of the reform project.

The content of the nobles' addresses casts doubt on the contention in Soviet historiography that the autocracy was a "dictatorship of the nobility." Almost all the deputies rejected the Commission's draft. Some demanded a considerable reduction in the size of the peasants' allotments, while others, such as Unkovsky, wanted the immediate redemption of existing allotments, thereby limiting the bureaucracy's influence on the implementation of the reform. The addresses voiced demands for gentry participation in the Main Committee's final discussion of the peasant reform as well as in future decisions on important political issues. The author of one of the memoranda, Chamberlain Nikolai Bezobrazov, who was the nephew of Prince Aleksei Orlov, the chairman of the Main Committee, even declared that only "elected representatives make the government an autocracy." Without them, he wrote, "it bears the character of arbitrary rule; . . . it gropes its way and falls into traps set by the bureaucracy, which becomes the government's driving force and leader instead of its instrument."[27] The nobles' declarations angered Alexander II. His responses included: "fine sophistries"; "nonsense"; "see what ideas these gentlemen have in their heads"; and "he fully convinced me that people like him want to establish oligarchic rule in Russia."[28] At his instructions, the authors of the addresses received varying degrees of punishment. Unkovsky, for example, received "His Imperial Majesty's reprimand," while Bezobrazov was dismissed from service and banished to a remote province.

The penalties imposed on the deputies aroused the nobles' assemblies, the nobility's institutions of local self-government, which had the official right to petition the supreme power on all social and political issues. In 1859 they began submitting petitions of a constitutional nature. They openly counterposed the interests of society to those of the governmental bureaucracy. One of Unkovsky's colleagues called the nobles' assemblies "the sole legal guarantee against the arbitrariness of the bureaucracy, which oppresses everyone, understands nothing, accomplishes nothing, and fears everything. The bureaucracy, which has only its own personal advantages in view, is directly opposed to the interests of society as a whole."[29] The nobility's constitutional petitions streamed in almost without interruption until 1862; the last of them, the address of the nobles' assembly of Moscow Province, dated from 1865. In the mid-1860s, the center of the constitutional movement gradually shifted from the nobles' assemblies to the zemstvos, the new all-estate institutions of local self-government.

Why did representatives of the nobility call for the introduction of a constitution in Russia? For some, it was a matter of narrow self-interest, a desire to receive political power in compensation for the loss of their serfs. Others clearly recognized the danger that an emancipation based on the principles of the Editing Commission would upset the balance of social and political forces in the society. In a review of the Commission's work, Unkovsky wrote:

> If the government remains as before, the landowners' peasants will inevitably be subjected to the unbridled arbitrariness of the bureaucrats. In essence, it makes no difference whether they be serfs of a landowner or serfs of a bureaucrat, and it is even better to be a landowner's serfs . . . Only the moral elevation of their duties can attract the best men to government service. That moral elevation can be achieved only if they are independent. This is possible only if their work is open to the public and they are responsible to an independent judicial authority.[30]

Unkovsky in fact advanced a program for a far-reaching liberal transformation of the country based on the principle of participation by all the social estates.

Paradoxically, the program advocated by Unkovsky and his like-minded colleagues did not differ substantially from the principles of the Editing Commission's leaders. The latter, however, firmly opposed the nobility's efforts to seize the initiative in reforming the government. "Never, never, as long as I have the power," Nikolai Miliutin declared, "will I allow the nobility to claim any initiative in matters regarding the interests and needs of the people as a whole. Concern for their welfare belongs to the government. The initiative in undertaking any reforms for the good of the country belongs to the government and only to the government." Leading associates of the enlightened bureaucracy, such as Konstantin Kavelin and Iury Samarin, opposed the introduction of a constitution on the assumption that it would constrict the autocracy's reform efforts and lead to the nobility's domination over the peasantry.[31] The clashes between the nobles' deputies and the Editing Commission opened a rift between potential allies, the enlightened bureaucracy and the liberal nobility, and undermined the position of Miliutin and his supporters.

The consequences of that rift quickly made themselves felt. Conservative magnates continued to exert pressure on the tsar. After Rostovtsev died in

February 1860, in part as a result of the enormous nervous strain of his work on the reform, Count Viktor Panin, a vehement opponent of emancipating the serfs with land, was appointed chairman of the Editing Commission. Under conservative pressure, the Commission made serious concessions, reducing the peasants' allotments and increasing the redemption payments. The position of the peasants underwent a further deterioration when the reform project came before the Main Committee and the State Council. The basic principles of the reform remained intact, but with significant amendments. The reform process nonetheless culminated on February 19, 1861, when Alexander II, on the sixth anniversary of his accession to the throne, signed the Manifesto on the Abolition of Serfdom and the Statute on the Peasants Being Freed from Serfdom.

A less happy fate awaited the reformers themselves, men who had devoted all their energy, knowledge, and ability to planning the peasant reform. The government entrusted the implementation of the reform to their staunch opponent, Petr Valuev, who assumed the post of minister of internal affairs. The Editing Commission was disbanded as soon as its work was over. Those of its members who came from other cities were ordered to leave Petersburg immediately. Miliutin and Lanskoi were dismissed within a month and a half of the proclamation of the Manifesto of February 19. Lanskoi died soon after his dismissal. Miliutin, whose intense labor on the reform and abrupt dismissal upon its completion undermined his health, took a year's leave of absence and went abroad. The government recalled him to active state service for a second time when insurrection broke out in Poland in 1863. There, on the western border of the empire, Miliutin and his old comrades-in-arms, Cherkassky and Samarin, were able to carry out a more consistent peasant reform, using it to undercut the position of the local gentry. Miliutin's agrarian reform in Poland oddly combined liberal-democratic elements and centralizing and Russifying tendencies. This was his last service to the state. A stroke in 1866 ended his activity, and he died in 1872 at the age of fifty-four.[32]

The reform had a considerable impact on public consciousness in Russia and abroad. The largely peaceful emancipation of the serfs appreciably enhanced the authority of the autocracy and of Alexander II personally. European and American public opinion responded favorably to the reform, and Americans contrasted the circumstances of the Russian emancipation with the military conflict surrounding the abolition of slavery in the United States. The elimination of serfdom greatly expanded the opportunities for the development of capitalism in Russia and on the whole gave the country social stability for the next fifty years.

At the same time, the reform also had important negative features. Above all, the principles of the reform of 1861 were foreign to the peasants' own outlook.[33] Although most peasants accepted the reform calmly, tensions began to build up beneath the surface. The emancipation seemed yet another confirmation of the peasant myth of the tsar as their "little father" and "defender," but the peasants could not accept such prominent features of the reform as the preservation of gentry landholding and the redemption of their allotments. In the peasant's mind, the land belonged to everyone, and only those who worked it had the right to use it. When the provisions of the reform were announced, the peasants began to suspect that the tsar had been deceived, and "the lords [had] substituted their own emancipation" for the tsar's. More than half of the landlords' peasants refused to sign the regulatory charters, the agreements with the landowners confirming the provisions of the emancipation. (In such cases, the charters took effect unilaterally at the demand of the landowners.) Rumors arose among the peasants of a "scheduled hour" or "promised hour" when the tsar would announce the "real" emancipation to them, without redemption payments or reduced allotments. At times, the uneasy mood of the peasants erupted into insurrections that required armed force to suppress. The best-known instances occurred in the villages of Bezdna, in Kazan Province, and Kandeevka in Penza Province.

The onerous provisions of the reform, and especially the open rebellions of the peasants, stimulated an opposition movement within the intelligentsia. Its leaders had long felt dissatisfied with what they regarded as excessive concessions to the landowners in the planning of the reform. Nikolai Chernyshevsky, the leading writer for *The Contemporary*, became the ideological leader of the radical camp, to which most of the intelligentsia belonged. (Alexander Herzen at this time occupied an ambivalent position, wavering between the liberals and the radicals.) The program of Chernyshevsky and the radicals included giving the peasants the major share of the land, minimal redemption payments or none at all, and preservation of the peasant commune. The radicals viewed the commune as the embryo of a future socialist order. They advocated increasingly extreme tactics to achieve their program and in the end concluded that Russia needed a peasant revolution.

To what extent were Chernyshevsky and his followers justified in their criticism of the peasant reform? To be sure, the reform had been based on a number of compromises which the radicals rejected in principle. At the same time, their criticism had some merit. Most important, the peasants acquired their land under extremely burdensome conditions. "Cut-offs," that is, reductions in the peasants' pre-reform allotments, which the enlightened bureaucrats had exerted every effort to prevent, became the norm as a result of conservative pressure. In the country as a whole, the peasants lost about twenty percent of their previous allotments. The significance of the cut-offs was most striking in the black-earth provinces, where land was particularly valuable. The peasants' losses there ranged from 30 percent of their allotments in Kharkov, Kazan, and Simbirsk provinces to 44 percent in Samara Province.[34] Many scholars believe that the reduced allotments severely hampered the establishment of independent peasant farming and often failed to guarantee the peasants even a bare subsistence. Rapid population growth in the second half of the nineteenth century led to a further reduction in the size of the peasants' allotments, from an average of 13.8 to 7.0 acres.[35] By the turn of the twentieth century, social tensions in the Russian countryside had reached an explosive level.

The redemption operation also aggravated the plight of the peasants because the authorities used this provision, formally a market transaction, to replenish the drastically depleted state treasury. Unlike the governments of Austria and Prussia, which ruled countries similar to Russia in their political and social structure, the autocracy did not invest a single ruble in the peasant reform. On the contrary, it profited from it. Characteristically, in the period when the reform was being implemented, the government expended one-third of its budget on military needs and one-sixth on the conquest of the Caucasus.[36] The state immediately paid the landowners between 75 and 80 percent of the amount of the redemption, in the form of state bonds. The peasants then repaid that sum to the state, with 6 percent interest, over the next forty-nine years. From the outset, the redemption sums included compensation to the landowners not only for the land but also for the loss of their unpaid serf labor, considerably increasing the size of the redemption. The peasants' redemption payments actually lasted forty-five years, until the revolution of 1905. During this time they paid an amount double the initial value of the redemption.[37] Moreover, the government automatically subtracted the landowners' existing debts to the state from the redemption sums that they received, making it much more difficult to establish an entrepreneurial system of agriculture on the gentry estates.

The agrarian sector of the Russian economy by no means remained stagnant after the abolition of serfdom. Enterprising landowners and some well-to-do peasants used their economic freedom to develop an active commercial agriculture. Peasant entrepreneurs increased their landholdings by buying up gentry lands. The grain harvest doubled in the second half of the nineteenth century. In the 1890s half the net grain harvest reached the market. In the four decades from 1861–65 to 1901–5, the value of grain exports increased almost eightfold, from 56.3 million to 447 million rubles.[38]

The bulk of the peasantry, however, did not engage in truly commercial farming. They entered the market only under pressure from the government, which forced them to sell not only their surplus but a portion of their needed grain in order to pay their taxes. The peasants' own allotments obviously did not suffice to fulfill their obligations to the state. They had to lease land from the gentry on highly disadvantageous terms, working the gentry's estates with their own equipment. This arrangement impeded the growth of labor productivity in agriculture and condemned the Russian village to poverty and semi-starvation.

The low productivity and backward technology of the agricultural sector had another cause as well. The preservation of the peasant commune severely restricted the personal rights of the peasants. In 1861 the former serfs ceased to be the property of the gentry and received the right to appear in court, conclude contracts, establish commercial and industrial enterprises, and transfer to other social estates. "Peace mediators," special officials independent of the local administration, supervised the demarcation of the lands of the gentry from those of the peasants.[39] Still, peasants remained subject to corporal punishment, furnished the army's recruits until 1874, paid the "soul tax" until the mid-1880s, and had limited freedom of movement. The commune retained collective responsibility for the payment of the peasants' taxes and other obligations.

Peasant courts and forms of peasant self-government, such as village and cantonal elders and assemblies, replaced the landowners' police and administrative powers over their former serfs. Those institutions also bore the marks of the transitional era. On the one hand, the archaic principle of separating the social estates applied to the village and cantonal assemblies, in that they dealt exclusively with the peasantry. Peasant courts operated on the basis of customary law, which differed considerably from standard legal norms. On the other hand, those institutions linked the peasants to broader spheres of public life. Through their new institutions of self-government, peasants served as jurors in court cases and as members of the zemstvos, the all-estate local self-government institutions established in 1864.

The authors of the peasant reform made a deliberate decision to preserve the commune and a separate system of administration for the peasantry. They intended them only as temporary measures, however, aimed at protecting the peasants from pressure by their former masters, the landowners, and helping them avoid a rapid loss of their land and economic ruin under market conditions. They anticipated that steps would be taken later on to weaken both the separate system of peasant self-government and the power of the commune over the individual peasant. Their expectations were not borne out, however. In the 1880s and the 1890s, a period of political reaction, the government came to regard the commune and peasant separateness as principles of social stability in the countryside and set out to reinforce them. By the end of the nineteenth century it was clear that the need for further agrarian change had grown acute. Would it come about through reform or through revolution?

Chapter 5

The Great Reforms: Sources and Consequences

Count Sergei Uvarov, minister of public education under Nicholas I and one of his most talented officials, said of serfdom: "This tree has put down deep roots, and both the Church and the throne have given it shade. It cannot be uprooted." In Uvarov's opinion, the abolition of serfdom would inevitably entail political change. "The question of serfdom is closely related to the question of autocracy and even of the monarchy. They are two parallel forces that developed together. They have a single historical origin, and their legitimacy is identical."[1]

The Great Reforms implemented in the 1860s and the 1870s under the guidance of the enlightened bureaucracy sought to refute Uvarov's view. The enlightened bureaucrats understood, of course, that the abolition of serfdom would bring with it social and administrative changes. They assumed, however, that those changes would first affect the "lower stories" of the social edifice and, far from limiting autocratic power, would strengthen it. Reality justified their expectations only in part. The reforms of the 1860s and the 1870s created a system in which the absolute power of the monarch coexisted with an independent judiciary, a relatively free press, and local self-government. Their coexistence was fraught with profound contradictions that pointed to the necessity of extending the reforms to the "upper stories" of the political system by introducing representative government.

The first of the Great Reforms after the abolition of serfdom, the zemstvo reform of January 1, 1864, created rural institutions of self-government in the provinces and districts. The law of June 16, 1870, created parallel urban institutions, the municipal dumas.[2] The need for urban reform had arisen in Russia with the development of market relations, the turbulent process of urbanization, the increasing complexity of the urban economy, and widening social disparities in the towns.[3] The municipal dumas, which had first been proposed in 1862, took eight years to establish, while the creation of the zemstvos occurred immediately after the emancipation of the serfs. Why did the rural reform take place so quickly, and what role did rural self-government play in Russian history?

The primary reason for the rapid pace (by Russian standards) of the rural reform was the need to fill the "power vacuum" that the emancipation created in the provinces. Under serfdom, the landowners were not just the owners of the peasants but were responsible for their welfare. The landowners were supposed to give their serfs economic assistance, feed them in times of famine, and provide for their medical needs and education. Before the abolition of serfdom, the provision of those services had been extremely meager, especially in the areas of health and education, but after 1861 the need for them grew substantially. The growing capitalist economy increased the demand for a skilled labor force in the agricultural sector. The almost universal illiteracy of the peasants, the lack of agronomic and veterinary services in the villages, and the recurrent epidemics among both humans and livestock became intolerable. Because the bureaucratic apparatus lacked the capacity to provide social services in the provinces, the only alternative was the introduction of local self-government.[4]

The autocracy had an additional reason for taking this step. As already noted, the constitutional movement among the gentry reached its peak at the end of the 1850s and beginning of the 1860s. The government reasoned that giving society, and most of all the gentry, some autonomy in economic and social affairs promised to divert the public's attention from political matters. Minister of Internal Affairs Petr Valuev reflected this thinking. The primary value of the zemstvos, he remarked sarcastically, was that they would "provide activity for a considerable portion of the press as well as those malcontents who currently stir up trouble because they have nothing to do."[5]

Russian society, of course, saw through the government's maneuver, and not everyone approved of it. On the whole, however, especially at first, society welcomed the introduction of the zemstvos. Konstantin Kavelin, the outstanding representative of Russian liberalism, asserted in 1865: "The whole of our immediate future depends on the success of the zemstvos, and our readiness for a constitution depends on how well they work." The French writer Anatole Leroy-Beaulieu, who had a wide circle of acquaintances in Russia, related the words of the Russians with whom he spoke: "We have begun to erect an edifice from its very foundation . . . We will build it stronger and higher than you [Europeans] have built your fragile structures."[6]

If the edifice of constitutionalism were to grow from the foundation of the zemstvo, however, several contradictions built into its design would have to be overcome. The most significant were those related to the system of zemstvo representation. In creating institutions of self-government, the planners of the reform had to take into account the official division of society into estates and the enormous gaps between the levels of education and well-being of the different strata of the population. The authorities considered this problem in the early stages of planning for the reform, entrusted to a commission formed in 1859 under the leadership of Nikolai Miliutin in the Ministry of Internal Affairs. The commission conceded primacy to the gentry as the wealthiest and most educated estate. At the same time, however, it secured a fairly substantial position for the peasantry and anticipated the zemstvo's transformation into an institution that would truly represent all the estates. Valuev, who assumed responsibility for the preparation of the reform upon his appointment as minister of internal affairs in 1861, took a different view. Valuev felt that after the abolition of serfdom the gentry landowners should rule in the provinces, on the English model. "The masses can be compared to sand, not to solid ground," Valuev wrote in his memorandum "On the Internal Situation of Russia" in 1862. "In vain would we seek firm support in them . . . Only property in larger quantities, landed property that ties its owner to a locality . . . can serve the state as a fully conservative element." Valuev's political program envisaged a major redirection of the government's focus from the lower strata of society to the upper strata, a repudiation of the course that the enlightened bureaucracy had pursued while preparing the peasant reform. He wrote, "On February 19, 1861, the imperial sun brightly illuminated and warmed the valleys. The time has come to illuminate and warm the heights and outlying areas."[7] Valuev's plan included a consultative representative assembly and a broad compromise with the non-Russian elites in the borderlands of the empire, particularly the Polish and Baltic German nobilities, to supplement the predominance of the gentry in the zemstvos. Valuev was able to exert some influence on the zemstvo reform, but on the whole the zemstvos created in 1864 were based on the principles that Miliutin had advocated.

The reform of 1864 established zemstvos on two levels, the district and the provincial. Every three years the population of a district elected deputies to a district zemstvo assembly, and the district assemblies in turn elected the deputies to a provincial zemstvo assembly. The district and provincial zemstvo assemblies elected the executive boards of the zemstvos from their own ranks. As a sign of gentry dominance, the chairman of the zemstvo assembly had to be the local marshal of the nobility. The zemstvo electoral system gave even more weight to the gentry. The Statute on Zemstvo Institutions divided the electors in the districts into groups, or curias. The first curia, consisting of private landowners, mainly gentry, had the greatest degree of representation. The second curia consisted of the owners of urban real estate, and the third of communal peasants. The third curia, which did not have a property requirement for voting, was restricted to members of the peasant estate. As a result of this unequal system of representation, after the first zemstvo elections in 1865–67 the gentry received 41.6 percent of the seats in the district assemblies and 74.2 percent of the seats in the provincial assemblies. Peasant representatives constituted 38.5 percent and 10.6 percent of the deputies at the district and provincial levels, respectively: merchants, 10 percent and 11 percent; clergy, 6.5 percent and 3.8 percent; and petty townspeople, 0.5 percent at each level.[8] By the end of the second decade of the zemstvo's existence, however, this picture of almost complete gentry predominance had changed considerably.

The authors of the zemstvo reform had provided for the possible enlargement of non-gentry representation. Well-to-do peasants, townspeople, and merchants could attain membership in the first curia by purchasing land as private property. The growth of market relations in Russia fostered such transfers, especially in areas of intensive industrial development (the central region) and entrepreneurial agriculture (the Volga region and the steppe region of the south). In the district zemstvo assemblies of Moscow Province, for example, by 1886 the representation of merchants had grown by half, from 15 to 24 percent, and the share of peasant proprietors had more than doubled, from 2.6 to 5.5 percent. In Nizhny Novgorod Province, the share of merchant deputies had increased from 7 to 14 percent, and that of peasant proprietors from 1 percent to 4.8 percent. Peasant proprietors in Tauride Province increased their representation from 1 percent to 14 percent. Similar developments occurred in Vladimir, Kostroma, Kaluga, Kherson, and Saratov provinces. In 1865, non-gentry property owners predominated in 16 out of 260 district zemstvos, but in 1886 the number had risen to 47.[9] The development of capitalism substantially altered the social structure of Russia and inevitably affected the composition and activities of the local self-government institutions.

The growing ranks of zemstvo employees, the so-called "third element" or "zemstvo intelligentsia," had an even greater impact on the functions and social makeup of the zemstvos. (The "first element" consisted of government officials, and the "second element," the elected deputies of the zemstvo assemblies.) The zemstvo's need for trained specialists stemmed directly from the essence of the zemstvo reform. When the administration created the zemstvos, it hastened to rid itself of responsibility for the few social services it provided. These consisted mostly of the schools, hospitals, and pharmacies under the jurisdiction of the Ministry of State Domains and the Offices of Public Welfare, which Catherine II had created in her reform of provincial government. To maintain these institutions, the zemstvos hired doctors, medical assistants (feldshers), and teachers, and later agronomists, veterinarians, insurance agents, and other professionals. The Statute on Zemstvo Institutions allowed the zemstvos to hire such employees and to levy taxes on the local population to pay their salaries.[10]

The need to identify sources of tax revenue and create a rational system of tax assessments gave rise to one of the most important activities of the zemstvos, the collection of statistics. At first the zemstvo statisticians confined themselves to practical tasks, but with time their work began to encompass the most diverse aspects of Russian provincial life. On the whole, the second half of the nineteenth and the beginning of the twentieth centuries saw the confident development of the zemstvo's activities and a corresponding growth of the zemstvo intelligentsia. By the beginning of World War I, the zemstvos had created about 40,000 schools and 2,000 hospitals with 42,500 patients. From the 1860s to the 1880s alone, zemstvo statisticians appraised 3.5 million peasant households and 38 million desiatinas of land. Between 1864 and 1913 the budget for the zemstvos grew from 14.7 million rubles to 253.8 million, as expenditures on public education and health continued to increase. By the beginning of the twentieth century, the "third element" consisted of sixty thousand people. A large number of them, including 62 percent of the teachers, came from the lower classes: petty townspeople, peasants, and the lower clergy. About 63 percent of rural teachers were women.[11]

The zemstvo intelligentsia altered Russian public life. As doctors, agronomists, statisticians, and other zemstvo employees, educated Russians came into contact with the vast peasant population. Their experience, unprecedented in Russia's history, gave the zemstvo intelligentsia an elevated conception of its mission, one that transcended the mere fulfillment of professional duties. Western Europe, wrote one of the zemstvo doctors, "developed medical assistance as a personal matter between a patient and the doctor serving him on the basis of professional and commercial principles. Russian zemstvo medicine arose as a purely social matter. The assistance a zemstvo doctor renders is not a personal service at the patient's expense but an act of philanthropy, a public service."[12]

Messianic elements in the outlook of the zemstvo intelligentsia supplemented its altruism, which served as a powerful stimulus to carry out its low-paid cultural and educational work in the countryside. At the same time, the altruism and humanitarianism characteristic of the zemstvo intelligentsia often gave rise to radical and even revolutionary sentiments. In all its daily activities, the "third element" came face to face with the people's poverty and distress. Because it was excluded from politics and thus from participation in governmental decision making, however, the zemstvo intelligentsia failed to understand the full complexity of the problems associated with efforts to improve people's lives.

These characteristics turned the zemstvo intelligentsia into fertile soil for anti-governmental tendencies of various sorts. Revolutionaries often sought jobs as zemstvo feldshers, midwives, or statisticians in order to spread revolutionary propaganda among the peasants. Zemstvo workers themselves frequently disseminated revolutionary views. According to a police report from Saratov province, "These people, nursing a feeling of discontent, . . . look with secret dissatisfaction at everything that stands higher than they do in society. With their false understanding of the people's welfare, especially those who were previously instilled with liberalism and have not yet broadened their ideas about the life of the people, they may, lacking supervision in remote areas, . . . act in a harmful manner in these circumstances."[13] Opposition-minded teachers presented a particular danger to the government. Their work had a direct influence on the peasants' consciousness and threatened to undermine the patriarchal traditions and religious precepts on which the peasant worldview rested.

The anti-governmental sentiments of the "third element" often found support among the deputies of the zemstvo assemblies. Unlike the "third element," the deputies tended to hold liberal rather than radical views. Their opposition arose from the limitations that the administration imposed on the activities of the zemstvos. When the zemstvos were created, they received considerable autonomy. They not only had the right to hire employees and collect taxes, but they could make decisions independently within their sphere of competence, and when necessary they could complain to the Senate about the actions of the administration. In the absence of a system of representation in the central government, the zemstvos' prerogatives inevitably came into conflict with the autocratic principle of the governmental apparatus. The result was continual strife between the administration and the zemstvos.

Some statesmen had foreseen this danger and in the mid-1860s proposed the creation of a central representative assembly to supplement the zemstvo reform. As mentioned earlier, Valuev drafted one of those proposals in 1863. Valuev's plan called for a "congress of state deputies" attached to the State Council, with both appointed members and elected delegates from the provincial zemstvos and the large cities. Gentry landowners were to form an absolute majority of the state deputies. The congress would discuss the draft of the state budget and laws proposed by the government, and some of its members would be included in the State Council. The decisions of the congress as well as of the State Council were to be strictly advisory in nature.

Grand Duke Konstantin Nikolaevich put forward a somewhat different proposal in 1866. Under his plan, the State Council would convene congresses of deputies from the provincial zemstvos and provincial nobles' assemblies for preliminary consideration of petitions from the institutions of self-government as well as other questions of local significance. Alexander II confirmed neither of these proposals.[14]

The need to "crown the edifice," that is, to complete the zemstvo reform by summoning a nationwide representative assembly, became clear, and the proposals to create such an institution were moderate. Why, then, did Alexander II stubbornly reject political reform? Undoubtedly, traditional conceptions of autocracy that Alexander had inherited from Nicholas I played a major role, but there were other considerations as well. Alexander had good reason to fear that the peasants would interpret the introduction of a representative body as a limitation on the power of the tsar to the benefit of the gentry. The result might be a peasant uprising. In 1861 Alexander told Otto von Bismarck, then Prussia's ambassador to Russia, "Throughout the country, the people see the monarch as the emissary of God, as a paternal and all-powerful master. That feeling, which has an almost religious force, is inseparable from my person . . . To give up the sense of power that the crown gives me would open a breach in the halo which the nation possesses."[15] In a conversation in 1865 with Pavel Golokhvastov, one of the representatives of gentry constitutionalism, Alexander based his rejection of a national assembly on the grounds of concern for the integrity of the empire. "I give you my word," the emperor said, "that I would be prepared to sign any constitution right now, at this desk, if I were convinced that it was useful for Russia. But I know that if I were to do so today, Russia would fall to pieces tomorrow."[16] Only at the very end of his reign, in 1881, did Alexander approve a proposal for nationwide representation drawn up by Minister of Internal Affairs Mikhail Loris-Melikov. However, the tsar's death at the hands of a terrorist cut short the implementation of this plan. (See chapter 7.)

It should be noted that Alexander was not alone in his opposition to a representative assembly. Such eminent representatives of Russian liberalism as Iury Samarin, Konstantin Kavelin, and Boris Chicherin expressed similar reservations. In Samarin's opinion, the broad development of local self-government and civil liberties should precede representation on the national level. "For the time being we cannot have a popular constitution," he declared, "and a constitution that is not popular, that is, one that establishes the domination of a minority operating without the authorization of the majority, is a lie and a deception."[17] Whatever the motives for opposing nationwide representation, however, its absence condemned the administration to an endless and fruitless war with the zemstvos.

The first salvos in the war rang out in 1866, soon after the creation of the zemstvos, when the authorities unilaterally limited the zemstvos' ability to levy taxes on the local population in order to finance their work. The government ruled that in the towns, taxes could be assessed only on real estate, not on the capital or profits of commercial and industrial establishments. The Petersburg provincial zemstvo assembly opposed the government's decision and demanded that henceforth only "the joint forces and simultaneous labor of the central administration and the zemstvo" should decide matters relating to local self-government. One of the deputies, Count Andrei Shuvalov, made use of the conflict to assert the need for a central representative body. "A question resolved separately in different zemstvo assemblies," he declared, "may have the same defect, that is, of being decided unilaterally." In response, the government resorted to repression. It temporarily suspended the Petersburg zemstvo, exiled Shuvalov abroad, and banished Nikolai Kruze, the chairman of the zemstvo board, to the town of Orenburg in the southern Urals.[18]

The government continued to take measures aimed at limiting the activity of the zemstvos. In 1866 provincial governors received the right to withhold confirmation of zemstvo officials on the grounds of political unreliability, and in 1879 they were given authority to dismiss zemstvo employees or to prevent them from being hired. The governor had to authorize publications of the zemstvos, municipal dumas, and nobles' assemblies. A measure of 1867 required the chairmen of zemstvo assemblies to prevent discussion of political issues. A series of decrees made zemstvo doctors, feldshers, and teachers administratively subordinate to the appropriate governmental departments. In 1869 and 1873, respectively, the government created the posts of inspector and director of public schools, enabling it to intensify its supervision of the zemstvo schools. The authorities rejected, or left unanswered, all petitions by the zemstvos to create a nationwide zemstvo newspaper or to convene inter-provincial zemstvo congresses, even to address purely practical needs such as combating livestock epidemics. By the end of the 1870s relations between the zemstvos and the administration were tense and hostile.

Conflict also marked relations between the administration and the new courts created by the Judicial Statutes of November 20, 1864. The judicial reform was no less important than the zemstvo reform, and it embodied liberal principles to an even greater degree. The reform of 1864 had political significance in that it limited the power of the autocrat in the judicial realm. Like the zemstvos, the new courts owed their existence to the abolition of serfdom.

The judicial system that existed prior to 1861 had arisen under Peter I and Catherine II and conformed fully to the principles of the "well-ordered police state" that prevailed at the time. The pre-reform system included separate courts for the different social estates, an investigative process conducted without the participation of the litigants, and written legal proceedings. By the middle of the nineteenth century, as the society grew more complex, it had become increasingly clear that the system was no longer functional. The history of the pre-reform courts is filled with stories of trials that lasted not for years but for decades, and officials who lost or even deliberately destroyed dozens of court records.[19] The government had broached the question of judicial reform in the 1840s, but within both society and government, different views arose as to the principles on which the reform should be based.

The spectrum of opinion can be reduced to two general points of view. Some high officials sought to combine the legal procedures of pre-reform Russia and contemporary Western Europe. The enlightened bureaucrats, concentrated in the Ministry of Justice and the State Chancellery, resolutely opposed them. Prince Dmitry Obolensky, an enlightened bureaucrat close to Grand Duke Konstantin Nikolaevich, declared that "for a profound juridical awareness of the people's rights openness (*glasnost'*) is essential, without which that awareness can never be acquired. Therefore, if you want to achieve your objectives, you must be allowed the means." The legal and judicial principles that had developed in Western Europe, he maintained, "are not the property of any one country but belong to all mankind."[20]

The very process of drafting the reform helped to overcome the opposition of the conservatives. The planning was widely publicized, and preparatory materials were published and reviewed by scholars and practicing jurists in Russia and abroad. The government commissioned translations of European legal codes and dispatched several of the reform's planners to Western Europe to study procedures there. Prominent scholars and judicial officials were invited to participate in the preparation of the reform, including Sergei Zarudny, an assistant state secretary of the State Chancellery; Dmitry Rovinsky, the procurator (public prosecutor) of Moscow Province; and Konstantin Pobedonostsev, the senior secretary of the general assembly of the Senate's Moscow departments. The need to create a new, integrated judicial system entirely different from the pre-reform courts soon became clear. The Judicial Statutes of 1864 were designed, as Alexander II said in his decree, "to establish courts in Russia that will be speedy, just, merciful, and equal for all my subjects."[21]

What methods did the Judicial Statutes employ to create such courts? One of their most important innovations was the "peace court," or arbitration court, which presided over petty civil and criminal cases. The peace court, operating in accordance with accelerated and simplified procedures, relieved the higher judicial organs of a large number of minor lawsuits and greatly reduced the amount of red tape in the Russian court system. The justices of the peace, who had to meet a property and educational requirement, were elected by municipal dumas in the larger cities and by district zemstvo assemblies. Thus the judicial, zemstvo, and municipal reforms of the 1860s and the 1870s turned out to be interconnected.

The cases within the competence of the peace court were relatively minor, but they were the most prevalent, for they generally involved matters of everyday life. The application of regular legal procedures to these cases raised the Russian population's level of legal culture. In the words of the liberal journalist Vladimir Bezobrazov, the peace court introduced legal principles "into a sphere of social relations where not even a hint of law had previously existed, nor even a conception of the possibility of law." Grigory Dzhanshiev, a historian of the Great Reforms, wrote:

> Instead of a rude shout and a punch to the jaw, [the ordinary Russian] encountered a cordial justice of the peace who addressed everyone respectfully and listened attentively. He judged everyone equally: the distinguished lord, the general, the admiral, the millionaire, and the peasant in bast sandals. He stuck up for the "little man," even if he had to clash with the authorities or with a rich and powerful opponent. Instead of the old adage "the law was not written for us," the common people began to say "now we're ordered not to fight," "the justice of the peace won't pat you on the back for that," and "now everyone is equal before the court."[22]

The principles underlying the crown courts, which dealt with more serious infractions of the law, represented an even greater innovation. The judicial statutes created two levels of crown courts: the circuit courts and the judicial chambers. The circuit courts conducted trials by jury. Most civil and criminal cases came before the circuit courts, and the judicial chambers functioned as courts of appeal from the circuit courts. In the judicial chambers the verdict was handed down not by jurors but by so-called "estate representatives": the marshal of the nobility, the cantonal elder, and the town mayor. In a limitation of the principles of the Judicial Statutes, the government gave the judicial chambers jurisdiction over cases dealing with the press and some political crimes. The Senate retained its role as the ultimate guardian of legality and created cassation departments to carry out this function. A serious defect of the new judicial system was that, like the zemstvos, it operated only in the European territories of the Russian Empire.

The courts were independent of the administration. Neither crown judges, who were appointed by the emperor, nor judicial investigators could be removed, thus guaranteeing the courts' impartiality. The judicial process was now oral, public, and adversarial, with a procurator representing the prosecution and an attorney representing the defense. A bar association with a corporate structure was established. It was independent of the government, and the most famous attorneys, such as Vladimir Spasovich and Fyodor Plevako, enjoyed wide popularity with the public.

The institution of juries was a particularly important addition to the judicial system. Representatives of the zemstvos and the municipal dumas drew up the jury rolls without the participation of the administration. The provincial governor merely verified the lists. He could remove an individual from the list of jurors, but he had to give reasons for his decision. Jurors had to meet a property requirement, but it was very modest. A special procedure drew peasants into the ranks of jurors. Elected officials of the system of peasant self-government also participated in the work of the courts.

The historian Alexander Afanasiev calculated that in 1883, in the twenty provinces of European Russia excluding the cities of Moscow and Petersburg, peasants constituted 57.4 percent of the jurors; nobles and civil servants, 14.9 percent; merchants, 9.4 percent; and petty townspeople, 18.3 percent.[23] The broad representation of peasants on juries made this institution one of the most democratic in the country. It is not surprising that opponents of the judicial reform scornfully referred to jury trials as "street justice."

The actions of juries inevitably reflected the distinctive characteristics of the peasant mentality. Peasant jurors were excessively indulgent in regard to crimes against female honor and abuses by officials, for example, but they showed no mercy when it came to religious offenses. The number of acquittals increased sharply before important Christian holidays. In the majority of cases, however, jury verdicts were just and well-founded, generally reflecting a balanced view of a particular case. The jury courts' openness to the public, their adversarial character, their independence of the administration, and their close ties to the society prompted a warm public response. They proved to be one of the finest elements in the life of post-reform Russia. Trials in which wealthy and high-ranking individuals appeared as defendants resonated throughout the country, for in earlier times such people would doubtless have been able to avoid judicial punishment. Examples include the trial in 1874 of a retired Guards officer, V.M. Kolemin, for running a gambling den; the 1874 trial of the Abbess Mitrofania, a former baroness who had ties to the imperial court, for forging promissory notes; and the 1875 trial of the millionaire merchant S.T. Ovsiannikov for committing arson in order to collect insurance.[24] On the whole, the post-reform courts helped to raise the level of legal culture in Russian society, strengthen its sense of legality, and guarantee individual rights. Even after the reform of 1864, however, remnants of the past persisted in the judicial sphere, particularly in the separate peasant courts, which dealt exclusively with peasant cases. At the same time, tensions steadily built up between the new judicial institutions and the state administration.

Some of the tension arose because of the way in which conflicts between the administration and the periodical press had been resolved. The reform of April 6, 1865, freed periodicals from preliminary censorship. It created a new set of relations between the administration and the press, in which the courts played an important role. The government's censor now reviewed the contents of periodicals only after publication. If he found something in them that he deemed illegal, he could bring a court action against the editor, the author, or the publisher. In addition to prosecution, the government could issue an administrative warning to the periodical. After a third warning the government suspended the publication for six months, after which the minister of internal affairs had the right to petition the Senate to prohibit it entirely.[25]

The reform of 1865 transferred censorship functions from the Ministry of Public Education to the Ministry of Internal Affairs, a sign of the growing public and political importance of the periodical press. Valuev, who had jurisdiction over censorship after 1865, at first tried to utilize the courts to exert pressure on publishers. Those attempts failed. In the absence of a cabinet system of government, the Ministry of Justice acted independently of the Ministry of Internal Affairs, and any conflict between them inevitably affected prosecutions of the press. Under the statutes of 1864 the courts themselves enjoyed too much autonomy to submit to manipulation. When the administration prosecuted a publication, the court demanded clear evidence of a violation of the law, which was usually very difficult to find.

The first judicial trials of the press, in 1866, ended by exonerating the defendants or imposing light sentences on them. In response, the government in effect gave up attempts to try publications in the courts and turned instead to new forms of administrative pressure. In 1868 the Ministry of Internal Affairs was allowed to forbid the retail sale of periodicals, and in 1873 to prohibit discussions in the press of any social or political issues. The press, in turn, learned how to circumvent such prohibitions by resorting to Aesopian language, allegories, and the reprinting of foreign material. By the end of the 1870s the press, like the zemstvos, was locked in conflict with the authorities.[26]

Similar antagonism existed between the government and the new courts, primarily as a result of the political trials of the 1860s and the 1870s. Beginning in the early 1860s, the authorities had to contend with the growth of a revolutionary movement within the intelligentsia. As was the case with the press, they tried to utilize the courts to strengthen their position. The historian Nikolai Troitsky calculated that more than 220 political trials took place from 1866 to 1895. As a rule, they drew a great deal of public attention.[27] Although political cases usually were not subject to jury trials, in other respects the trials of revolutionaries followed the basic principles of the Judicial Statutes of 1864. As public, adversarial proceedings, they gave the accused the opportunity to expound their views. In some cases the openness of these trials helped the authorities, but for several reasons it soon began to work against them.

Under the authoritarian system that prevailed in Russia, virtually any act of political protest was subject to prosecution. Therefore, in an open trial the government found it difficult to prove the criminal nature of the defendants' activities. The difficulty was especially great when those activities involved no actual deeds but remained on the level of ideas and discussions. Even when revolutionaries fought openly against the authorities, they could always argue in court that under Russian conditions such action was justified because legal protest was impossible. Foreign observers found that argument particularly compelling. The prominent revolutionary Sergei Kravchinsky (better known under the pseudonym Stepniak) declared bluntly that Russian revolutionaries were "the men of [17]93 and [17]89 in France whom the whole of Europe takes as its models."[28] By contrast, the arguments of the prosecution, crude and unconvincing as a rule, amounted to claims that the revolutionaries were "immoral" and "self-interested." Such allegations could not be proved in court.

As a result, instead of tarnishing the reputation of the revolutionaries in the estimation of Russian and foreign public opinion, the trials enhanced it. Inevitably, juries handed down a large number of not-guilty verdicts in political trials. From 1866 to 1878, the courts acquitted 165 out of 433 defendants.[29] Not surprisingly, the conservative and reactionary press began to demand that the principles of the 1864 judicial statutes should not apply to political cases. As early as the beginning of the 1870s the conservative journalist Mikhail Katkov condemned the "placidity" of judges, the "showing-off" of lawyers, and an atmosphere in which "the prisoners' dock becomes a tribune from which seditious speeches pour forth."[30]

The source of Katkov's wrath was the realization on the part of the revolutionaries that an open trial gave them the opportunity to propagandize their views. Their attorneys, willingly or not, assisted the revolutionaries' propaganda efforts. To defend the accused at political trials, lawyers either had to minimize and distort their views, a tactic unacceptable to the revolutionaries, or try to vindicate them. In an 1878 memorandum to the emperor, a highly placed police official wrote: "Not a single trial of crimes against state power occurs without the defense counsel pointing out the administration's obsolescence, its imperfection, or its other defects, which are represented either as the cause of the crimes or as grounds for justifying them."[31]

Irritated by the politicization of the legal profession, the authorities began to attack its rights, as well as the rights of the courts as a whole. Both the judiciary and the bar responded with growing hostility to the government. The antagonism between the courts and the administration broke out into the open during the trial of the revolutionary Vera Zasulich, who shot and seriously wounded Fyodor Trepov, the governor of St. Petersburg, in 1878. (Trepov had ordered the flogging of a political prisoner.) The authorities treated it as a criminal case of attempted murder and submitted it to a jury trial, certain of a favorable outcome. Zasulich's lawyer, Petr Aleksandrov, took full advantage of the opportunities that the statutes of 1864 provided. In jury selection, he rejected conservatively inclined merchants and large landowners in favor of petty civil servants and members of the intelligentsia. He turned his defense into an indictment of the authorities. According to contemporary memoirs, "he put Trepov on trial rather than Zasulich." In the end, the jury acquitted Zasulich. Her trial, a reflection of society's lack of trust in the government, represented a major defeat for the authorities in their struggle against the revolutionaries.

When the authorities saw that judicial prosecution of the revolutionaries had failed, they began to curtail the rights of the new courts and make greater use of extrajudicial forms of repression. The law of May 19, 1871, allowed the minister of justice, in agreement with the chief of the security police, to impose administrative penalties. By 1880 the number of administrative exiles, according to official figures, had reached twelve hundred.[32] The same law turned over the conduct of inquiries (in effect, investigations) in political cases to the police. On June 7, 1872, the government set up a special court for political cases, the Special Office of the Governing Senate, to which many of the provisions of the 1864 statutes did not apply. In 1878 all trials for crimes against government officials, even those that were not political, were removed from the competence of juries. On August 9, 1878, as revolutionary terror increased, the government handed over all cases of crimes against the state to military courts.

This trend culminated in the Regulation concerning Measures for the Protection of State Security and Public Tranquillity of August 14, 1881, after the death of Alexander II. The minister of internal affairs could now declare any part of the country to be in a state of "reinforced" or "extraordinary" protection. In regions under "extraordinary protection" the administration had the right to prohibit all gatherings, suspend periodicals, close educational institutions, dismiss employees of local self-government institutions, and arrest, exile, or hand over to a military court any individual on grounds of political unreliability.[33] At first the regulation was a temporary measure, for a duration of three years, but it was regularly extended and, in Vladimir Lenin's words, turned into "the real Russian constitution."

Lenin was not alone in recognizing the importance of this measure. In the opinion of the historian Richard Pipes, "in the early 1880s, all the elements of the police state were present in imperial Russia," and in the early twentieth century the imperial government "moved into the even more sinister realm of totalitarianism." "After 14 August 1881," according to Pipes, "Russia ceased to be an autocratic monarchy in any but the formal sense," and real power passed into the hands of the political police.[34] Such a categorical conclusion is hardly warranted. Although many of the principles of the Judicial Statutes of 1864 were seriously curtailed, the foundations of the legal order that had been laid in the 1860s remained in effect. The press continued to influence public life. Despite numerous attempts, the government in the 1880s did not fundamentally limit the operation of the judicial mechanisms of the 1860s outside of the political realm.[35] Nevertheless, the period after the death of Alexander II, the 1880s and the early 1890s, witnessed a significant retreat from the principles that the Great Reforms had introduced into Russian life in the 1860s and the 1870s. Obviously, the revolutionary movement was an important factor in the government's turn to reaction. It is necessary to examine the history of that movement if we are to understand the nature of the political situation Russia faced at the turn of the twentieth century.

Chapter 6

Russia's Economy and Finances after the Emancipation of the Serfs

The peasant reform fundamentally transformed Russian social relations and gave rise to new administrative and judicial institutions. Inevitably, it exerted a profound influence on the economy as well. The reformers of the 1860s and the 1870s believed that the economy on the whole should follow the Western path of development and embrace the principles of private property, free competition, entrepreneurship, and hired labor. Mikhail Reutern, the future minister of finance and a prominent representative of the enlightened bureaucracy, wrote in 1860: "The opportunity to seek one's own advantage without excessive constraints, and the conviction that the fruits of hard work are the inalienable possession of the worker, will develop in the intelligent Russian people the qualities with which it is endowed."[1] The authors of the peasant reform regarded market mechanisms as the principal means of increasing Russia's economic well-being.

To a certain degree, post-reform reality justified the reformers' hopes. As noted previously, the production of grain for sale, both on the domestic market and abroad, grew in the second half of the nineteenth century. The use of hired workers, which absorbed the labor force of impoverished peasants, expanded. The production and sale of agricultural machinery and improved farm implements rose perceptibly. From the 1870s to the 1890s the annual production of iron plows in Russia increased more than fivefold. From the 1860s to the 1890s the number of seasonal agricultural workers migrating to other districts for wage labor showed a similar increase, from 700,000 to 3.6 million.[2]

One important indicator of the Russian economy's evolution was the growth of non-gentry private landownership as the gentry steadily lost its monopoly on private landholding. In 1861 the noble estate owned 87 million desiatinas of land, but by the beginning of the twentieth century it held only 52 million. The proportion of gentry holdings in private landownership as a whole had fallen from 80 percent to 50 percent, while peasant holdings grew from 5 percent to 20 percent.[3] Farming gradually became more commercial and entrepreneurial. Not only agricultural products but land and labor were becoming commodities. The regional specialization of agriculture, which had begun to emerge before the emancipation, intensified. Ukraine, the Black Sea area, and the Volga region became the main centers of commercial grain production. Bessarabia, Ukraine, and the steppe region north of the Caucasus led in the production of sugar beets. Commercial flax, meat, and milk production predominated in the central industrial and northern provinces of European Russia. These developments attested to Russia's evolution toward a market economy.

However, serious impediments stood in the way of further progress. The very structure of the 1861 reform was responsible for the gradual nature of Russia's economic development after the abolition of serfdom. As Peter Gattrell has aptly remarked, "Peasant emancipation was a complex process, not just a straightforward act of legislation."[4] The redemption procedures were not fully implemented until the beginning of the 1880s, and the peasants' redemption payments lasted until 1905. The commune, the separate status of the peasant courts and peasant self-government, and collective responsibility for the payment of the peasants' obligations all persisted. Even impoverished peasants were not allowed to give up their allotments. The authors of the peasant reform regarded these restrictions as temporary measures designed to smooth the peasants' transition to the new market economy. As time went on, however, these archaic principles had an increasingly negative impact on economic development.

The redemption operation and the peasants' lack of land proved even more harmful. To pay their redemption fees, peasants were forced to rent land from the landowners, for which they paid by working the landowners' fields. This system of "labor payment," a modified form of the compulsory labor service that had existed under serfdom, seriously retarded the growth of labor productivity in agriculture. Working the lord's land, peasants had no interest in the fruits of their labor, and their own farming often suffered from neglect.

The labor-payment system had a deleterious effect on the landowners as well, for it allowed them to receive an income without investing in their own agriculture. Many landowners reduced their former serfs to desperate straits by depriving them of vital resources, such as pastures or watering places for their cattle. Aleksandr Engelhardt, a landowner and well-known chemist who was an expert on Russian agriculture, wrote at the beginning of the 1880s: "Matters have reached the point at which even the value of an estate is determined not by the inherent quality of its land but by the way in which it is situated in relation to the peasants' allotments and the extent to which it hems them in."[5]

Under these conditions, the crop yields of most peasant farms were bound to remain low. At the beginning of the 1860s, the net grain harvest (excluding seed) was roughly 20 puds (1 pud = 36 lbs.) per peasant "soul." At the end of the 1890s it had risen to only 26 puds.[6] The government's rigid taxation policy made the situation even worse. By forcing the peasants to sell their grain to pay their redemption fees, it condemned a considerable number of them to semi-starvation. The amount of grain remaining in the hands of the peasants at the beginning of the twentieth century ranged from one-third to one-ninth of the grain held by peasants in the developed countries of the West. "We do not sell our surplus grain," Engelhardt attested. "We export our daily bread, the grain we need for our own sustenance."[7] As an inevitable consequence, mass famine became a regular occurrence in the countryside from the end of the 1860s onward.

Famine might have been avoided if the government had allowed entrepreneurial peasant farmers greater freedom to develop, particularly by loosening the fetters that bound them to the commune, but it did not. The ruling circles looked with suspicion on the rising stratum of rural entrepreneurs, the "kulaks" (literally, "fists"). They regarded these peasants as potential competitors of the gentry landowners, and they feared the prospect of a mass landless proletariat. Moreover, the authorities viewed the commune, with its collective responsibility, as a convenient instrument for administering the countryside and exacting redemption payments and taxes from the peasants. The government not only retained the many restrictions that communal life imposed on peasant entrepreneurial activity but even intensified them. The law of December 14, 1893, for instance, prohibited individual peasants from withdrawing from the commune even after they had completed their redemption payments.

The commune's existence in turn preserved archaic agricultural techniques and methods of land use. Periodic redistributions of land to take account of changes in the composition of peasant families continued, as did the system under which each peasant household held its land in the form of numerous strips in different fields.

Numerous administrative restrictions impeded the development of peasant entrepreneurship. These included the peasant courts and the system of peasant self-government as well as the passport system, which hindered free-dom of movement. Under these circumstances, Russia could not compete on an equal footing with Western grain producers, despite its enormous agricul-tural potential. "The American sells his surplus, while we sell our daily bread," Engelhardt wrote.

> The American is free both as regards his land and as regards himself, and he can do as he pleases on his farm. He has neither a zemstvo chairman, nor a police superintendent, nor a village constable over him. No one tells him when or what to sow, how to drink, eat, sleep, or dress, but we have a regulation for everything . . . The American farmer knows how to work, is scientific about everything, and is educated . . . Our peasant knows only how to work, but he has no understanding of anything, no knowledge, and no education.[8]

The problems afflicting agriculture after the Emancipation also had a nega-tive impact on the development of industry. At the beginning of the 1860s Russia experienced an industrial slump that continued until the end of the decade. Capital investment, exports, and domestic trade also encountered difficulties. Turnover at the Nizhny Novgorod fair, the largest in Russia, fell from 105 to 98 million rubles in 1860–61, and surpassed the pre-reform level only in 1864. The metallurgical industry of the Urals, which was based on serf labor, was particularly hard hit. In 1860–62 the production of Urals pig iron fell from 14,500 to 10,400 puds. Not until 1870 did it exceed the pre-reform level.[9] Although industrial development began to revive in 1870, it failed to meet the country's needs. Imported industrial goods satisfied many of Russia's economic requirements. In the 1860s imported metals, metal goods, and machinery constituted 10 percent of Russian imports, but by the end of the 1870s that figure had doubled. From the late 1860s onward, Russia's trade balance showed a persistent deficit.[10]

In confronting the country's post-reform economic problems, Russia's rulers tried to pursue a policy of economic liberalism. They encouraged pri-vate initiative and private enterprise and relaxed state regulation of economic activity. They implemented this policy particularly in the industrial, com-mercial, and fiscal areas. Indeed, in the 1860s and the 1870s pre-revolution-ary Russia may have experienced the most consistent application of liberal economic principles in its history. The results vividly displayed both the ad-vantages and shortcomings of the liberal approach. Liberal economic prin-ciples enjoyed popularity within the Russian government in the 1860s and the 1870s primarily because the enlightened bureaucrats, who gained con-siderable influence at the beginning of the 1860s, based their economic views on the principles of free trade and the ideas of the Manchester School, which dated back to Adam Smith. Although these ideas were losing authority in the West by the 1860s, the enlightened bureaucracy continued to hold them in high regard. Reaction against the excessive regulation of economic life in the reign of Nicholas I also generated sympathy for the principles of free trade. Finally, the emphasis on private initiative was a matter of dire necessity. In the wake of the unsuccessful Crimean War, the treasury was in a nearly catastrophic state. The government simply did not have the means to carry out the sorely needed modernization of the economy.

These circumstances determined the activities of Mikhail Reutern, a typical representative of the enlightened bureaucracy, who served as minister of finance from 1862 to 1878. He came from a noble family of modest means, graduated from the Tsarskoe Selo Lyceum (high school), which produced many Russian administrators, and was an active participant in the Russian Geographical Society. The future minister of finance was a close acquaintance of Nikolai and Dmitry Miliutin, Aleksandr Golovnin, and other reformers, and shared their views. During the preparation of the peasant reform he took an active part in the work of the Editing Commission. In the second half of the 1850s Reutern became a member of Grand Duke Konstantin Nikolaevich's circle, and the grand duke played a decisive role in Reutern's appointment as finance minister.

Before taking up his post, Reutern traveled to England, France, the United States, and Prussia. The United States made the greatest impression on him. He found similarities between the national characteristics of Russians and Americans: "mechanical skill, the ability to adjust to circumstances and surmount unexpected obstacles, spirit, and boldness." In his opinion, "both peoples combine an ardent love for their country with an inclination to roam the wide world, to migrate." Reutern remained an Americanophile, and his friends nicknamed him "the Yankee." On the whole, Reutern and his fellow enlightened bureaucrats regarded the Western countries as a model for Russia to emulate. Reutern deplored the absence in Russia of "the initiative and enlightened enterprise that have covered England and America with a network of excellent means of communication and, without waiting for directions or assistance from the government, search out every method of increasing productivity."[11]

The principles of "initiative and enlightened enterprise" underlay the activities of the Ministry of Finance under Reutern. To secure favorable conditions for the development of private initiative, Reutern proposed a number of significant changes in the economic system. The ministry drew up plans to create a system of private credit, to privatize some state domains, and to limit state expenditures on unproductive projects. The most important aspect of the ministry's program was fiscal reform: the establishment of a balanced budget, the creation of a new taxation system based on an income tax, and the stabilization of the currency. Finally, the public was to receive more information about the state's finances.

In 1862 the government began to publish a list of its revenues and expenditures. Russia's rulers had long considered this an extremely dangerous, almost revolutionary step. They feared that disclosure of the real state of the Russian budget might prove a shock to society. The Finance Ministry official who was directly responsible for publishing the budget refused to do so and handed in his resignation. In fact, publication of the budget figures increased trust in the government both at home and abroad and improved the empire's credit in international financial markets.

The enlightened bureaucrats regarded the policy of openness as a way of strengthening the position of the state.[12] Openness was not the same as freedom of speech in the Western sense, however. The enlightened bureaucrats used it in pursuit of practical objectives. Aleksandr Golovnin, who served as minister of public education from 1861 to 1866, argued that the selective and provisional disclosure of certain elements of the government's activities would stimulate public discussion to the benefit of the authorities. It would furnish information when important legislative measures were being drafted and would increase society's trust in the administration.[13] Openness could not be kept within such narrow confines, however. It was bound to become an independent force, slip out from under the control of its creators, and to some degree turn against them. Nevertheless, in 1855–65 the policy of openness was a positive step.

Another measure, introduced in 1862, also had a positive effect: the principle of "unity of funds," a governmentwide system of accounting and bookkeeping. The administration failed to follow this principle consistently, however, as it did not monitor the financial activities of state-owned railroads or state-subsidized private railroads, an important item of expenditure in the state budget at the beginning of the 1860s. The administration continually engaged in so-called "over-budget allowances," that is, appropriations that exceeded previously established departmental estimates of expenditures. For all its efforts, the Ministry of Finance also failed to achieve a decisive breakthrough in the struggle against the traditional vices of the Russian fiscal system: embezzlement of state funds, arbitrariness, and waste.

The Ministry of Finance under Reutern nevertheless persisted in its encouragement of private economic initiative. Of particular importance was the abolition of the state monopoly on the mining and sale of salt in 1862 and the tax farming of alcoholic beverages in 1863. The latter measure eliminated a major source of corruption in the governmental apparatus. Previously the tax farmer, in return for paying a certain sum to the treasury, bribed officials and received a virtually unchecked monopoly on the sale of liquor in a particular geographical area. Now, this business was open to free competition in return for specified payments to the treasury in the form of excise taxes and license fees.[14] The elimination of the tax farms helped to increase state revenues. It also freed up a considerable amount of private capital and redirected it into the most productive branches of the economy, such as banks, railroads, foreign trade, and oilfields.

The formation of a private credit system, which the Ministry of Finance vigorously promoted, also helped to redirect private capital investment. The State Bank, established in 1860, became the center of a network of private commercial banking. In 1862 the government confirmed the regulations for the establishment of public municipal banks, and in 1863 it approved the statutes of the first private institution for short-term credit, the Petersburg Mutual Credit Society. In 1864 the government helped to create the first corporate bank, also in the capital. By the mid-1870s Russia had more than forty corporate banks, holding 40 percent of the country's savings deposits, while the State Bank held 30 percent.[15]

The Ministry of Finance paid especially close attention to industrial development. The government lowered taxes on industry and rural enterprises and made it easier for individuals to take up commercial and industrial occupations, although merchants and artisans retained their traditional estate organizations, created by Peter I and Catherine II. Foreigners active in trade and industry enjoyed the same rights as Russian subjects. Reutern assisted industry with loans, and he was the first finance minister to begin consulting with businessmen and including them in discussions of legislative proposals. The Ministry of Finance initiated all-Russian industrial exhibitions, in Moscow in 1865 and in Petersburg in 1870. Thirteen new commodity and stock exchanges came into existence, as well as a Council of Trade and Manufacturing under the Ministry of Finance.

Meanwhile, social policy stagnated, especially in the countryside. In the 1860s and the 1870s the government failed to replace the archaic peasant "soul tax" with an income tax and merely shifted some of the tax on "souls" onto agricultural land and urban real estate.[16] The authorities were so concerned with balancing the budget and stabilizing the currency that they even raised the soul tax several times. The Ministry of Finance displayed little initiative in agricultural affairs. Although Reutern was well-informed about the plight of the peasants, knew that they lacked sufficient land and were overburdened with redemption payments,[17] and ordered his ministry to conduct research on the peasant economy with a view to lowering the redemption fees, his initiatives produced no practical results. Proposals for the gradual elimination of communal landholding and revision of the passport system were not implemented. Nothing was done to regulate relations between factory owners and workers.

The Finance Ministry's lack of attention to agriculture, the foundation of the Russian economy, accounted in large part for the failure of one of its principal objectives, monetary reform. Reutern first tried to achieve convertibility for the ruble in 1862. Using his personal connections with Western bankers, he took out a loan of 15 million pounds sterling from the London and Paris Rothschilds. In April 1862 the government declared the free exchange of banknotes for bullion. The reforming finance minister was doomed to disappointment in this endeavor, however, for the amount of the loan proved insufficient for the size of the operation. The political situation did not help. Unrest in Poland, which had been growing steadily since the mid-1850s, erupted into open insurrection in January 1863. The value of the ruble and of Russian securities on international exchanges immediately collapsed. The holders of banknotes began to demand that they be exchanged for gold. In November 1863 the Ministry of Finance, having lost tens of millions of rubles, had to suspend convertibility and resort to the inflationary expedient of issuing masses of paper rubles without gold backing.

Russia's negative balance of international trade made the country's economic and fiscal situation even worse. The trade imbalance reflected the free-trade principles of the Ministry of Finance, which lowered import tariffs on a number of goods. The balance of payments also suffered from the unrestrained expenditures of Russian travelers abroad, whose numbers grew fivefold between 1866 and 1875. The state's increasing indebtedness led to ever larger interest payments and dividends to Western creditors. These developments dealt a serious blow to the reputation of the finance minister.

The changing balance of forces within the government created serious problems for Reutern. By the mid-1860s the contradictory results of the peasant reform, the Polish insurrection, and the rise of a revolutionary movement within Russia had considerably undermined the position of the enlightened bureaucrats. Grand Duke Konstantin Nikolaevich, who became viceroy of Poland in 1862, tried to pursue a liberal policy there but was unsuccessful and had to withdraw to the background. Dmitry Karakozov's attempt to assassinate Alexander II in April 1866 did much to turn the government toward reaction. (See chapter 7.) Some of "Konstantin's men," such as Golovnin and Minister of Justice Dmitry Zamiatnin, lost their ministerial posts. Count Petr Shuvalov, head of the Third Section since 1866, now became the leading figure in the government. Like Konstantin Nikolaevich before him, Shuvalov dreamed of being an "informal prime minister," but he had his own view of Russia's future. He believed that the provincial nobility, as the most educated and prosperous estate, should play the primary role in post-reform Russia. Minister of Internal Affairs Valuev, Shuvalov's most important ally in the government, provided the theoretical basis for his plans.[18] With Valuev and his other allies, Shuvalov went on the offensive against the last enlightened bureaucrats in the government, Reutern and Dmitry Miliutin.

Not simply an opportunistic attempt to redistribute spheres of influence, this attack was part of a larger program. Along with measures to benefit the provincial gentry, "Shuvalov's men" demanded greater administrative centralization, more rigorous censorship, greater powers for the police, and the dismissal of liberal professors from the universities. They proposed to give more power to the governors, including control over the local offices of the Ministry of Finance, and to establish a Gentry Land Bank to subsidize the landowners. In the spring and summer of 1866 Reutern came very close to dismissal. Faced with the latest wave of pressure from Shuvalov's men, Reutern firmly demanded protection for his ministry from outside attacks. Alexander II, in an effort to end the quarrels among his ministers, ordered Reutern to draw up a memorandum spelling out a long-term plan for the Finance Ministry's activities.

Reutern's memorandum expressed the enlightened bureaucracy's traditional belief that only reform from above could ward off revolution. "The history of every nation," he wrote, "attests that revolution can be averted by timely reforms that grant the nation by peaceful means what it seeks in revolution, that is, the elimination of outworn forms and deep-rooted abuses." The difficulties inevitable in the initial stages of reform must not bring them to a stop. "Much more time, trouble, and sacrifice is required," he warned, "before Russia can complete its transition and establish itself firmly on new, rational foundations." Only consistent reform in every area of public life, Reutern emphasized, would enhance Russia's prestige in the eyes of the world and guarantee its economic prosperity. "If we act in this way, we can hope that in the course of a few years Russia's economic forces will gather strength. The reforms that constitute Your Imperial Majesty's glory will not be brought to a halt for lack of resources, but on the contrary will yield abundant fruit. Russia will finally emerge stronger and richer than ever from the anxious transitional period that naturally and inevitably follows changes in the civil and economic structure."[19]

Reutern skillfully drew a connection between further reforms and Russia's financial stability, which was Alexander's foremost priority. He argued that the steady implementation of reform would stop the flight of capital from Russia, draw foreign capital into the country, and make Russian industry an attractive field of investment. In his memorandum he advocated continuation of the liberal program. The government should exercise maximum restraint in its expenditures and direct them into productive areas, should not intervene in conflicts between other countries, and should increase existing taxes until it could introduce an income tax. Reutern considerably strengthened his position in the eyes of the emperor. At the end of 1866 the government accepted the memorandum as its long-range program, and Reutern continued his work as minister of finance for another dozen years.

The most urgent item in the Finance Ministry's program in the late 1860s and the early 1870s was railroad construction. The Crimean defeat had brought home to Russia's rulers the pressing need for railroads, from both an economic and a strategic standpoint. In the late 1850s the government had attempted to draw private capital into railroad construction, but with meager results. The construction of railroads by the state also proved slow and expensive. The Ministry of Finance now proposed a "middle way": railroad construction would be entrusted to private capital, but the state would provide encouragement in every way possible. In 1867 the government established a special fund for the support of private railroad construction, to which it contributed the proceeds from the sale of Alaska and the privatization of several state-owned rail lines. The state offered firm profit guarantees to the entrepreneurs to whom it granted concessions for the building and operation of railroads. Factories for the production of rails, locomotives, and railroad cars received considerable state support. The authorities anticipated that as railway construction proceeded, the entrepreneurs would repay the sums they had borrowed and continually replenish the special fund.

Railroad construction not only played a major role in Russia's economic growth but also illustrated Russia's distinctive pattern of industrial development. In the leading countries of Europe, especially in England, the railroads formed the capstone of the industrial economy, but in Russia they served in large part as its foundation. By connecting the different regions of the country, the railroads fostered regional economic specialization, stimulated the production of goods, and developed foreign and domestic markets. The impetus that they gave to the population's mobility was of particular significance. As Peter Gatrell has put it, the construction of railways helped to free Russia from the burden of its vast spaces, just as the abolition of serfdom freed the Russian peasants from the burden of involuntary labor.[20] The very process of building and operating railroads created demand for metal, machinery, coal, wood, oil, and hired labor. In the 1890s as much as 36 percent of the country's coal, 44 percent of its oil, and 40 percent of its metal went to supply the needs of the railroads.[21]

The question of which railroads to build provoked sharp debate within the government. The military wanted to give priority to lines that had strategic significance, while representatives of the Ministry of Finance emphasized economic needs. A certain compromise was eventually reached. The railroads built at the beginning of the 1870s linked the grain-producing regions with navigable rivers and ports on the Black and Baltic seas. At the same time, these lines permitted the transfer of troops from the center of the country to the western frontiers. Moscow became the center of the railway network, with lines extending to Kiev and Kharkov via Kursk, to Rostov and Odessa via Kharkov, to Vologda via Yaroslavl, and to Saratov via Tambov. At the end of the 1870s construction began on railroads in the Urals and Transcaucasus, on the peripheries of European Russia.

· The advantageous terms of the government's concessions to private entrepreneurs and the huge state subsidies created an enormous railroad boom that continued until the mid-1870s. Dozens of new companies sprang up. Foreign capital poured into Russia. Between 1865 and 1875 the railroad network grew from 3,800 to 19,000 versts. The number of joint-stock companies in the areas of banking, industry, and trade rose just as quickly. At the height of the boom in 1870–73, 259 companies with capital of 516 million rubles were founded, including 39 commercial banks and 14 land banks. The progress of private entrepreneurship encouraged the Ministry of Finance to draft a reform of Russia's archaic corporate law, which required governmental permission for each new joint-stock enterprise.[22] The railroad boom stimulated the rise of new industrial regions, including the Donets Basin (Donbass) and Baku. The treasury's bullion reserves tripled between 1867 and 1875, raising the possibility of reviving the monetary reform.

Just as the liberal economic policy was achieving its greatest success, however, the system's internal contradictions inexorably surfaced. The drawbacks of the liberal approach appeared most clearly in the railroad sector, which seemed to constitute the Finance Ministry's principal achievement. The feverish competition for concessions gave rise to speculative companies, massive misappropriation of funds, and corruption. The complete freedom that the entrepreneurs enjoyed in the construction and operation of the railways served as a powerful impetus to abuses. Contrary to the authorities' plan, reimbursements from the private companies failed to replenish the railroad fund. Many companies generated no profits, so that they could not repay the subsidies. The government was forced to draw on the state budget to finance construction. The annual payments of millions of rubles in guaranteed capital for the private lines quadrupled from 1871 to 1881, causing budget deficits and an increase in Russia's foreign state debt.

The government received little compensation for its painful sacrifices. Despite intensive construction activity, the railroad industry did not meet the country's economic or strategic needs. Managed by dozens of private companies, the rail network did not form a unified whole. In their pursuit of increased profits, the railroad "barons" worried little about the quality or feasibility of the lines. They built tracks carelessly, in violation of technical standards. By bribing officials, entrepreneurs were able to operate unfinished lines. Thanks to their monopoly on rail transport, they could set freight rates arbitrarily, to the detriment of the Russian economy.

Stock speculation flourished in the credit sector. Private banks engaged less in the financing of trade and industry than in the lucrative business of issuing company stocks. In 1874 the industrial and financial crisis that had swept Europe reached Russia, causing a decline in commodity prices, a slowdown in the rate of growth of basic branches of industry, and the curtailment of commercial activity. The bankruptcy of the Commercial Loan Bank, the second largest bank in Moscow, touched off a massive run on deposits. When the railroad fund became completely exhausted, in 1876, the government stopped granting new concessions. The stock-market crash and the industrial crisis shook the confidence of foreign business circles in Russia's finances. The value of the ruble and of Russian bonds immediately plummeted. Foreign capital fled the country.

The events of the mid-1870s revealed the weaknesses of the private-enterprise system as it functioned in Russia. The distinctive features of Russian capitalism that would continue to characterize it in subsequent decades had become clear. The weak development of entrepreneurship and the limited scale of private capital made extensive state intrusion in the economy inevitable. The state encouraged and nurtured the market sector, both by granting concessions and by providing subsidies, tax advantages, credit, and large state orders. The result was a significant limitation of the principle of free competition. A businessman's profit often depended less on skillful management than on close ties to the tsarist bureaucrats and the opportunity to receive state funds. The Russian Marxist Georgy Plekhanov wrote that the Russian bourgeoisie "has developed lungs which require the clean air . . . of self-government, but at the same time it has not yet atrophied its gills, with the help of which it continues to breathe in the turbid water of decaying absolutism."[23] Small in numbers and closely tied to autocratic power, the Russian bourgeoisie long remained politically passive, unable to provide a solid base for an influential liberal movement.

The enormous profits acquired in large part at the expense of the state acted as a corrupting force on the Russian bourgeoisie. It characteristically pursued excessive rather than moderate profits, and its sense of social responsibility remained weak, as evidenced by the intensive exploitation of its workers. Anti-bourgeois sentiment, which had long been ingrained in Russian popular consciousness, grew stronger as a result. Many authors in the late nineteenth and the early twentieth centuries wrote that Russians were convinced of the "iniquity of money," and that they valued the principles of equality and justice far more than success in business. As the philosopher Semyon Frank commented in 1923, Russians did not have "the worldview of a property owner, that is, a disinterested and impersonal belief in the sanctity of property."[24]

By the mid-1870s the negative consequences of the liberal economic policy had become so apparent that the Ministry of Finance reverted to strict state regulation of economic life. The ministry took steps to limit loans issued by banks and to curb the creation of joint-stock companies. A law of 1872 prohibited the establishment of new banks in cities where such banks already operated. Reutern refused to implement the proposal, drafted by a ministerial commission, to reform the laws on the formation of joint-stock companies. These measures unfolded against a background of growing international tension. Insurrections by the Slavic peoples of the Balkans in the mid-1870s confronted Russia with the prospect of a new war. The necessity of embarking on large-scale military activity exacerbated the state's need for financial resources. An edict at the end of 1876 required the payment of customs duties in gold currency. Given the current value of the ruble, that meant a 30-percent increase in duties and a turn toward protectionism in Russian tariff policy.

The Russo-Turkish War that broke out in April 1877 dealt a severe blow to Russia's finances and made it impossible to realize the major objective of the liberal economic policy, the introduction of a stable currency. Reutern tried his best to avert Russia's entry into the war. In a memorandum to Alexander II, he argued that war would lead to "the devastation of our fiscal and economic interests," the flight of foreign capital, and the bankruptcy of many enterprises and banks.[25] He failed to convince the emperor, who replied testily to Reutern's claim that funds were lacking: "Resources exist, but you have to be able and willing to obtain them." The finance minister had to take the well-worn path of borrowing from the State Bank, increasing the state debt, and issuing more paper currency. These policies had grave consequences. Between 1877 and 1880 Russia's state debt rose by 1.5 billion rubles. The amount of bullion supporting the ruble decreased by half, and the ruble's value sank to a new low.

Reutern took the collapse of his hopes for Russia's economic revival as a personal blow. His health deteriorated. In July 1878, after the Congress of Berlin, which ended the war, Reutern resigned. He left his successor a "financial testament" that he had written in February 1877. In his evaluation of the poor state of the country's economy, he noted the destructive consequences of feverish stock speculation. "The experience of all countries," he wrote, "shows that such a development inevitably provokes a reaction, that is, a crisis. Along with truly useful enterprises come a great many that are thoroughly useless or are badly designed and unprofitable. Speculation, which is often highly unscrupulous, exploits the public's propensity for enterprises and creates companies having as their objective not what is indicated in their prospectuses but only the defrauding of their gullible shareholders." Reutern considered it expedient to stop encouraging company formation and "to avoid anything that might once again produce a feverish stimulus to industrial and corporate enterprises."[26]

In view of the exhaustion of the railroad fund and the impossibility of contracting profitable foreign loans, Reutern felt that no new lines should be constructed in the immediate future. To protect the interests of trade and industry, he recommended an increase in tariffs and a reduction in imports. In the difficult financial circumstances that the recent war had created, Reutern recognized that it was futile to hope for stabilization of the currency in the near future. His testament showed that he had retreated from his former free-trade views. Life had confounded all his previous calculations. Protectionist ideas became increasingly popular both in Russia and abroad.

The shift from liberal principles to increased state regulation of the economy dominated the Finance Ministry's economic policy in the 1860s and the 1870s. The overall results of that policy were mixed. On the one hand, the government made great strides in the creation of a Russian railroad network. It introduced some liberal economic measures aimed at the stimulation of private enterprise, such as abolishing liquor tax farming and the salt monopoly, adopting a liberal tariff policy, propagating commercial banks, and, most of all, creating a concession system for the construction of railroads. At the same time, the authorities were forced to recognize the risks of shifting the burden of financing industry and transportation to the private sector. The government had failed to consider certain specific features of the country's economy: the weakness of the bourgeoisie, the severe shortage of capital, and the limited capacity of the internal market. Economic policy also had to take into account the most significant characteristic of Russia's historical development, the powerful and highly intrusive influence of the state in every aspect of public life.[27] These factors led the government to reverse its economic policy. The mid-1870s marked a return to large-scale state regulation of the economy. The government reined in company formation, ended the granting of railroad concessions, and erected high tariff barriers. In the 1880s and the early 1890s this approach firmly established itself in government policy. By the beginning of the twentieth century, a distinctive economic system prevailed in Russia, which combined elements of a market structure with the traditionally powerful regulatory role of the state.

Chapter 7

The Opposition Movement in Post-Reform Russia: From "Thaw" to Regicide

On March 1, 1881, in the center of St. Petersburg, "on a public thoroughfare, in broad daylight, at the focal point of the entire government,"[1] Alexander II, the sole monarch of his dynasty to be awarded the title of "Liberator," died at the hands of a terrorist. Russians at the time could not help wondering why the tsar who had freed the peasants from serfdom fell victim to revolutionaries acting in the name of the people and dedicated to their welfare. The mood of Russian society in the twenty years since the emancipation had undergone a paradoxical evolution. The first steps by the authorities to introduce the peasant reform called forth "boundless optimism that for many people turned into utter intoxication,"[2] but gradually the spirit of opposition grew so strong that it culminated in an outburst of revolutionary terror. Why did the Great Reforms, intended to move society in a liberal direction, in many respects produce the opposite result? Can the reforms of the 1860s and the 1870s be considered a cause of social instability? Could Russia have followed a different path? To answer these questions, we must examine the history of the opposition movement in the second half of the nineteenth century.

After Russia's defeat in the Crimean War, the government significantly loosened the constraints on society. A "thaw" began, one sign of which was an invigorated press. Another was the revitalization of social organizations: existing associations grew more active, and a variety of new ones arose in the late 1850s and the early 1860s. Critical political and social issues came under discussion at the Free Economic Society, the Russian Geographical Society, and even an organization seemingly as remote from politics as the

Chess Club. The activities of the Literary Fund, founded in 1858, ranged far beyond the cultural sphere. The Sunday-school movement for adult literacy and the Committee on Literacy of the Free Economic Society expanded their efforts. Student unions and various charitable organizations emerged.[3] Russia was making considerable progress in the creation of a civil society. At the same time, the new social organizations soon began to display an oppositional and even revolutionary political orientation. In 1862 a secret society called Land and Liberty, an outgrowth of the Literary Fund and the Chess Club, sought to prepare a peasant revolution. Although the society lasted until 1863 and dissolved itself without waiting for peasant disturbances to break out, it served as the first step in the development of a revolutionary underground that would operate throughout the reign of Alexander II.

This movement arose primarily because of the distinctive Russian social structure, specifically the extreme weakness of a "middle class," that is, the bourgeois strata that served in the West as one of the main supports of a civil society. In Russia, the space between the common people and the noble and bureaucratic ruling circles was occupied since the reign of Nicholas I by an intelligentsia composed of "men of all ranks," that is, of individuals drawn from a variety of social backgrounds, who for the most part espoused radical views. In the words of Nikolai Berdiaev, the eminent philosopher and historian of social thought, the Russian intelligentsia could not be considered a strictly socio-economic phenomenon. It was "an idealistic class, a class of people wholly captivated by ideas and prepared in the name of those ideas to face prison, exile, and execution."[4] The intelligentsia consisted of individuals from various social estates who had broken with previous traditions and were ready for a radical transformation of the world. The government unwittingly contributed to the development of the intelligentsia's radical outlook by excluding it from the political realm. As a result, the intelligentsia adopted an intolerant, uncompromising attitude toward the existing system. The intelligentsia's intermediate position between the state and the people also contributed to its radical outlook. It became a kind of religious order, with its own rules of behavior, sages, and way of life.

Because it rejected autocratic power and the existing social system in Russia, the intelligentsia could not declare its views openly until the "thaw." The relaxation of governmental controls revealed the existence of reservoirs of hatred that had accumulated for many years. The ideological evolution of Nikolai Chernyshevsky is indicative in this respect. Chernyshevsky was the leading writer for the journal *The Contemporary*, continuing the tradition of Vissarion Belinsky, one of the Russian intelligentsia's spiritual leaders. Chernyshevsky greeted with approval and even rapture the first steps by the authorities to abolish serfdom. Subsequently, however, he grew disappointed with the government and began to criticize the reform, denouncing the bureaucratic manner in which it was planned, the class selfishness of the landowners, and the burdens the redemption process imposed on the peasants. Chernyshevsky's younger colleague at *The Contemporary*, Nikolai Dobroliubov, went further, branding the liberals "superfluous men." Dobroliubov's attacks elicited protests even from Alexander Herzen, who defended his friends in the philosophical circles of the 1840s from the reproaches of the young radicals. Disillusioned with liberalism and the limited results of the government's reforms, Dobroliubov and Chernyshevsky began to place their hopes on a popular revolution that would lead to the creation of a socialist system in Russia.

The views of Chernyshevsky and Dobroliubov (who died of tuberculosis in 1861 at the age of twenty-five) did not represent the final stage in the development of Russian radicalism. Dmitry Pisarev, who became the leading writer for the journal *The Russian Word* in 1861, added to the ideological arsenal of radicalism. In Pisarev's opinion, the pinnacle of social development was the liberation of the individual personality from all constraints, whether imposed by authority, by tradition, or by social and family ties. Reason must be the sole basis of human activity. "The final word of our youthful camp," he proclaimed, "is that what can be smashed should be smashed; what survives the blow is good, and what breaks into smithereens is rubbish. In any case, hit right and left. No harm will or can come of it."[5]

Pisarev's mode of thought, which came to be called "nihilism," from the Latin *nihil*, or "nothing," won broad support among the intelligentsia in the 1860s. In the 1860s and the 1870s young members of the intelligentsia inspired by Pisarev's appeals and by the characters in Chernyshevsky's novel *What Is to Be Done?* tried to organize their lives according to allegedly "rational principles." They contracted fictitious marriages with the goal of emancipating girls from "parental tutelage." They set up cooperative sewing and bookbinding workshops, where they attempted to earn their living by their own labor and to put into practice the principle of communal property. Most such efforts failed.

Nihilism, it should be noted, dealt with the inner life and everyday existence of the individual and did not relate directly to the demand for social and political revolution. Nevertheless, Pisarev's struggle against authority and his appeals to "strike right and left" clearly encouraged the development of a revolutionary frame of mind.

Overt action against the established order was not long in coming. University students, who comprised the part of the intelligentsia most sensitive to any sort of social change, became the bearers of protest. Significant changes in the student body took place after the accession of Alexander II. In 1855–56 the lifting of most of the restrictions that Nicholas I had imposed on the universities led to an influx of students and auditors. The audiences that filled the lecture-halls became considerably more variegated and the atmosphere in the universities more restive. The authorities grew increasingly worried and intensified their surveillance of the students. The government limited the admission of needy students to the universities and punished infractions of university rules more severely. As a result, disturbances erupted at the universities of Moscow, Petersburg, and Kazan in the autumn of 1861. The police broke up student demonstrations in Moscow and Petersburg and arrested hundreds of students.

Protests against restrictions on academic freedom coincided with the start of the peasant reform and the suppression of peasant uprisings. In 1861 a memorial service for peasants who had been killed in the village of Bezdna took place at Kazan University. Professor Afanasy Shchapov, an historian, gave a fiery speech against social oppression that resonated widely with the public.

The rise of the student movement determined the next turn in the government's policies. In 1862 Aleksandr Golovnin, an enlightened bureaucrat and a close associate of Grand Duke Konstantin Nikolaevich, became minister of public education.[6] Under his leadership, the government adopted a liberal university statute on June 16, 1863, and a statute for the high schools on November 19, 1864.[7] The new regulations declared the universities and high schools open to students from all social estates. University autonomy, which Nicholas I had abolished, was restored. The introduction of liberal principles was not consistent, however. The statute of 1863 granted significant prerogatives to university faculties, but it did not give the students corporate rights. This became one of the sources of unrest in the post-reform universities.

Student disturbances were not the only manifestations of political protest in Russia. Despite the new freedoms enjoyed by the press, opportunities for the legal expression of political views remained limited. Underground proclamations began to circulate. The "manifesto campaign" of the early 1860s reflected the radicalization that was characteristic of the intelligentsia's political movements. The series of manifestos that opened the campaign and appeared under the title *The Great Russian* in June, August, and October 1861, was fairly moderate in tone. The authors proposed the use of peaceful methods to obtain a constitution, such as the presentation of addresses to Alexander II, and felt that the basic principles of the peasant reform needed to be reexamined. They wanted to give the "cut-offs" back to the peasants and have "the entire nation" assume the cost of the redemption process. In contrast, the radical manifesto *To the Young Generation* of September 1861 demanded the distribution of all land to the peasants, a political amnesty, the replacement of the standing army by a popular militia, and broad self-government both at the center of the country and in the provinces. The authors proclaimed, "We do not need an emperor anointed in the Cathedral of the Assumption but an elected elder who will receive a salary for his services . . . To be sure, we would not want matters to go as far as a violent revolution. But if it cannot be otherwise, not only will we not reject a revolution, we will gladly call on the people to help carry it out."[8]

The radicalism of the manifesto campaign reached its peak in the leaflet *Young Russia*, issued in May 1862 by a group of students under the leadership of Petr Zaichnevsky. Its authors demanded the destruction of all existing social and political institutions, including marriage and the family. They declared that Russia faced insoluble contradictions between the "oppressed and plundered people" and the "imperial party."

> There is only one way out of this oppressive, terrible situation: revolution, a bloody and implacable revolution, a revolution that will radically change all the foundations of contemporary society without exception and will destroy the defenders of the present order . . . Soon, soon the day will come when we will unfurl the great banner of the future and with a loud cry of "Long live the social and democratic Russian republic!" we will advance to the Winter Palace to exterminate those who dwell there.[9]

The appearance of *Young Russia* coincided with a series of great fires in Petersburg and in towns along the Volga, which gave rise to rumors of a vast "conspiracy of nihilists." Although the investigation of *Young Russia* turned up only a small circle of students under Zaichnevsky's leadership, the government resorted to harsh repressive measures. It suspended *The Contemporary* and *The Russian Word* for eight months and in 1866 closed them for good. It brought the Sunday-school movement in the factories under the control of the authorities. In the summer of 1862 the police arrested Pisarev, Chernyshevsky, and several other radical leaders. Chernyshevsky was implicated in the composition of one of the revolutionary manifestos. Although never found guilty, he was sentenced to hard labor followed by exile in Siberia. Pisarev, also accused of writing a manifesto, spent more than four years in solitary confinement. Soon after his release he drowned while swimming in the Neva River in St. Petersburg.

Events in the Kingdom of Poland, on the empire's western frontier, contributed to the rise of a conservative mood in society and the government. A relaxation of Russian rule in Poland had followed Alexander II's accession to the throne, including an amnesty for political prisoners and preparations for administrative autonomy. However, the government rejected any thought of independence for Poland. The Polish opposition movement, financed and supported by the extensive Polish emigration in Western countries, grew steadily more radical.

In 1863 armed rebellion broke out in Poland. The bitterness of the fighting on both sides, the demand of the insurgents for restoration of the Commonwealth within the 1772 borders, and the attempts by Western powers to exert diplomatic pressure on Russia elicited an upsurge of patriotic sentiment in Russian society, which rallied around the government. Addresses to Alexander II streamed in from noble assemblies, peasant societies, zemstvos, universities, and other organizations. Mikhail Katkov, the editor of the newspaper *Moscow Gazette*, became the hero of the day. Katkov renounced his former liberal views and demanded harsh punishment for both the Poles and the nihilists. The nihilists themselves, who had maintained ties with the Polish insurgents, were seriously discredited. The circulation of Herzen's *Bell*, which supported the uprising, went into decline. It ceased publication in 1867.[10]

The attempt on Alexander's life by a university student named Dmitry Karakozov in April 1866 drove the government even further to the right. The authorities viewed the assassination attempt as a symptom of profound flaws in the system of public education. Aleksandr Golovnin, the liberal minister of public education, was dismissed. In an imperial rescript of May 13, 1866, to Prince Pavel Gagarin, the chairman of the Committee of Ministers, the emperor stated: "It pleased God to reveal before the eyes of Russia the consequences to be expected from aspirations and states of mind insolently infringing on everything that Russia has held sacred from time immemorial: religious beliefs, the foundations of family life, obedience to the law, and respect for constituted authorities." Alexander's rescript laid down in the clearest terms the task of asserting ideological influence on Russia's youth and on society as a whole: "I have already given instructions that [the education of the young] be directed in a spirit of true religion, respect for the rights of property, and observance of the fundamental principles of public order."[11]

The government entrusted that task to Golovnin's successor, Count Dmitry Tolstoi,who continued to serve also as supreme procurator of the Holy Synod, the official in charge of the Orthodox Church.[12] The core of Tolstoi's policy, a program of "classical education" devised by Katkov, consisted of the greatly intensified teaching of dead languages (Latin and ancient Greek) in the secondary schools, to deter students from "superficial philosophizing" and shield them from exposure to topical social and political issues. The high-school reform of 1871 introduced the classical system. At the same time, the authorities strengthened their control over the zemstvo primary schools, stepped up their surveillance of high-school and university students, and began to revise the University Statute of 1863.[13] Tolstoi's policy failed to achieve its objectives. Unrest continued in the universities, and the radical movement, after a certain decline at the end of the 1860s, reemerged on an even larger scale under the new ideological banner of "Populism." Before that occurred, however, a noteworthy episode took place in the late 1860s and the early 1870s that proved to have great significance for the subsequent evolution of the radical movement. In an outburst of revolutionary extremism, an organization emerged called The People's Reprisal, under the leadership of Sergei Nechaev, a teacher of religion in a parish school who had audited classes at St. Petersburg University.

Extremist tendencies had their roots in the circumstances under which the Russian radical movement arose. Faced with an all-powerful state, many radicals concluded that victory in the political struggle required them to copy and replicate the state's authoritarian methods. Within the extremist circle of Nikolai Ishutin, to which Karakozov belonged, arose a terrorist group called Hell, which saw its mission as committing regicide, manipulating liberals and other opposition forces, and punishing traitors in its midst. According to the group's statutes, the revolutionary must "give up all personal enjoyment, concentrate within himself hatred and malice toward evil, and live by and take pleasure in this aspect of life." Subordinates must strictly obey their superiors. The statutes declared: "If any member should be asked by the entire association . . . to hang a stone around his neck and jump into the water, that order would have to be carried out."[14]

Extremism and authoritarianism found their most complete embodiment in the activities of Nechaev, who set out to create his own revolutionary organization at the end of 1868. Nechaev believed that all means were justified in the revolutionary struggle, including deception, forgery, blackmail, and provocation. He established contact with Russian revolutionary émigrés in Europe and made a great impression on Mikhail Bakunin, one of their leaders. Bakunin had participated in the Westernizer circles of the 1830s and emigrated in 1840. Arrested in 1849 for his role in an insurrection in Saxony, he was extradited to Russia and spent years in prison and Siberian exile. After escaping from Siberia in 1861, he became the foremost theoretician of Russian anarchism. With Bakunin's help, Nechaev equipped himself with the mandate of the Revolutionary European Alliance, a nonexistent organization that represented only Bakunin and several of his fellow anarchists, all of them members of the First International. Nechaev returned to Russia and in the name of the Revolutionary Alliance began recruiting members to his organization.

As part of his effort, Nechaev fabricated tales of his escape from the

Peter and Paul Fortress, extracted pledges of complete obedience from his followers, and distributed leaflets to acquaintances, thereby exposing them to persecution by the authorities. Gradually, Nechaev's methods began to draw protests from his associates. In an attempt to nip mutiny in the bud, and also to create a "bond of blood" among the members of his organization, Nechaev demanded that they murder one of the doubters, a student named Ivan Ivanov. The crime soon came to light and became the subject of a notorious court trial. Nechaev himself fled abroad, but the Swiss authorities extradited him to Russia as a common criminal, and he ended his days in the Peter and Paul Fortress.

The trial of the Nechaevists in 1871 provoked a sharp debate within Russian society. Radicals refused to see the "Nechaev Affair" as a typical reflection of the revolutionary movement. The well-known journalist Nikolai Mikhailovsky characterized it as "a sad, mistaken, and criminal exception."[15] The great writer Fyodor Dostoevsky held a different opinion. He regarded the Nechaev Affair as a symptom of a profound spiritual illness that had seized the revolutionary intelligentsia. Dostoevsky expressed his view in the novel *The Devils* (also known as *The Possessed*), which was based on documents presented at the Nechaev trial. Subsequent events proved him correct. Although most revolutionaries repudiated Nechaev's methods as "immoral," the very logic of the revolutionary struggle drove them toward the use of violence and compulsion. This tendency led inevitably to the adoption of revolutionary terror. Before the radical movement turned to terrorism, however, it went through a stage of development inspired by a different interpretation of Populism.

The doctrine of Populism, which took shape in the late 1860s and the early 1870s, combined several ideas that had been circulating within the intelligentsia for a decade.[16] They included the theory of peasant socialism based on the commune, which Herzen and Chernyshevsky had developed, and the concept of the "critically thinking individual," which derived from Pisarev's ideas. Bakunin's views, which he expounded in his *Statism and Anarchy* of 1873, played a major role in the formulation of Populism. Bakunin rejected state power of any kind, whether authoritarian or democratic, on the grounds that it would inevitably serve as an instrument for oppressing the individual. All these ideas appealed to the intelligentsia but had hitherto existed separately, without coalescing into a unified whole.

Petr Lavrov, a journalist who had participated in the revolutionary movement of the 1860s, took the decisive step of integrating them into a coherent ideology. Lavrov elaborated his views in a series of articles published in 1868 under the title "Historical Letters." According to Lavrov, the intelligentsia, having acquired its culture and education at the people's expense, owed a debt to the people. The intelligentsia existed "to repay that debt," that is, to explain to the people what their true interests were and to lead them to socialism.

The doctrine of the intelligentsia's debt to the people gave the disconnected ideas of the radicals a long-awaited cohesiveness and endowed the actions of the intelligentsia with a powerful moral imperative. The life and activities of the "men of all ranks" now acquired a high moral purpose that impelled them to sacrifice themselves in the struggle against the existing system. The revolutionaries began to act with almost religious enthusiasm. In their devotion to the people's welfare, they willingly suffered imprisonment, hard labor, even execution. They often gave up their material privileges, renounced their high social positions, and subjected themselves to strict self-deprivation. They practiced voluntary poverty, donating their personal property to the revolutionary cause. In many respects, the Populist revolutionaries curiously resembled the medieval ascetics who steadfastly rejected personal well-being in the name of higher objectives.[17]

Seized by an almost religious zeal, the Populists believed that they had a mission to save the Russian peasantry from the "horrors" of capitalist development: pauperization, separation from the land, enslavement by capital, and harsh exploitation. They felt that the intelligentsia, through heroic effort, could change the course of Russian history. Furthermore, this had to be done immediately, because capitalism, which the Populists believed had been artificially implanted in Russia from above, was making rapid progress. One of the leaders of Russian Populism, Petr Tkachev, wrote: "The commune is already beginning to disintegrate. The government is exerting all its strength to destroy and ruin it completely. The peasantry is giving rise to a class of kulaks, landowners, and renters of the peasants' and landowners' land—a peasant aristocracy . . . That is why we cannot wait . . . we must allow no delay, no procrastination. Now—or in the far distant future, perhaps never!"[18]

This first stage of Russian Populism gave rise to an astonishing, historically unique event, the massive "going to the people" movement by the intelligentsia. In the spring of 1874 waves of students and other young people, with no overall leadership, fanned out to the countryside. Several thousand activists made their way to thirty-seven provinces. Some of the Populists had in mind a long-term educational campaign to spread socialist ideas among the peasants. Others, adhering to Bakunin's doctrines, considered the countryside fully ripe for revolt. As one contemporary put it in his memoirs, they "went out to select emplacements for future artillery."[19] The peasants failed to justify the hopes of either group. They proved unreceptive to socialist ideas and often turned the propagandists over to the police. The authorities arrested some 4,000 individuals, 770 of whom underwent further interrogation. In 1877, 193 defendants were brought before a court in what became one of the most famous political trials in post-reform Russia.

What drew the Populist revolutionaries to the Russian peasantry? Why did they seek so stubbornly to merge with the people, whom one propagandist called "those dear strangers whose acquaintance I had so long yearned to make"?[20] As previously noted, the worldview of the intelligentsia resembled a religious faith. Although its members renounced any belief in God, they still needed an unquestioned object of reverence and worship. "The people" served that need. Poor and oppressed, they bore within themselves the seeds of a new and just order, socialism. Sergei Kravchinsky, a revolutionary leader during the 1870s, called the "going to the people" movement "a kind of crusade." It displayed "the infectious and all-consuming character of religious movements." The participants sought "not only to achieve specific practical objectives but at the same time to satisfy a profound need for personal moral purification."[21] There is ample evidence of the revolutionaries' extraordinarily emotional and exalted attitude toward the people. One of them always capitalized the word when he wrote it. Another "spoke of the people with tears in his eyes and nervous gesticulations," while a third compared his "love for the peasant" to "the mystery of the Eucharist."[22]

The quasi-religious mentality of the revolutionaries contrasted sharply with the traditional religion that the people themselves professed. The peasants interpreted their poverty and suffering not as the consequences of an unjust social system but as the product of their own sinfulness. To the Populists' call for an overthrow of the existing order, the peasants responded that "the people themselves are to blame for everything" because "they are all drunkards and have forgotten God." The peasants did have a communal outlook, and they hoped for a redistribution of the land, but they expected the fulfillment of their hopes to come from the tsar, whom they regarded as a sacred figure, and not from revolutionaries who came from the city and reminded them too much of their hated "masters." It is not surprising that the peasants reacted angrily to the Populists' attacks on the tsar and often handed them over to the police.[23]

Although we might expect the failure of the "going to the people" movement to have sobered the Populists, the revolutionaries could neither renounce their deification of the people nor subject their views to a fundamental reexamination. Even after 1874 they made truly heroic efforts to get their message through to the peasants in one way or another. To disseminate their views they settled down in the countryside as statisticians, midwives, teachers, or artisans to bring themselves closer to the peasants. Some obtained positions as clerks in the local zemstvos. They undertook campaigns in the Volga region and the Urals, where peasant uprisings had occurred long before, and in the settlements of religious dissenters: the Old Believers and sectarians.

In 1876 the Populists formed a unified revolutionary organization called Land and Liberty, named to honor the first society of that name, formed in the 1860s, to coordinate revolutionary activities throughout Russia. The leadership of the new organization consisted of prominent Populists, among them Georgy Plekhanov, Andrei Zheliabov, Sofia Perovskaia, and Sergei Kravchinsky. In accordance with Bakunin's precepts, Land and Liberty proclaimed as its goal a free federation of self-governing communes and a peasant revolution triggered by propaganda in the countryside as its basic means of struggle. To arouse the peasants, the organization energetically formed Populist "settlements" in the countryside, and it published and distributed revolutionary newspapers, pamphlets, and leaflets. All its efforts proved fruitless, however. Faced with the passivity or even hostility of the people, the revolutionaries essentially had only one recourse: to give up their propaganda campaign among the peasants and concentrate on the seizure of state power.

Some revolutionaries already advocated this strategy. In the early 1870s Petr Tkachev, Nechaev's former associate who had emigrated to the West, urged the revolutionaries to give up their hopes for a popular uprising and devote their efforts to creating a disciplined revolutionary organization that would carry out a coup d'état.[24] Only by seizing state power, Tkachev asserted, could the revolutionaries introduce socialism into Russian life. Their immediate task must therefore be "to turn the current conservative state into a revolutionary state."[25] Such appeals, which reflected a lack of trust in the revolutionary potential of the people, had found little response among the Populists. As hopes for a peasant insurrection faded, however, the Populists found themselves drawn to Tkachev's views.

The government's harsh measures against any expression of opposition helped to turn the Populists in this direction. A broad wave of arrests followed the "going to the people" movement. The prisoners spent three years in solitary confinement before being brought to trial, during which time ninety-three of them died, went mad, or committed suicide.[26] Although a large number of the defendants were acquitted, they were all sentenced to administrative exile after the trial. The revolutionaries responded in kind to the government's repressions. In January 1878 Vera Zasulich attempted to assassinate the governor of St. Petersburg. That was followed by the murder of several high-ranking officials, including the chief of the secret police, Nikolai Mezentsev. In April 1879 a revolutionary named Aleksandr Soloviev, acting without the approval of Land and Liberty, made an unsuccessful attempt on the life of Alexander II. The Populists now had to decide which tactic to pursue in their revolutionary campaign. In the summer of 1879 Land and Liberty split into two organizations, the Black (that is, Total) Repartition and the People's Will. The Black Repartition, headed by Georgy Plekhanov, chose the traditional strategy of educating the people, but the police soon destroyed it. The People's Will, under the leadership of Andrei Zheliabov and Sofia Perovskaia, concentrated entirely on acts of individual terror.[27]

How did the People's Will justify its turn to terror, to a political struggle that manifestly diverged from the doctrines of classical Populism? The group's leaders argued that in view of the peasants' passivity, individual terror was the only means of making the transition to socialism. It was necessary first to seize state power and then, under conditions of political freedom, to instill socialist ideas in the people. Political murder, to be sure, appeared dubious from a moral standpoint, but the People's Will declared that under an autocratic regime it had no other means of struggle. At the same time, the group resolutely condemned political terror in democratic countries. After President James A. Garfield of the United States was assassinated in July 1881, the People's Will declared: "In a country where individual freedom offers the possibility of an honest ideological struggle . . . political murder is a manifestation of the same spirit of despotism that we have made it our task to destroy."[28]

As for Russia, the Populists believed that the autocratic structure of the government made it not only unavoidable but possible to seize power by means of individual terror. They argued that the autocracy "hung in mid-air," lacking solid support from any stratum of society. By killing the dignitaries who held key posts in the state, the revolutionaries believed, they would sow chaos and confusion in the ruling circles. The governmental machinery would collapse, and they could take power. A Constituent Assembly, elected in an atmosphere of broad political freedom, would be convened after the revolution.

Russia's political system, in which the emperor held the basic levers of power, soon made him the prime target of political terror. On August 26, 1879, the anniversary of Alexander's coronation, the Executive Committee of the People's Will passed a death sentence on him and began to hunt him down. At the end of 1879, having dug a tunnel over forty yards long to a railroad track, the revolutionaries planted a mine and detonated it under the tsar's train. The explosion derailed the train, but the tsar was not on board and no one was hurt. In February 1880 they set off a bomb in the tsar's residence, the Winter Palace, killing and wounding several dozen soldiers of the palace guard. The tsar again emerged unscathed. Only on March 1, 1881, did they succeed in killing him, when bomb-throwing terrorists, at the cost of their own lives, blew up the tsar's carriage on the Catherine Canal in Petersburg.

The impotence of the autocracy's police apparatus in its battle against a mere handful of terrorists astonished contemporaries. (The Executive Committee, which planned and carried out the assassination, consisted of no more than fifteen people.) It has also been the subject of sharp debate among historians. Most agree that a large part of the explanation is that moderate elements in the society sympathized with the revolutionaries. A governmental conference called in April 1879 to discuss measures to fight terrorism concluded: "almost all more or less educated people appear apathetic in the current struggle of the government against a relatively small number of evil-minded people."[29] This unprecedented situation led the authorities to consider changes in the way the state implemented its policies, and it became the stimulus to major reforms.

Initially, the government reacted to the Populist terror in traditional fashion, by increasing repression. After the murder of police chief Mezentsev in August 1878, the authorities transferred political trials to the military courts. The attempt on Alexander's life in the spring of 1879 led to the appointment of governors-general in Petersburg, Kharkov, and Odessa, in addition to those already existing in Moscow, Kiev, and Warsaw. The governors-general received extraordinary powers to deal with the revolutionaries. At the same time, the government broadened the application of the death penalty. From August 1878 through August 1879 fourteen executions took place. None of these measures had an appreciable effect. Along with its policy of repression, however, the government gradually began to seek a compromise with the public. In August 1878 the government began to turn to the public for help in the struggle against the revolutionaries.

The government's appeal elicited a flood of petitions from institutions of local self-government, particularly the zemstvo assemblies. As elected bodies, they regarded themselves as authentic representatives of society. In 1878–79 seventy-four zemstvo addresses reached the government, five of them containing political demands.[30] The zemstvo liberals pointed out that moderates were not so much unwilling as unable to render assistance to the authorities. "While anarchist ideas are disseminated both in the underground press and by word of mouth," the address of the Chernigov zemstvo declared, "society is deprived of the means of expressing its opinion. There is no public opinion, for there is no publication to express it. No press exists which, free of the fear of administrative punishments and guided by the interests and urgent needs of society, . . . might arouse a sense of initiative, a sense of self-preservation, and a desire to support the foundations of the state system." The Tver zemstvo asserted that the weakness of legal principles, scorned by both the terrorists and the administration, prevented a successful struggle with the revolutionaries. "Confidence in the force of law, safeguarded by the courts, is wavering. The courts and the law no longer protect the individual, who is entirely subject to the arbitrariness of the administration."[31]

At first, the authorities ignored these statements and even subjected their authors to persecution. As the failure of repressive measures to combat the terrorists became clear, however, some officials within the government began to voice the need to reach out to society. Count Mikhail Loris-Melikov made the most consistent effort to achieve this objective.

Loris-Melikov rose to the highest reaches of the government during the last cycle of terrorist violence. After the explosion in the Winter Palace in 1880, the authorities decided to abandon the unsuccessful tactic of dividing extraordinary powers among the governors-general. Instead, they now concentrated power in the fight against the revolutionaries in a special body, the Supreme Administrative Commission, and appointed Loris-Melikov to head it. He was an army general, a hero of the Russo-Turkish War of 1877–78. As governor-general of Astrakhan and then of Kharkov, he proved to be an energetic and flexible administrator. Even before taking up his high post in Petersburg, Loris-Melikov had formulated a concrete political program that envisaged a broadening of society's rights and a resumption of the Great Reforms.[32]

Loris-Melikov recognized that the policy of repression had exhausted itself, and he set out to make concessions to the moderates in society in order to win them over to the government's side. The authorities adopted a more tolerant attitude toward the zemstvos and the press, and allowed the publication of several new journals and newspapers. Loris-Melikov insisted on the removal of Dmitry Tolstoi, the hated minister of public education, and he organized a series of audits by the Senate to uncover defects in the administrative structure. He curtailed the use of administrative exile, and at the same time centralized and regularized the activities of the police. The Third Section of His Majesty's Own Imperial Chancellery was abolished, and the Ministry of Internal Affairs assumed its functions.

Loris-Melikov intended his policy to culminate in the creation of a representative body that would draft proposals to extend and develop the Great Reforms. He stressed that its proposals would not infringe on autocracy. In a report to Alexander II on January 28, 1881, he wrote: "The organization of popular representation in forms borrowed from the West is inconceivable for Russia. Those forms are not only alien to the Russian people, they may even destabilize all of their basic political views and introduce utter confusion."[33] The general insisted that his project had purely pragmatic objectives, to determine the opinions of knowledgeable people concerning the country's needs and to reveal the most acceptable means of continuing reform. Temporary Preparatory Commissions, which would include elected deputies from the

Count Mikhail T. Loris-Melikov. Engraving.

zemstvos and the largest cities, were to meet in Petersburg. The commissions would discuss only those questions that the government presented to them, and they would be strictly consultative. All in all, however, the commissions might have served as the embryo of true parliamentary institutions.

While advancing his proposal, Loris-Melikov gathered around him a circle of like-minded officials and gradually turned into an informal prime minister. He had the backing of War Minister Dmitry Miliutin and Finance Minister Aleksandr Abaza as well as support on many issues from Grand Duke Konstantin Nikolaevich, the chairman of the State Council. On the whole, the period of Loris-Melikov's ascendancy represented the high point of the enlightened bureaucracy's influence within the government. In August 1880, Loris-Melikov declared a successful end to the struggle against terrorism, and the Supreme Administrative Commission was dissolved. Loris-Melikov now became minister of internal affairs, while retaining many of the additional powers of a prime minister. Russia seemed closer than ever to convening a representative body and creating a cabinet form of government. Subsequent events, however, showed that Loris-Melikov had been unduly optimistic.

Not everyone in the government trusted Loris-Melikov's declarations that his proposals were politically inoffensive and had nothing in common with Western parliamentarism. An influential group of Loris-Melikov's opponents emerged in the higher echelons of the government, centered around Grand Duke Aleksandr Aleksandrovich, the heir to the throne. Konstantin Pobedonostsev, the most important figure in this group, had taken part in the preparation of the judicial reform of 1864, but as one of the grand duke's mentors he had subsequently abandoned liberalism and adopted reactionary views.[34] In the opinion of Pobedonostsev and his supporters, any attempt to introduce representative government in Russia would undermine the unlimited nature of autocracy, initiate a struggle for power, and lead to a weakening of the state and its ultimate disintegration. Pobedonostsev had initially approved of Loris-Melikov's policies, especially the centralization and rationalization of the police apparatus. Loris-Melikov, in turn, facilitated Pobedonostsev's appointment as supreme procurator of the Holy Synod. As Loris-Melikov's reform plans unfolded, however, Pobedonostsev became an increasingly bitter opponent. For some time, Loris-Melikov attributed little significance to Pobedonostsev's opposition, but the count had made a major political miscalculation.

Another mistake, one that was to prove crucial, was to underestimate the efforts of the revolutionary underground. The long pause in terrorist activity after the explosion in the Winter Palace did not signal the end of the revolutionaries' activities. They were merely gathering their strength for a decisive blow. Zheliabov and other leaders of the People's Will had been arrested thanks to the efforts of the newly reorganized secret police, but several major figures, including Sofia Perovskaia, remained at liberty. She now organized the last, and fatal, attempt on Alexander's life. The death of the Tsar-Liberator meant the political defeat of Loris-Melikov and his supporters and the failure of his reform program. Soon after Alexander III acceded to the throne, he issued the Manifesto of April 29, 1881, on "the unshakable institution of autocracy." The dismissal of Loris-Melikov, along with Miliutin and Abaza, soon followed.

A similar fate, complete political defeat, awaited the revolutionaries, who had at last achieved their long-sought goal of killing the autocrat. Contrary to the Populists' expectations, the death of the tsar led neither to a mass popular insurrection nor to the collapse of the state apparatus. Within a few weeks the government arrested and executed the organizers of the assassination, including Perovskaia, and the police almost entirely destroyed the People's Will. This conclusion to the terrorists' efforts had important consequences both for the authorities and for the revolutionary movement. The government, now firmly controlled by conservatives, would no longer undertake major reforms on its own initiative, except in economic policy. Russian statesmen would long be forbidden to make references to Western experience and liberal principles. As for the revolutionaries, Populism would fail to regain its previous authority in their eyes. To be sure, at the beginning of the twentieth century there would be a revival of Populist organizations in Russia, but they would have to share influence on the intelligentsia with a new revolutionary current, Marxism, which posed a much greater threat to the autocracy. Both of these circumstances—the government's unwillingness to reform and the generational change within the revolutionary movement—made new social upheavals in Russia inevitable.

Chapter 8

Russia and the World, 1856–1900

"Russia is not angry; Russia is concentrating." With these words, Prince Aleksandr Gorchakov, who succeeded Count Nesselrode as foreign minister in 1856, defined the essence of Russia's foreign policy after the Crimean War. The main task of Russian diplomacy now was to keep the country at peace to enable the empire to carry out domestic reforms, revive its military power, and reclaim its former authority in foreign affairs. The government did not fully succeed in carrying out that task, however. Despite all its diplomatic efforts, Russia in the second half of the nineteenth century was drawn into several international conflicts that exacerbated the country's social and political contradictions and dealt a blow to the reform process. Events demonstrated that the Russian Empire lacked the capacity to regain the status and power that it had enjoyed earlier in the century.

One reason for its failure was the great gap between Russia and the West in levels of industrial development. Try as it might, the government failed to eliminate the disparity. Even after the railroad boom of the 1870s, Russia's rail network remained far smaller than that of the West. In 1894 Russia had 64 kilometers of railroad track per 10,000 square kilometers of territory, an amount one-sixteenth that of England, one-twelfth that of Germany, and one-fifth that of the United States.[1] In 1875 Russia produced less than 16,000 tons of steel, while Germany and England produced 303,000 and 719,000 tons respectively. Russian industry satisfied only 60 percent of the country's demand for coal and 20.5 percent of its demand for locomotives. Russia's foreign trade was less than 4 percent of the world total, below that of such countries as Belgium and Holland.[2] Not surprisingly, the condition of the

Prince Aleksandr M. Gorchakov. Photograph.

economy severely affected the long-planned modernization of the empire's military forces. With enormous effort, the government had succeeded in carrying out a twofold transformation of the navy, from sail to steam and from wooden to ironclad vessels, by the end of the 1870s. However, the disparity in the numbers of ships between Russia and the Western countries (England, France, and later Germany) inevitably grew. The rearmament of the army proceeded with difficulty. In the mid-1890s, Russia lagged behind not only France and Germany but even Austria-Hungary in the number of artillery weapons per infantry battalion.[3]

In addition to the problems of rearming the military forces, serious difficulties arose in reorganizing them. Dmitry Miliutin, the brother of Nikolai Miliutin, took charge of the military reforms. As minister of war from 1861 to 1881, he became one of the empire's leading statesmen. Despite Miliutin's strong position in the government and Alexander II's personal confidence in him, the reforms proved to be a protracted enterprise. Only a few came to fruition in the 1860s: a reduction in the term of service, the creation of a system of military districts, a reorganization of military courts and military academies along the lines of their civilian counterparts, and an increase in the powers of commanders of the military districts, which helped to decentralize military administration and make it more flexible and efficient.

The key reform, universal military service, came about only in 1874, under the impact of France's defeat in the Franco-Prussian War. All Russian men now became subject to military service at the age of twenty-one, for a term of four years in the army or seven years in the navy. Depending on an individual's level of education, the term of service could be reduced to three months. In addition, illiterate recruits received an elementary education. In the words of contemporaries, the army thus became an important surrogate school. The introduction of universal military service for men of all estates seriously reduced the privileges of the nobility. It patently contradicted Peter III's Manifesto on the Freedom of the Nobility of 1762 and Catherine II's Charter to the Nobility of 1785, which had made service by the "well-born estate" strictly voluntary. Despite the distinctly progressive character of the military reforms, however, they retained a number of archaic features. In particular, appointments to high command posts remained the prerogative of the emperor and often depended on personal favoritism rather than professional qualifications. The reforms themselves became the subject of considerable debate within society. Some critics accused Miliutin of undermining the army's esprit de corps and diminishing its fighting capacity.[4]

The obstacles to military reform and its equivocal results, as well as the weakness of the economy, dictated that the Russian government exercise extreme caution in the international arena. Immediately after the Crimean

Count Dmitry A. Miliutin. Photograph

War, Russia began to draw closer to its recent enemy, France, at that time the most influential power in continental Europe. The government calculated that the rapprochement with France would help it to eliminate the restrictive provisions of the Peace of Paris. The two countries acted in concert on several international issues. Russia supported France when the latter, together with the Kingdom of Sardinia (Piedmont), declared war on Austria in 1859. Russia thereby "punished" its unfaithful Austrian ally, which had taken a hostile position toward Russia during the Crimean War. However, the Russo-French rapprochement of the late 1850s proved neither firm nor long-lasting.

Although France obtained Russia's support on particular issues, it was not prepared to satisfy Russia's principal desire, assistance in revising the terms of the Peace of Paris. As Gorchakov, a proponent of the Russo-French rapprochement, was forced to admit, "The assistance that the Tuilleries cabinet rendered us was, to tell the truth, insincere and highly limited."[5] Napoleon III's contacts with Russia served above all as a means to achieve his own objectives. The Polish rebellion of 1863 made that especially clear. In an effort to exploit the principle of national self-determination in his own interests, the French emperor interceded with Alexander II on the Polish issue and raised the question of granting Poland broad autonomy.

In March 1863 European states led by England and France proposed that the Russian government restore the Polish Constitution of 1815 and proclaim a political amnesty. In June they proposed a conference of the countries that had participated in the Congress of Vienna to discuss the Polish question. They accused the Russian government of violating the conditions under which Poland had become part of the Russian Empire after the defeat of Napoleon. A large-scale anti-Russian campaign unfolded in the Western press. These developments aroused indignation in numerous circles of Russian society, which regarded the actions of the Western powers as interference in Russia's internal affairs. The public reaction enabled the Russian government to reject the demands of England and France. By mobilizing sizable forces and announcing plans for broad social reforms in Poland, the government suppressed the insurrection. Relations with France deteriorated. They worsened further when a Polish émigré named Antoni Berezowski attempted to assassinate Alexander during his visit to the World Exposition in Paris in 1867.

By the beginning of the 1870s the Russo-French rapprochement was essentially defunct, and Alexander himself had adopted a distinctly anti-French position. The Russian emperor made his attitude clear during the Franco-Prussian War of 1870–71, when he remained deaf to appeals for help from the French, who were going down to defeat. Alexander's attitude was not the product of cold calculation. It had an emotional source in memories of the

Crimean War and even of Napoleon I's invasion of Russia. The French government protested the shelling of Paris by the Prussian army with the words: "this bombardment is a return to barbarism and should arouse the universal indignation of civilized governments and nations." When Alexander received word of this protest, he wrote in the margins of the report: "And what about the Kremlin, which they blew up!"[6]

Russia observed a formal neutrality during the Franco-Prussian War, but the sympathies of its ruling circles, or, in any event, of Alexander II, were manifestly on the side of Prussia. According to Dmitry Miliutin's memoirs, after each Prussian victory Alexander sent a congratulatory telegram to King William. He also sent so many St. George Crosses (the highest Russian military order) to Prussian officers that complaints and mockery arose within the Russian public. Despite Russia's neutrality, Russian officers, doctors, and field hospitals served in the Prussian army. In 1873, soon after the conclusion of the war and the formation of the unified German Empire, Russia and Germany concluded a treaty that Austria-Hungary adopted in the same year. This Three Emperors' League represented to a certain degree Russia's return to its traditional foreign-policy alignment with the conservative powers of Central Europe.

Rapprochement with Germany enabled Russia to attain its most important foreign policy objective: abrogation of the restrictive clauses of the Peace of Paris. At the end of 1870 Gorchakov took advantage of the defeat of France, the chief guarantor of the treaty, to declare Russia's refusal to observe the disarmament of the Black Sea. To justify this step, Russia cited numerous instances of Turkey's violation of the disarmament provisions. Russia also pointed out the changes that had taken place since 1856 in the conditions of warfare, particularly the introduction of new and more destructive armaments, such as ironclad naval ships. Despite England's protests, the European powers accepted Russia's declaration, and the London Conference of 1871 confirmed it.

The Three Emperors' League also helped Russia to resolve some important foreign-policy problems. It safeguarded the country's European frontiers as Russia advanced into Central Asia, and it secured Austria-Hungary's neutrality during the Russo-Turkish War of 1877–78. From its inception, however, the League was riddled with profound contradictions. During the 1870s, Russia restrained Germany from a definitive rout of France, naturally to Germany's dissatisfaction. The sharp conflict between Russia and Austria-Hungary in the Balkans continued to fester. On the whole, despite the Three Emperors' League, Russia's position in Europe remained shaky, and a considerable part of Russian society had the impression that Russia was almost totally isolated internationally.

Russia's difficult external situation gave rise to an intensification of anti-Western sentiments in social thought. Nikolai Danilevsky's book *Russia and Europe* (1869) vividly expressed those sentiments. The author, an eminent biologist, attempted to apply the concepts of the natural sciences to social life. In his opinion, the fundamental differences between Russia and Western Europe precluded any fruitful borrowing of elements of Western culture. Russia, he wrote, "is not a participant either in European good or in European evil . . . Neither sincere humility nor sincere pride allows Russia to consider herself part of Europe."[7] Danilevsky regarded Western Europe as a separate Romano-Germanic world, a separate civilization, the foundations of which were completely alien to Russia. Russia had its own unique principles and its own destiny: to lead an independent civilization, the Slavic world.[8]

Danilevsky's theory resembled Slavophilism, but there were essential differences between them. His program lacked the messianism of the Slavophiles. He did not believe that Europe could be "saved" by adhering to the principles of Slavic culture and social life, nor did he desire Europe's salvation. He believed that Russia should concentrate on pursuing its own national objectives, first and foremost the conquest of Constantinople, which was to be the center of a future Slavic federation.

Danilevsky's ideas were an attempt to take account of certain developments in the international environment in the 1860s, particularly the growing sympathy for Russia among the Slavic peoples under the rule of Austria-Hungary and Turkey. National self-consciousness, on the rise among the Slavs, manifested itself vividly in 1867 at the All-Russian Ethnographic Exhibition and Slavic Congress in Moscow, to which the various Slavic lands sent delegations. In Russia itself, a Slavic Committee under the chairmanship of Mikhail Pogodin had existed in Moscow since 1858, and similar institutions arose in Petersburg, Kiev, and Odessa. The committees addressed mainly cultural issues, such as providing aid to churches and schools in the Balkans and assistance to Slavic students studying in Russia. Their activities also had a distinctly political coloration, however. The Slavic Committees maintained close contacts with Russian consuls in the Balkans and established ties with participants in the Slavic national-liberation movement.[9] In the late 1870s the Slavic Committees would play an important part in the struggle of the Balkan Slavs against Turkey. Until then, however, Russian foreign policy was considerably more active on the empire's eastern frontiers, in Central Asia and the Far East.

Russian diplomacy turned its attention to the eastern parts of the empire in the second half of the nineteenth century as a direct result of the Crimean War. The naval forces that England and France had deployed on Russia's remote ocean frontiers, the White Sea and the Sea of Okhotsk, had shown that in the event of a serious conflict the country could not defend its entire coastline. The notion that Russia was destined to remain a continental power and not a sea power gained greater currency. Under the influence of similar ideas, Russia in 1818 had declined to acquire the Hawaiian Islands. Likewise, after the Crimean War, the Russian government considered it essential to make significant concessions. It now agreed to earlier U.S. proposals that it cede Alaska and the Aleutian Islands to the United States.

The mid-1860s marked the high point of friendly relations between Russia and the United States. During the Civil War, Russia supported the North, unlike Britain and France. Russian public opinion on the whole sympathized with the Northern side, and some Russian volunteers fought in its army. In 1863 the Russian government sent naval squadrons to New York and San Francisco to demonstrate its solidarity with the Northern states. In turn, American society was sympathetic toward Russia. After Karakozov's attempt to assassinate Alexander II, Congress unanimously adopted a resolution congratulating the tsar. A special American delegation to Russia, headed by Assistant Secretary of the Navy Gustavus Fox, received a warm welcome.[10]

The sale (in effect, the grant) of Alaska and the Aleutian Islands to the United States for 7.2 million dollars, or 11 million rubles, took place in March 1867.[11] The financial aspects of the transaction were not the major consideration for Russia. The basic reasons for the sale were Russia's need to rid itself of possessions that it could not defend in the event of war with a naval power, and its desire to weaken England's position in North America while at the same time avoiding potential clashes with the United States. The sale of Alaska allowed Russia to concentrate its efforts on extending its frontiers in the Amur and Ussuri regions in the Far East and assimilating its new territories there.

The colonial subordination of China by Britain and France in the "opium wars" of the 1840s–60s provided the impetus for Russia's thrust to the Far East. As China gradually lost its independence, the European powers posed a threat to Russia's possessions in Siberia. The mouth of the Amur River, which Russia regarded as the "gateway to Siberia," was the subject of particular anxiety. Nikolai Muraviev, the governor-general of Eastern Siberia, declared, "Russia will not tolerate the occupation by any foreign power of the mouth of a river whose upper reaches flow along Russian possessions."[12] The Russian government therefore raised the question with China of a precise demarcation of the border between them.

Under the Treaty of Aigun (1858), Russia acquired from China the territory along the left bank of the Amur. Two years later, the Treaty of Peking ceded to Russia the Pacific coastal region, called the Ussuri District. Intensive settlement of the new territories ensued, and the cities of Blagoveshchensk, Khabarovsk, and Nikolaevsk arose. The city of Vladivostok, founded in 1864, became Russia's major outpost on the Pacific Ocean. The acquisition of these Far Eastern territories enabled Russia to secure full possession of Sakhalin Island, which it had administered jointly with Japan. In exchange for Sakhalin, Japan in 1875 received all the Kurile Islands.

As in the Far East, the issue of borders posed serious problems in Central Asia, another area of Russian expansion in the second half of the nineteenth century.[13] Several factors impelled Russia's advance into Central Asia: Russian capitalism's need for markets and raw materials, especially cotton; the government's desire to protect the empire's southern borders against armed incursions from the Central Asian states; and competition with England, which had brought Persia (Iran) and Afghanistan under its control in the 1850s.

As an important crossroads of international trade routes, populated by Turkic and Iranian tribes, Muslim Central Asia had long found itself within the Russian government's field of vision. Russia periodically sent trade missions and diplomatic embassies to the region, but the Central Asian states— the khanates of Khiva and Kokand and the Emirate of Bukhara—resisted contact. Thus the entire mission sent to Khiva by Peter the Great under the leadership of Prince Aleksandr Bekovich-Cherkassky was put to death by order of the khan. Significant obstacles remained in subsequent years. Russian merchants had to pay double or sometimes even quadruple the customs duties that their Muslim counterparts paid. Armed bands from Khiva and Kokand plundered merchant caravans, attacked Russian settlements, and enslaved their inhabitants. These circumstances long impeded the development of close relations between Russia and Central Asia.

The situation changed considerably in the mid-nineteenth century. The Kazakh tribes inhabiting the lands between Russia and Central Asia had now come under Russian rule. At the same time, England's economic penetration of Central Asia had intensified. The Russian government began to step up its activities in Central Asia in order to prevent its rival from entrenching itself in the region. Unlike Western colonial expansion, in which "the flag followed capital," in Russia's expansion "capital followed the flag," that is, military and political encroachment preceded economic penetration.[14]

Most historians today believe that England had no plans for the conquest of Central Asia, nor did Russia have such designs on India, as ruling circles in England frequently charged. Both powers expanded into Central Asia out of fear of the other.[15] Russia also wanted to weaken England's position in Europe, especially during the Polish insurrection, when Russia faced the real prospect of a new European war. The prominent Russian diplomat Count Nikolai Ignatiev, director of the Asiatic Department of the Ministry of Foreign Affairs, believed that "to preserve good relations with England, we must show her, at least once, that we can move from a passive position and cause her substantial harm in the event of a breach." Dmitry Miliutin in 1863 declared that "a demonstration in Central Asia will draw England's attention away from Poland."[16]

In the mid-1860s Russia embarked on a military advance into Central Asia. In 1864 Russian troops struck a blow at the Khanate of Kokand by taking the cities of Turkestan and Chimkent. The immediate objective was to join the two defensive lines that separated Russian possessions from the Central Asian states, the Orenburg line and the West Siberian line, and to establish firm state borders in Central Asia. The Russian military leadership in Central Asia considered further conflict inevitable, however. In 1865 General Mikhail Cherniaev, the commander of the Russian forces in Central Asia, seized Tashkent, the major city in the Kokand Khanate, on his own initiative. "General Cherniaev has taken Tashkent," wrote an exasperated Petr Valuev, who opposed territorial seizures and advocated peaceful relations with England. "No one knows why or for what purpose . . . There is an wanton element in everything that is going on in the borderlands of our empire."[17]

The seizure of Tashkent drew Russia into conflict with the Emirate of Bukhara, which claimed part of the territory of Kokand. A series of battles brought the important urban centers of the emirate under Russian rule. In 1868 the weakened states of Central Asia were forced to conclude unequal treaties with Russia that deprived them of the right to conduct an independent foreign policy while preserving their internal autonomy. In 1873 the Khanate of Khiva, surrounded on all sides by Russian troops, concluded a similar treaty. In 1876 the Khanate of Kokand, where an insurrection against Russia had broken out, was abolished. Russia annexed the lands of the khanate and included them in a new administrative unit, the Governor-Generalship of Turkestan.

Russia completed its annexation of Central Asia with the subjugation of the Turkmen tribes that recognized the authority of the Khiva Khanate but were in fact independent. In 1881 Russia captured the fortresses of Geok-Tepe and Ashkhabad. Four years later Russian troops occupied the settlements of Merv and Kushka, at the southernmost point of the Russian Empire. The capture of the oasis of Merv brought Russia into conflict with the Emir of Afghanistan and with the English, who stood behind him. A series of clashes between Russian and Afghan forces led to an agreement in 1885 to divide control of Central Asia. The agreement recognized Afghanistan as part of England's sphere of influence, while Russia annexed the lands of the Turkmen tribes.

The conquest of Central Asia completed the territorial formation of the Russian Empire. It raised with particular urgency the question of how to administer a huge multi-ethnic and multi-religious state. The painful experience of the Caucasus War impelled the Russian authorities to approach this question with considerable caution. General Konstantin Kaufman was appointed to head the Turkestan District in 1867. He proposed a thorough study of local forms of land relations "that might be brought into conformity with the practices prevailing in other parts of the empire, while corresponding to the needs of the people and if possible without violating age-old popular conceptions of land law."[18] The Russian administration tried as much as possible to preserve local customs while cautiously introducing changes that served the interests of the Russian state. In the territories it annexed in Central Asia, Russia carried out a land reform that limited the rights of the local aristocracy and somewhat improved the situation of the lower classes. The Russian authorities built hospitals, libraries, and schools and began to disseminate secular culture while observing religious toleration. Nevertheless, the desire of the Petersburg government and the local administration to observe traditional customs was not always reflected in the daily practices of lower and middle-ranking officials, who often tolerated coercion and arbitrariness in the treatment of the local population.

The attitude of the Russian public and governmental administrators toward the empire's new Asian territories combined two divergent elements: on the one hand, the notion, borrowed from West European thought, of Russia's "civilizing mission," and, on the other, a recognition of "Asiatics" as their equals, with customs and cultural traditions of value in their own right. Neither of these approaches wholly predominated, and Russian policy displayed features of both right up to 1917.[19] In many respects, of course, objective circumstances dictated a relatively high degree of tolerance by Russia of local customs and practices, for the continental character of the empire meant that developments taking place at its center and on its peripheries were directly linked.

Russia's successful drive to the east did nothing to resolve the problems facing the country in Europe. The turn toward Asia in the 1860s and the 1870s could only be a passing episode because all the Russian Empire's vital interests lay in Europe. At the end of the 1870s Russia embarked on a more active European policy. Closely connected with the "Slavic question," it resulted in a diplomatic reorientation by Russia and a search for new allies.

The exacerbation of the Slavic question in the mid-1870s grew out of the complex social, political, and ethnic developments within the Ottoman Empire. Despite the victory of the Turks, in alliance with England and France, over Russia in the Crimean War, their empire continued to weaken and to lose its former political status in the second half of the nineteenth century. The sultan's government attempted to rally the elite of Ottoman society by channeling its energies into the struggle against the "common enemy," the Balkan Slavs backed by Russia. At the beginning of the 1870s the Turkish government sharply curtailed the educational rights of the Slavic peoples and increased their tax burden. In response, insurrections broke out among the Slavs in Bosnia and Herzegovina in 1875 and Bulgaria in 1876. The Ottomans suppressed the uprisings with immense brutality.

These events produced an unusually stormy reaction in Russian society. There was an upsurge of public activity of a sort that Russia had scarcely seen since the Napoleonic invasion. Demonstrations of solidarity with other Orthodox peoples who expected Russia's help, and demands to bring them under Russian protection, were clear signs that Russia's national consciousness had grown considerably since the abolition of serfdom. The feeling of solidarity with the Balkan Slavs seized literally all strata of society. Russians donated millions of rubles to benefit the Slavs. The thousands of volunteers who set out for the Balkans included eminent representatives of science and culture, such as the writer Vsevolod Garshin, the artist Vasily Polenov, and the doctors Nikolai Pirogov and Sergei Botkin. Fyodor Dostoevsky took an active part in the public campaign in support of the Slavs.

"Peasants who have barely learned to read syllable by syllable are poring over all the newspaper accounts that fall into their hands," the Simbirsk police administration reported. According to the memoirs of contemporaries, soldiers in rearguard units begged "with tears in their eyes" to be sent to the front.[20] Slavic Committees collected funds for the Balkan Slavs, purchased weapons and shipped them to the Balkans, transported volunteers to the war, and sent their own agents to the insurgents. The activities of the Slavic Committees in fact began to slip out from under the government's control. They came to exert a considerable influence on public opinion and to a certain extent even on Russian foreign policy. The situation demanded an immediate response by the authorities.

Alexander II was at first highly dubious about intervening in the events in the Balkans, and even more about engaging in a new war with Turkey. The Tsar-Liberator shared his father's hostility to insurrectionists of any sort as "rebels against legitimate authority." Alexander had no desire to repeat the fate of Nicholas I, whose intervention in a conflict over the "Eastern Question" had led to the catastrophic collapse of his reign. The emperor also took into account the difficult state of Russia's finances, the unfinished military reforms, and the inevitability of a hostile reaction to a new war by the European powers, especially England and Austria-Hungary. The pressure of public opinion on the government became so great, however, that even the

autocratic monarch could not withstand it. In 1875–76 the Russian government undertook diplomatic efforts, on its own and in concert with European
states, to settle the conflict in the Balkans. In April 1877, after failing to
receive a positive response from Turkey, Russia declared war.

The Russo-Turkish War of 1877–78 became a test of the military reforms
Russia had introduced in the 1860s and the 1870s, and of the modernization
of its war industries. The results were contradictory.[21] On the one hand, the
railroad network that had been built in the previous two decades enabled the
rapid transportation of troops to the theater of military operations. The cross-
ing of the Danube River also proved successful. On the other, the army supply system, which had been entrusted to private contractors, proved glaringly
deficient. High military appointments were still the prerogative of the emperor, and many Russian commanders fell below the required standard. The
Russian army had talented military leaders, such as Iosif Gurko, Mikhail
Dragomirov, and Mikhail Skobelev, but they occupied secondary posts and
were unable to influence the high command. The battles for the Turkish fortress of Plevna highlighted the organizational defects of the Russian army.
The Russians failed three times to storm the fortress and succeeded in cap-
turing it only after a prolonged siege.

Plevna displayed the weaknesses of Russia's military forces to the country's
adversaries and spurred them on to greater activity. As the English historian
A.J.P. Taylor accurately remarked, "Plevna . . . gave the Ottoman empire
another forty years of life."[22] When the Russian army began to advance toward Constantinople after the capture of Plevna, England brought its ships
into the Sea of Marmara and declared that it would not allow the seizure of
the Turkish capital. Russia's pride and prestige suffered an even greater blow
after the conclusion of the war. Russia and Turkey signed a preliminary peace
agreement at San Stefano, a suburb of Constantinople. The Treaty of San
Stefano created an extensive Bulgarian state, enlarged the territory of Serbia
and Montenegro, and granted Romania full independence from Turkey. Russia received the mouth of the Danube and territory on the Black Sea coast of
the Caucasus. England and Austria-Hungary, however, refused to recognize
the terms of the San Stefano Treaty and insisted that an all-European congress review them. Lacking influential allies in Europe, Russia had to accede
to their demand. The Congress of Berlin in 1878 significantly reduced the
territory of Bulgaria. Russia's adversaries also made important territorial gains
at Turkey's expense: England acquired Cyprus, and Austria-Hungary received
Bosnia and Herzegovina.

The decisions of the Congress of Berlin provoked an outburst of indignation in Russia. Many who had supported the Balkan Slavs openly demanded
war with England and Austria- Hungary and harshly criticized official diplo-

General Mikhail D. Skobelev. Photograph.

macy for the concessions Russia made in Berlin. Ivan Aksakov, the chairman
of the Moscow Slavic Committee, proclaimed: "The duty of loyal subjects
orders us to hope and to believe, but the duty of loyal subjects also orders us
not to keep silent in these days of lawlessness and injustice which have raised
a barrier between the tsar and the land."[23] Not a trace remained of the enthusiasm that had previously gripped the whole of society. The contradictory
outcome of the war and Russia's concessions diminished the government's
authority within the country and contributed to the social and political crisis
that led ultimately to the assassination of Alexander II.

Russia also experienced profound disappointment in its relations with the
Balkan states of Serbia and the newly formed Bulgaria. It should be noted
that Russia played a decisive role in the construction of the Bulgarian state.
Under the leadership of Prince Vladimir Cherkassky, a former colleague of
Nikolai Miliutin, the creation of administrative institutions and courts and
the organization of transportation, postal services, education, and public health
all made considerable progress. Military consultants from Russia oversaw
the creation of a Bulgarian army. A large-scale agrarian reform took place.
The process of state building in Bulgaria culminated in the introduction of a
highly liberal constitutional structure, one of the paradoxes of Russian foreign policy. Russia itself, of course, had no constitution at this time. Thanks
to these measures and its mission to liberate the Slavs, Russia enjoyed great
authority in the Balkans. Quite rapidly, however, that authority began to wane.

As in the time of Nicholas I, the Russian government frequently exerted
crude pressure on the Balkan states and even resorted to outright dictation.
Russia's Western adversaries actively exploited each miscalculation by the
Russian government and emphasized the archaic nature of Russia's autocratic political order and system of social estates. Moreover, as in the 1830s
and the 1840s, the weakness of Russia's economic position in the Balkans
became apparent. The young Balkan states needed massive infusions of capital
and industrial goods as well as markets for their own industry. The Western
states, and especially Austria-Hungary, thanks to its geographical proximity,
were able to meet those needs. Gradually but inexorably the governments of
the Balkan states loosened their ties with their recent liberator, Russia, and
began to reorient themselves toward Austria-Hungary. By the mid-1880s
Russia had lost its dominant position in the Balkans and had even broken
diplomatic relations with Bulgaria. A symbolic expression of this state of
affairs was the toast that the new Russian tsar, Alexander III, proposed to
"Russia's sole ally in Europe, the prince of Montenegro."[24]

The unexpected and discouraging outcome of Russia's liberation mission
and its loss of influence in the Balkans led to new interpretations of Russia's
role in the world. Konstantin Leontiev, a thinker and writer with long service

in Russia's diplomatic legations in the Balkans,[25] expounded his views in his book *The East, Russia and the Slavs*, published in two volumes in 1885–86. In contrast to Nikolai Danilevsky, Leontiev remained skeptical of the notion of creating a federation of all the Slavs under Russia's leadership, on the grounds that it might hasten the penetration into the Slavic world of liberal and democratic ideas from the West. "All the Southwestern Slavs without exception are democrats and constitutionalists," he claimed. "They share . . . an inclination to equality and liberty, that is, to ideals that are either American or French." The solution he envisaged was to preserve and cultivate among the Slavs the traditions of "Byzantinism," by which he meant the habit of submission to a strong authoritarian government, strict social hierarchy, and a mystical and ascetic Christianity. Consequently, Russia should not hasten to undermine Turkey's position in the Balkans. "The closer to us a nation is by blood and language, the more we should maintain a wise separation, without breaking ties with them . . . The ideal should be not merger but attraction at a calculated distance."[26]

Another outstanding thinker of the second half of the nineteenth century, Vladimir Soloviev, the son of the historian Sergei Soloviev, started from very different premises. Soloviev at first stood close to the Slavophiles, but he subsequently rejected their doctrines because of what he called their "national egotism." Such egotism, he maintained, determined the failure of Russian foreign policy, for it prevented Russia from gaining firm authority in the Balkans. Russia should not aggressively contrast itself to the West and reject the principles of Western culture. On the contrary, Russia should incorporate Western achievements into its own spiritual experience and try to surpass them, combining the East's elevated spirituality and mystical contemplativeness with the West's principles of law and order and guarantees of personal liberty. Russia's mission, Soloviev argued, its "national idea," was to become a vast bridge between West and East. To carry out that mission, Russia should base its actions on unselfish principles. It should renounce the seizure of territory and the oppression of other peoples, the Poles above all, in its domestic policy. "To repent of its historical sins and satisfy the demands of justice," Soloviev wrote, "to renounce national egotism by giving up Russification and recognizing unqualified religious freedom—that is the only way for Russia to prepare itself . . . to fulfill its real national idea."[27]

By the mid-1880s, as a result of the break in relations with Bulgaria and the hostility of England and Austria-Hungary, Russia found itself nearly isolated politically, just as it had been at the time of the Crimean War. Relations with its longtime ally, Germany, had steadily cooled after the Congress of Berlin. Although Otto von Bismarck, the German chancellor, declared that he would act as an "honest broker" at the congress, his unsympathetic attitude toward Russia had been apparent. Germany invariably supported its ally Austria-Hungary, whose interests in the Balkans clashed irreconcilably with those of Russia. Germany itself had begun an economic and political penetration of Turkey. The Three Emperors' League had collapsed by the end of the 1880s. Russia could not afford to remain isolated for long, however. The government undertook an intensive search for new allies, which culminated in the conclusion of an agreement with France in the early 1890s.

Contemporaries regarded the alliance between the French Republic and the Russian autocratic monarchy as a major historical paradox. It evoked a great number of responses, some ambivalent, some skeptical, and some openly negative. " 'God Save the Tsar' and the 'Marseillaise'—that is like Christ's Resurrection being celebrated in a synagogue," Minister of Finance Sergei Witte wrote to the well-known conservative journalist Prince Vladimir Meshchersky in 1899. "To any Frenchman, our autocracy represents barbarism, and our tsar is a despot. To us, their notorious *égalité, fraternité*, and so forth, is an advertisement for the banker Blok printed every day in all the Russian newspapers. The French parliament is a blasphemy of common sense and a colossal self-deception."[28] The visit of a French naval squadron to Russia in 1891 created a sensation when the Russian autocrat stood as the "Marseillaise," the national anthem of the French Republic, was played. Despite its seemingly paradoxical character, however, there were good reasons for a Russo-French alliance.

Geopolitical circumstances, above all, brought about the rapprochement of the two countries. In 1879 Austria and Germany signed a military agreement, parallel to the Three Emperors' League, which Italy adopted in 1882. This created a bloc of Central European powers. The alliance of France and Russia, situated at the western and eastern extremities of Europe, formed a natural counterweight to that bloc. Economic and financial factors also played a large role. French capitalists had begun making large-scale investments in Russian industry in the 1880s. The Russian government turned to the French authorities more and more often for its loans. The French ambassador to Russia, Antoine-René-Paul Laboulaye, declared: "The alliance of Russia, which is rich in people, and France, which is rich in money, represents an enormous force."[29]

While the economies of Russia and France at the end of the nineteenth century complemented each other quite well, deep conflicts existed between the economies of Russia and Germany. German tariffs to defend the country's internal market against Russian grain had provoked retaliatory measures by Russia against German industrial goods. Both countries raised their import duties several times in the course of the 1880s. The German government took steps that closed the Berlin stock exchange to the sale of Russian securities. Tensions between the two countries steadily increased.

The alliance between France and Russia, formalized in a series of separate agreements in 1891–94, appeared to many contemporaries as a step toward peace in Europe.[30] Even those who were on the whole critical of the autocracy agreed. The celebrated historian Vasily Kliuchevsky, in a speech devoted to the memory of Alexander III, said: "European civilization did not take sufficient care to secure its peaceful development. For its own safety it housed itself in a powder magazine. More than once, from various directions, a burning fuse approached this dangerous arsenal, and each time the solicitous and patient hand of the Russian tsar quietly and carefully deflected it . . . Europe acknowledged that the tsar of the Russian people was also a sovereign of international peace."[31]

The alliance and the fact that Russia engaged in no major wars in the 1880s and the early 1890s won Alexander III the sobriquet of "the Peacemaker" in conservative circles. However, the "peace" created by the Russo-French agreement of the early 1890s was based on profound contradictions. For a time it consolidated the balance of power in Europe, but it also contributed to the formation of opposing military and political blocs. In that respect it served as an important step toward World War I, a war that was fated to bring the history of the Russian Empire to a close.

Chapter 9

Under the Banner of Unshakable Autocracy

We have already referred several times to Alexander III, the son of Alexander II, who came to the throne when a terrorist's bomb killed his father in 1881. As we have seen, under Alexander III Russia carried out a major shift in its foreign policy, from its traditional alliance with Germany to an alignment with France. While still heir to the throne, Alexander Aleksandrovich had shown conservative sympathies, and upon coming to power he initiated a review of the innovations of the 1860s and the 1870s. Clearly, the era of Alexander III, from 1881 to 1894, played a vital role in the history of Imperial Russia. His reign marked the last period of protracted political stability in the empire, a time when the authorities still had the opportunity to mitigate, if not resolve, many of the problems that faced the country. They failed to do so. Beginning in the mid-1890s, social, political, ethnic, and religious tensions began to snowball, producing a full-scale crisis. The revolutionary upheavals of the early twentieth century buried the Romanov monarchy and ushered in the new Soviet period of Russian history.

To a considerable degree, these destructive upheavals resulted from the "counter-reforms" that aimed at revising the innovations of the 1860s and the 1870s. The counter-reforms abolished some of the institutions that Alexander II had introduced, such as university autonomy and the peace courts, and distorted others, including peasant self-government, the zemstvos, the municipal dumas, and trial by jury. The counter-reforms revealed the weakness of the reform process in Russia, which lacked any firm guarantees or a broad social base. The government undermined the innovations of previous decades without encountering significant resistance. In the long term, however, the counter-reforms had serious consequences. They contradicted

Emperor Alexander III. Photograph.

the course of development on which the country had embarked after the abolition of serfdom, and they aggravated relations between the government and society. In effect, they were an attempt to turn back the clock, for the government chose to depend on the most reactionary segments of Russian society. This state policy reflected both the contradictory and inconsistent results of the mid-century reforms and the personal characteristics of Emperor Alexander III.[1]

As the second son of Alexander II, Alexander III had not been prepared to reign. He became heir to the throne only at the age of twenty, after the death of his older brother, Nicholas. Only then did he begin to receive an extensive education, and until the end of his life he displayed serious gaps in his knowledge. The peculiarities of Alexander's intellect exacerbated his educational deficiencies. Although strong-willed and honest, he had a highly inflexible mind that led him to oversimplify reality. He came of age in the mid-1860s, when the contradictory results of the reforms were becoming apparent: the difficult circumstances of the emancipated peasantry, the conflicts between the administration and the institutions of self-government, the rise of the revolutionary movement, and the embezzlements and other abuses that marked the era of "concession fever." Alexander began to criticize his father's reforms, and his antipathy to liberal principles and attempts to follow Western models steadily increased.

The conservatives in his entourage confirmed his views. Alexander developed particularly close relations with his former tutor, Konstantin Pobedonostsev.[2] In the 1870s the heir's court became a center of attraction for various forces that were unhappy with the government's policies. They included not only outright reactionaries but men of broader views, such as Pan-Slavists and Slavophiles who did not reject reform but wanted to give it a distinct national character. Through Pobedonostsev, Alexander made the acquaintance of Fyodor Dostoevsky, studied the works of Iury Samarin, and attentively followed the activities of Ivan Aksakov. At a time when European models were influencing government policies, reactionaries and conservatives of various stripes formed a united front. Alexander criticized Dmitry Miliutin's military reforms for violating Russia's historical traditions, and in the mid-1870s the heir and his entourage demanded an active Russian policy in the Balkans. When military operations began, Alexander went to the Balkans and in 1877–78 commanded a large Russian military unit, the Rushchuk Detachment.

In the social and political crisis that marked the late 1870s and the early 1880s, Alexander demanded a ruthless campaign against the revolutionaries and the formation of a dictatorship to pursue it. He played an important part in the creation in 1880 of the Supreme Administrative Commission that Mikhail Loris-Melikov headed. In the first months of the "dictator-ship," Alexander and Loris-Melikov maintained fairly close relations. As Loris-Melikov began to give priority to liberal and reformist principles, however, they grew estranged. The assassination of Alexander II seriously undermined Loris-Melikov's position and ultimately led to his dismissal, if not immediately.

On first coming to the throne, Alexander III did not openly declare his political course.[3] Loris-Melikov's reform plan, which Alexander II had ap-proved, was in a sense the political testament of the deceased emperor, and it was awkward for his son to disregard it. Fear of the terrorists persisted, and their strength remained unknown. Zemstvos and private individuals addressed numerous petitions to the emperor insisting that reform must continue. Per-sonally, however, Alexander III was not inclined to adopt liberal measures, and the conservatives encouraged him to oppose them. Mikhail Katkov wrote articles blaming the liberals for the death of the Tsar-Liberator, while Pobedonostsev deluged Alexander with letters urging him to dismiss the "lib-eral dictator." At a March 8 meeting to discuss Loris-Melikov's plan, Pobedonostsev gave a thunderous speech denouncing the innovations of the 1860s and the 1870s as fruitless and harmful chatter, and the plan itself as an attempt to introduce a constitution, "an instrument of all kinds of injustice, an instrument of all kinds of intrigue . . . a deception based on a foreign model that is unsuitable for Russia."[4]

The statements of Katkov and Pobedonostsev gave Alexander the support he needed to reject any liberal plans. Convinced that the revolutionary un-derground had exhausted its strength, he finally sided with the conservatives. On April 29, 1881, he issued the Manifesto on Unshakable Autocracy, writ-ten by Pobedonostsev. "Amid our great sorrow," the manifesto proclaimed, "the voice of God commands us to take up vigorously the task of governing . . . with faith in the strength and truth of the autocratic power that we have been called upon to affirm and safeguard for the popular good from any infringement."[5] Loris-Melikov rightly interpreted the manifesto as an indi-cation that his plans were unacceptable and submitted his resignation. His close associates, Finance Minister Aleksandr Abaza and War Minister Dmitry Miliutin, also relinquished their posts. Thus the first resignation in Russian history of a "cabinet," a government of like-minded ministers, took place. Grand Duke Konstantin Nikolaevich, chairman of the State Council, naval minister, and prominent patron of the enlightened bureaucracy, resigned as well. The manifesto of April 29 was the most important ideological docu-ment of Alexander III's reign. The principle of "unshakable autocracy" that it proclaimed made a reexamination of the reforms of the 1860s and the 1870s inevitable.

The policy of counter-reform took shape gradually. The administration of Nikolai Ignatiev, who served as minister of internal affairs in 1881–82, was a transitional stage between Loris-Melikov and the policy of reaction. Ignatiev, an eminent diplomat and an active proponent of Pan-Slavism, had been ambassador to Turkey. As minister he pursued a program that was an odd combination of nationalist rhetoric and measures to benefit the masses. He proposed that the government utilize the peasants' monarchist instincts, arguing that improvements in their economic position would draw them closer to the throne. He therefore sought to continue the social and economic policies of Loris-Melikov. Ignatiev's administration implemented or planned a series of important agricultural measures that had first been proposed under Alexander II. The law of December 28, 1881, brought the remainder of the former privately owned serfs into the redemption process and lowered the redemption payments; the law of May 22, 1881, made it easier for peasants to rent state lands; and the soul tax was abolished between 1882 and 1886. Most of these measures were the work of the leading Russian reformer Nikolai Bunge, the minister of finance. His efforts also led to the establishment of a Peasant Land Bank, on May 18, 1882, to assist peasants in enlarging their allotments. Further legislation increased the taxation of the propertied classes and prepared the way for the introduction of an income tax.

Because Ignatiev had come into office after the publication of the Manifesto on Unshakable Autocracy, he devoted considerable effort to strengthening the power of the state. During his administration, the Regulation concerning Measures for the Protection of State Security and Public Tranquillity of August 14, 1881, discussed in chapter 5, went into effect. Stricter police controls led to the complete defeat of the revolutionary underground. The government sharply curtailed the rights of the Jews, whom it viewed as the bearers of destructive tendencies. The anti-Jewish "pogroms," organized attacks that broke out in the southwestern provinces of the Russian Empire in 1881–82, served as grounds for the measures against the Jews. The government claimed that the Jews themselves were responsible for the pogroms because they "exploited" the local population. The Temporary Rules of May 3, 1882, prohibited Jews from settling outside the cities and small towns and from selling liquor on Sundays or Christian holidays. The registration of real-estate agreements and of powers of attorney for the administration of real estate issued in the names of Jews ended. The anti-Jewish provisions were subsequently expanded. In 1887 the government issued a circular that set percentage quotas for Jews in secondary schools and institutions of higher education. Jews could not be appointed as court investigators or be admitted to the bar. In the early 1890s massive numbers of Jews were expelled from the interior provinces of Russia.[6]

Ignatiev's policy did not consist only of repression, however. While shoring up autocratic power, he also sought to expand its social base. On the local level he adopted a tolerant attitude toward the zemstvos and even invited zemstvo experts—admittedly, not elected but appointed by the government—to discuss certain administrative issues. Ignatiev intended his policies to culminate in the convocation of an Assembly of the Land, a consultative body of representatives modeled on the assemblies of pre-Petrine Russia. The plan was for a huge conference of three thousand individuals directly elected by the social estates, that is, the nobles, merchants, and peasants. Ignatiev's idea was that the Assembly of the Land would strengthen the tsar's authority without imposing limitations on it and without subjecting Russia to the negative aspects of parliamentarism, such as the conflict of political parties and the rise of professional politicians cut off from the people. The Assembly of the Land, Ivan Aksakov wrote, is a special type of representation capable of "shaming all the constitutions in the world. It is broader and more liberal than they are, while at the same time it maintains Russia's historical, political, and national foundations."[7]

The advocates of an Assembly of the Land were so sure of success that they had already drawn up a special plan to supply newspaper articles and reports on its meetings to the foreign press. For inveterate defenders of autocracy like Katkov and Pobedonostsev, however, the autocratic political system was clearly incompatible with any form of representation. Katkov initiated a campaign in the press against the Assembly of the Land, and Pobedonostsev again addressed letters to the tsar. "If will and authority pass from the government to any popular assembly whatsoever," he wrote, "the result will be a revolution, the ruin of the government, and the ruin of Russia."[8] The arguments of the conservatives convinced the emperor to reject Ignatiev's plan. In May 1882 he dismissed Ignatiev and replaced him with Dmitry Tolstoi. As minister of public education in the 1860s and the 1870s, Tolstoi had earned a reputation as a zealous defender of conservative and authoritarian principles. "The very name of Count Tolstoi," Katkov exulted, "is itself a manifesto and a program."[9] Tolstoi's appointment marked the government's definitive turn to a policy of reaction.

Before giving an account of that policy, however, we need to discuss the activities of Nikolai Bunge, who served as minister of finance until the end of 1886. Bunge occupied a peculiar position in Alexander III's government. An eminent economist, a proponent of Western theories, and a participant in the planning of the peasant reform of 1861, he had risen to the heights of power at a time of increasing conservatism. On the eve of Alexander III's accession, Bunge was serving as deputy minister of finance under the economic liberal Aleksandr Abaza, and when Abaza fell from power it appeared that Bunge also would lose his post. In the social and economic sphere, as distinct from the political, however, the autocracy had less room for maneuver. Because the authorities feared disruption of the national economy and the possibility of social upheavals, they felt obliged to continue the economic policies that Loris-Melikov had initiated. The task of pursuing those policies fell to Bunge, who succeeded Abaza as finance minister.

Although an adherent of economic liberalism, Bunge naturally had to tailor his actions to the conservative course that Alexander III's government was pursuing. Also, he drew a lesson from the negative consequences of Reutern's policies. State intervention in the economy, which had already begun under Reutern, intensified under Bunge. The authorities began to impose stricter controls on commercial banks and other corporations, steadily increased customs duties, and greatly expanded the construction of state-owned railroads as well as the government's purchase of privately owned lines. By the early 1890s two-thirds of Russia's railroads belonged to the state.[10] Nevertheless, Bunge's strategic objective remained what it had been under Alexander II, the development of market relations. He wrote: "The state would be embarking on a dangerous path if it . . . engaged in those branches of industry that private entrepreneurs have successfully pursued, if it took it into its head to monopolize mining, mills, and factories . . . The intrusion of the state into industrial enterprise would mark the start of the unlimited power of the administration to set prices, a power hitherto unknown and one which, of course, would be mightier than any possible coalition of capitalists."[11]

Bunge's fear of "the unlimited power of the administration" arose in large part from the dissemination in the late nineteenth century of socialist theories that proclaimed the necessity of abolishing private property. An unconditional opponent of socialism, he regarded socialist theories as "an evil that would destroy morality, duty, liberty, and the individual." Those theories appeared particularly dangerous because the workers' movement, which was well developed in the West, had already made its appearance in Russia. The first significant actions by industrial workers that drew the attention of Russian society came at the end of the 1870s. In 1885 a major strike broke out at the Morozov textile factory outside of Moscow. Well organized and stubborn, the strikers elected their own leaders and presented the factory administration and the authorities with collective demands. The leaders of the strike were tried before a jury, which acquitted them on all counts. The government was forced to satisfy some of the strikers' demands. To prevent the growth of worker discontent, Bunge believed, the government should take steps "not only to protect each member [of the working class] from accidental calamities but to eliminate discord and conflicts of interest between capital and labor, on the one hand, and among the workers themselves, on the other."[12]

At Bunge's insistence, the government began to pass labor legislation. Laws of 1882 and 1885 regulated the working conditions of women and juveniles and introduced a system of factory inspectors to enforce the regulations. A law of 1886 specified the procedures for hiring and firing workers, the payment of wages, and the levying of fines by the factory owners. In Bunge's opinion, these regulations represented just the first step toward resolving the worker question. He intended to follow them with a series of broader measures to improve workers' living conditions, to allow profit sharing, and even to begin legalizing trade unions. He proposed the adoption of laws on sanitary conditions in the factories, obligatory industrial training, accident insurance, the investigation of disputes between workers and factory owners, the establishment of mutual-assistance funds, and the construction of workers' housing, bathhouses, laundries, cafeterias, and reading rooms.

Bunge's plans and policies elicited growing hostility from the conservatives, who declared him "part of the party that went down to defeat on April 29, 1881." The conservatives claimed that Bunge's policies "whetted the appetites" of the masses, incited them to make greater and greater demands, and gave rise to unrealistic expectations. Pobedonostsev called the agrarian reforms of the early 1880s "a waste of state funds and the introduction of corrupting principles into the people's consciousness." Katkov scornfully declared that all Bunge's "wisdom" came out of "German books." The Moscow journalist presented a program for the creation of a "national economy" that included a sharp increase in protective tariffs, state intervention in the country's economic life, greater circulation of paper money, and a state monopoly on certain forms of economic activity.[13] Pressure from the conservatives forced Bunge to resign his post on January 1, 1887.

Bunge's departure and the abandonment of the social programs he was planning had dire consequences. The prominent physics professor and corporate executive Ivan Vyshnegradsky, who replaced Bunge, ignored the social aspects of his predecessor's activities. Instead, he concentrated exclusively on achieving the fiscal goal of a balanced budget through an increase in taxes and a positive trade balance.[14] Vyshnegradsky adamantly pressed the peasants for back taxes and redemption dues and forced them to sell their grain at low prices in order to increase exports. He described the essence of his program with the slogan "We ourselves will eat less, but we will export." The results quickly made themselves felt. Weakened by heavy taxes, the peasant economy exhausted its reserves and was unable to withstand a natural calamity. In 1891–92 a vast famine struck a number of Russian provinces, followed by a cholera epidemic. The famine and epidemic killed an estimated 500,000 people.[15]

To make matters worse, the autocracy adopted a series of measures in the second half of the 1880s and the early 1890s aimed at preserving the patriarchal and communal practices of peasant life. The expectation that the Emancipation of 1861 would enable the peasants to become individual landowners failed to materialize. The authorities came to view the commune and the institutions associated with it, such as large families and collective responsibility, as the best means of maintaining stability in the countryside. A law of March 18, 1886, increased the power of the head of the family (the *bolshak)* and made it considerably harder for younger family members to create separate households. An 1889 law made it more difficult for peasants to emigrate. A law of December 14, 1893, abolished the provision of the Emancipation Statute that permitted a peasant to separate from the commune upon completion of his redemption payments. Peasants were prohibited from mortgaging their allotments or renting them to anyone outside the commune. These laws did not improve the peasants' situation or prevent the social stratification of the peasantry, but they did hinder peasants' efforts to develop commercial agriculture. The agrarian legislation, in combination with the relentless exaction of resources from the peasants, technological stagnation in agriculture, and the unrelenting increase in the size of the peasant population, contributed to the outburst of mass discontent that gripped the Russian countryside at the beginning of the twentieth century.

The government's political and ideological policies also fostered social tensions. Many of these policies bore the stamp of Konstantin Pobedonostsev, who occupied a special place in the conservative camp. Although he was a decided opponent of liberal principles, he was skeptical of a reactionary revision of the institutions that had been created in the 1860s and the 1870s. When the first counter-reform, the University Statute of 1884, was under discussion, he declared: "Why create a new institution . . . when the old one is impotent only because the people in it are not doing their work properly?"[16] Pobedonostsev feared legislative or administrative change, even a reactionary one. His remedy was to focus on the "re-education" of society, on its spiritual regeneration. From 1880 onward, he served as supreme procurator of the Holy Synod. In that capacity he took energetic steps to strengthen the Orthodox Church as it struggled against secular tendencies that had been developing in Russia since the time of Peter the Great and had triumphed in Europe by the end of the nineteenth century. In the 1880s and the early 1890s he helped to create up to 250 churches and 10 monasteries each year. The number of white clergy, or priests, grew in those years by 20 percent, to 56,900, while the number of black clergy, or monks, grew by 64 percent, to 45,500. The growth of church schools for the common people was particularly striking. By 1894 the number of such schools had increased sevenfold, to 31,835, and the number of pupils enrolled in them had increased ninefold, from 105,317 to 981,076.[17]

Pobedonostsev regarded the religious outlook, with its doctrines of patience, humility, and submission to authority, as the greatest obstacle to the spread of destructive revolutionary ideas. Therefore he sought ways to strengthen the influence of religion on society. Besides expanding the network of parish schools, he urged the clergy to deliver more sermons. He encouraged the formation of church brotherhoods, the publication of spiritual literature, the building of churches in the old Russian style, and the holding of church festivals for the masses. Most of those efforts proved fruitless. The secularization of Russian life had advanced too far. The attempt to impose religious influence on society had little effect on the common people and aroused dissatisfaction in educated circles. Despite measures to revitalize the Church, it remained under strict bureaucratic control. The clergy showed little enthusiasm for Pobedonostsev's educational programs. Administrative pressure to rouse the clergy from its lethargy had the opposite effect, increasing its resentment of the secular authorities. The growing dissatisfaction in the Church with Pobedonostsev's policies expressed itself in 1905 in demands by both the episcopate and the parish clergy to abolish secular control of the Church. They called for restoration of the canonical structure of church administration that Peter I had abolished, that is, a patriarch and periodic church councils. The clergy's opposition to the existing system of church–state relations would become an important element in the social and political crisis of the early twentieth century.

Pobedonostsev's religious policies had an even more damaging impact on the borderlands of the Russian Empire. Besides advocating greater influence for the Orthodox Church on Russian society, Pobedonostsev strove to fortify its position in the non-Orthodox regions. In the 1880s and the early 1890s the Orthodox Church expanded its influence. Orthodox missionaries often made use of the coercive powers of the state in carrying out their activities against Islam and Tibetan Buddhism in the eastern parts of the empire. The Russian authorities continued to exert pressure on Catholicism in Poland and the western provinces and even began to persecute the Lutheran Church in the relatively peaceful Baltic region.[18] Pobedonostsev's policies failed. His attempts to spread Orthodoxy by force alienated many otherwise loyal and conservative-minded people. Instead of fostering the unity of the Russian Empire, religious persecution generated social and political unrest and prepared the way for the empire's disintegration.

The failure of Pobedonostsev's policies led to the gradual decline of his authority in the government. His hostility to administrative reform, combined with the equivocal results of his religious and ideological policies, bewildered many conservatives, who found his approach strange and capricious. The suspicion arose that Pobedonostsev had a "nihilistic mentality" that rendered him incapable of putting forth a positive program. By the end of the 1880s the supreme procurator had lost much of his influence. Nevertheless, the authorities did not entirely renounce the policies he had initiated. The government of Alexander III continued to regard them as the ideological counterpart of the legislative and administrative changes it was pursuing, that is, the counter-reforms.

The government's onslaught on dissent was the most important step in preparing for the counter-reforms. All the conservatives agreed that this was essential. On August 27, 1882, the government issued new Temporary Rules on the Press that greatly expanded administrative control over periodical publications. A committee composed of the ministers of justice, public education, and internal affairs and the supreme procurator of the Holy Synod could now shut down any periodical by decree, without a court trial. Over the next several years, the authorities closed many newspapers and journals that espoused left-liberal or radical views. The minister of internal affairs had the right to prohibit discussion in the press of sensitive social and political issues, such as the agrarian question, conflicts between the zemstvos and the administration, and student unrest. The government purged libraries of "harmful" publications, including books by Nikolai Dobroliubov, Dmitry Pisarev, Louis Blanc, Karl Marx, Herbert Spencer, and Adam Smith.[19] In a symbolic expression of its break with earlier policies, the government in 1886 prohibited any mention in the press of the twenty-fifth anniversary of the abolition of serfdom.

Conservatives regarded the universities, as well as the press, as a source of destructive ideas. They sincerely believed that a mistaken approach to education had contributed to the social and political upheavals of the previous decades. In the late 1870s Katkov and his associates drew up a proposal for university counter-reform, and at the beginning of the new reign the government began to discuss it. The plan called for greater administrative control over the content of education as well as the daily life and social composition of the student body. Government officials were to be in charge of giving examinations, thereby permitting them to control not only the level of students' knowledge but the content of professors' lectures. The authorities would have the right to confirm examination requirements and curricula. The proposal abolished the university court and created inspectors independent of the faculty to supervise the students.[20] Finally, it limited the number of lower-class students admitted to universities and secondary schools. In 1887 the government abolished preparatory classes for the high schools and issued its famous circular on "the children of cooks." The circular recommended exclusion from the high schools of "the children of coachmen, cooks, laundresses, and petty shopkeepers, whose offspring, except for the unusually gifted, should not rise above the social station to which they belong."[21]

The government intended not only to control the content of education but to restructure university administration. The university counter-reform eliminated the election of professors, deans, and rectors and greatly limited the rights of the University Council. The government regarded the abolition of university autonomy as a rehearsal of sorts for subsequent counter-reforms. Implementing the university counter-reform proved difficult, however. Important changes in the law, such as the revision of the university statute, required a decision by the State Council, the highest legislative-review body of the Russian Empire. In the 1880s the State Council contained some retired government ministers who still shared the views of the enlightened bureaucracy. Naturally, they opposed the university counter-reform.[22]

Even such a staunch conservative as Pobedonostsev opposed Katkov's proposal, on the grounds that it would undermine the scholarly standards of the universities and reduce their administration to chaos. In the end, the State Council confirmed the new university statute only through behind-the-scenes maneuvering. At the insistence of Katkov and his supporters, the tsar convened a special meeting that excluded all opponents of the measure except Pobedonostsev. The supreme procurator had to bow to the pressure of Katkov's adherents. The new statute, adopted with a few concessions, received Alexander III's confirmation on August 15, 1884. The university counter-reform reflected the degree to which destructive tendencies had penetrated the governmental apparatus of the Russian Empire. From then on, Russia's monarchs would increasingly circumvent official bureaucratic channels. They would rely on personally trusted advisers from outside the government, set ministers against each other, and provoke inter-departmental discord. Such practices contributed to the steady breakdown of the autocratic system and its administrative structure.

The university counter-reform increased the prerogatives of the administration, but it did not resolve the conflicts between the authorities and the university faculties. Those conflicts deepened and then erupted with renewed force at the beginning of the twentieth century. Student unrest also continued to fester. A wave of student disturbances broke out in Russian universities in 1886–87. From the mid-1890s onward, university disorders and strikes followed one another in rapid succession. Under Alexander III, however, they remained a distant prospect. The conservatives believed that the adoption of the new university statute represented a significant victory, one that opened the way to the restoration of strong authoritarian rule. "Rise, gentlemen," Katkov triumphantly proclaimed, "the government is in session, the government is returning!"[23]

After achieving revision of the university statute, the conservatives turned their attention to a more difficult task, the counter-reform of local self-government. The first step was to increase the influence of the nobility and enhance its public functions. The government began to change its social policy immediately after rejecting Ignatiev's concept of a "popular autocracy." Upon his appointment as minister of internal affairs, Dmitry Tolstoi told the tsar that he did "not recognize a peasant Russia." Then he added, referring to the nobility: "Your ancestors created Russia, but they created her with our hands."[24] Alexander III was inclined to regard such sentiments favorably. In response to a wave of petitions from conservative-minded landowners, the government set out to shore up the economic position of the gentry. In 1885, on the hundredth anniversary of Catherine the Great's Charter to the Nobility, the government established a Gentry Land Bank, which issued loans to landowners on preferential terms. In the following year, a Law on the Hiring of Agricultural Labor considerably expanded the rights of landowners over peasants hired to work for them. The imperial rescript on the anniversary of the Charter to the Nobility stated: "We recognize it as a blessing for the benefit of the state that Russian nobles, now as in former times, have continued to occupy the preeminent position in military leadership, in local courts and self-government, in selfless care for the needs of the people, and, by their example, in the spread . . . of sound principles of public education."[25]

In 1885 Aleksandr Pazukhin, a district marshal of the nobility from Simbirsk province, published an article in Katkov's *Russian Herald* that provided a theoretical basis for the government's new pro-gentry course. Pazukhin criticized Alexander II's reforms and demanded changes in the institutions they had created. In his opinion, the reforms had weakened the gentry's role as the natural link between the autocracy and the people and had eroded social stability in Russia. The intelligentsia came to occupy the gentry's place, even though it rejected historical tradition and was hostile to autocracy. "If we see a great evil in the previous reign's destruction of the system of social estates," Pazukhin wrote, "then the task of the present reign should be to restore what was destroyed."[26] The revival of the system of social estates, he argued, should accompany the strengthening of authoritarian rule and limitations on the independence of the courts and local self-government. In combining restoration of the system of social estates with the reinforcement of autocratic power, Pazukhin identified both the social basis of the forthcoming counter-reforms and the means of implementing them. Soon after publishing this article, Pazukhin was appointed director of the chancellery of the ministry of internal affairs. He played an important part in preparing the counter-reforms.

The first target of counter-reform was the system of peasant self-government. The need for reform had in fact been recognized for some time. The authors of the Emancipation Statute of 1861 had regarded the social exclusiveness of peasant institutions as a temporary measure, and by the 1880s those institutions were clearly an anachronism. Ignatiev initiated a reform project that would have substantially diminished the separate status of peasant self-government by giving the all-estate zemstvos far-reaching prerogatives in local affairs, but the government's adoption of a pro-gentry policy brought his project to a halt. Pazukhin's new program for the reform of local administration, by contrast, preserved the separate status of peasant institutions. In addition, it subordinated them to the authority of "land captains," officials drawn from the local gentry who were under the jurisdiction of the Ministry of Internal Affairs.[27]

Pazukhin's plan cut short the expansion of peasant autonomy that the Emancipation Statute had envisaged. The decision that the authorities made at the beginning of the 1880s to reject representative government now made the gentry the sole connecting link between the government and the peasants, who formed the great majority of the Russian population. The government's economic support of the local gentry strengthened the landowners' tutelage over the peasants still further.

The government's desire to preserve the traditional patriarchal practices of peasant life, which manifestly contradicted the needs of the time, required the peasants' subordination to strict authoritarian control. The powers granted to the land captains enabled them to assert that control. They had the right to overrule any decision by a peasant court or institution, to remove peasant judges and officials, to fine the peasants, to arrest them for short periods, and to subject them to corporal punishment. The power that the landowners now wielded over the peasants resembled pre-1861 practices to such a degree that rumors spread among the peasants of the impending restoration of serfdom.

The concentration of judicial and administrative authority in the hands of the land captains led to the abolition of the peace courts throughout most of the Russian Empire, a serious violation of the principles of the judicial reform of 1864. The judicial counter-reform, one of the most important elements of the conservatives' plans, succeeded in part. A law of May 25, 1885, limited the irremovability of judges by creating a body called the Highest Disciplinary Court. The law of February 12, 1887, curtailed the openness of court sessions to the public. Laws of April 28 and July 7, 1889, raised the qualifications for jurors and narrowed the competence of jury courts. Wholesale judicial counter-reform did not occur, however. A commission for a comprehensive review of the Judicial Statutes was appointed only in 1894, and the social unrest that began at the time cut short its activities.[28]

Now that officials appointed by the government supervised the system of peasant self-government and combined both judicial and administrative functions, the stage was set for counter-reform of the zemstvos. Pazukhin drafted a proposal to strengthen representation by social estate and to limit the zemstvo's autonomy from the government. He planned to abolish the executive boards of the zemstvos and replace them with district and provincial administrative offices, the staff of which would be selected by the governor and work under his supervision. Pazukhin's proposal was so radical that it frightened many conservatives in the government. Pobedonostsev opposed abolishing the zemstvo boards. He wrote, "One may ask the purpose of this fundamental distortion, as it seems to me, of the original concept of the legislation, and the restoration in local economic administration of precisely the bureaucratic principle that it would be desirable . . . to avoid there."[29]

The opponents of Pazukhin's proposal feared the growth of uncontrolled bureaucratic power as well as disruption of the zemstvos' economic activities. The proposal encountered serious opposition when it came before the State Council. In the end, the authorities concluded that it was unnecessary to abolish the zemstvo boards and to press for the complete abolition of zemstvo autonomy.

The new Regulation on Zemstvo Institutions of June 12, 1890, nevertheless considerably expanded the administration's control over the zemstvos as well as the role of social-estate membership in zemstvo elections. The new system of zemstvo elections mandated by the Regulation of 1890 cut short a trend that had begun in the 1860s and the 1870s, the incorporation of new bourgeois elements into the zemstvos. The Regulation deprived certain categories of the population of voting rights and reduced the size of the zemstvo assemblies. The first curia, which previously included all landowners, now consisted exclusively of nobles, and the property requirement for voting in this curia was greatly reduced. At the same time, the property requirement for voting in the second curia, which consisted of urban electors, rose substantially. The peasants in effect lost their electoral rights. Now they could only submit lists of candidates for the zemstvo assemblies, from which the governor selected the deputies on the recommendation of the land captains. All told, about half the voters lost the right to vote, and the nobles now held an absolute preponderance in the district zemstvo assemblies. This change had a particularly harmful effect on the work of the zemstvos, for there were often too few noble landowners in the first curia to elect deputies. The activities of the reorganized zemstvos suffered as a result, focusing less than before on peasant interests.[30]

Because the zemstvo managed to retain its status as an institution of self-government, it continued to come into conflict with the administration even after the counter-reform. The clashes died down under Alexander III, only to flare up again in the mid-1890s.

On June 11, 1892, the municipal dumas underwent a counter-reform similar to that of the zemstvos. The new law substantially raised the property requirement for voting, thus considerably reducing the number of municipal voters. Not just the lower classes but the middle strata of the towns, such as civil servants, petty traders, and entrepreneurs, lost the right to vote. Noble homeowners and wealthy bourgeois now predominated in elections. Under these provisions, the number of voters fell by between one-half and three-quarters in most of the towns. No more than 0.7 percent of the population participated in elections in Moscow and Petersburg. Like the zemstvos, the dumas came under strict state control. The provincial governor now oversaw nearly all the decisions of the institutions of self-government, both urban and rural. He had to confirm the members of the zemstvo and duma boards in office, and they were now considered to be in state service.[31]

The changes introduced in the 1880s and the early 1890s enhanced the importance of the traditional social estates, undermined the reforms of the 1860s and the 1870s, and enabled the government to assert a much greater degree of control over society. Supporters of Alexander III, citing the absence of major revolutionary disturbances during his reign, regarded the restoration of order as the emperor's greatest service. From the conservatives' point of view, Alexander was the "Peacemaker" in internal affairs as well as in the international arena. The "pacification" that his reign achieved, however, was in large part illusory. The preservation of the system of social estates and of the patriarchal and communal customs of the peasantry contradicted the accelerated pace of industrial development that the government itself was encouraging. The pursuit of two divergent social and economic policies was bound to have tragic consequences, the first sign of which was the famine of 1891–92. Curtailing the rights of the zemstvos, the courts, the universities, and the press embittered relations between the administration and society and prepared the ground for wide-ranging political conflict. Finally, ethnic and religious persecutions strained the government's relations with the population in the borderlands of the Russian Empire. By the end of Alexander III's reign, Russia stood on the brink of major upheavals; it had truly become a knot of contradictions. The task of untying that knot fell to Alexander's son, Nicholas II.

Chapter 10

Nicholas II: A Policy of Contradictions

On January 17, 1895, Nicholas II, fated to be the last emperor in Russian history, began his reign with an address to delegations from the zemstvos, towns, nobility, and Cossacks: "I know that of late, in some zemstvo assemblies, voices have been heard of people carried away by senseless dreams of the participation of representatives of the zemstvos in matters of internal administration. Let it be known to all that I, while devoting all my strength to the good of the nation, will safeguard the principle of autocracy just as firmly and steadfastly as did my late unforgettable father."[1]

Russia faced a historic choice in the reign of Nicholas II. Would the country follow the path of reform or revolution? Would the old order remain standing or collapse? By the turn of the twentieth century, the many contradictions that were slowly gathering in Russian life had tied themselves into a single knot, making a peaceful outcome of the crisis extremely difficult. The personal characteristics and political outlook of Nicholas II, especially his uncompromising adherence to the principle of unlimited autocracy, played a major role in causing about the eventual revolution.[2]

As the eldest son of Alexander III, Nicholas had been destined for the throne since childhood. He received a thorough education in, among other things, foreign languages, law, economics, and military science. His teachers included the best educators of the day. However, Nicholas lacked any practical experience in government. Alexander III had counted on gradually preparing his son for the throne and for a long time gave him no governmental responsibilities. The untimely death of the Tsar-Peacemaker thrust his son to the pinnacle of power without the preparation that he needed, and from the beginning Nicholas's inexperience had an adverse effect on

Emperor Nicholas II. Photograph.

the functioning of the bureaucratic apparatus. In addition to his lack of familiarity with governmental affairs, the tsar was physically unimposing—he was short and suffered from shyness. To contemporaries, Nicholas II looked like "a pathetic provincial actor playing an emperor, a role for which he was unsuited."[3]

Nicholas himself realized that he did not have the personal qualities his high state position required. More than once he remarked with bitter irony that he had been born on the day of Job the Sufferer, and indeed misfortune would follow him throughout his life. He preferred his family circle, where he was profoundly and unconditionally happy, to affairs of state. Soon after he came to the throne, he married Princess Alix of Hesse-Darmstadt, who became Alexandra Fyodorovna upon her adoption of Orthodoxy. To the end of his days, he remained bound to her by a deep and sincere love. "All my life the worst has always come to pass, precisely what I feared most," Nicholas wrote in his diary after his accession, "but along with such irremediable sorrow, the Lord has also rewarded me with a happiness of which I could not even have dreamt, in giving me Alix."[4] Nicholas's character and attitudes would seem to have created suitable conditions for limiting the tsar's power and introducing constitutional government. That course, however, was unacceptable to Nicholas II.

As the son of Alexander III and a pupil of Konstantin Pobedonostsev, Nicholas was deeply convinced that autocracy was a form of power that had been handed down from on high; it was a sacred gift, and he had an obligation to bequeath it unchanged to his heir. "I myself will bear the burden of power that was placed on me in the Moscow Kremlin. I will account for my power before God."[5] That statement, which Nicholas made during one of the official ceremonies at his accession, perfectly expresses the essence of his worldview. His own understanding of the relations between state and society also made him a defender of autocracy. The last emperor never doubted that the "simple folk" remained sincerely devoted to tsarist power, and that demands for political reform came solely from an intelligentsia that had cut itself off from its roots in the people. He therefore believed that the best way to maintain social and political stability in the country was to be as firm and unyielding as possible in preserving tsarist authority.

Nicholas's wife reinforced his political views. Unlike her husband, Alexandra possessed a strong will and an imperious character. As a granddaughter of Queen Victoria of England, she had been brought up at Victoria's court and might have been expected to bring the influence of constitutional ideas to bear in Russia. Just the opposite occurred, however, and in Russia she became a fierce and uncompromising champion of autocracy. That outlook gained support from her devotion to Orthodoxy, which in her mind was inseparable from conservative ideas, and from her hostility to the high society of St. Petersburg. She believed that the bearers of true religious feeling came from the common people, and she welcomed various "prophets," "elders," and "soothsayers" to the palace. The best known of those prophets was Grigory Rasputin, a Siberian peasant who enjoyed immense authority in the eyes of Nicholas and Alexandra while undermining the authority of the monarchy with his scandalous behavior outside the palace.

Nicholas and his wife opposed nearly all the political trends of their time. They were enraptured with the pre-Petrine era, a time, according to the Slavophiles, when society was permeated with deep religious feeling and the tsar lived in peace and unity with the people. Contrary to long-standing tradition, Nicholas named his only son Alexis. The name had not been given to heirs to the throne since the tragic death of Peter the Great's son, who was executed for participating in a conspiracy against his father. Nicholas encouraged the building of churches in the pre-Petrine style, and in 1903 he gave a grand costume ball at the palace at which the imperial couple and the aristocracy appeared in traditional Russian dress.[6] Unlike most of his predecessors on the throne, Nicholas regarded Peter the Great, the founder of the empire, with manifest disapproval. "This is an ancestor whom I love less than the others because of his enthusiasm for Western culture and his flouting of all purely Russian customs," the tsar declared. "Foreign ways cannot be implanted all at once, without recasting them. Perhaps that was a transitional era and it was necessary, but I find it unappealing."[7]

Nicholas had even less sympathy for those who wanted to transform Russia along Western lines. Liberals who had expected the young tsar's accession to the throne to moderate the government's policies were bitterly disappointed. In his speech of January 17, 1895, Nicholas spelled out the course his government would follow. The authorities immediately began to attack the zemstvos, which were considered the driving force of the opposition. Over the next several years, the government sharply curtailed the competence of the zemstvos. It limited their right to levy taxes, created obstacles to their publishing activities and their contacts with one another, halted their statistical research, and removed famine relief from their jurisdiction. The Ministry of Internal Affairs subjected the most opposition-minded zemstvos to irksome inspections and refused to confirm many well-known zemstvo leaders in their posts.

The authorities harshly suppressed any protest by workers, peasants, students, and ethnic minorities. At the same time, the government continued to support the authority of the local gentry as the main pillar of the throne. A Special Conference on the Needs of the Noble Estate met from 1897 to 1901 "to secure to the preeminent estate the predominant significance it has had for the fate of the country since time immemorial."[8] The conference resulted in several measures to strengthen the state's financial support for the landowners. The defense of conservative principles and the tightening of repression could not resolve the problems the country faced, however. Socio-economic pressures and a growing opposition movement forced the government to make tactical concessions, one of which was the proposal in 1896 by Minister of Internal Affairs Ivan Goremykin to establish zemstvos in the Western Region (*Zapadnyi krai*) and several other borderland provinces.

The idea of introducing zemstvos in the Western Region was closely connected with the autocracy's overall policy toward ethnic minorities in the 1880s and the 1890s. As part of the turn to conservatism in the reign of Alexander III, the government had begun to curtail the autonomy of the empire's borderlands and to unify and Russify the imperial administration. In addition to discrimination against the Jews, this policy included limiting the rights of the Muslim population of the Volga and Urals regions, replacing the Caucasian Viceregency in the Transcaucasus with the regular system of imperial administration, and abolishing the traditional administrative, police, and judicial institutions of the Baltic provinces. At the turn of the century, the authorities extended the policy of unification and Russification to Armenia and Finland. New regulations in the early 1900s abolished the autonomy of the Armenian Church and placed its property under state control. In 1899–1901, the government began to attack Finland's extensive constitutional rights. It limited the jurisdiction of the Finnish Diet (parliament), introduced the use of the Russian language in Finnish administrative institutions, abolished the separate Finnish army units, and began to appoint Russians to Finnish administrative posts.[9]

The Western Region, which included Lithuania, Belorussia, and parts of Ukraine, territories that had previously belonged to Poland, occupied a special place in the autocracy's ethnic policy. Ever since the Polish insurrection of 1830–31, St. Petersburg had sought to undermine the influence of the local Polish Catholic elites and more fully integrate the region into the empire. The imperial authorities regarded as their main source of support the local Ukrainian and Belorussian peasants, who were Orthodox and whose language was close to Russian. The peasants, however, had little cultural or economic influence in the region. To give them a greater role, Goremykin proposed that the zemstvos to be established in the Western Region should retain the electoral system of 1864, under which all landowners, not just nobles, voted in the first curia. That arrangement would have represented a compromise between the official ethnic policy and the liberal principles of the Great Reforms. Conservative sentiment in the government was so strong, however, that it precluded even this modest step. One of the most influential dignitaries who opposed Goremykin was Minister of Finance Sergei Witte. "One does not place one's bet on both the red and the black squares at the same time," he wrote in a memorandum to the tsar. "It is inappropriate to speak on the one hand of the development of social initiative and the principle of self-government, and to plan its territorial expansion, while suppressing all initiative . . . One cannot create liberal forms without giving them a corresponding content."[10] In fact, Witte accused his colleague of seeking to undermine the foundations of autocracy. Goremykin lost his battle with Witte and was forced to resign in 1899.

It should be pointed out that the clash between Witte and Goremykin was less an ideological confrontation than the product of an inter-departmental rivalry that in many ways determined the policies of the autocracy at the turn of the century. In the 1890s the Ministry of Finance had accumulated a great deal of authority within the bureaucracy, eclipsing the Ministry of Internal Affairs. In a time of rapid industrialization, economic issues took on increased significance in the government's policies. By the end of the decade, the Ministry of Finance, besides exercising jurisdiction over the budget and taxation, supervised industry and the banking system, regulated relations between workers and factory owners through the system of factory inspectors, and managed commercial ports, the border guards, a network of professional training institutions, and Russia's trade representatives abroad. As a result of his department's extensive responsibilities, Witte confidently began to behave like an informal prime minister. We must therefore examine the character of this outstanding official, who played such an important role in Russia's economic and political history.[11]

One of the most talented of Nicholas II's officials, Witte in many respects was the exact opposite of his monarch. Whereas Nicholas turned his face to the past, Witte, through all the ups and downs of his career, stayed firmly in touch with the present. His father, a nobleman who served as a high official in the Caucasian Viceregency, suffered financial ruin as a result of unsuccessful investments in the Transcaucasus mining industry. Left without resources, Witte had to take a "plebeian" job in the administration of the Southwestern Railroad upon graduating from university. There he made a brilliant career. His university education in mathematics helped him to improve the system of freight rates, introduce various technical innovations, and reorganize the administration, thereby significantly increasing the profitability of the company. In 1889 he was invited to enter the government as director of the Department of Railroads in the Ministry of Finance. The department offered too few opportunities for such an ambitious politician, however, and in 1892 he became minister of transport and just a few months later minister of finance. Witte displayed enormous energy in that post. He devoted his efforts particularly to the rapid industrialization of Russia, with the intention of catching up to the leading industrial countries of the West within ten years. What was the reasoning behind his program?

First, he sought to end Russia's dependence on the West for technology and raw materials, because the need to import machinery, coal, and metal placed a heavy burden on the Russian economy. Second, as always, military and strategic considerations played an important role. Finally, Witte assumed that industrial development would serve as the basis for the country's rearmament and general economic growth. "In the history of the material culture of every state," he emphasized, "the development of industry is rightly considered a vital factor in the economic life of the people. Exclusively agricultural countries are correctly acknowledged to be poorer than those in which the people's labor finds diverse applications and thereby creates new sources of prosperity."[12]

Witte understood that in an agricultural but capital-poor country like Russia heavy industry would have to be largely an artificial creation. He wrote to the tsar: "The circumstances of our country required intensive state intervention in the most diverse aspects of social life, fundamentally distinguishing it from England, for example, where everything is left to private initiative . . . and where the state merely regulates private activity."[13] Under Witte, the state used various methods to influence the economy. It gave entrepreneurs huge subsidies and credits, state orders, and tax privileges. It also protected Russian industry with tariffs, which reached their peak under Witte. Increased tariffs imposed a burden on Russian consumers, who had to pay higher prices for imported products. To Witte, however, that was inevitable: "Great tasks demand great sacrifices."

Witte's industrialization program exacted "great sacrifices" from the population in other ways as well. Consumers had to pay high excise, or indirect, taxes on salt, matches, and sugar, and on the purchase of alcohol from the government. In the 1890s revenues from these indirect taxes grew by 42.7 percent.[14] At Witte's insistence, the sale of alcoholic beverages, which had always played an enormous role in Russia's financial system, passed entirely into the hands of the state when it introduced the so-called "liquor monopoly." The proceeds from this monopoly grew steadily, and by 1913 they were almost three times as large as the revenue from all direct taxes put together. As a result, the state budget with some justification came to be called the "drunken budget."[15]

Witte's greatest achievement, the introduction of the gold standard in 1897, also required sacrifices from the population. In preparation for the transition to a gold ruble, the government for many years extracted resources from the peasants in order to ensure a positive balance of trade. Like all of Witte's undertakings, the adoption of the gold standard had highly contradictory effects. It increased the flow of foreign capital into Russia, but at the same time it severely penalized the producers and exporters of grain, Russia's basic export, who had previously benefited from the low exchange rate of the Russian ruble relative to foreign currencies.

Witte's opponents, particularly among the provincial gentry, sharply criticized his policies and accused him of ruining Russian agriculture. The most astute critics argued that industrial growth had to be based on rising demand, which required expansion of the internal market. The prominent economist and government official Vladimir Gurko wrote in the newspaper *New Times,* "Are we really in a position to reverse that order by creating industry first and only then guaranteeing a market for its products by increasing the well-being of the masses?"[16] Witte, however, feeling that he had the support of Nicholas II, long ignored the criticism. To Nicholas, Witte's program seemed a covert way of resolving the country's problems without resorting to far-reaching social and political reforms.

At the turn of the twentieth century, it seemed to many Russians that the program was fulfilling the emperor's expectations. In fact, the results of Witte's activities stagger the imagination. Between 1893 and 1899 the production of ferrous metal and machinery almost tripled, as did the production of oil and coal. Russia could now dispense almost entirely with the importation of metals. The amount of railroad track almost doubled. The industrial boom of the 1890s produced about 40 percent of Russia's railroads and industrial enterprises, more than 60 percent of the joint-stock companies, and 85 percent of the foreign companies active in Russia in 1900. Foreign capital investment increased significantly. France and Belgium were the leading foreign investors in the Russian economy, mainly in metallurgy and coal mining in the south of Russia (now Ukraine). The English invested in the Baku oilfields, the copper industry of the Urals and Central Asia, and gold mining. German capital predominated in the heavy industry of Poland and the Baltic region.[17]

The government's finances made impressive gains under Witte. Both the income and expenditures of the state budget doubled between 1893 and 1903: income rose from 1.46 billion to 2.32 billion rubles, and expenditures from 947 million to 1.883 billion rubles.[18] The growth of the state budget far exceeded the growth in national income and therefore did not correspond to the population's level of well-being. The flow of funds into the treasury, however, enabled the government to finance large industrial projects that would not yield an economic return in the near future. The greatest of those projects was the construction of the Trans-Siberian Railroad from the Urals to Vladivostok, a distance of more than 5,000 miles. The Trans-Siberian was built in the record time of ten years, from 1891 to 1901. It linked the European part of Russia to the Far East and began to draw the vast undeveloped expanses of Siberia into the economic life of the country.

The creation of large industrial enterprises, both state-owned and private, was one of the most important consequences of Witte's industrial policy. Big factories, funded by foreign investment and equipped with advanced technology, arose particularly in the Donbass and Baku. They were accompanied by modern forms of industrial organization, such as stock and commodity exchanges and monopolistic groupings. Syndicates were especially widespread in Russia at the turn of the century. These combinations of enterprises, which allocated orders, purchases of raw materials, and markets among themselves, included the Company for the Sale of Products of Russian Metallurgical Factories, created in 1902, and similar organizations in the manufacture of pipe, coal, and railway cars, founded two years later. Organizations of industrialists also grew in importance, the largest of which was the Association of Industry and Trade, established in 1906.

A group of Petersburg banks dominated the financial sphere: the Russo-Asiatic Bank, the Petersburg International Bank, the Azov-Don Bank, the Commercial-Industrial Bank, and the Russian Bank for International Trade. The "big five" accounted for almost half of all the capital and assets of Russia's corporate banks. The concentration of capital in Russian commercial banks surpassed that of banks in the developed capitalist countries. On the eve of World War I, industrial-financial groups based on industrial and banking monopolies began to emerge. The Russo-Asiatic Bank group, for example, included a military-industrial conglomerate that owned the Putilov factory, an oil concern, large railroad companies, machine plants, and metal and coal mines. Monopolies began to develop close ties with government agencies. Russia resembled the advanced countries of the West in the degree to which its leading branches of heavy industry formed monopolies and in the organizational forms that those monopolies assumed.[19]

Despite all Witte's efforts, the gap between Russia's level of industrial development and that of the West persisted because Russia had started from such a low point. By some measurements, such as labor productivity and industrial production per capita, the gap assumed major proportions. In 1898 England produced thirteen times as much pig iron per capita as Russia; Germany produced eight times as much, and France almost four times as much. In the same period, England produced fifty-three times as much coal, Germany almost twenty-five times as much, and France almost nine times as much as Russia.[20] Nevertheless, the country had taken an impressive step forward in its industrial development. By the beginning of the twentieth century, Russia had a higher industrial growth rate than any other country and

Russia: Basic Economy, 1909–1913

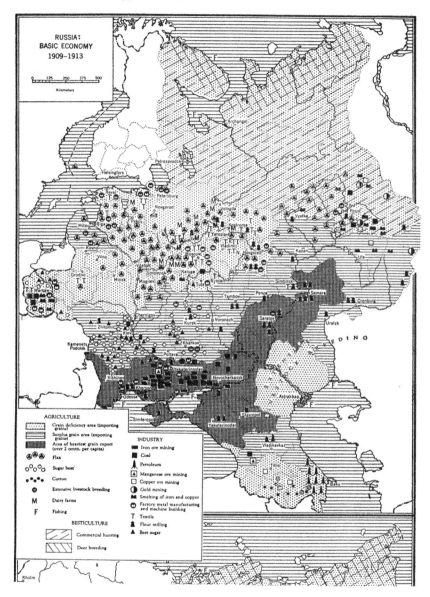

Source: Lyashchenko, Peter I. *History of the National Economy of Russia to the 1917 Revolution.* Trans. By L.M. Herman; introd. By Calvin B. Hoover; maps redrawn under the supervision of Leonard H. Dykes. American Council of Learned Societies Devoted to Humanistic Studies. Russian Translation Project. Series 4. New York: Macmillan, 1949. By permission of the American Council of Learned Societies

briefly led the world in oil production. Russia's share of world industrial production rose from 4 percent in the early 1890s to 7 percent in 1914. Russia was now one of the five most industrially developed countries, behind the United States, Germany, and England but roughly on a par with France.

In the early years of the twentieth century, however, Witte's economic system began to falter, starting with the world economic crisis of 1900–1903. By integrating Russia into the world economic system, Witte exposed it to the periodic crises of overproduction characteristic of capitalist economies. Unlike the countries of the West, which were able to emerge from the crisis of 1900–1903 relatively quickly, Russia experienced a prolonged depression. The plight of Russian agriculture, still the foundation of the country's economy, was largely to blame. As Witte's critics had warned, the agricultural sector, exhausted by rapid industrialization, could not provide a large enough domestic market to absorb the products of industry. Nor was it possible for the state to draw more resources from the impoverished countryside. Agricultural productivity, held back by primitive farming methods and technology, remained low. The peasant population continued to increase, exacerbating the problem of overpopulation. Ominous signs of the deepening agrarian crisis included growing arrears in the peasants' obligations to the state, harvest failures, and mass famines in 1897, 1898, and 1901.

By the end of the 1890s Witte recognized the danger posed by the gap between Russia's rapidly growing industrial sector and its primitive agriculture. He believed that the key to agricultural improvement lay in changing the legal position of the peasants to grant them full rights, increased economic independence, and liberation from the shackles of the commune. He urged the dismantling of the system, created in the late 1880s and the early 1890s, that limited the peasants' rights and increased the state's supervision of them. He believed that these measures would "complete the emancipation of the peasantry" and transform the peasant "from a half-person into a person."[21]

In making his proposal, Witte did not address the most important problem facing Russian agriculture, the peasants' need for more land, which might have been resolved by reducing the gentry's landholdings. Nevertheless, even in its modest form Witte's proposal worried Nicholas. Russia's ruling circles regarded the preservation of patriarchal principles in the countryside as the surest guarantee of social stability. In addition, the authority of Alexander III, whose memory Nicholas sincerely revered, stood behind the traditional agrarian policy. Finally, in touching on agrarian affairs, Witte encroached on the jurisdiction of the Finance Ministry's traditional rival, the Ministry of Internal Affairs. From 1902 on, the head of that ministry was Viacheslav Plehve, an energetic statesman who had the capacity to deliver a sharp rebuff to Witte.

Plehve, like Witte, came from the provincial service nobility, but his career had followed a very different path.[22] After graduating from the university he entered the judiciary and at the beginning of the 1880s became procurator of the St. Petersburg judicial chamber. As head of the Department of Police in the early 1880s, he played a decisive role in crushing the remnants of the People's Will. His success in wiping out the revolutionary underground convinced him that repressive measures were effective and that vigorous steps had to be taken to strengthen the authoritarian system of government. Plehve believed that "playing at constitutionalism must be nipped in the bud." To his opponents he argued that "tsarist power enjoys great prestige among the people, and the sovereign has a loyal army."[23]

The views of Witte and Plehve stemmed from such fundamentally different principles that any compromise between them was impossible. Witte, who regarded the development of capitalism as "a universal and immutable law," argued that "what is happening now in Russia is what happened at the appropriate time in the West: [Russia] is making the transition to a capitalist system." Plehve countered that "Russia has its own distinct history and social structure," and "there is every reason to hope that Russia will avoid the yoke of capital, the bourgeoisie, and class struggle." Whereas the minister of finance urged the government to "lead the masses" and satisfy the needs of society through reform, the minister of internal affairs asserted that such a policy would merely undermine public order. "If it is not within our power to alter the historical course of events that is leading to instability in the state," he maintained, "then we must erect barriers to it in order to restrain it, instead of swimming with the current and always trying to be ahead of it."[24] Because he was not strong enough to resolve the argument between his ministers, Nicholas allowed them to act independently. In 1902 the administration created two new governmental bodies to discuss agrarian problems: a Special Conference on the Needs of Agricultural Industry, which Witte headed, and an Editorial Commission to Examine Peasant Legislation, under the leadership of Plehve's closest associates in the Ministry of Internal Affairs.

To secure the broadest possible support for their plans, Witte and Plehve set up networks of local committees representing each of their ministries in the provinces and districts. Witte's Conference created a particularly elaborate network of more than six hundred committees. The Conference dealt with issues relating to peasant self-government, the courts, civil and criminal law, and forms of land tenure. Most of the local committees declared themselves in favor of "eliminating the separate status of the peasants in regard to their rights in general, and to administrative and judicial procedures in particular." They also favored freeing the peasants to leave the commune, "helping village communes make the transition to individual ownership of homesteads and farms," broadening opportunities for "individual entrepreneurship," and instilling in the peasants a sense of property ownership and respect for the property of others. The resolution of one local committee read:

> The Kiev district committee considers it necessary to address the frequently expressed fear that allowing the peasants to dispose of their property might lead to the buying up of their land by more well-to-do individuals and the formation of a landless proletariat. The committee does not share that fear for the following reasons. First, the formation of a class of landless peasants is inevitable, because the population is growing, whereas landed property is definitely and quite narrowly limited. Second, if the state attempted to preserve the right of landownership for the entire rural population, a much greater danger would arise: the danger of turning the mass of the population into a proletariat possessing too little land, and the fragmentation of the land into tiny scraps that could not be cultivated.[25]

Other committees issued similar declarations.

The Manifesto of February 26, 1903, which Nicholas timed to coincide with the birthday of the late Alexander III, attempted to take into account the work of the Conference. The emperor promised to find "ways to make it easier for individual peasants to leave the commune" and to take measures "to abolish collective responsibility, which inhibits the peasants." However, he proclaimed that the government's basic agrarian policy remained "the inviolability of the communal system of peasant land tenure."[26] The government did introduce some rural reforms in the early years of the twentieth century. It prohibited cantonal courts from administering corporal punishment, abolished collective responsibility, and made it easier for peasants to emigrate. Although these changes were of some benefit, they did nothing to resolve the agrarian question.

The Manifesto of February 26 represented a serious defeat for Witte. The finance minister's influence within the government had noticeably diminished by this time. He was blamed for ignoring the interests of agriculture, for the painful consequences of the industrial crisis of 1900–1903, and even for "encroaching on the responsibilities not only of other ministries but of the autocracy itself."[27] From the beginning of 1903 the activity of Witte's Conference had begun to wane. In August 1903 Witte was dismissed and transferred to the honorary and powerless post of chairman of the Committee of Ministers. Plehve, the conservative, had won the battle over the agrarian question.

Although the proposal that Plehve had the Editing Commission draw up formally acknowledged the decay of the commune since 1861 and expressed a benevolent neutrality toward the well-to-do peasants, its recommendations were profoundly conservative, even reactionary. The plan proposed classifying as inalienable property not only the allotments that the peasants had received in 1861 but land that they had purchased as individuals. It favored increasing the powers of the land captains, rural judges, and the head of the extended patriarchal family. It called for the extension of the special restrictions imposed on the peasant estate to members of other social estates who lived in the countryside, such as petty townspeople. It advised the curtailment of the operations of the Peasant Land Bank, which helped peasants to buy and resell land obtained from the nobility. Peasants would in effect be prevented from leaving the commune because they would have to renounce their allotments without compensation. The ministry's proposal elicited protests even in conservative circles. Plehve was accused of trying "completely to enserf the peasants and to separate them entirely from the other estates."[28]

Plehve's plan, which in fact lacked any positive program, left the autocracy with no option but to continue the policy of strengthening authoritarian rule and intensifying repression. With redoubled energy, Plehve set to work suppressing peasant disturbances, attacking the zemstvo opposition, and limiting the autonomy of the borderlands. He continued to curtail Finland's autonomy and undermine the rights of the Armenian Church. Anti-Jewish pogroms broke out in the southwestern provinces amid numerous complaints from the public that the army and police did nothing to stop them. Meanwhile, the Ministry of Internal Affairs drafted a plan that would have given the governors virtually unlimited power over their provinces. Plehve's assassination by a terrorist's bomb in July 1904 was a clear sign that a revolution was approaching.

Russia's defeat in the war with Japan in 1904–5 made that revolution inevitable. The origins of the Russo-Japanese War go back to the second half of the nineteenth century, when Russia acquired the Amur and Pacific Coast regions, vast territories that had previously belonged to China. The next logical step for Russia was to obtain an ice-free port in the Far East that would serve as a transportation terminal for the whole Siberian and Far Eastern region. The need for such a terminal became particularly urgent once the construction of the Trans-Siberian Railroad began. Witte insisted on concluding a treaty with the Chinese government in 1896 under which the eastern branch of the Trans-Siberian, the Chinese Eastern Railway, ran through the northern Chinese possession of Manchuria.

Russia now began to consolidate its position in China and the Far East, a policy that Nicholas wholeheartedly supported as a way of raising Russia's international prestige. As heir to the throne, Nicholas had traveled through

Russo-Japanese War, 1904–1905

Source: *A History of Russia*, Seventh Edition, Nicholas V. Riasanovsky and Mark Steinberg, p. 375. Copyright © 1963, 1969, 1977, 1984, 1993, 2000, 2004 by Oxford University Press, Inc. Used by permission of Oxford University Press, Inc.

Siberia and the countries of Asia and chaired the committee for the construction of the Trans-Siberian Railroad. As noted in chapter 8, at the beginning of the twentieth century Russia was able to pursue an active foreign policy only in the Far East. In the Balkans and the Middle East, the influence of Germany and its ally Austria-Hungary was growing rapidly. In Central Asia, sharp conflicts with England constrained Russian activity. Under these conditions, Russia's ruling circles embraced the ideology of "Asianism" as a distinctive program in foreign policy. The Asianists claimed that Russia had an inner spiritual affinity with the countries of Asia, which could serve as the basis for Russian influence.

Prince Esper Ukhtomsky, a poet and journalist who had accompanied Nicholas on his tour of the Far East, expressed the doctrine of Asianism.[29] According to Ukhtomsky,

> Beyond the Altai Mountains, beyond the Pamir Mountains, lies a mysterious, uncharted realm, unknown to science, just like pre-Petrine Rus, with its rich tradition and inexhaustible love of the miraculous, with its humble submission to natural and other calamities imposed for sinfulness, with the mark of stern greatness on its entire spiritual makeup . . . For the Great Russian state there is no other way out. Either we must become what destiny has summoned us to be from time immemorial, a major force in the world, combining West and East, or we will tread the path of decline, without glory and universally ignored. If this becomes our fate, Europe will crush us with its external superiority, and the Asiatic peoples, unless we awaken them, will be even more dangerous than the ethnic minorities in the western regions of the Russian Empire.[30]

Russia's rulers, of course, had strong motives of their own for penetrating the Far East, aside from the ideas of the Asianists. Witte consistently advocated such a course. In his opinion, northern China should become not just the transportation terminal for Siberia and the Far Eastern region but a zone of Russian economic influence. He believed that it offered investment opportunities for Russian capital and a market for Russian industrial products. Because he understood the danger that Russia might be drawn into a war, he insisted on strictly peaceful methods of penetration, such as railroad concessions, the establishment of banks, and trade agreements with the Chinese government. Despite Witte's intentions, however, the very fact of Russia's growing influence in China brought it into contention with countries that had their own spheres of influence there, primarily England and Japan.

Conflict with Japan first arose in the mid-1890s. Japan defeated China in 1894 and took control of some Chinese territory, including Korea and the Liaotung Peninsula, with its strategically important naval base of Port Arthur. Russia, with the support of the other European powers, forced Japan to relinquish the territories it had conquered. Russia then established itself in Port Arthur in 1898 and built a branch of the Chinese Eastern Railway to the town. Japan regarded Russia's behavior as an act of treachery. Public opinion in the Western countries, especially the United States and England, considered Russia's actions aggressive and began to side with Japan.

The activities of a circle of adventurers with close personal ties to Nicho-

las II added to the tensions. Their leader, a retired guards officer named
Aleksandr Bezobrazov, regarded himself as a master politician. In an effort
to increase Russian influence in Manchuria and northern Korea without the
aid of official diplomacy, the Bezobrazov circle formed a company to obtain
a timber concession and bring Russian soldiers into Korea in the guise of
woodcutters. Convinced of Russia's absolute military predominance,
Bezobrazov behaved provocatively toward Japan. Plehve gave him considerable support in the belief that "a victorious little war" would create a "healthy"
atmosphere in Russia and help to avert a revolution. All these calculations
were profoundly mistaken. Bezobrazov had not taken into account the need
to defend Russia's western borders and the impossibility of transferring a
large contingent of troops to the remote region of the Far East.[31] By the early
twentieth century Japan, which had begun to modernize along Western lines
in the 1860s, had completed a vast industrial boom, created powerful military forces, and was only waiting for a suitable pretext to begin a war.

On January 27, 1904, Japanese squadrons, without a declaration of war,
attacked Russian ships in Korea and raided Port Arthur. The start of the war
immediately exposed the numerous defects in the organization of Russia's
military organization and administrative system. The Russian navy was considerably inferior to the Japanese fleet in the quality and speed of its ships
and in the range of their artillery. Only a single branch of the Trans-Siberian
Railroad, which was not yet working at full capacity, linked the theater of
military operations with central Russia. Many of the Russian generals were
passive and lacked initiative. A system of "dual power" made the situation
even worse: military leadership was divided between Admiral Evgeny
Alekseev, the viceroy of the Far East, and Aleksei Kuropatkin, the commander
of the Manchurian Army. The military command allowed the Japanese to
land unopposed in Korea and to blockade Port Arthur.

The Russian generals, afraid of being cut off from the Chinese Eastern
Railway, their sole link with Russia, engaged in delaying tactics as their forces
fell back to the north. This had a devastating effect on troop morale. The
war's objectives were unclear to the Russian army, which for the first time
consisted largely of short-term recruits who were not inclined to reckless
self-sacrifice. In a series of battles along the Sha-ho River and at Liaoyang
and Mukden, Russian forces suffered serious defeats. Having destroyed
Russia's Pacific Squadron, the Japanese assaulted and captured Port Arthur
at the end of 1904.

The war culminated in the destruction of the so-called Second and Third
Pacific Squadrons, consisting of ships of the Baltic Fleet that had been sent
from Europe for the relief of Port Arthur. By the time the squadrons reached
the Far East, Port Arthur had already fallen, and the expedition no longer

served any purpose. In May 1905 the Japanese navy engaged the Russian ships in the Tsushima Straits and annihilated them without losing a single ship of its own. The Tsushima disaster and Russia's other military defeats dealt a severe blow to the country's international standing. For the first time, Russia had suffered defeat at the hands not of a European power but of a little-known Asiatic state. Doubts arose not only about Russia's military power but about the stability of its domestic order. Even conservatives came to realize the need for profound social and political changes.

American mediation brought the Russo-Japanese War to an end with a peace treaty signed on August 23/September 5 in Portsmouth, New Hampshire. The Russian delegation, headed by Sergei Witte, succeeded in rejecting the most onerous Japanese demands, including the payment of an indemnity, but Russia's losses remained substantial. Russia ceded the southern half of Sakhalin Island to Japan and lost its rights to the Liaotung Peninsula and Port Arthur. The loss of southern Sakhalin hampered communications with Kamchatka and Chukotka, Russia's possessions in northeastern Siberia. The Peace of Portsmouth deprived Russia of free access to the Pacific, and for some time to come the tsarist government was unable to conduct an active policy in the Far East. Finally, the Russo-Japanese War precipitated the revolution of 1905.

Chapter 11

Opposition and Revolution

The mid-1890s marked the beginning in Russia not only of a new reign but of mass unrest, which would continue right up to the Bolsheviks' consolidation of power in the early 1920s. The long period of change from above, when the state took the initiative in social and political reform, came to an end. The patriarchal sleep of the masses, the social stability that proponents of Russia's uniqueness regarded as its most important difference from the West, receded into the past. Society's steadily increasing pressure on the government led to the first Russian revolution, in 1905–7. The revolutionary events, however, clearly displayed distinctive Russian features. It was not the bourgeoisie that played the leading role, as in the West, but the peasants and the industrial proletariat. On the whole, radical left-wing parties were more prominent participants in the revolution than liberal groups and organizations.

It would be a mistake, of course, to underestimate the importance of liberals in the social and political struggles at the turn of the twentieth century.[1] The institutions of local self-government had become the driving force of opposition to the government in the 1860s and the 1870s, and they continued to make a significant contribution. In fact, the late 1890s and the early 1900s saw an upsurge of zemstvo opposition. Expansion of the zemstvo's activities and the strengthening of its financial base clashed with the government's attempts to curtail local self-government. Influential zemstvo figures, many of whom were large landowners with extensive contacts at court and in the administration, began to seek ways of influencing the government's policies. They created informal circles for the discussion of measures "to secure the free development of local life" and "to resist the pressure of the Petersburg bureaucracy." A good example was the Symposium (*Beseda*) that existed from 1899 to 1905. It included numerous representatives of the Russian aristocracy, such as princes Pavel and Petr

Dolgorukov, Prince Dmitry Shakhovskoi, and counts Vladimir Bobrinsky and Pavel Sheremetev.[2]

Participants in the zemstvo opposition held a variety of political views. Some of them wanted to retain the unlimited power of the tsar and rejected only the "domination of the bureaucracy." They desired a representative body to advise the government on legislation and guarantees of so-called "non-political liberties" such as freedom of speech and conscience. Their program embodied the old Slavophile notion that "the power of government belongs to the tsar, but the power of opinion belongs to the people." Dmitry Shipov, the chairman of the zemstvo board of Moscow province, was their most prominent spokesman. The so-called "Slavophile" position enjoyed limited support in zemstvo circles, however. More influential were the Dolgorukov brothers, Shakhovskoi, the veteran zemstvo activist Ivan Petrunkevich, and other advocates of constitutional change, who called for the creation of a legislative assembly and a government accountable to parliament.

The zemstvo opposition traditionally expressed its views in addresses and petitions to the tsar. Nicholas II had given his "senseless dreams" speech of January 1895 in reply to some of these petitions. As time went on, the zemstvo opposition, dissatisfied with the narrow framework of informal discussion circles and the submission of petitions, began to form semi-legal and illegal organizations on a nationwide scale, the largest of which was the Union of Zemstvo Constitutionalists founded in 1903. The turn to conspiratorial activity marked a significant new stage in the evolution of the Russian liberal movement and a change in its relations with the government. An equally important change took place in the social composition of Russian liberalism at the turn of the century. A new social force, the intelligentsia, began to take over the leadership of the liberal movement from the zemstvo activists.

Professional associations of teachers, doctors, lawyers, engineers, and other occupational groups, which had grown in numbers and importance, formed the social base of "intelligentsia liberalism." University students played a particularly prominent role in Russian public life.[3] As the most mobile part of the intelligentsia and the most responsive to new currents of thought, students actively protested against anything that seemed to violate freedom and social justice. Thus the way the police behaved while breaking up a demonstration in 1899 produced disturbances at St. Petersburg University that immediately won the support of students in several other Russian cities. The government's clumsiness and the strained situation throughout the country created a tense atmosphere in the universities in which outbreaks of unrest could occur at any time. An almost uninterrupted series of student demonstrations, political meetings, and "strikes" (mass boycotts of classes) took place from the late 1890s to the end of the 1905 revolution.

To use Ivan Turgenev's terms, the "sons" expressed their discontent in mass meetings and strikes in the universities, while the "fathers," the representatives of the professions, used their corporate organizations as a weapon of struggle. Conferences and congresses of teachers, agronomists, and doctors refused to confine themselves to discussions of professional matters. They often adopted political resolutions that demanded limits on the powers of the bureaucracy, the removal of restrictions on various forms of public activity, and the expansion of the right of self-government. When the revolution began, members of the professions began to create their own political organizations, which united in May 1905 in the so-called Union of Unions. The founders of the Union of Unions included the most prominent representatives of intelligentsia liberalism, such as the historians Pavel Miliukov and Aleksandr Kizevetter and the lawyer Vasily Maklakov. They subsequently headed the Constitutional Democratic Party, popularly known as the Kadets, which formed the left wing of the liberal spectrum and played a major role in the political life of the early twentieth century.

The spokesmen of the liberal intelligentsia were considerably more resolute than their zemstvo colleagues. They insisted on the introduction of social reforms, including an eight-hour workday, legalization of trade unions, resolution of the agrarian question, and changes in policy toward the non-Russian peoples of the empire. Their concern with social issues owed a good deal to the Marxist background that many of them shared. The economist Petr Struve and the philosophers Nikolai Berdiaev and Sergei Bulgakov, among others, had participated in the Marxist movement and come under the strong influence of Marxist ideology. Like Miliukov, they accepted the possibility of encroaching on private property rights. Their agrarian program, in particular, proposed a partial transfer of the nobility's land to the peasants. In political matters, the liberal intelligentsia stood for the creation of a representative legislature and an executive power responsible to parliament. Finally, it wanted to grant cultural autonomy to the various ethnic minorities of the empire.

The question of non-Russian minorities, a particularly salient issue at the turn of the twentieth century, occupied a prominent place in the program of Russian liberalism. The policy of centralization and Russification of the borderlands under Alexander III and Nicholas II had aroused sharp protest from the minorities, whose ethnic consciousness increased in magnitude and strength as capitalism intensified. In the late 1880s non-Russian parties began to advance demands ranging from guarantees of cultural autonomy to secession from the Russian Empire. Some organizations, such as the Muslim leagues and the Polish National Democratic Party of Roman Dmowski, espoused liberal principles. Most, however, held revolutionary socialist views, such as the Clarion (*Hnchak*) and Federation (*Dashnaktsutiun*) in Armenia, the Polish Socialist Party of Józef Piłsudski, and the General Union (*Bund*) of Jewish Workers in Lithuania, Poland, and Russia.[4] By including the demand for cultural autonomy in their program, the Russian liberals hoped to seize the initiative from the radicals in regard to ethnic policy.

Intelligentsia liberalism also borrowed some of the radicals' tactics, one of the characteristics that distinguished it from the old zemstvo liberalism. Whereas the zemstvo liberals generally had tried to stay within the confines of legality, the liberal intelligentsia moved boldly beyond them. Thus their illegal journal *Liberation*, founded in Germany in 1902, sought to unite the various currents of the opposition movement. The editor of the journal was Petr Struve, a leading representative of intelligentsia liberalism and former Marxist. *Liberation* conducted its campaign against the authorities by publishing all sorts of secret documents received from sympathetic officials at court and in the bureaucracy. In January 1904 the illegal Union of Liberation made its appearance, uniting the liberal intelligentsia and adopting a more radical position than the Union of Zemstvo Constitutionalists. The Union of Liberation even cooperated with the revolutionaries. In September and October 1904 representatives of the Union of Liberation and members of Russian revolutionary and ethnic parties held a conference in Paris. They minimized their ideological differences and passed resolutions calling for "the elimination of autocracy" and its replacement by "a free democratic system based on universal suffrage" and, for all minority ethnic groups, "freedom of national development, guaranteed by law."[5]

At the time of the Paris conference the autocracy was in crisis, beset by pressure from the liberal opposition, Russia's defeats in the war with Japan, and the general state of unrest in the country. Not only the adherents of the Union of Liberation but the more moderate zemstvo liberals were up in arms. In November 1904 a semi-legal All-Russian Zemstvo Congress took place in Petersburg. The congress adopted highly political resolutions calling for the abolition of "extraordinary protection," an end to administrative repression, political amnesty, broader rights for the zemstvos, the elimination of restrictions based on ethnicity, religion, and social estate, and, above all, the introduction of a constitutional system. At the same time, a "banquet campaign" took place. The banquets, which celebrated the fortieth anniversary of the judicial reform of 1864, served as forums for political speeches and demands for constitutional reform. According to the Department of Police, more than 120 banquets, with about fifty thousand participants, took place in thirty-four cities.[6] Nicholas II highly disapproved of such activities, but because of the tense atmosphere in the country he had to reconcile himself to them for the time being.

In view of the government's glaring failures in both domestic affairs and foreign policy, the authorities even made an attempt to satisfy the liberals by putting some of their proposals into effect. Prince Petr Sviatopolk-Mirsky, who became minister of internal affairs in August 1904 after the assassination of Plehve, set out to pursue a policy of accommodation. Sviatopolk-Mirsky's brief administration lasted until January 1905. Depending on their political sympathies, contemporaries variously termed it "a breath of spring," "a time of trust," "the first step forward in a hundred years," or "an era of permissiveness." Sviatopolk-Mirsky had previously served as assistant minister of internal affairs and as a provincial governor. Upon his appointment as minister of internal affairs, he sought to reach out to moderates. "My administrative experience," he declared, "has led me to the deep conviction that fruitful governmental work must be based on sincere goodwill and sincere trust toward public and estate-based institutions, as well as toward the population in general."[7] Sviatopolk-Mirsky's program resembled that of Mikhail Loris-Melikov, adapted to new conditions. For example, Sviatopolk-Mirsky gave his tacit approval to the zemstvo congress of November 1904. Subsequent events, however, showed that Sviatopolk-Mirsky's efforts came too late. In the strained atmosphere of the early 1900s, both the left and the right wings greeted any attempt at moderate reform with acute hostility and doomed it to failure.

At the end of November 1904, perhaps to smooth over the tsar's adverse reaction to the resolutions of the zemstvo congress, Sviatopolk-Mirsky presented Nicholas with a detailed report on his proposed program. At the heart of the report was a rejection of the reactionary course the government had followed since the time of Alexander III. "Our domestic policy course," the report emphasized, "even though applied more or less consistently for over twenty years by men who often had great talent and political experience, has not produced the expected results."[8] Because a reactionary policy did not meet the country's real needs, a return to the principles of the Great Reforms was essential, Sviatopolk-Mirsky believed. His proposals included increasing the autonomy of the zemstvos, drawing new elements of the population into zemstvo elections, easing the restrictions on ethnic and religious minorities, ending administrative persecution of the press, abolishing the peasant commune, and raising the social status of the peasantry.

Sviatopolk-Mirsky realized, of course, that such broad reforms required changes in the way the government operated. Inevitably, his report included the creation of a representative assembly. He tried to disguise the constitutional nature of this step by claiming that it was fully compatible with the preservation of autocracy. "While responding to the demands of the time," this innovation "would also conform precisely to the principles of our system of government, without violating them in any way and without even representing anything new." However, the dignitaries who discussed the report at a governmental conference were well aware of the implications of the proposed reforms. Nicholas's uncle, Grand Duke Sergei Aleksandrovich, the governor-general of Moscow, declared that the Fundamental Laws of the Russian Empire prohibited the tsar from changing the political system. Konstantin Pobedonostsev argued that "autocracy is not just of political significance but also has a religious character, and the sovereign does not have the right to limit the mission that Divine Providence has assigned to him." These arguments fully accorded with Nicholas's own views. "The peasants will not understand a constitution," he told the conference; "they will understand only that the tsar's hands have been tied, and then—good luck, gentlemen."[9] The conference rejected Sviatopolk-Mirsky's proposal. The imperial decree of December 12, 1904, which summed up the results of the government's deliberations, omitted any mention of a representative assembly and contained only a vague promise of future reforms.

The December 12 decree was a major political defeat for Sviatopolk-Mirsky and a portent of his imminent dismissal. The government now lacked any positive program in the face of a steadily approaching revolution. It was no longer possible to establish contact between the authorities and the liberal camp, which was growing implacably hostile to the government. Nevertheless, what actually touched off the revolution was not the actions of the liberals but the protest of factory workers.

The labor movement emerged as a distinct factor in Russian public life at the end of the 1870s and the beginning of the 1880s. By the mid-1890s it had become an object of intense interest to both the government and various social and political forces. In size, the industrial proletariat remained insignificant compared to the peasantry, numbering only 1.9 million, or 1.5 percent of the population, in 1897. Nonetheless, it represented a powerful force. The workers were concentrated in the most important urban centers, and many of them worked in huge plants and factories. The rapid growth of large industry, combined with low worker productivity, made Russian industry more highly concentrated than in the West. At the beginning of the twentieth century 46 percent of the workers in the various branches of industry worked in the 589 largest enterprises in the country.[10] Because many industrial workers were literate, they had access to revolutionary propaganda. The severe conditions under which they lived and worked, including low wages, a long workday, poor housing, and neglect of health and safety measures, made that propaganda attractive to them. In many cases, poor working conditions reflected real problems. Russian industrialists, latecomers to world capitalism, could not export capital to overseas colonies and make relatively easy profits there. They had to exploit their workers harshly in order to hold their own in international competition.

For some time, the government made almost no attempt to limit the exploitation of Russian workers. In fact, the authorities curtailed the labor laws introduced in the early 1880s by Minister of Finance Nikolai Bunge. Russia's rulers believed that relations between Russian workers and factory owners had a special "patriarchal" character that distinguished their country from the West. Even Witte shared that belief for a time. He wrote in an official report in 1895: "Patriarchal relations between factory owner and worker prevail in our industry. Such paternalism often finds expression in the owner's solicitude for the needs of the workers and employees in his factory, in the care he takes to preserve concord and harmony, and in the simplicity and justice of their relationship. When moral law and Christian feelings underpin that relationship, there is no need to resort to written law and compulsion."[11] The notion that Russia's unique character made labor laws unnecessary was a major miscalculation, one that cost the government dearly.

Massive worker unrest in major Russian cities and industrial regions began in the mid-1890s and continued until the end of the revolution of 1905. In 1896 the so-called "Petersburg industrial war" broke out, a textile workers' strike that gained the support of metalworkers in the capital and workers at numerous enterprises in that province. The strikers began by demanding to be paid for the days that had been declared holidays on the occasion of Nicholas II's coronation, and then presented more general demands, such as a shorter workday. In the early 1900s worker protests became part of the May Day celebrations and often took on a political cast. The strike of the Obukhov steelworkers in Petersburg in May 1901, which came to be known as the "Obukhov defense," spilled over into armed clashes with troops and police, a clear symptom of the social tension that was building up in the country. During the industrial crisis of the early 1900s, worker protests frequently enveloped the majority of enterprises in a town or even a region, as in the strikes of 1902 in Rostov-on-Don and 1904 in Baku, and the general strike of 1903 in southern Russia, in which some 200,000 workers in the main industrial centers of Transcaucasia and Ukraine took part.[12]

Worker strikes, mass meetings, and demonstrations became an important part of public life, often interacting with urban middle-class protests by white-collar workers and intelligentsia. The industrial workers' protests found an echo in the countryside, because many workers retained close ties to villages where they had relatives, friends, and often an allotment of land in the commune. The peasants' land hunger and tax burden created favorable conditions for the rise of rural discontent, and at the beginning of the twentieth century peasant disturbances increased in frequency. The largest uprising occurred in 1902 in Left-Bank Ukraine (Kharkov and Poltava provinces) and resulted in the destruction of gentry estates, the plundering of seed grain and equipment, and mass encroachments on the nobility's land. The unrest spread to 165 villages with a population of 150,000 and required more than 10,000 soldiers to suppress it.[13]

The government tried to relieve the tension by introducing some social reforms. New labor legislation in 1897 reduced the maximum workday in industry to eleven and a half hours. In 1901 workers at state enterprises who were disabled on the job became eligible for pensions. Legislation in 1903 made industrialists responsible for accidents to their workers and established factory elders to serve as intermediaries between the workers, the factory owners, and the authorities. These measures failed to achieve their goal, however. Revolutionary organizations, particularly Marxist groups, steadily gained influence over the workers.

The rise of Marxism in Russia marked an important stage in the development of the revolutionary movement. Georgy Plekhanov, the central figure in the spread of Marxist ideology that began in the 1880s, had been an active participant in the Populist movement and one of the leaders of the Black Repartition.[14] After he fled Russia, Plekhanov and other émigré revolutionaries founded the Emancipation of Labor Group in Switzerland in 1883. The organization devoted most of its efforts to translating and disseminating the works of Marx, Engels, and their followers. The Russian revolutionaries' turn to Marxism was no accident. They sought to comprehend the reasons for the failure of the People's Will and to understand why the peasants had proved unreceptive to its revolutionary and socialist principles. Using Marxist logic, Plekhanov concluded that, as a class of small proprietors, the peasants could not independently carry out a revolution. Moreover, under the impact of capitalist development the peasantry was breaking down into a bourgeoisie and a proletariat, and only the latter could serve as a social base for a Russian revolution. Russia could not avoid the European path of capitalist development. Proud thoughts of leaping directly into socialism from a world of semi-serfdom must be abandoned. There was no basis for supposing that "our country possesses any charter of uniqueness that history has bestowed upon it for merits of which no one is aware."[15]

Plekhanov's doctrine brought new inspiration to the Russian revolutionary movement. In the words of Nikolai Berdiaev, in the 1880s and 1890s the "emotional and sentimental" type of Populist revolutionary gave way to the tougher and more intellectually sophisticated type of Marxist revolutionary.[16] Many Russians were shocked at the readiness of Plekhanov's adherents to "reconcile themselves" to the sufferings of the peasants as a necessary product of capitalist development, their denial of the intelligentsia's ability to influence the course of history, and their scorn for the traditions of Populism. They charged that Plekhanov's writings "spit on the blood that heroes had shed," and there were even instances of the public burning of his books.[17] However, it was impossible to ignore the questions that Plekhanov raised and the indisputable evidence of the social stratification of the peasantry, the rapid progress of industry, and the growth of the urban proletariat. The adherents of Populism had to develop a new ideology that would enable them to remain loyal to their old ideals while acknowledging the new facts of Russian life. That ideology was the achievement of Viktor Chernov, the leading theoretician of the Socialist Revolutionary (SR) Party, formed in 1901 out of scattered Populist groups.[18]

In contrast to the old classical Populism, Chernov conceded that capitalism was developing in Russia. He refused, however, to regard it as a positive phenomenon. In Chernov's view, the negative consequences of capitalism in Russia, such as mass impoverishment, increased exploitation, and economic anarchy, far outweighed its positive aspects, such as the creation of large-scale economic enterprises in town and countryside. The full development of capitalism in Russia appeared unlikely because the objective conditions for it were lacking. The "toiling peasantry," composed of small and middle peasants, stubbornly held its own in the face of commercial and monetary conditions that were breaking it down. The poor or middle peasant who worked his own land could join the struggle for a new order with the help of the revolutionary intelligentsia. With the victory of the revolution, "socialization of the land" would "draw" the peasants to socialism. The new order would divide the land equally among those who worked it, prohibit the buying and selling of land, and end the use of hired labor in agriculture. After the overthrow of autocracy, cooperative associations of various kinds would arise in the countryside, and a socialist economy would begin to take root.

Unlike the Marxists, who devoted themselves to inciting the industrial proletariat, the Socialist Revolutionaries acted in the name of the so-called "toiling class," which included the factory workers, the small and middling peasants, and the intelligentsia. The SRs viewed revolutionary terrorism as the principal method of uniting this diverse coalition and rallying its forces to the anti-tsarist cause. Acts of terrorism, they believed, would show society that the authorities were vulnerable and would disorganize the governmental apparatus. From the beginning of the 1900s on, the SRs waged an extensive and notorious terrorist campaign.[19] A special group within the party called the Combat Organization carried out terrorist acts. It enjoyed considerable autonomy and long eluded the police. The terrorists killed eminent dignitaries one after another, among them Minister of Public Education Nikolai Bogolepov in 1901; two ministers of internal affairs, Dmitry Sipiagin in 1902 and Viacheslav Plehve in 1904; and Grand Duke Sergei Aleksandrovich in 1905. The police regarded the SRs as the main enemies of the regime and concentrated their efforts on the struggle against them. Subsequent events showed that a far greater danger came from the adherents of Marxism: the Social Democrats, and especially their radical wing, the Bolsheviks.

By the mid-1890s a considerable segment of the Russian intelligentsia had adopted Marxist ideology. The reception of Marxism in Russia was complicated. One part of the intelligentsia rejected the revolutionary side of Marxism and focused on its economic theories, which sought to demonstrate the historically progressive character of capitalism in comparison to the patriarchal economy based on serfdom and communal agriculture. These so-called "legal Marxists," most notably Petr Struve, Nikolai Berdiaev, and Sergei Bulgakov, subsequently joined the liberal camp. Not all members of the intelligentsia, however, viewed Marxism merely as an historical interpretation of capitalism and a justification for the necessity of evolutionary development. The revolutionary aspect of Marxism, which Marx himself had emphasized, attracted a good deal of attention in Russia. In the 1880s the proponents of revolutionary Marxism began to create Social Democratic circles modeled on the workers' parties of Western Europe. The first congress of Russian Social Democrats, held in Minsk in 1898, proclaimed the establishment of a party, but the police arrested all of its participants before they could actually create a unified party organization. The second congress, which took place in Brussels and then in London in 1903, finally succeeded in founding the Russian Social Democratic Workers' Party (RSDRP), whose members were known as the SDs.

The new party's first steps showed that even the revolutionaries understood Marx's doctrines in different ways. Disputes arose over the timing of a socialist revolution, the tactics that the party should employ, and the proletariat's potential allies in the revolutionary struggle. Some SDs, including Plekhanov and Iuly Martov, believed that a socialist revolution could take place in Russia only after a prolonged period of capitalist development, during which objective forces, such as the formation of large industry and the growth of the proletariat, would create the preconditions for socialism. In the first stage of the revolutionary process, after the overthrow of autocracy, Russia would have to adopt a constitutional, or "bourgeois-democratic" political system, and liberal parties would take power. In this period the SDs would play the role of a parliamentary opposition, making use of trade unions, the press, cultural and educational societies, and other legal methods of political struggle to defend the workers' interests.

The radical SDs held very different views. Their leader was Vladimir Ulianov, better known under his pseudonym Lenin, who had been Martov's comrade in Social Democratic circles and previously one of Plekhanov's followers.[20] Lenin and his adherents refused to wait out the indefinite period of time during which, in Plekhanov's words, "Russian history will mill the flour for the pie of socialism." In Lenin's opinion, the waiting period until the socialist revolution could be shortened by mobilizing all the oppressed elements of the population, both the working class and the poorest peasants, to overthrow autocracy. The revolutionary party, a small but conspiratorial and disciplined organization capable of seizing power and initiating a socialist order from above, would play the central role in carrying out the revolution. The question of how to organize the party produced the first major schism in the ranks of Russian Social Democracy. Martov and Plekhanov favored a party with a relatively large membership and a democratic structure, while Lenin insisted on rigorous organization and discipline. Lenin's followers won a majority of votes in elections to the party's leadership committees and took the name "Bolsheviks," meaning "the men of the majority." Their opponents came to be called "Mensheviks," or "the men of the minority."

The formation of the Bolshevik faction demonstrated how acute the social and political tensions in Russia had become. Bolshevism incorporated certain elements of the Populist tradition, such as conspiratorial tactics and a belief in the intelligentsia's ability to direct the course of social development, and combined them with the Marxist notion that social development was subject to immutable laws. Some historians regard Lenin as the successor to Pavel Pestel, Sergei Nechaev, and Petr Tkachev, revolutionaries who believed that they could put the centuries-old traditions of Russian authoritarianism at the service of the revolution and use them "for the good of the people." Vladimir Lenin proved to be an extremely dangerous opponent of the Russian autocracy and of the entire Russian social and political order.

The 1905 revolution gave the Bolsheviks and the other revolutionary parties an opportunity to test their views in practice. The clumsiness of the authorities themselves provoked the outbreak of the revolution. In the early years of the twentieth century the government began to create legal working-class organizations in an effort to bring the workers' movement under its control and to undermine the social base of the revolutionary parties. The best known of these "unions" operated in Moscow under the direction of Sergei Zubatov, who headed the local branch of the Okhrana (the political police). Zubatov unions arose also in Petersburg, Kharkov, Tver, and other cities. In Ukraine and Belorussia Zubatov's agents created the Jewish Independent Workers' Party to rival the Bund.[21] The Zubatov unions opened workers' "tearooms," or clubs, created mutual-assistance funds, and arranged lectures on such topics as the West European labor movement. The Zubatov organizations briefly enjoyed great popularity among the workers, but they ultimately failed. The attempts by Zubatov's agents to intervene in strikes as mediators between the workers and the factory owners aroused the dissatisfaction of influential industrialists. As a result, the authorities severely curtailed the operations of the Zubatov unions, and Zubatov himself lost his job. The failure of this experiment showed once again that the autocracy lacked any positive program for dealing with the approaching revolution.

A Petersburg version of the Zubatov unions, the Assembly of Russian Factory and Mill Workers, led to an even greater disaster. Created in 1903 under the leadership of a priest named Georgy Gapon, the organization had attracted more than ten thousand members by the end of 1904. Gapon, an adventurer and a demagogue as well as a talented orator and preacher, sought to use the influence of his organization for his own objectives. At the beginning of 1905, in the midst of a growing wave of strikes, Gapon hit upon the idea of a mass procession to present the tsar with a petition stating the needs of the workers. The revolutionaries, who had infiltrated the Gapon organization and played an important part in it, insisted that the petition include radical demands for a political amnesty; the abolition of all social, ethnic, and religious restrictions; and a Constituent Assembly elected by universal suffrage. Such a petition was unacceptable to the tsar. The procession to the Winter Palace on January 9, 1905, ended in tragedy. When the police and troops failed to block the procession, they opened fire. Estimates of the number killed and wounded range from 160 to 1,600. The events of January 9, which came to be known as "Bloody Sunday," ignited the first Russian revolution.

The outbreak of the revolution revealed the extent to which social animosities had accumulated in the preceding decades.[22] The strike movement immediately intensified. Between January and April 1905, 800,000 workers went on strike in various Russian cities. Close to 200,000 participated in May Day strikes.[23] In the spring and summer, insurgent peasants in central Russia, Poland, the Baltic region, Ukraine, and Georgia burned gentry estates, drove away the nobles or even killed them, and plundered their property. In some places they created self-styled "peasant republics," regions in which all agents of the government were expelled and elected peasants took power. The disturbances affected even the military, which until then had been the loyal bulwark of the autocracy. In June 1905 a mutiny broke out on a battleship of the Black Sea fleet, the *Potemkin*, which remained in the hands of the insurgents for eleven days.

The unprecedented scale of the unrest took the autocracy by surprise. Attempts to suppress the disturbances by force proved unsuccessful at first because the government did not have enough troops at its disposal until the conclusion of the war with Japan. Moreover, the authorities were unsure of the army's reliability, and no one within the government was capable of assuming responsibility for mass repressions. Sergei Witte, the chairman of the Committee of Ministers, whose importance grew considerably during the revolution, presented a clear alternative to the tsar: if he could not establish a dictatorship, then he had to make concessions in the form of radical political reforms. The crucial reform would have to be the creation of a representative assembly.[24]

On February 18, 1905, the tsar issued a rescript to Minister of Internal Affairs Aleksandr Bulygin in which he declared his intention, which until now had been unthinkable, of creating a consultative assembly called the State Duma. It was to be elected on the basis of unequal suffrage: that is, different strata of the population, depending on their property ownership and social estate, would choose different numbers of deputies. In the tense revolutionary atmosphere, this concession satisfied no one. The left-liberal intelligentsia, including the Union of Liberation, the Union of Unions, and a considerable segment of the Union of Zemstvo Constitutionalists, demanded a legislative parliament based on universal suffrage. There was also widespread support for a Constituent Assembly, which would draft a constitution.

In contrast, the masses demanded far more than parliamentary government. Revolutionary soviets (councils) arose in the spring of 1905, first in the cities and then in the countryside and among the military mutineers. The soviets, organs of direct democracy composed of representatives of the masses, usually acted under the leadership of the revolutionary parties. The first soviet appeared in May 1905 during a textile workers' strike in the city of Ivanovo-Voznesensk in Moscow Province. The Petersburg and Moscow soviets achieved the greatest fame during the revolution. Leon Trotsky, who was to become a major figure in the revolution of 1917 and one of the leaders of the Bolshevik Party, played an important part in the Petersburg Soviet in 1905. Dispensing with complex procedures, the soviets decided on issues that directly affected people's lives. For example, they forced price reductions in the towns, divided the gentry's land in the countryside, and secured housing for workers. The creation of the soviets indicated that while the people rejected the old autocratic and bureaucratic government, they regarded the parliamentary alternative of the liberals with skepticism.

Widespread discontent with the existing order and the desire for rapid change reached their climax in the nationwide political strike of October 1905, in which over a hundred million people took part. In hundreds of Russian cities, factories shut down, economic activity came to a halt, educational institutions closed, postal and telegraph services ceased, and transportation facilities stood idle. The government found itself in an untenable position and had to make the crucial political concession. On October 17, 1905, the tsar issued a manifesto that promised the establishment of a legislative assembly and granted fundamental civil liberties, including freedom of speech, conscience, assembly, and the press. Earlier, on April 17, the tsar had issued a decree giving his subjects the right to choose their religious affiliation and to leave the Orthodox Church. Hundreds of thousands of people in the non-Russian areas of the empire took advantage of this right to convert from Orthodoxy to other faiths.[25] One important consequence of the Manifesto of October 17 was the formation of a ministerial cabinet, the Council of Ministers. The first chairman of the new Council of Ministers, in effect the prime minister, was Sergei Witte, who was succeeded in April 1906 by Ivan Goremykin.

The creation of a legislative assembly for the most part satisfied the liberals, who began gradually withdrawing from the revolution. The revolutionary parties viewed events very differently, however. In late 1905 and early 1906 they organized armed uprisings, the most famous of which was the "Moscow insurrection" of December 1905. Uprisings erupted also in Nizhny Novgorod, Kharkov, Rostov-on-Don, Novorossiisk, Krasnoiarsk, Chita, and other cities. By then, however, the government had large contingents of troops available, and it was able to take advantage of the split in the ranks of its opponents and slowly bring the revolution to a halt. To suppress the armed uprisings, the authorities made widespread use of terror, including military field courts, composed of army officers, which swiftly tried cases involving resistance to the government and as a rule imposed death sentences. The revolutionaries also engaged in widespread terror. In addition, considerable loss of life resulted from the mass disturbances and from inter-ethnic conflicts, such as anti-Jewish pogroms in Moldavia, Belorussia, and Ukraine, and clashes between Armenians and Azerbaijanis in Transcaucasia.[26] Historians estimate that between 1905 and 1907 the death toll from the revolution ran into the tens of thousands.[27]

Despite the resistance of the revolutionaries, disturbances diminished during 1906 and 1907. Historians regard the dispersal of the Second State Duma in June 1907 as the endpoint of the revolution. (The following chapter examines the activities of the First and Second Dumas.) The results of the revolution were profoundly contradictory. On the one hand, it brought the country the reforms it had long awaited, including a legislative assembly, a cabinet system of government, and basic civil liberties. Legal political parties, trade unions, and other public organizations began to emerge, and censorship diminished considerably, though it did not entirely disappear. Workers achieved higher pay and a sizable reduction in the length of the workday in factories and mills. In the countryside, the peasants won a reduction in land rents and, most important, the abolition of redemption payments at the end of 1905. On the other hand, the modernization of the country came at a very high price. The terror greatly diminished the value of human life. The same revolutionary force and violence that had wrested reforms from the autocracy, posed a serious threat to future political stability. The maintenance of stability depended in large part on the government, which in the wake of the revolution faced the task of introducing critical reforms, above all in agriculture.

Chapter 12

On the Eve of Great Changes

Before turning to the reforms that the government introduced after the revolution of 1905–7, we need to explore their social, political, and legal context. The most important element of that context was the State Duma, the representative assembly promised by the Manifesto of October 17. The government issued specific laws that determined the structure of the assembly: the statute of December 11, 1905, on elections to the State Duma, and the statutes of February 20, 1906, on the State Duma and the State Council.[1] A considerable segment of Russian society, particularly the liberals, hailed the creation of the Duma as an important turning point in the country's history, a landmark on Russia's road to Westernization, and the culmination of a century of struggle for popular representation. The conviction was widespread that the changes taking place were irreversible. Nevertheless, the political system that emerged at the end of 1905 and the beginning of 1906 contained serious problems from the start.

After agreeing to a representative assembly in response to the pressure of the revolution, the bureaucracy imposed a number of limitations on its powers, using as models the most conservative constitutions of the time, those of Germany, Austria, and Japan.[2] Like the parliaments of those countries, the Duma could not directly influence the actions of the government, which was responsible only to the monarch. The Duma's legislative and budgetary powers were severely restricted because the State Council and the emperor had to confirm any law passed by the Duma, and certain items in the state budget were "reserved," meaning that the Duma could not discuss them. The emperor retained the right to issue laws "in exceptional circumstances" when the legislature was not in session, although the legislature subsequently had to confirm them. Finally, the two chambers of the legislature, the Duma and the State Council, rested on very different principles, leading to continual conflict between them. The statute on the State Council gave it legislative powers equal to those of the Duma. The tsar continued to appoint half the membership of the State Council, with the other half elected by various public organizations and by institutions representing the social estates: the Academy of Sciences and the universities, the Holy Synod, the noble assemblies, the zemstvo assemblies, and commercial and industrial organizations. The government intended the State Council, with its complex composition, to serve as a conservative counterweight to the State Duma.

The Duma had such limited powers that many contemporaries did not consider it a full-fledged parliament and spoke jokingly of Russia's "constitutional autocracy." The new edition of the Fundamental Laws of the Russian Empire, issued on April 23, 1906, just four days before the Duma's first session, reflected the new political system's internal contradictions. The Fundamental Laws continued to refer to the "autocratic" power of the tsar, although the text omitted the word "unlimited." Despite the juridical ambiguity, however, the country now had a real legislative assembly that faced the challenge of reconciling divergent social and political interests, expanding and strengthening the social base of the monarchy, and increasing public trust in the government. The Duma's success depended on how broadly it represented the various social strata. In this respect, however, the electoral law of December 11, 1905, introduced yet another serious complication.

The monarchy unconditionally rejected the liberal slogan of universal, direct, and equal suffrage. Voting was indirect in all the curias, or categories into which voters were divided. Some elements of the population had no electoral rights at all.[3] The new electoral system gave significant advantages to the wealthy upper classes: the landowners and bourgeoisie. For example, one landowner's vote equaled those of three bourgeois, fifteen peasants, and forty-five workers. Even so, the peasants, by virtue of their overwhelming numbers, elected about 40 percent of the Duma deputies. That was the intention of the government, which counted on the peasant deputies' traditional monarchist sentiments to counterbalance the liberals and revolutionaries. One of the participants in the governmental conferences on the eve of the Duma's first meeting related in his memoirs that "Witte undoubtedly expressed the general view when he said: 'Thank God we will have a peasant Duma.' "[4]

The assembly was indeed a "peasant Duma" in the sense that the agrarian question, the central issue for the millions of Russian peasants, figured prominently in its deliberations, but it still did not meet the government's expectations. Ominous signs appeared at the opening session, which took place in the Winter Palace on April 27, 1906. According to the memoirs of Minister of Finance Vladimir Kokovtsov, the majority of the deputies "who as though

on purpose demonstratively occupied the front rows, close to the throne, . . .
consisted of Duma members in workers' smocks or shirts. Especially prominent was a tall fellow who wore a worker's smock and high polished boots,
and examined the throne and everyone around it with an insolent and deri-
sive air."[5] These representatives of the people formed a sharp contrast to the
tsar's glittering entourage, which consisted of generals and dignitaries in
parade uniforms and numerous courtiers bearing the gem-studded state re-
galia. This symbolic confrontation foreshadowed the vigorous conflicts that
arose in the course of the Duma's activities. Contrary to the hopes of the
authorities, the peasants did not rally behind the government, and their deputies in the Duma formed part of the opposition.

By the beginning of the twentieth century the peasants' traditional
worldview no longer guaranteed their loyalty to the throne. Uppermost in the
minds of the peasants were specific economic demands, above all the demand for land. The Kadets, whose program called for a partial expropriation
of gentry estates to benefit the peasants, held 153 of the 448 seats in the
Duma. Another 107 deputies formed the Toilers' (*Trudoviki*) Group, which
shared many of the views of the Socialist Revolutionary Party.[6] At one of the
first sessions of the Duma, each of these two major opposition groups presented its own project for resolving the agrarian question. Whereas the Kadets
proposed only a partial curtailment of the gentry's landholdings, the Toilers'
Group put forth a much more radical demand for equal use of the land by
those who worked it. The Toilers' Group proposed the expropriation of all
privately held land that exceeded a certain labor norm, a plan that amounted
to the gradual elimination of private landownership. The government found
both projects totally unacceptable. It declared that "the principle of the in-
alienability and inviolability of property is . . . a fundamental bulwark of the
state's existence throughout the world."[7]

A host of other issues besides the agrarian question divided the government and much of the Duma. The deputies presented proposals to abolish the
State Council, to broaden the legislative powers of the lower chamber, and to
establish the accountability of ministers to the Duma, a measure that would
have given Russia a full-fledged parliamentary system. "The executive power
must be subordinated to the legislative power," demanded the lawyer Vladimir
Nabokov, one of the leaders of the Kadets. Many deputies called for a general political amnesty. At the first session of the Duma, the veteran zemstvo
oppositionist Ivan Petrunkevich declared: "Honor and conscience demand
that the first free word spoken from this rostrum be dedicated to those who
sacrificed their life and liberty for Russia's political freedom. A free Russia
demands the liberation of all those who have suffered for freedom."[8]

The government gradually realized that it could not work with such an assembly. On July 8, 1906, the authorities dissolved the First Duma, accusing it of "inciting sedition." In protest, some of the Kadet and Toilers' deputies withdrew to autonomous Finland and issued a call for civil disobedience by the populace. Their appeal, called the Vyborg Manifesto after the town in which it was issued, met no response, however.

Although the government had dissolved the First Duma, it did not intend to abolish the assembly itself. In the autumn of 1906 it held elections to the Second Duma on the basis of the previous electoral law. As a result of their bitter experience, the Kadets conducted themselves much more cautiously in the Second Duma, which convened on February 20, 1907. Their slogan now was "safeguard the Duma." Their new tactics brought them no success, however, because they lacked a majority in the Second Duma, with only 98 out of the 518 deputies. In contrast, the radical left-wing groups considerably increased their representation: the Social Democrats had 65 deputies, the Socialist Revolutionaries 37, and the Toilers' Group 104. Right-wing groups also increased the number of their deputies, from 15 to 63. As a result, the Second Duma, opposing the government on most issues, was fragmented and virtually unable to function. The authorities once again faced the prospect of dissolving the Duma. They realized, however, that if they conducted new elections on the basis of the old electoral law, the conflicts would continue. Only a change in the electoral law would resolve the impasse, but that course entailed several negative consequences.

First of all, according to the Fundamental Laws of 1906, the government could not change the electoral law unilaterally. Such a change required the agreement of the Duma, which was unobtainable. The only alternative was a forcible violation of the legal system. Furthermore, changes in the electoral law would make the suffrage even more unequal than it was, thereby further undermining the fragile system of representation. The political situation in the country would deteriorate. By the summer of 1907, however, the government felt that it had no choice. On June 3 the authorities dissolved the Duma, accusing the Social Democratic deputies of participating in a military conspiracy. On the same day, the government issued a new electoral law. The manifesto on the dissolution of the Duma stated: "Only the power that granted the first electoral law, the historical power of the Russian tsar, has the right to rescind it and replace it with a new one."[9] The nature of the elections changed greatly. The new law reduced the number of peasant representatives by half and the number of worker representatives even more. One landowner's vote now equaled 4 votes of the upper bourgeoisie, 68 votes of the petty townspeople, 260 peasant votes, and 543 worker votes. The number of peasant electors in the indirect voting system declined from 42 percent to 22.5 percent, while the number of landowner electors rose from 31 percent to 50.5

percent. The number of deputies from Poland and the Caucasus declined by two-thirds.

The authors of the new electoral law candidly termed it "shameless," recognizing that it violated all the principles that would have made the Duma an authentic expression of the interests of the population at large. Evidently, they believed that in the tense atmosphere of revolutionary Russia this "shameless" law was the heavy price that had to be paid to achieve a more or less constructive assembly. The elections to the Third Duma in the autumn of 1907 directly reflected the changes in the electoral law. The Octobrists, who stood to the right of the Kadets and had previously been a negligible force, now became the largest party in the Duma, with 148 of the 448 deputies. Right-wing groups had 144 deputies, the Kadets only 54. On reform proposals the Octobrists voted with the Kadets to create a left-liberal majority, while on repressive measures they swung to the right. Thanks to the so-called "Octobrist pendulum," the Duma succeeded in passing several government-sponsored initiatives.

In the eyes of most Russians, the new electoral system diminished the legitimacy of the Duma and cast doubt on the legality of any measures it might pass. The Duma henceforth represented mainly the small wealthy strata of society and lacked firm ties with the lower classes. Under these conditions, the introduction of far-reaching social reforms aimed at expanding a prosperous middle class in Russia became particularly urgent. That was the objective of Petr Stolypin, who became chairman of the Council of Ministers in July 1906.

A broad spectrum of political forces, from extreme conservatives to proponents of moderate reform, hailed the rapid political ascent of Stolypin, the last major statesman of tsarist Russia. They all expected him to carry out elements of their own programs. The historian David Macey wrote of Stolypin: "An independent public figure . . . who combined the qualities of a modernizing landowner, a marshal of the nobility, and a government official, he symbolized the unity of social and governmental forces that alone made possible a revolution of consciousness,"[10] that is, a rejection of ingrained bureaucratic habits of mind in the formulation of policy.

Stolypin came from an ancient noble clan that went back to the sixteenth century, and he was related to many famous Russian families, including the Suvorovs, the Gorchakovs, and the Lermontovs. The Stolypins owned estates in Kovno, Saratov, Penza, Kazan, and Novgorod provinces, a total of more than seven thousand desiatinas. After graduating from St. Petersburg University, Stolypin held various offices in the Ministry of Internal Affairs and in local administration, and in 1904 he was appointed governor of Saratov Province. As governor, he distinguished himself in

1905 by waging a fierce and uncompromising struggle with the revolutionaries and resolutely suppressing agrarian disorders. The qualities he displayed, as well as his membership in a wealthy old noble family, helped Stolypin to make a brilliant career. He was soon appointed minister of internal affairs and then, at the age of forty-four, became Russia's youngest head of government.[11]

Nicholas and his entourage, of course, expected Stolypin to wage an energetic battle against the revolution, and he fully justified their hopes. In response to an attempt on his life by a wing of the SR Party, Stolypin established military field courts that speedily tried cases of resistance to the authorities. In 1907–9, the military field courts sentenced 2,681 people to death, an average of 70 per month.[12] Stolypin conducted himself self-confidently in the Duma, firmly replying to attacks by the left-wing deputies with such phrases as "You can't intimidate me," and "You need great upheavals, but we need a Great Russia."[13]

Unlike the intransigent conservatives, however, Stolypin fully understood that he could not suppress the revolution with punitive measures alone. "In Prussia and Austria, where the government overcame a revolution, it succeeded not just by applying physical force but by assuming the leadership of reforms even while asserting force," the prime minister declared. "To direct the creativity of the government entirely to devising police measures is a sign of impotence on the part of the authorities."[14] In fact, Stolypin pursued a dual program in which repression provided the essential foundation for the introduction of moderate political reforms. His program included not only agrarian reform but broader powers for the zemstvos, changes in the zemstvo electoral system to draw in prosperous peasants, greater civil rights for the peasantry, abolition of the land captains, and restoration of the peace courts. In addition, he planned to expand freedom of conscience, to establish a state insurance system for workers, and gradually to introduce universal primary education.

Social and political circumstances after 1907 on the whole favored Stolypin's plans. The revolution had exhausted the population. Between 1905 and 1907 it had endured a vast wave of violence and destruction, and it welcomed many of the steps the government took to restore order. Mass antigovernment action, including workers' strikes, gradually declined after 1907. In 1908, 176,000 workers went on strike, but in 1910 the number fell to 47,000.[15] The revolutionary parties underwent a profound crisis. A dispute between "liquidators" and "recallers" split the Social Democrats. The "liquidators" proposed to abolish or sharply curtail the party's revolutionary underground organization in favor of legal activity, while the "recallers" wanted to recall the SD deputies from the Duma and concentrate entirely on underground activities. The Azef Affair, in which Evno Azef, a longtime leader of the SR Party, was unmasked as a police agent, left the Socialist Revolutionaries deeply shaken.

The intelligentsia, the eternal enemy of the existing order, found itself gradually drawn into it as legal public organizations like the zemstvos and the municipal dumas expanded their activities. In 1895–1912 the zemstvos' budget grew from 65.8 million to 220 million rubles, and that of the cities to 297 million rubles. By the mid-1910s the zemstvos administered an extensive network of schools, hospitals, agronomic and veterinary services, and credit and savings institutions, all of which required a large professional staff. The institutions of urban self- government also needed large numbers of educated employees to administer new facilities such as telephone, streetcar, and streetlight systems. Cooperative institutions grew rapidly. In 1914 Russia had about thirty thousand credit, producer, and consumer cooperatives, with twelve million members. Deposits in credit cooperatives reached 304 million rubles.[16]

A collection of articles entitled *Landmarks*, which appeared in 1909 and quickly went through five editions, offered a philosophical interpretation of these changes. The authors— Nikolai Berdiaev, Sergei Bulgakov, Mikhail Gershenzon, Aleksandr Izgoev, Bogdan Kistiakovsky, Petr Struve, and Semyon Frank—were prominent opposition figures, and many of them were former Marxists. Their essays reflected the profound changes that had taken place in their outlook and mode of thought. They criticized not specific elements of the revolutionary ideology but the very foundations of the radical intelligentsia's worldview. According to the *Landmarks* authors, the intelligentsia was seeking to liberate people externally before they had become free internally. That was no accident, for in the opinion of the authors the intelligentsia was inherently hostile to slow, stubborn effort and wanted "to leap into the realm of the future" in one bound. In its struggle for a "radiant future," the radical intelligentsia applied a double standard: it was intolerant of disagreement with its own views but readily resorted to violence against its enemies. Its favorite theory, socialism, emphasized the redistribution of material goods and minimized the importance of creative activity. Thus the intelligentsia's worldview condemned to sterility the revolutionaries' desperate struggle "for the happiness of the toiling people."[17]

Although the intelligentsia greeted *Landmarks* with bitter denunciations, the controversy that the collection aroused demonstrated the timeliness of its views. Increasing numbers of social and political figures were abandoning the idea of demolishing existing institutions in favor of slow, gradual change. The left wing of the liberal camp, the Kadets, lost some of its influence, and right-liberal views and organizations began to play a larger role. The most important of those organizations was the Union of October 17, or Octobrist Party, the largest group in the Third and Fourth Dumas.[18]

Although liberal, the Octobrists considered the demands of the Kadets excessive and wanted to distance themselves categorically from the revolutionary movement. They declared: "Our party's goal is to rally a circle of people around the government for united, fruitful, and creative work."[19] The first leader of the party was Dmitry Shipov, a large landowner and prominent zemstvo figure, followed by Aleksandr Guchkov, who came from a famous dynasty of Old Believer textile manufacturers in Moscow. The party's membership consisted of moderate zemstvo and municipal duma activists, landowners, and prominent government officials. It also included bankers and industrialists, such as Nikolai Avdakov and Emmanuel Nobel, and well-known intellectuals, such as the lawyer Fyodor Plevako and the historians Vladimir Gere and Vasily Sergeevich. The social base of the Octobrist Party was better defined but much narrower than that of the Kadets.

The Octobrists' ideology was evident from their name: they adhered to the principles of the Manifesto of October 17, 1905. Eager to promote the gradual development and refinement of those principles, the Octobrists regarded a constitutional monarchy as the best political structure for the country, with a property qualification for parliamentary elections and a government responsible only to the tsar. Control of the executive power by the monarch, they felt, was not only a long tradition in Russia but also "a pledge of its organic development on the basis of its thousand-year past."[20] They opposed granting extensive cultural autonomy to the non-Russian peoples of the empire. While recognizing the importance of trade unions, they were skeptical of giving workers the right to strike, and they argued that in view of Russia's industrial backwardness, an eight-hour workday would lead to a sharp rise in prices and make Russian goods uncompetitive. Finally, on the agrarian question, the Octobrists rejected any massive expropriation of privately owned land and stressed the importance of individual peasant landownership and the abolition of the commune.

The Octobrists provided the government with significant support in the Duma, for one of Stolypin's favorite ideas was breaking up the commune. Stolypin consistently advocated resolving the agrarian question by changing the peasants' relationship to the land rather than by enlarging their allotments. The prime minister, like his Octobrist allies, believed that the peasants' troubles stemmed from a relative, not an absolute lack of land, as they failed to make use of the land they already possessed. Although the Russian peasants' allotments were comparable in size to those of West European peasants or even larger, they produced low yields because the commune shackled the peasantry. Stolypin argued that expropriating the landowners' estates, as the Kadets and Toilers' Group proposed, would not satisfy the peasants' land hunger because population growth in the countryside would soon simply "eat up" the additional land.

Stolypin proposed to solve the peasants' problems by unleashing their initiative, giving them a sense of ownership and increased incentives to make more productive use of their land. In 1904 the future prime minister wrote: "If we provide an outlet for the energy and initiative of the best forces in the countryside, and if we give the industrious farmer the opportunity to acquire a separate piece of land, first for a trial period and subsequently in full ownership, . . . then alongside the commune, wherever it still exists, an independent, prosperous peasant, a stable representative of the land, will emerge." Such an agrarian reform would change the mentality of the peasants, make them less receptive to revolutionary propaganda, and give them "a healthier view of other people's property rights."[21] The destruction of the commune would have the added advantage of reducing the ability of the peasants to take collective action against the landowners and the government.

The emphasis that Stolypin placed on agrarian reform reflected his attention to social rather than just political change. "We must begin by replacing the eroded foundation stones, and do it in such a way as to strengthen the whole structure without undermining it," he declared.[22] Stolypin's reform program represented a culmination and completion of the reforms of the 1860s and the 1870s.

During the revolution of 1905–7, Stolypin laid the groundwork for his agrarian reform. The Manifesto of November 3, 1905, abolished the peasants' redemption payments for their allotments and expanded the operations of the Peasant Land Bank. On November 4, 1906, the government issued a law creating land-tenure commissions in the provinces and districts. Decrees of August 12 and 27, 1906, transferred some state lands and crown lands to the Peasant Land Bank for sale on preferential terms to the peasants living on them. A decree of October 5, 1906, abolished the most significant limitations on the rights of peasants as compared to members of other estates. Finally, the celebrated decree of November 9, 1906, allowed a peasant to leave the commune while retaining possession of his allotment land. The Duma subsequently confirmed the decree, which became law in 1910.

Under this law, a peasant who withdrew from the commune could demand a unitary piece of land, called an *otrub*, equivalent to the scattered strips of his allotment. If the peasant moved his house, livestock, and equipment from the village to his new land, he created a farmstead (*khutor*), like an American farm. The formation of farmsteads was the ultimate objective of Stolypin's agrarian reform. He asserted: "As long as the peasant is poor, as long as he does not own land as his personal property, as long as he finds himself forced to remain in the clutches of the commune, he will stay a slave, and no written law will give him the blessing of civil freedom."[23]

Stolypin realized that weakening the commune would make it impossible for all the peasants to remain on the land. Inequality and stratification would inevitably result when the peasants personally owned their allotment land and could buy and sell it. Serious measures were required to prevent the development of social tensions. Stolypin predicted that some of the peasants who lost their land would find work in the growing industries of the cities. For others, he planned a large-scale program of emigration to the eastern areas of the empire, Siberia, the Far East, and Central Asia. Emigration would foster the economic development of newly acquired regions, increase the number of Russians in the borderlands, and remove the most hapless, embittered, and potentially rebellious peasants from overpopulated central Russia.

Stolypin's agrarian reform lasted about seven years, up to the outbreak of World War I, and in quantitative terms it was notably successful. In 1906–14, 35 percent of peasant households, or 3.5 million, declared their intention to withdraw from the commune. Twenty-six percent, or 2.5 million, completed their withdrawal, and about 400,000 households, or one-sixth of those that withdrew, created farmsteads. In the course of the reform, the Peasant Land Bank sold 11 million desiatinas of gentry land and 4 million desiatinas of state and crown land. Of the 3.3 million peasants who migrated eastward, 2 million succeeded in setting up their own farms.[24]

An appreciable growth in agricultural production accompanied Stolypin's agrarian program, although its actual causes remain in dispute. Some historians argue that the reforms themselves made a less important contribution than favorable climatic conditions and lower peasant taxes. Whatever the explanation, Russia's rural economy achieved considerable success in 1907–13. The sown area grew by 10 percent and grain exports by 30 percent. The average annual grain harvest was half again as large as in the preceding thirty years: 74 million tons compared to 49 million. The use of mineral fertilizer doubled, and the use of agricultural machinery more than tripled.[25]

The growth in agricultural production helped raise the population's standard of living, as reflected, for example, in increased savings-bank deposits and greater per capita consumption of industrial products and foodstuffs. The expansion of the internal market in turn initiated a new industrial boom. The average annual increase in industrial production in 1907–13 reached 9 percent. Pig-iron production grew by 64 percent, steel by 82 percent, and coal by 50 percent.[26] The country seemed firmly on the road to peaceful development. Stolypin declared: "Give us twenty years of external and internal peace, and you will not recognize Russia."[27]

Despite the country's socio-economic and political progress, however,

Grain Yields on Peasant Allotments, 1909–1913

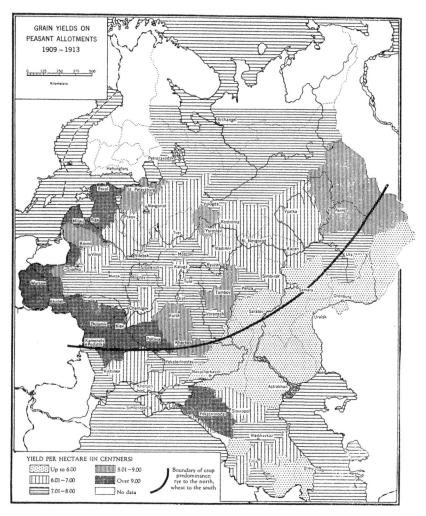

Source: Lyashchenko, Peter I. *History of the National Economy of Russia to the 1917 Revolution.* Trans. By L.M. Herman; introd. By Calvin B. Hoover; maps redrawn under the supervision of Leonard H. Dykes. American Council of Learned Societies Devoted to Humanistic Studies. Russian Translation Project. Series 4. New York: Macmillan, 1949. By permission of the American Council of Learned Societies.

alarming signs began to appear. Stolypin's agrarian program itself caused many problems. On the whole, the reform answered the needs of the country and increased the chances for a peaceful outcome to the crisis. The changes had been so long delayed, however, that in order to carry them out the government had to exert a good deal of administrative pressure on the peasantry. In David Macey's words, "despite Stolypin's slogans, such as 'enrich yourselves' and 'reliance on the strong and the sober,' the reforms both preserved and in some cases expanded the traditional governmental system of bureaucratic tutelage, chiefly by creating an enormous bureaucratic apparatus specifically to implement the reforms."[28] The Stolypin reforms enjoyed the most success in areas where commercial production was already well developed, such as New Russia (Tauride, Ekaterinoslav, and Kherson provinces), the Northwest (Petersburg, Pskov, and Smolensk provinces), and the Lower Volga (Saratov and Samara provinces). They had the least success in the non-black-earth provinces. The authorities often forced entire villages to create individual farms, even where communal practices were still of importance to the peasants. In some regions, historians have found, the commune had begun to transform itself into a producers' cooperative, and it retained its traditional function as a mutual-assistance institution in difficult times. Under these circumstances, the government's efforts to force its will on the peasants only exacerbated tensions in the countryside.

The major defect of the reform was its lack of financial resources. The government's expenditures on re-equipping the army and repaying the state's debts left inadequate funds to support the new peasant farms and the Siberian settlers. As a result, many peasants who attempted to create independent farms were financially ruined and lost their land. Half a million of the 3.5 million peasants who emigrated east of the Urals failed to establish themselves there and had to return to European Russia. Despite the government's efforts, the peasants continued to dream of a "black [total] repartition" and regarded the landowning nobility as their main enemy. Making good use of these sentiments, the revolutionaries gradually expanded their activities in the countryside. Paradoxically, however, the radicals posed less of a threat to Stolypin than groups that ostensibly had a vital interest in maintaining a stable order in the Russian Empire: the conservative gentry and the radical nationalists, or "Black Hundreds."

The Black Hundreds (a derogatory term coined by their opponents and derived from medieval Russian history) arose as a direct consequence of the revolution of 1905–7.[29] These organizations attracted elements of the population that suffered from the upheavals and feared their spread: conservative nobles, traditionalist merchants, small traders, and part of the working class. These ill-assorted groups rallied to one central idea: militant nationalism.

The Black Hundreds regarded the ethnic minorities of the Russian Empire as the main perpetrators of the revolution. They especially hated the Jews, who, they believed, made up the majority of the opposition parties. The anti-Semitic and anti-Polish appeals of the Black Hundreds also won them broad support among the peasants in the western provinces, although their influence in central Russia was limited.

Attacks on Jews and revolutionaries by urban and rural mobs marked the beginning of the revolution, and particularly the publication of the October 17 manifesto. The mobs carried out pogroms against the Jews, attacked anti-governmental demonstrations and political meetings, and murdered several prominent opposition figures. In an effort to organize and channel the spontaneous actions of the masses, nationalist leaders created political organizations such as Aleksandr Dubrovin's Union of the Russian People and Vladimir Purishkevich's Union of the Archangel Michael. Leaders of the Black Hundreds figured prominently in the Second and especially the Third State Dumas. They demanded greater prerogatives for the monarch, restrictions on the opposition parties, and curtailment of the rights of the non-Russian ethnic groups in the borderlands.

At first the Black Hundreds welcomed Stolypin's energetic actions and hailed his harsh measures to suppress the revolution. He appreciated the militant nationalism that inspired the Black Hundreds, for he too considered the extensive rights of the ethnic minorities a threat to the unity and stability of the state. His administration renewed the attack on Finland's autonomy, which had been fully restored during the revolution. The law of June 17, 1910, on procedures for approval in Finland of laws that pertained to the empire as a whole, removed several issues from the competence of the Finnish Diet, including regulations on freedom of assembly and association, legislation on the press, and school curricula. The law of 1911 on the introduction of zemstvos in the western provinces created "national," or ethnic, curias, that is, separate voting for "Russian" (meaning Belorussian and Ukrainian) electors at the expense of the Polish landowners. Stolypin began the process, which was completed in 1912, of detaching the so-called Kholm District, predominantly Ukrainian in population, from the Kingdom of Poland. Because Stolypin coupled his nationalist measures with social and political reforms, however, the Black Hundreds grew increasingly suspicious of him. They believed that his reforms would destroy the Russian monarchy's traditional sources of support, the patriarchal outlook of the peasants and the predominance of the local gentry.

An influential conservative organization, the Council of the United Nobility, established in 1905, also grew dissatisfied with Stolypin's policies. Opposition from conservative gentry circles posed a danger to Stolypin because many of their members belonged to the aristocracy and had direct access to the tsar. Nicholas, who at first supported his energetic prime minister unreservedly, also shared many of the conservative opposition's grievances against Stolypin. Moreover, a powerful and independent governmental leader simply did not conform to the preconceptions of Nicholas II, who continued to regard himself as the unconditional source of executive authority. Stolypin's independent actions as prime minister inevitably encroached on areas that the tsar considered his sole prerogative, such as foreign policy and military affairs. "It seems to me that he wants to take my place," Nicholas once said of Stolypin to his intimate circle.[30]

By 1911, shortly before his murder at the hands of a terrorist, most observers felt that Stolypin's dismissal was imminent.[31] Stolypin's assassination owed much to certain measures the government had taken to combat revolution. Even before Stolypin took office, the authorities made extensive use of agents provocateurs, members of anti-governmental groups who came over to the side of the government and supplied it with information on the revolutionary underground. Some of those individuals served both the government and the revolutionary parties at the same time, organizing assassination attempts on their own employers, the heads of the Ministry of Internal Affairs. The classic example of a double agent was Evno Azef, who for many years directed the Combat Organization of the SR Party. The obvious danger in the use of such agents led many public figures and government officials to demand its elimination, but Stolypin continued the practice. As a result, he himself fell victim to an agent provocateur. His assassination took place in September 1911, in Kiev, where he was attending celebrations in connection with the dedication of a memorial to Alexander II. The inexplicably negligent police allowed a young lawyer named Dmitry Bogrov, who was both a Socialist Revolutionary and a secret agent of the police, to approach Stolypin in a theater and shoot him at point-blank range.

Stolypin's death revealed the country's increasingly troubled state. The improvements in the standard of living and in the social and political system had come too late. Rising social tensions manifested themselves in new peasant disturbances and the revived worker and student movements. In 1911 the authorities' attempt to tighten control over higher education led to a mass resignation by professors at Moscow University, followed by a student strike. In 1912 the so-called "Lena incident" shocked the country. Troops fired on striking workers at the British-owned Lena River goldfields in Siberia, killing or wounding over four hundred men. This event precipitated a wave of protest strikes involving more than 300,000 workers. In 1913 and the first half of 1914 two million workers went on strike, more than in the revolutionary year of 1905.[32]

The results of the elections to the Fourth State Duma in the autumn of 1912 did not favor the government. The Octobrists, who had undergone an internal crisis during the Third Duma, lost 98 of their 154 deputies, although they remained the largest party in the Fourth Duma. The number of deputies from opposition groups, both on the left and on the right, increased. Even the once loyal Octobrists now opposed the government, feeling that it had lost all political initiative after Stolypin's death and could no longer respond effectively to the challenges facing the country. Aleksandr Guchkov, the leader of the Octobrists, declared in 1913: "We are living through a historical drama in which we must defend the monarchy against the monarch, the church against the church hierarchy, the army against its leaders, and the authority of the government against the representatives of that authority."[33]

Conclusion

Despite the growth of social and political tensions in Russia, a new revolution and the fall of the monarchy were by no means inevitable in 1914. Within the "old regime," destructive tendencies clashed with clear signs of stabilization, and the outcome of their struggle was not foreordained. The event that tipped the scales to the side of revolution was Russia's entry into World War I. The war itself resulted from uneven rates of development among the great powers, an imbalance that sharply intensified at the beginning of the twentieth century. Although Russian interests were not directly involved in the coming conflict, the country could not remain on the sidelines and had to participate in a war that would have far-reaching consequences.

The main participants in the international rivalry of the early twentieth century were Germany, a new imperialist power, on the one hand, and England and France, the old colonial powers, on the other. Germany came late to the colonial division of the world. It sought new markets, sources of raw material, and opportunities to invest its capital, and it strove to control major trade routes. England and France, naturally, did not wish to yield their colonial preeminence.

Russia, which was well aware of its lack of preparedness for war and its vulnerable geopolitical situation, tried to conduct itself with the utmost restraint. Hoping to avoid being drawn into a European conflict, Russia had shifted the focus of its foreign policy to the Far East at the turn of the century. Russia also tried to reduce international tensions in Europe. In 1899, on the initiative of the Russian government, an international disarmament conference convened at The Hague. Most of Russia's diplomatic efforts proved fruitless, however. The Hague Conference adopted a number of resolutions on the rules of war, but it could not prevent the growth of international conflict. Russia's "withdrawal" from Europe to the Far East, of course, ended with its catastrophic defeat in the war with Japan. As time went on, Russia's inevitable participation in a world war, and thus its need for allies, became increasingly clear. The choice of allies was no simple matter for Russia's rulers, however.

At the beginning of the twentieth century Russia had serious disagreements with both Germany and England, the leaders of the two rival political and military blocs in Europe. In the 1890s economic conflicts had arisen between Russia and Germany. Germany waged a tariff war with Russia, raising import duties on Russian grain while obtaining favorable treatment for its own industrial goods. In addition, Germany was actively asserting its influence in the region of the Black Sea Straits, which was of great strategic importance to the Russian Empire. Relations with England were also complicated because England opposed Russia in Central Asia and supported Japan during the Russo-Japanese War. Faced with growing danger from Germany, however, England in the early 1900s greatly improved its relations with France. That facilitated a rapprochement between England and Russia because in the early 1890s Russia and France had established a military alliance and close economic cooperation.[1]

An additional factor that drew Russia toward alliance with England and France was the rise of patriotic sentiment within the liberal opposition. Liberals who had previously been uncompromising adversaries of the autocracy began to adopt a more conservative stance and actively discussed Russia's national interests and the best means of defending them. "There is only one way to create a great Russia," Petr Struve wrote in 1912, "and that is to direct all our efforts to the region that is most susceptible to the real influence of Russian culture. That region is the entire Black Sea basin, meaning all the European and Asiatic countries that border on the Black Sea."[2] Struve and his like-minded associates believed that the growing needs of Russian capitalism required the country to fortify its position in the Balkans. That policy inevitably brought Russia into conflict with Austria-Hungary, which enjoyed German support. By the beginning of the twentieth century control over the Balkans had become a matter of survival for Austria-Hungary because the growing ethnic movements of the Balkan Slavs were undermining the "patchwork empire" from within.

The conflicts with Germany and Austria-Hungary ultimately impelled Russia's rulers to choose an alliance with England and France. In 1907 England and Russia concluded an agreement that resolved their old antagonisms in Central Asia. They assigned Afghanistan to the English zone of interest, divided Persia into two spheres of influence, and recognized Tibet as an independent state. Russia officially joined the Anglo-French alliance,

Russia in World War I, 1914 to the Revolution of 1917

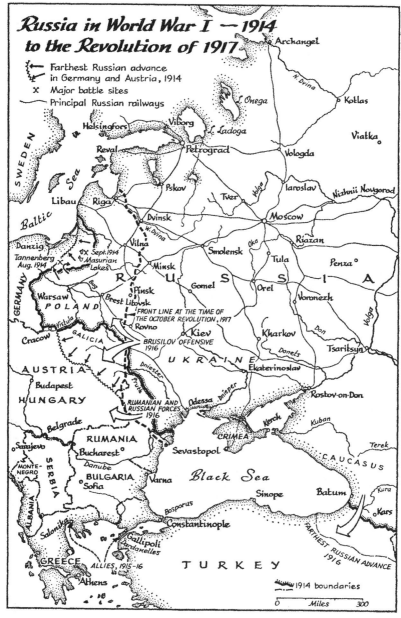

Source: A History of Russia, Seventh Edition, Nicholas V. Riasanovsky and Mark Steinberg, p. 393. Copyright © 1963, 1969, 1977, 1984, 1993, 2000, 2004 by Oxford University Press, Inc. Used by permission of Oxford University Press, Inc.

called the Entente, which had been concluded in 1904. In turn, Germany and Austria-Hungary actively sought to diminish Russia's diplomatic influence in the Balkan states and increased their presence in Turkey. The Balkan states themselves—Greece, Bulgaria, Romania, Serbia, and Montenegro—were constantly fighting each other in an effort to enlarge their territory, and through agreements with the Great Powers they drew them into their conflicts. Under these circumstances, one spark was enough to ignite a conflagration.

On June 15/28, 1914, Gavrilo Princip, a member of a Serbian nationalist organization, assassinated the heir to the Austrian throne, Archduke Francis Ferdinand. Austria-Hungary and Germany felt prepared for military action and decided to use the assassination as a convenient pretext for going to war. The Austrians presented Serbia with a ten-point ultimatum that patently violated its sovereignty. They demanded, for example, that Serbia allow Austrian officials access to Serbian territory in order to investigate the planning of the assassination, and that the Serbian government punish officials, officers, and professors on lists that the Austrians would provide. Full acceptance of the ultimatum would have amounted to capitulation by Serbia and a serious diplomatic defeat for its ally, Russia. On Russia's advice, the Serbs accepted most points of the ultimatum, but Austria-Hungary considered the reply unsatisfactory and declared war on Serbia. Russia began a general mobilization, which led to the breaking of relations with Germany. Soon, the alliance system drew most of the European powers into the war. France entered on Russia's side; and England, Italy, Romania, and eventually the United States joined France and Russia. Bulgaria and Turkey supported Austria-Hungary and Germany.

Many observers predicted that Russia's participation in the war would lead to the fall of the old regime. At first, however, events on the battlefield went relatively well for Russia. Although an attempt to attack East Prussia failed, the Russians gained significant victories on the Austrian front. Russia occupied Galicia and Bukovina, took the cities of Lvov and Chernovtsy as well as the powerful fortress of Przemysl, and seized key passes in the Carpathian Mountains. The Russian army prepared to invade Hungary. Military actions in the Transcaucasus against Turkey were also successful.[3] In the winter of 1914–15, however, the German high command radically revised its strategy and shifted its basic military operations from the western to the eastern front. Russia's military position sharply deteriorated.

The events of 1915 revealed the serious gaps in Russia's modernization and the shortcomings of its heavy industry. Despite the rapid pace of Russian industrialization in the late nineteenth and early twentieth centuries, Russia had not caught up to the leading countries of the West. The state-owned military factories produced only 600,000 shells in 1914, while the front required 42 million annually. The density of the railroad network in European Russia was one-tenth that of Germany. These deficiencies manifested themselves during the large-scale offensive that Germany and Austria-Hungary undertook against Russia in the spring of 1915. Russia's opponents achieved overwhelming superiority in military technology and munitions, with two and a half times as many machine guns, four and a half times as many light weapons, and forty times as many heavy weapons.[4] The Russians had to withdraw from Galicia, Bukovina, Poland, and parts of Belorussia and the Baltic provinces. Between May and September 1915 the Russian army lost about 2.5 million men.

The military defeats had an immediate social and economic impact on Russia. The relatively thin rail network could barely handle the floods of troops and refugees and the shipment of munitions. The large cities began to experience food shortages. The shift of resources from the production of consumer goods to heavy industry shattered the domestic market and led to inflation. The peasants found it unprofitable to sell their grain. The mobilization of a significant part of the peasant population made matters worse by curtailing agricultural production. Refugees, wounded soldiers, newly mobilized recruits waiting to be sent to the front, and ordinary citizens suffering from the hardships of war formed an embittered, confused mass demanding rapid and decisive improvements.[5] Russia needed a firm government able to react quickly to the problems facing the country and take steps to resolve them. The political system, however, may have been the most fragile element of the old older.

The unstable nature of the political structure that had emerged after the revolution of 1905–7 did not manifest itself immediately. The declaration of war produced an outburst of national unity and a temporary cessation of political conflict. All the political parties except the Bolsheviks expressed support for the war. Pavel Miliukov, an implacable opponent of the government, declared in the name of the Kadet Party that the war was being fought "for the liberation of our homeland from foreign invasion, for the liberation of Europe and the Slavs from German domination, and for the liberation of the entire world from the intolerable burden of armaments."[6] The Russian army's defeats in 1915, however, immediately revealed the ephemeral nature of the sense of national unity. The opposition parties, which now included the Octobrists and other right-liberal groups, renewed the struggle against the government. They felt that they had a solid basis for their political attack, for they not only asserted the need to fight the enemy and defend Russia's national interests but declared that they could do it better than the government.

The main weapons in the hands of the opposition parties were the public organizations that had arisen in 1914 and 1915: the All-Russian Union of Zemstvos and the All-Russian Union of Towns, which formed the Union of Zemstvos and Towns (known as Zemgor), and the War Industries Committee.[7] The primary functions of Zemgor, under the chairmanship of Prince Georgy Lvov, a Kadet, were to provide assistance to refugees and wounded soldiers, and to supply the front with food, boots, and clothing. The War Industries Committee, chaired by Aleksandr Guchkov, mobilized private industry for the war effort. Both organizations commanded extensive networks of local committees with tens of thousands of personnel. Although Zemgor and the War Industries Committee were supposed to engage in purely technical matters, in the hands of the opposition they gradually turned into something like a parallel government and began to play a key role in major areas of economic and social life. The opposition made use of them in its campaign to wrest control of the executive power, from which the Fundamental Laws of April 23, 1906, had excluded members of the legislature.

The emperor, who jealously defended his right to exercise absolute executive authority, found their efforts totally unacceptable. He was firmly convinced that even in peacetime, let alone under the exceptional conditions of a war, the government must remain under the monarch's control. The government imposed restrictions on the operations of Zemgor and the War Industries Committee, angering their participants. Even influential generals and government officials found it difficult to understand the confrontation between the tsar and the liberals. They felt that in wartime a spirit of compromise should prevail, and that all efforts should focus on victory at the front. Agreement, however, proved even harder to achieve than on the eve of the war. The government began to engage in "ministerial leapfrog": between July 1915 and February 1917, Russia had four prime ministers, six ministers of internal affairs, three ministers of foreign affairs, four ministers of war, and four ministers of justice.[8] The instability of the government exasperated society and hampered the conduct of the war.

As the situation worsened both at the front and in the rear, the stakes in the political struggle rose steadily and forced the two sides to resort to increasingly radical measures. In August 1915 the majority of Duma deputies united in the so-called Progressive Bloc, which demanded political reforms and control over the government.[9] The government was so discredited in the eyes of society that representatives of a wide range of political opinions supported the Progressive Bloc's demands: the leaders of Zemgor and the War Industries Committee, many of the zemstvos and municipal dumas, some organizations of the nobility, and even deputies of the State Council. In its effort to achieve power, the opposition began to employ highly dubious methods. It spread rumors of attempts by court circles to conclude a separate peace with

Germany on terms disadvantageous to Russia, and of contacts between Empress Alexandra, who was a German princess by birth, and the German high command. A speech in the Duma by Pavel Miliukov in November 1916 resonated throughout the country. Although he based his speech entirely on unverified information, Miliukov punctuated his attack on the government with the repeated question: "Is this stupidity, or is it treason?"

The tsar, in turn, increasingly shut himself off from society. He isolated himself within a narrow circle of people he personally trusted and lost all understanding of the real situation in the country. In August 1915 he made the fateful decision to assume supreme command of the army and left for the front. In Nicholas's absence, important governmental affairs fell into the hands of Alexandra. A sickly woman inclined to mysticism, she firmly believed in autocratic power and had a poor understanding of Russia's system of government.

Grigory Rasputin, a rogue from Siberia who represented himself as a holy man and a "prophet," exerted enormous influence on Alexandra. She believed that he possessed the God-given power to treat the hemophilia that afflicted the imperial couple's only son, Alexei. Rasputin's closeness to the empress enabled him to engage in political intrigue, influence state appointments, and distribute lucrative military contracts. Rasputin's rise completed the tsarist family's alienation not only from society and the government but from its own relatives, the grand dukes, as well as military commanders and courtiers.[10] Opposition leaders and military circles began to draw up plans for a palace coup d'état to remove the emperor and empress from power and transfer the throne to a member of the dynasty more sympathetic to the opposition. In December 1916 some aristocrats murdered Rasputin. In the end, however, mass disturbances in Petrograd, as the Germanic-sounding St. Petersburg had been renamed at the start of the war, and not a palace coup determined the fate of the old regime. Political meetings and worker demonstrations gained the support of broad segments of the population. After a few days, troops began to join the insurgents. Nicholas tried to send loyal military detachments to Petrograd and attempted to return to the capital himself, but his train was stopped outside the city. Army commanders and Duma leaders, believing that they firmly controlled the situation in the country, used this opportunity to seize power. On March 2, 1917, Nicholas II was forced to abdicate.[11]

The fall of the monarchy at the end of February and the beginning of March 1917 gave the opposition forces the opportunity to realize their long-held plans for radical social and political reforms. The leaders of the Duma formed a Provisional Government, which became the official center of power after Nicholas's abdication. The Provisional Government reflected the interests of "privileged Russia," that is, the upper strata of society that had elected most of the Duma deputies. Not everyone in Russia trusted the "capitalist ministers." From the very beginning of the revolution, the Petrograd Soviet, which represented the lower classes, began to operate as a kind of parallel government. The existence of "dual power" in the capital undermined the stability of the country and raised the danger of a political crisis. At first, however, the Provisional Government and the Petrograd Soviet maintained fairly amicable relations. The Mensheviks and SRs, who led the Soviet, believed that conditions were not yet ripe for the establishment of socialism in Russia, and that the country would have to pass through a long period of capitalist development. During that time, the liberals would hold power, and they themselves would assume the role of a political opposition.

The initial cooperation between the Provisional Government and the Soviet fostered an atmosphere of national unity that seemed conducive to peaceful change. The leaders of the Provisional Government announced a series of reforms, including elimination of ethnic and religious restrictions, abolition of the death penalty and of the old organs of repression, and greater powers for the institutions of local self-government. The government began to prepare a land reform and for the election of a Constituent Assembly. The masses, however, embittered and war-weary, were unwilling to await the future benefits of reform and demanded immediate improvements. The Bolsheviks promised radical change and energetically expanded their activity in Russia after the fall of the monarchy. Neither the liberals who initially led the Provisional Government nor the moderate socialists who replaced them proved able to cope with the problems facing the country. Government ministers changed with dizzying frequency. In the midst of economic ruin and political crisis, the Bolsheviks came to power on October 25/November 7, 1917.

The Bolsheviks immediately took steps to curtail political freedom, suppress their opponents, and uproot the elements of civil society and the rule of law that they had inherited from the old regime. Their creation of a strictly authoritarian form of rule and their mobilization of the country's resources for military purposes enabled them to win the Civil War of 1918–20. The repressive and dictatorial methods that the Bolsheviks applied to their political adversaries gradually came to define the atmosphere within the party as well. A fierce struggle for power took place within the Bolshevik leadership in the 1920s and the early 1930s, culminating in the absolute rule of Joseph Stalin.

The Bolshevik leaders used their authoritarian political system to unite most of the old Russian Empire into the Union of Soviet Socialist Republics, which played an increasingly important role in international affairs. In the late 1920s and the early 1930s, the USSR initiated an industrialization program that finally enabled the country to catch up to the leading states of the West in industrial development. The USSR's industrialization program significantly increased the country's military power and turned it into one of the most powerful states in the world. For millions of Soviet citizens, the country's industrial success, even if considerably exaggerated in official propaganda, demonstrated the correctness of the Bolsheviks' ideas and the soundness of the changes they had introduced. The significance of the industrialization of the 1930s for the victory of the Soviet Union in World War II is a key factor in evaluating the legitimacy of the Bolsheviks' policies, and it remains a matter of sharp dispute. Most Soviet and Russian historians claim that without the Bolshevik industrialization program the USSR would have been unable to defeat Nazi Germany. Holland Hunter and Janusz Szyrmer, however, have argued that the collectivization of agriculture and the centralized bureaucratic administration of the national economy retarded Soviet economic development. In their opinion, the USSR prevailed over Germany despite the changes of the 1930s, not because of them.[12]

In any event, the price of the industrialization drive of the 1930s was extremely high. The collectivization of agriculture, by eliminating individual peasant farming, brought the resources of the countryside under the complete control of the state, which exploited them for industrial purposes. The formation of the new economic system entailed the massive application of forced labor. The repressions of the 1930s sent millions of prisoners to concentration camps, where they were forced to work in inhuman conditions. In the end, Stalin's industrialization program, despite the enormous sacrifices it exacted, was unable to secure a lasting advantage for the Soviet Union in its rivalry with the West. In the mid-1950s the leading Western countries entered a new post-industrial stage of development and once again left the Soviet Union behind.

As contacts with the West increased, economic stagnation, widespread alienation from the political system, and the inability of the Soviet economy to guarantee an acceptable standard of living undermined the Soviet population's confidence in the validity of communist ideology. Alternative programs of development began to circulate, reflecting a range of views from liberalism to right-wing nationalism. In the mid-1980s the Soviet leaders' introduction of far-reaching reforms threw the country's social, political, and economic system into turmoil. The Communist Party steadily lost its grip on the country and was ultimately removed from power. At the end of 1991 the USSR disintegrated. The Russian Republic, which as the Russian Federation became an independent country, experienced a profound social and political crisis, much like the situation in 1917. The similarities led to a renewed interest in history and to a search in the past for answers to urgent current problems.

What lessons might we draw from an analysis of Russia's development in the nineteenth and the early twentieth centuries? In the last century of tsarist Russia the old regime made a prolonged effort to respond to the challenges of the time. It tried to adapt to the rise of industrialization and the spread of democratic institutions in the West. Russia entered a new stage of modernization requiring changes in the traditional pillars of Russian life, autocracy and serfdom, which in earlier stages had served as the basis of governmental reform efforts. A new development, characteristic of the nineteenth century, was society's desire to play a part in determining the country's future. Society had previously been a passive instrument in the hands of the government, but now it became an actor in its own right, as the upsurge of nationalist sentiment during the Napoleonic Wars demonstrated.

Although the events of 1812–14 raised the question of a comprehensive reform of the Russian social and political order, the process of reform proved long and complex. The Decembrist movement, an early attempt by opposition forces to seize the initiative in renovating the country, ended in failure and led to the authoritarian regime of Nicholas I. For some time, society remained cut off from politics. The result, however, was a remarkable development of social thought. The ideas and theories of the philosophical circles of the 1830s and the 1840s interacted with the attempt of the best representatives of the bureaucracy to combine the foundations of Nicholas's regime with moderate social and administrative reforms. Only Russia's defeat in the Crimean War made reform a reality, however, by diminishing Russia's power in international affairs, which had influenced every aspect of the country's life after the Napoleonic period. The joint efforts of the educated public and the enlightened bureaucracy ultimately produced the reforms of the 1860s and the 1870s.

The Great Reforms abolished serfdom, created independent courts and institutions of local self-government, introduced universal military service, and eliminated preliminary censorship. Initiated by the autocracy, the reforms vividly displayed both the positive and negative sides of reform from above. On the one hand, Russia's renovation in the 1860s and the 1870s proceeded under state control and was relatively peaceful. The Great Reforms advanced the development of a civil society, promoted economic competition and a market economy, and contributed to the industrial boom of the later nineteenth century. The autocracy took steps toward the creation of a state based on the rule of law. On the other hand, the reforms were half-hearted. They preserved vestiges of serfdom, which made Russia's economic development in the second half of the nineteenth century extremely painful for the masses. The principle of autocracy repeatedly came into conflict with the new institutions that the reforms had created.

The government's growing repression was in large part a defensive response by the autocracy to the rise of political opposition and the emergence of the revolutionary movement. The bloody outcome of the political crisis of the late 1870s and the early 1880s inevitably retarded modernization. For many years the government refused to grant the peasants equal rights and freedom to leave the commune, and it failed to lower the barriers between the social estates and expand the powers of local self-government. A new crisis arose, which culminated in the revolution of 1905–7. The revolution displayed many of the negative features that would distinguish Russian history for much of the twentieth century. For the first time in many decades, the country experienced mass violence and terror, international conflict, and political murder. As subsequent events showed, the old regime was unable to overcome the consequences of the revolution and restore lasting social and political stability to the country.

Many historians believe that the reforms introduced in the course of the revolution of 1905–7 came too late to set Russia on the road to peaceful development. Nevertheless, it would be wrong to claim that the old regime at the beginning of the twentieth century was doomed. In the last decade of the monarchy's existence, Russia made significant advances in the social, economic, and political spheres. Legal political parties emerged, representative institutions and trade unions arose, and the press enjoyed much greater freedom. Petr Stolypin's agrarian reform encouraged private property ownership and a market economy, helped to settle outlying areas of the empire, and stimulated a new boom in industry and agriculture. Even Russia's entry into World War I did not mark the beginning of a steady descent into revolution. The fierce contention of various currents of social development determined the fate of the old regime, and its ultimate outcome was the product of numerous historical circumstances.

The same could be said of Russia's current stage of development. The fall of the communist order plunged the country into a deep crisis, and it is still straining to find its place in the contemporary world. The Soviet government's destruction of the foundations of a civil society, self-government, and the separation of powers makes it difficult to create democratic political institutions. The disintegration of the Soviet Union greatly complicated Russia's international position, and the tortuous process of creating a capitalist economy exacerbates social tensions. Clearly, many of the problems facing Russia today have historical precedents, and the country must draw fully on its past experience in trying to solve them.

Notes

Introduction

1. P.A. Valuev, "Duma russkogo (vo vtoroi polovine 1855 g.)," *Russkaia starina*, No. 5 (1891), p. 354.

2. Leontii Dubel't, quoted in *Golos minuvshego*, No. 3 (1913), p. 141.

3. V.O. Kliuchevskii, *Sochineniia*, 9 vols. (Moscow, 1987–90), 1:65.

4. See S.V. Dumin, "Drugaia Rus' (Velikoe kniazhestvo Litovskoe i Russkoe)," in *Istoriia Otechestva: liudi, idei, resheniia. Ocherki istorii Rossii IX–nachala XX v.*, ed. S.V. Mironenko (Moscow, 1991), pp. 76–126.

5. According to the calculations of V.M. Kabuzan, cited by Andreas Kappeler, at the beginning of the nineteenth century Ukrainians and Belorussians formed the second largest group in the population after Russians (about 30 percent). Next came Poles (7 percent), the peoples of the Baltic and Volga regions (each group constituting 4–5 percent), Jews (2.5 percent), and Finns (2 percent). The population of Russia also included nomadic peoples of the steppe and the peoples of the North and Siberia, who were few in number. See Andreas Kappeler, *The Russian Empire: A Multiethnic History*, trans. Alfred Clayton (Harlow, UK, 2001), pp. 114–18.

6. See V.V. Kargalov, *Vneshnepoliticheskie faktory razvitiia feodal'noi Rusi. Feodal'naia Rus' i kochevniki* (Moscow, 1987), pp. 218–61.

7. Quoted in ibid., p. 220.

8. See V.B. Kobrin and A.L. Iurganov, "Stanovlenie despoticheskogo samoderzhaviia v srednevekovoi Rusi," *Istoriia SSSR*, No. 4 (1991), pp. 54–64.

9. A.L. Iurganov, "U istokov despotizma," in *Istoriia Otechestva: liudi, idei, resheniia*, ed. Mironenko, pp. 42–43.

10. Kargalov, *Vneshnepoliticheskie faktory*, pp. 173–217.

11. The question of the Golden Horde's influence on Russia has been examined extensively in George Vernadsky, *The Mongols and Russia* (New Haven, 1953); and Charles V. Halperin, *Russia and the Golden Horde: The Mongol Impact on Medieval Russian History* (Bloomington, IN, 1987).

12. A.I. Gertsen [Alexander Herzen], "O razvitii revoliutsionnykh idei v Rossii" (1850), *Sobranie sochinenii*, 30 vols. (Moscow, 1956), 7:13.

13. Quoted in Iurganov, "U istokov despotizma," p. 35.

14. The theses of Soloviev and Platonov are set forth in their major works: S.M. Solov'ev, *Istoriia Rossii s drevneishikh vremen*, 29 vols. (St. Petersburg, 1851–78), Vol. 6; and S.F. Platonov, *Ocherki po istorii Smuty v moskovskom gosudarstve XVI–XVII vv.* (St. Petersburg, 1899). For a short exposition of Kobrin's argument, see his essay "Ivan Groznyi: Izbrannaia Rada ili oprichnina?" in *Istoriia Otechestva: liudi, idei, resheniia*, ed. Mironenko, pp. 127–62.

15. D.S. Likhachev and Ia.S. Lur'e, eds., *Poslaniia Ivana Groznogo* (Moscow, 1951), pp. 142, 143, 213.

16. See B.N. Mironov, *Istoriia v tsifrakh* (Leningrad, 1991), appendix and tables 1–3.

17. S.M. Solov'ev, "Publichnye chteniia o Petre Velikom (1872)," in his *Izbrannye trudy. Zapiski* (Moscow, 1983), p. 57. *Dvorianstvo*, like the French *noblesse* and the German *Adel*, refers to the privileged social group just below the titled aristocracy. In English, "nobility" refers to the upper stratum and "gentry" to the lower stratum of this group.

18. Kliuchevskii, *Sochineniia*, 2:372.

19. See A.M. Sakharov, ed., *Istoriia Rossii: s nachala XVIII do kontsa XIX v.* (Moscow, 1997), pp. 42–46, 155–60, 184–95 (sections written by L.V. Milov).

20. Quoted in Kliuchevskii, *Sochineniia*, 5:8.

21. B.V. Anan'ich and E.V. Anisimov, eds., *Petr Velikii. Vospominaniia. Dnevnikovye zapisi. Anekdoty* (Moscow, 1993), p. 309.

22. "Tolkovanie k stat'e 20 Voinskogo ustava 30 marta 1716 g.," quoted in N.P. Eroshkin, *Krepostnicheskoe samoderzhavie i ego politicheskie instituty (pervaia polovina XIX v.)* (Moscow, 1981), p. 47.

23. Robert Jones takes the view that Catherine, motivated primarily by her concern for the interests of the state, sought to use the nobility to create a reliable network of governmental agents in the provinces. Robert Jones, *The Emancipation of the Russian Nobility, 1762–85* (Princeton, NJ, 1973), pp. 26–36, 164–80, 188–96, 235–43, 273–87.

24. B.I. Krasnobaev, *Ocherki istorii russkoi kul'tury XVIII v.* (Moscow, 1987), pp. 37–88.

25. Quoted in I.K. Pantin, E.G. Plimak, and V.G. Khoros, *Revoliutsionnaia traditsiia v Rossii, 1783–1883* (Moscow, 1986), pp. 57–79.

26. Aleksandr Nikolaevich Radishchev, *A Journey from St. Petersburg to Moscow*, trans. Leo Wiener, ed. Roderick Page Thaler (Cambridge, MA, 1958), p. 209.

27. Arcadius Kahan, "The Costs of 'Westernization' in Russia: The Gentry and the Economy in the Eighteenth Century," *Slavic Review* 25, No. 1 (1966), pp. 40–66.

28. Aleksandr B. Kamenskii, *The Russian Empire in the Eighteenth Century: Searching for a Place in the World*, trans. and ed. David Griffiths (Armonk, NY, 1997), pp. 194–243.

29. Pugachev's "Emancipation Decree," July 31, 1774, in *Imperial Russia: A Source Book, 1700–1917*, ed. Basil Dmytryshyn, 2d ed. (Hinsdale, IL, 1974), p. 96.

30. Ibid.

31. For an analysis of Paul's policies, see N.Ia. Eidel'man, *Gran' vekov. Politicheskaia bor'ba v Rossii. Konets XVIII–nachalo XIX stoletiia* (Moscow, 1982).

32. Quoted in A.N. Sakharov, "Aleksandr I (k istorii zhizni i smerti)," in *Rossiiskie samoderzhtsy, 1801–1917*, ed. A.N. Bokhanov et al. (Moscow, 1993), p. 35.

33. A.A. Kornilov, *Kurs istorii Rossii XIX v.* (Moscow, 1993), p. 70.

34. See Marc Raeff, *Michael Speransky: Statesman of Imperial Russia, 1772–1839* (The Hague, 1957), pp. 378–82.

35. M.M. Speranskii, *Plan gosudarstvennogo preobrazovaniia* (Moscow, 1905), p. 33.

36. Kornilov, *Kurs istorii Rossii XIX v.*, pp. 65–69, 75–76.

37. For an analysis of Karamzin's views, see Iu.M. Lotman, *Sotvorenie Karamzina* (Moscow, 1987); and N.Ia. Eidel'man, *Poslednii letopisets* (Moscow, 1983).

38. Richard Pipes, ed. and trans., *Karamzin's Memoir on Ancient and Modern Russia: A Translation and Analysis* (Cambridge, MA, 1959), pp. 184, 139.

39. Ibid., 140, 193.

Chapter 1: On the Path to Reform

1. Herzen, *Sobranie sochinenii*, 7:22.

2. For an analysis of issues relating to the War of 1812, see B.S. Abalikhin and V.A. Dunaevskii, *1812 god na perekrestkakh mnenii sovetskikh istorikov, 1917–1987* (Moscow, 1990).

3. Quoted in M.V. Nechkina, *Dekabristy* (Moscow, 1984), p. 64. The basic work on this subject in Soviet historiography is Nechkina's *Dvizhenie dekabristov*, 2 vols. (Moscow, 1955).

4. *Izbrannye sotsial'no-politicheskie i filosofskie proizvedeniia dekabristov*, ed. I.Ia. Shchipanov, comp. S.Ia. Shtraikh, 2 vols. (Moscow, 1951), 1:491.

5. Quoted in S.G. Pushkarev, *Rossiia 1801–1917. Vlast' i obshchestvo* (Moscow, 2001), p. 126. The first edition of this book was published in English in the United States: S.G. Pushkarev, *The Emergence of Modern Russia, 1801–1917*, trans. Robert H. McNeal and Tova Yedlin (New York, 1963).

6. See Pantin, Plimak, and Khoros, *Revoliutsionnaia traditsiia v Rossii*, pp. 84–88, 93–95.

7. *Polnoe sobranie zakonov Rossiiskoi imperii. Sobranie 1-e, s 1649 do 12 dekabria 1825 goda*, 49 vols. (St. Petersburg, 1830–1916; hereafter *PSZ*-1), Vol. 23, No. 25943.

8. N.V. Minaeva, *Pravitel'stvennyi konstitutsionalizm i peredovoe obshchestvennoe mnenie Rossii v nachale XIX v.* (Saratov, 1982), pp. 185–201; and S.V. Mironenko, *Samoderzhavie i reformy. Politicheskaia bor'ba v Rossii v nachale XIX v.* (Moscow, 1989), pp. 184–97.

9. Quoted in Mironenko, *Samoderzhavie i reformy*, p. 157.

10. In 1819 a governor-generalship was created consisting of five central provinces (Tula, Orlov, Voronezh, Tambov, and Riazan). It was meant to serve as the first step toward the division of Russia into lieutenancies. The government sounded out the situation in Left-Bank Ukraine (Chernigov and Poltava provinces), hoping to prod the local gentry into emancipating their serfs and possibly to revive the traditional "Cossack" form of self-government. The authorities also introduced self-government in Bessarabia (eastern Moldavia), which Russia had annexed on the eve of Napoleon's invasion. See ibid., pp. 78–89, 96–99, 163, 178.

11. Ibid., p. 77.

12. Quoted in A.N. Pypin, *Obshchestvennoe dvizhenie v Rossii pri Aleksandre I*, 4th ed. (St. Petersburg, 1908), p. 392.

13. N.P. Eroshkin, *Krepostnicheskoe samoderzhavie i ego politicheskie instituty (pervaia polovina XIX v.)* (Moscow, 1981), pp. 36–37.

14. On the Ministry of Religious Affairs and Public Education, see ibid., pp. 49–52. The traditional treatment of the activity of the Bible Society has been reexamined in a recent article by Stephen K. Batalden, "Printing the Bible in the Reign of Alexander I: Toward a Reinterpretation of the Imperial Russian Bible Society," in *Church, Nation and State in Russia and Ukraine*, ed. Geoffrey Hosking (London, 1991), pp. 65–78.

254 NOTES TO CHAPTER 1

15. See K.M. Iachmenikhin, "Aleksei Andreevich Arakcheev," in *Rossiiskie konservatory*, ed. A.N. Bokhanov et al. (Moscow, 1997), pp. 18–54.

16. Quoted in Nechkina, *Dekabristy*, p. 13.

17. At the death of the childless Alexander I, the throne should have passed to his brother Constantine, the next oldest of Emperor Paul's sons. During Alexander's lifetime, however, Constantine had renounced the throne. The third brother, Nicholas, should then have succeeded, but, for reasons that are not fully understood, Alexander had not published the manifesto announcing Nicholas's right to the throne.

18. See George Vernadsky, *La charte constitutionelle de l'Empire de Russie de l'an 1820* (Paris, 1933).

19. *Materialy po istorii SSSR dlia seminarskikh i prakticheskikh zaniatii. Osvoboditel'noe dvizhenie i obshchestvennaia mysl' v Rossii XIX v.*, ed. I.A. Fedosov, comp. V.A. Fedorov and N.I. Tsimbaev (Moscow, 1991), pp. 40–41.

20. Ibid., p. 40.

21. Nechkina, *Dekabristy*, p. 87; Pushkarev, *Rossiia 1801–1917*, p. 140.

22. Quoted in Pantin, Plimak, and Khoros, *Revoliutsionnaia traditsiia v Rossii*, p. 129.

23. *Materialy po istorii SSSR dlia seminarskikh i prakticheskikh zaniatii*, ed. Fedosov, p. 42.

24. Quoted in B.V. Anan'ich, ed., *Vlast' i reformy. Ot samoderzhavnoi k sovetskoi Rossii* (St. Petersburg, 1996), p. 256.

25. Quoted in W. Bruce Lincoln, *Nicholas I: Emperor and Autocrat of All the Russias* (Bloomington, IN, 1978), p. 86.

26. For analyses of the Third Section's activities, see Eroshkin, *Krepostnicheskoe samoderzhavie*, pp. 158–77; Sidney Monas, *The Third Section: Police and Society in Russia under Nicholas I* (Cambridge, MA, 1961); and P.S. Squire, *The Third Department: The Establishment and Practices of the Political Police in the Russia of Nicholas I* (Cambridge, 1968).

27. P.A. Zaionchkovskii, *Pravitel'stvennyi apparat samoderzhavnoi Rossii v XIX v.* (Moscow, 1978), pp. 67–70.

28. The most complete analysis of the phenomenon of "enlightened bureaucracy" is W. Bruce Lincoln, *In the Vanguard of Reform: Russia's Enlightened Bureaucrats, 1825–1861* (DeKalb, IL, 1982).

29. Eroshkin, *Krepostnicheskoe samoderzhavie*, pp. 142–58.

30. Ibid., p. 47.

31. See Richard Wortman, *The Development of a Russian Legal Consciousness* (Chicago, 1976).

32. In 1850 urban dwellers constituted 7.2 percent of the Russian population, compared to 39.5 percent in Great Britain, 14.0 percent in France, and 12.0 percent in the United States. In 1865 Russia had 62,000 kilometers of dirt and paved roads, compared to 210,000 in Great Britain and 260,000–270,000 in France and the United States. Most Russian towns had fewer than five thousand inhabitants. The basic forms of transport were still by water and cart, and markets remained the chief form of domestic commerce. See Mironov, *Istoriia v tsifrakh*, appendix and tables 4 and 42; and V.A. Fedorov, ed., *Istoriia Rossii XIX–nachala XX v.* (Moscow, 1998), pp. 20–22.

The growth in the number of mortgaged estates served as an index of the gentry's financial ruin. By 1859, 66 percent of the landowners' serfs were mortgaged to state credit institutions. Gentry indebtedness totaled 425.5 million rubles, which was double the annual revenue of the state budget. See Fedorov, ed., *Istoriia Rossii XIX–nachala XX v.*, p. 16.

33. On the activities of the Ministry of Internal Affairs, see Daniel Orlovsky, *The Limits of Reform: The Ministry of Internal Affairs in Imperial Russia* (Cambridge, MA, 1981).

34. Eroshkin, *Krepostnicheskoe samoderzhavie*, p. 181.

35. Quoted in M.O. Gershenzon, ed., *Epokha Nikolaia I* (Moscow, 1911), p. 13.

36. For a detailed discussion, see S.V. Mironenko, *Stranitsy tainoi istorii samoderzhaviia* (Moscow, 1990).

37. See V.Ia. Grosul, "Pavel Dmitrievich Kiselev," in *Rossiiskie reformatory, XIX–nachalo XX v.*, ed. A.P. Korelin (Moscow, 1995), pp. 77–115.

38. Quoted in A.A. Kizevetter, "Vnutrenniaia politika v tsarstvovanie Nikolaia Pavlovicha," in *Istoriia Rossii v XIX veke*, ed. Iu.O. Bem, 4 vols. (Moscow, 2001), vol. 1: *Doreformennaia Rossiia*, p. 220. This is a contemporary reprinting of works by leading Russian historians of the early twentieth century.

39. Quoted in M.M. Bogoslovskii, "Gosudarstvennye krest'iane pri Nikolae I," in ibid., p. 212.

40. The fundamental work on the reform of the state peasants is N.M. Druzhinin, *Gosudarstvennye krest'iane i reforma P.D. Kiseleva*, Vol. 1 (Moscow and Leningrad, 1946), Vol. 2 (Moscow, 1959).

41. Bogoslovskii, "Gosudarstvennye krest'iane," pp. 246–59.

42. Quoted in Zaionchkovskii, *Pravitel'stvennyi apparat*, pp. 111–12.

43. Quoted in Gershenzon, ed., *Epokha Nikolaia I*, p. 52.

44. Paraphrased in A.E. Presniakov, *Rossiiskie samoderzhtsy* (Moscow, 1990), p. 294.

45. A.F. Tiutcheva, *Pri dvore dvukh imperatorov. Vospominaniia, dnevnik, 1853–1882* (Moscow, 1990), p. 36.

Chapter 2: "A Time of External Slavery and Internal Freedom"

1. Kornilov, *Kurs istorii Rossii XIX v.*, p. 176; and *Entsiklopedicheskii slovar'. Rossiia* (Leningrad, 1991; repr. of 1898 ed.), p. 387.

2. The change is described in Cynthia Whittaker, *The Origins of Modern Russian Education: An Intellectual Biography of Count Sergei Uvarov, 1786–1855* (DeKalb, IL, 1984).

3. Fedorov, ed., *Istoriia Rossii. XIX–nachala XX v.*, p. 649.

4. See M.M. Shevchenko, "Sergei Semenovich Uvarov," in *Rossiiskie konservatory*, ed. Bokhanov et al., pp. 95–136.

5. On "Official Nationality," see Nicholas Riasanovsky, *Nicholas I and Official Nationality in Russia, 1825–1855* (Berkeley, CA, 1959).

6. S.S. Uvarov, *Desiatiletie Ministerstva narodnogo prosveshcheniia, 1833–1843* (St. Petersburg, 1864), p. 2.

7. A.L. Zorin, "Ideologiia 'pravoslaviia—samoderzhaviia—narodnosti' i ee nemetskie istochniki," in *V razdum'iakh o Rossii. XIX vek*, ed. E.L. Rudnitskaia (Moscow, 1996), pp. 105–28, emphasizes the connection between Uvarov's ideology and the concepts of European Romanticism.

8. Uvarov, *Desiatiletie Ministerstva narodnogo prosveshcheniia*, p. 4.

9. Shevchenko, "Sergei Semenovich Uvarov," pp. 111–18.

10. These phrases are from Uvarov's report on a census of Moscow University in 1832, a report to the emperor of 1833, and the report on his ten-year administration of the Ministry of Public Education. See N. Barsukov, *Zhizn' i trudy M.P. Pogodina*, bk. 4 (St. Petersburg, 1891), p. 83; Shevchenko, "Sergei Semenovich Uvarov," p. 106; and Uvarov, *Desiatiletie Ministerstva narodnogo prosveshcheniia*, p. 4.

11. S.P. Shevyrev, "Vzgliad russkogo na sovremennoe obrazovanie Evropy," *Moskvitianin*, No.1 (1841), p. 292.

12. N.I. Tsimbaev, " 'Pod bremenem poznan'ia i somnen'ia . . .' (ideinye iskaniia 1830-kh godov)," in *Russkoe obshchestvo 30-kh XIX v. Liudi i idei. Memuary sovremennikov*, ed. I.A. Fedosov (Moscow, 1989), pp. 29–34.

13. On the role of circles and salons in the social and cultural life of the 1830s and the 1840s, see B.F. Egorov, "Russkie kruzhki" and "Slavianofil'stvo, zapadnichestvo i kul'turologiia," in *Iz istorii russkoi kul'tury*, ed. A.D. Koshelev, 5 vols. (Moscow, 1996–2000), Vol. 5: *XIX vek*, pp. 463–75, 504–17.

14. On the influence of the philosophy of Schelling and Hegel on Russian intellectual life of the 1830s and the 1840s, see Andrzej Walicki, *The Slavophile Controversy: History of a Conservative Utopia in Nineteenth-Century Russian Thought* (Oxford, 1975), especially chap. 7.

15. Quoted in James H. Billington, *The Icon and the Axe: An Interpretive History of Russian Culture* (New York, 1966), p. 315.

16. Petr Iakovlevich Chaadaev, "Letters on the Philosophy of History: First Letter," trans. Valentine Snow, in *Russian Intellectual History: An Anthology*, ed. Marc Raeff (New York, 1966), pp. 167, 163, 164, 162.

17. P. Ia. Chaadaev, *Stat'i i pis'ma* (Moscow, 1989), p. 157.

18. See A.A. Levandovskii, *T.N. Granovskii v russkom obshchestvennom dvizhenii* (Moscow, 1989), pp. 118–25, 143–46.

19. For an analysis of the role of the universities in the formation of the reformers' outlook, see F.A. Petrov, "Rossiiskie universitety 40-kh XIX v. i deiateli Velikikh reform," in *P.A. Zaionchkovskii, 1904–1983 gg. Stat'i, publikatsii i vospominaniia o nem*, ed. Iu.S. Kukushkin (Moscow, 1998), pp. 205–19. See also Petrov, *Rossiiskie universitety v pervoi polovine XIX veka. Formirovanie sistemy universitetskogo obrazovaniia*, 4 vols. (Moscow, 1998–2001).

20. Levandovskii, *T.N. Granovskii*, p. 143–47.

21. Ibid., p. 102.

22. From the article "Rossiia do Petra Velikogo" (1841), in *Russkaia ideia*, ed. M.A. Maslin (Moscow, 1992), pp. 74, 75, 86.

23. Quoted in Levandovskii, *T.N. Granovskii*, p. 108.

24. Ibid., p. 105.

25. On the views of Kavelin and Chicherin, see Andrzej Walicki, *A History of Russian Thought from the Enlightenment to Marxism* (Stanford, CA, 1993), pp. 148–51.

26. Friendship circles, fashionable salons, and scientific societies played an active role in fostering such contacts in the 1840s. Especially important were the Petersburg circle of Westernizers headed by Konstantin Kavelin; the salon of Grand Duchess Elena Pavlovna, the wife of Nicholas I's brother; and the Russian Geographical Society, which operated from 1845 onward in the Ministry of Internal Affairs under the leadership of Grand Duke Konstantin Nikolaevich, the second son of Nicholas I. Many prominent representatives of educated society, such as Kavelin, Aksakov, and Samarin, served in the government in the 1840s. See Lincoln, *In the Vanguard of Reform*, pp. 91–101, 139–67.

27. I.V. Kireevskii, "V otvet A.S. Khomiakovu" (1839), in *Russkaia ideia*, ed. Maslin, pp. 69, 71.

28. A.S. Khomiakov, "O starom i novom" (1839), in ibid., p. 58.

29. See Levandovskii, *T.N. Granovskii*, pp. 138–49; N.I. Tsimbaev, "Moskovskie spory liberal'nogo vremeni," in *Russkoe obshchestvo 40–50–kh godov*

XIX v., Part I: *Zapiski A.I. Kosheleva*, ed. N.I. Tsimbaev and S.L. Chernov (Moscow, 1991), pp. 22–37.

30. N.I. Tsimbaev, *Slavianofil'stvo. Iz istorii russkoi obshchestvenno-politicheskoi mysli XIX v.* (Moscow, 1986), pp. 33, 122, 128–37.

31. K.S. Aksakov, "Ob osnovnykh nachalakh russkoi istorii" (1849), in *Materialy po istorii SSSR dlia seminarskikh i prakticheskikh zaniatii*, ed. Fedosov, p. 219.

32. K.S. Aksakov, "O tom zhe" (1850), in ibid., p. 222.

33. Konstantin Sergeevich Aksakov, "On the Internal State of Russia," trans. Valentine Snow, in *Russian Intellectual History*, ed. Raeff, p. 251.

34. Walicki, *A History of Russian Thought*, p. 97.

35. Tsimbaev, *Slavianofil'stvo*, p. 231.

36. The extent to which Westernism and Slavophilism correspond to the classical ideologies of West European political life, liberalism and conservatism, is an extremely complex question. In the opinion of Nikolai Tsimbaev, Westernism and Slavophilism constituted two branches of a single liberal movement. Andrzej Walicki saw the opposition of the Westernizers and Slavophiles as similar to the dialogue between European liberals and conservatives. The Slavophiles themselves, in particular Aleksei Khomiakov, highly valued the ideas and practices of the Conservatives in England. See Tsimbaev, *Slavianofil'stvo*, especially pp. 101 and 106–10; Walicki, *The Slavophile Controversy*, pp. 452–55.

37. Quoted in Tsimbaev, "Moskovskie spory," p. 14.

38. Ibid., p. 37.

39. *Materialy po istorii SSSR*, pp. 163–64.

40. Ibid., p. 167; Levandovskii, *T.N. Granovskii*, p. 168.

41. Vissarion Grigor'evich Belinskii, "Letter to N.V. Gogol," trans. Valentine Snow, in *Russian Intellectual History*, ed. Raeff, p. 254.

42. Shevchenko, "Sergei Semenovich Uvarov," p. 112.

43. Quoted in Tsimbaev, "Moskovskie spory," p. 39; see also Kornilov, *Kurs istorii Rossii XIX v.*, p. 192.

44. Herzen, *Sobranie sochinenii*, 5:12–13, and 6:206.

45. Quoted in Tsimbaev, "Moskovskie spory," p. 39.

Chapter 3: A Colossus with Feet of Clay

1. Quoted in Tsimbaev, " 'Pod bremenem poznan'ia i somnen'ia . . . , ' " pp. 32, 41; see also L.G. Zakharova, "Aleksandr II," in *Rossiiskie samoderzhtsy*, p. 174.

2. Marquis de Custine, *Letters from Russia*, trans. and ed. Robin Buss (London, 1991), p. 132.

3. See Vera Miltchina, " 'La Russie et ses ressources': une réfutation russe indite de 'La Russie en 1839' de Custine," in *L'Ours et le coq: Trois siècles de relations franco-russes*, ed. F.D. Liechtenan (Paris, 2000), p. 92.

4. On the "image of autocracy," see Richard Wortman, *Scenarios of Power: Myth and Ceremony in Russian Monarchy*, 2 vols. (Princeton, NJ, 1995–2000).

5. O.V. Orlik et al., eds., *Istoriia vneshnei politiki Rossii. Pervaia polovina XIX v.: ot voin Rossii protiv Napoleona do Parizhskogo mira 1856 g.* (Moscow, 1995), p. 210.

6. Ibid., p. 234.

7. Pushkarev, *Rossiia 1801–1917*, p. 206.

8. Ibid., p. 214; Presniakov, *Rossiiskie samoderzhtsy*, p. 298.

9. *Polnoe sobranie zakonov Rossiiskoi imperii. Sobranie 2-e, 1825–1881*, 55 vols. (St. Petersburg, 1830–1916; hereafter *PSZ-2*), Vol. 29, No. 28150; see also M.N. Pokrovskii, "Krymskaia voina," in *Istoriia Rossii v XIX v.*, ed. Bem, vol. 2: *Epokha reform*, pp. 34–38.

10. Quoted in G. Chulkov, *Imperatory* (Moscow, 1990), pp. 206, 209.

11. Kornilov, *Kurs istorii Rossii XIX v.*, pp. 167–74; and Pushkarev, *Rossiia 1801–1917*, pp. 100–102.

12. The successful development of particular branches of trade and industry in pre-reform Russia forms the basis of Peter Gatrell's contention that the abolition of serfdom in 1861 cannot be viewed as a major turning point in the country's economic development. See his "The Meaning of the Great Reforms in Russian Economic History," in *Russia's Great Reforms, 1855–1881*, ed. Ben Eklof, John Bushnell, and Larissa Zakharova (Bloomington, IN, 1994), pp. 84–101.

13. Pantin, Plimak, and Khoros, *Revoliutsionnaia traditsiia v Rossii*, p. 35. Kankrin is quoted in Walter M. Pintner, *Russian Economic Policy under Nicholas I* (Ithaca, NY, 1967), p. 139.

14. Pokrovskii, "Krymskaia voina," pp. 23–24.

15. N. Gvosdev, *Imperial Policies and Perspectives towards Georgia, 1760–1819* (Oxford, 2000).

16. For a general survey of Russian policy in Transcaucasia, see Kappeler, *The Russian Empire*, pp. 171–78.

17. Quoted in S. Ekshtut, "Aleksei Ermolov," *Rodina*, No. 3–4 (1994), pp. 27, 32.

18. See Firouzeh Mostashari, "Colonial Dilemma: Russian Policies in the Muslim Caucasus," in *Of Religion and Empire: Missions, Conversion and Tolerance in Tsarist Russia*, ed. Robert P. Geraci and Michael Khodarkovsky (Ithaca, NY, 2001), pp. 229–49.

19. On the Caucasus War, see the memoirs of the chief of staff of the Special Caucasian Corps, Dmitry Miliutin: *Vospominaniia, 1856–1860* (Moscow, 2004).

20. See Ruslan Gozhba, "Ot Kubani do Nila," *Rodina*, No. 3–4 (1994), pp. 130–34.

21. *Rodina*, No. 3–4 (1994), pp. 122–25; and Fedorov, ed., *Istoriia Rossii. XIX–nachalo XX v.*, pp. 206–7.

22. Pokrovskii, "Krymskaia voina," p. 583.

23. Orlik, ed., *Istoriia vneshnei politiki Rossii. Pervaia polovina XIX v.*, pp. 287, 283.

24. Pokrovskii, "Krymskaia voina," p. 8.

25. Orlik, ed., *Istoriia vneshnei politiki Rossii. Pervaia polovina XIX v.*, p. 316.

26. Fedorov, ed., *Istoriia Rossii. XIX–nachalo XX v.*, p.163.

27. Orlik, ed., *Istoriia vneshnei politiki Rossii. Pervaia polovina XIX v.*, p. 347.

28. *PSZ-2*, Vol. 23, No. 22087.

29. B.N. Chicherin, "Vostochnyi vopros s russkoi tochki zreniia," appendix to S.P. Trubetskoi, *Zapiski kniazia S.P. Trubetskogo* (St. Petersburg, 1906), pp. 132–33.

30. Quoted in "Zashchita politiki Rossii i polozheniia, priniatogo eiu v Evrope" (1854), *Russkaia starina* 7, No. 42 (1873), p. 805.

31. Pokrovskii, "Krymskaia voina," p. 14.

32. Ibid., p. 29.

33. See the letter of Henry Palmerston to George Aberdeen, 7(20) March 1854, in *The Later Correspondence of Lord John Russell, 1840–1878*, Vol. 2 (London, 1925), pp. 160–61.

34. Quoted in Presniakov, *Russkie samoderzhtsy*, p. 310. See also Theodor Schiemann, *Geschichte Russlands unter Kaiser Nikolaus I*, 2 vols. (Berlin, 1908).

35. Quoted in Pushkarev, *Rossiia 1801–1917*, p. 209.

36. N.N. Bolkhovitinov and V.N. Ponomarev, "Amerikanskie vrachi v Krymskoi voine," *SShA: ekonomika, politika, ideologiia*, No. 6 (1980).

37. Nicholas's sudden death gave rise to rumors that he had committed suicide. See N.Ia. Eidel'man, *Gertsen protiv samoderzhaviia. Sekretnaia politicheskaia istoriia Rossii XVIII–XIX vv. i vol'naia pechat'* (Moscow, 1984), pp. 9–19; and Igor' V. Zimin, "Physicians and Autocrats: The Perplexing Death of Nicholas I," *Russian Studies in History* 42, No. 3 (2003–4), pp. 8–25.

38. Tsimbaev, *Slavianofil'stvo*, p. 187.

39. See Levandovskii, *T.N. Granovskii*, p. 215.

Chapter 4: The End of Serfdom

1. Valuev, "Duma russkogo (vo vtoroi polovine 1855 g.)," p. 353.

2. Quoted in Pokrovskii, "Krymskaia voina," p. 71.

3. Tsimbaev, *Slavianofil'stvo*, p. 199.

4. W. Bruce Lincoln, *The Great Reforms: Autocracy, Bureaucracy, and the Politics of Change in Imperial Russia* (DeKalb, IL, 1990), p. 62.

5. Quoted in L.G. Zakharova, "Samoderzhavie i reformy v Rossii, 1861–1874," in *Velikie reformy v Rossii. 1856–1874*, ed. L.G. Zakharova, B. Eklof, and Dzh. [J.] Bushnell (Moscow, 1992), p. 43.

6. For a critique of this approach, see Abbott Gleason, "The Great Reforms and the Historians since Stalin," in *Russia's Great Reforms*, ed. Eklof, Bushnell, and Zakharova, pp. 1–16.

7. P.A. Zaionchkovskii, *Otmena krepostnogo prava v Rossii* (Moscow, 1954; 2d ed., 1960; 3d ed., 1968); Zaionchkovskii, *Provedenie v zhizn' krest'ianskoi reformy* (Moscow, 1958); and L.G. Zakharova, *Samoderzhavie i otmena krepostnogo prava, 1856–1861* (Moscow, 1984).

8. Terence Emmons, *The Russian Landed Gentry and the Peasant Emancipation of 1861* (Cambridge, 1968); and Daniel Field, *The End of Serfdom: Nobility and Bureaucracy in Russia, 1855–1861* (Cambridge, MA, 1976).

9. L.G. Zakharova, "Aleksandr II," in *Rossiiskie samoderzhtsy*, ed. Bokhanov et al., pp. 166–67.

10. Captain N.K. Merder, quoted in ibid., p. 169.

11. Ibid., p. 178.

12. *Golos minuvshego*, Bk. 5–6 (1916), p. 393.

13. Iu.F. Samarin, "O krepostnom sostoianii i o perekhode ot nego k grazhdanskoi svobode," *Sochineniia*, Vol. 2 (Moscow, 1878), p. 33.

14. Larissa Zakharova, "Autocracy and the Reforms of 1861–1874 in Russia: Choosing Paths of Development," in *Russia's Great Reforms*, ed. Eklof, Bushnell, and Zakharova, pp. 19–39; and V.L. Stepanov, "Mikhail Khristianovich Reitern," in *Rossiiskie reformatory*, ed. Korelin, pp. 150–51.

15. On the banking crisis as a factor in the preparation of the reform, see Stephen L. Hoch, "The Banking Crisis, Peasant Reform, and Economic Development in Russia, 1857–1861," *American Historical Review* 96, No. 3 (1991), pp. 795–820.

16. Zakharova, "Samoderzhavie i reformy," pp. 25, 27.

17. See L.G. Zakharova, "Rossiia na perelome (samoderzhavie i reformy 1861–1874 gg.)," in *Istoriia otechestva: liudi, idei, resheniia*, ed. Mironenko, pp. 304–5.

18. Statements by Rostovtsev and a passage from a memorandum of the Economic Section of the Editing Commission, in Zakharova, *Samoderzhavie i otmena krepostnogo prava*, pp. 164, 167, 173.

19. O. Trubetskaia, ed., *Materialy dlia biografii kn. V.A. Cherkasskogo*, Vol. 1, Bk. 2, Pt. 3 (St. Petersburg, 1904), Appendix 8, p. 43.

20. Cherkassky quoted in ibid., p. 44; see also Zakharova, *Samoderzhavie i otmena krepostnogo prava*, p. 112.

21. *Materialy Redaktsionnykh komissii*, Pt. 18 (St. Petersburg, 1860), pp. 3–8.

22. Zakharova, *Samoderzhavie i otmena krepostnogo prava*, pp. 129–31.

23. Evgenii V. Anisimov, *The Reforms of Peter the Great: Progress through Coercion in Russia*, trans. John T. Alexander (Armonk, NY, 1993).

24. Ibid., pp. 137–48.

25. A Council of Ministers was formally established in 1857, but it met under the personal chairmanship of the tsar and did not really become a working institution. See Anan'ich, ed., *Vlast' i reformy*, pp. 301–2.

26. P.A. Valuev, "Dnevnik," *Russkaia starina*, No. 11 (1891), p. 411.

27. Quoted in A.A. Kornilov, *Obshchestvennoe dvizhenie pri Aleksandre II (1855–1881). Istoricheskie ocherki* (Moscow, 1909), p. 62.

28. S.G. Svatikov, *Obshchestvennoe dvizhenie v Rossii, 1700–1895* (Rostov-on-Don, 1905), Pt. 2, pp. 12–17.

29. Quoted in Kornilov, *Obshchestvennoe dvizhenie pri Aleksandre II*, p. 64.

30. I. Ivaniukov, *Padenie krepostnogo prava v Rossii* (St. Petersburg, 1882), pp. 347–62.

31. Miliutin quoted in P.D. Stremoukhov, "Zametki odnogo iz deputatov pervogo prizyva," *Russkaia starina*, No. 4 (1900), pp. 142–43. On the bureaucrats' opposition to constitutionalism, see Kornilov, *Obshchestvennoe dvizhenie pri Aleksandre II*, pp. 120–21.

32. On Miliutin, see Anatole Leroy-Beaulieu, *Un homme d'État russe (Nicolas Milutine) d'après sa correspondance inédite* (Paris, 1884); and W. Bruce Lincoln, *Nikolai Miliutin: An Enlightened Russian Bureaucrat* (Newtonville, MA, 1977).

33. On the peculiarities of the peasant mentality, see Daniel Field, "The Year of Jubilee," in *The Great Reforms in Russia*, ed. Eklof, Bushnell, and Zakharova, pp. 40–57; and Field, *Rebels in the Name of the Tsar* (Boston, 1989).

34. M.N. Pokrovskii, "Krest'ianskaia reforma," in *Istoriia Rossii v XIX v.*, ed. Bem, 2:178–79.

35. Fedorov, ed., *Istoriia Rossii. XIX–nachala XX v.*, p. 284.

36. Zakharova, "Aleksandr II," pp. 186–87.

37. Fedorov, ed., *Istoriia Rossii. XIX–nachala XX v.*, p. 253.

38. Ibid., pp. 302–3; and Peter I. Lyashchenko, *History of the National Economy of Russia to the 1917 Revolution*, trans. L.M. Herman (New York, 1949), p. 737.

39. The peace mediators were drawn from the local gentry but were subordinated directly to the Senate. See Natalia F. Ust'iantseva, "Accountable Only to God and the Senate: Peace Mediators and the Great Reforms," in *Russia's Great Reforms*, ed. Eklof, Bushnell, and Zakharova, pp. 161–80.

Chapter 5: The Great Reforms: Sources and Consequences

1. Quoted in Presniakov, *Rossiiskie samoderzhtsy*, p. 279.

2. See V.A. Nardova, *Gorodskoe samoupravlenie v Rossii v 60–kh–nachale*

90–kh gg. (Leningrad, 1984); Nardova, "Municipal Self-Government after the 1870 Reform," in *Russia's Great Reforms*, ed. Eklof, Bushnell, and Zakharova, pp. 181–96; and L.F. Pisar'kova, *Moskovskaia gorodskaia duma, 1863–1907* (Moscow, 1998).

3. In the second half of the nineteenth century, the urban population increased from 6.1 to 16.8 million, while the population as a whole grew by 50 percent. The proportion of urban dwellers rose from 8 percent to 13.4 percent of the population. The concentration of population in the large cities accelerated. Each of the Russian capitals, Moscow and Petersburg, had more than a million inhabitants by the end of the century. See Fedorov, ed., *Istoriia Rossii. XIX–nachala XX v.*, pp. 305–7.

4. On the history of rural self-government, see V.F. Abramov, *Rossiiskoe zemstvo: ekonomika, finansy i kul'tura* (Moscow, 1996); L.S. Zhukova, *Zemskoe samoupravlenie i biurokratiia v Rossii: konflikty i sotrudnichestvo* (Moscow, 1998); and A.Iu. Shutov, *Zemskie vybory v istorii Rossii (1864–1917)* (Moscow, 1997). In Western historiography, see the collection of articles devoted to the history of the zemstvo: Terence Emmons and Wayne S. Vucinich, eds., *The Zemstvo in Russia: An Experiment in Local Self-Government* (Cambridge, 1982).

5. Valuev's memorandum of June 26, 1862, "O vnutrennem sostoianii Rossii," *Istoricheskii arkhiv*, No. 1 (1958), p. 144.

6. Quoted in Kornilov, *Obshchestvennoe dvizhenie*, p. 170; see also S.Ia. Tseitlin, "Zemskaia reforma," in *Istoriia Rossii v XIX v.*, ed. Bem, 2:182–93.

7. Valuev, "O vnutrennem sostoianii Rossii," p. 148.

8. B.B. Veselovskii, *Istoriia zemstva za sorok let*, Vol. 3 (St. Petersburg, 1910), pp. 49, 680–81.

9. L.G. Zakharova, *Zemskaia kontrreforma 1890 g.* (Moscow, 1969), pp. 16–26.

10. Western historians have studied the "third element" as part of the formation of professional groups and the emergence of a "middle class" and a civil society in Russia. See Harley Balzer, ed., *Russia's Missing Middle Class: The Professions in Russian History* (Armonk, NY, 1996); and Edith W. Clowes, Samuel D. Kassow, and James L. West, eds., *Between Tsar and People: Educated Society and the Quest for Public Identity in Late Imperial Russia* (Princeton, 1991).

11. G.A. Gerasimenko, *Zemskoe samoupravlenie v Rossii* (Moscow, 1990), pp. 14, 17, 32, 35; and N.M. Pirumova, *Zemskaia intelligentsiia i ee rol' v obshchestvennoi bor'be do nachala XX v.* (Moscow, 1986), pp. 168, 118, 129, 132, 142, 143, 155.

12. Pirumova, *Zemskaia intelligentsiia*, p. 23.

13. Ibid., pp. 80–81.

14. V.G. Chernukha, *Vnutrenniaia politika tsarizma s serediny 50–kh do nachala 80–kh gg. XIX v.* (Leningrad, 1978), pp. 15–67.

15. Zakharova, "Samoderzhavie i reformy," p. 40.

16. Quoted in Svatikov, *Obshchestvennoe dvizhenie v Rossii*, p. 58.

17. Kornilov, *Obshchestvennoe dvizhenie*, p. 120.

18. Quoted in Svatikov, *Obshchestvennoe dvizhenie v Rossii*, pp. 62–64.

19. See N.M. Kolmakov, "Staryi sud. Ocherki i vospominaniia," *Russkaia starina*, No. 12 (1886), pp. 514–16.

20. Quoted in M.G. Korotkikh, *Samoderzhavie i sudebnaia reforma 1864 g. v Rossii* (Voronezh, 1989), p. 54.

21. Ibid., p. 151.

22. G.A. Dzhanshiev, *Iz epokha Velikikh reform. Istoricheskie spravki* (Moscow, 1892), pp. 212, 216–17.

23. Afanas'ev, "Jurors and Jury Trials in Imperial Russia, 1866–1885," p. 221.

24. See A.F. Koni, *Na zhiznennom puti*, Vol. 1 (Moscow, 1913), pp. 17–26, 48–58, 70–78, and passim.

25. See M.K. Lemke, *Epokha tsenzurnykh reform, 1855–1865 gg.* (St. Petersburg, 1905); and Charles Ruud, *Fighting Words: Imperial Censorship and the Russian Press, 1804–1906* (Toronto, 1982).

26. V.G. Chernukha, *Pravitel'stvennaia politika v otnoshenii pechati. 60–70–e gg. XIX v.* (Leningrad, 1989), pp. 41–43.

27. N.A. Troitskii, *Bezumstvo khrabrykh. Russkie revoliutsionery i karatel'naia politika tsarizma, 1866–1882* (Moscow, 1978), p. 6.

28. Quoted in N.A. Troitskii, *Tsarizm pod sudom progressivnoi obshchestvennosti* (Moscow, 1979), p. 263.

29. Troitskii, *Bezumstvo khrabrykh*, pp. 89–90.

30. Ibid., p. 123.

31. Troitskii, *Tsarizm pod sudom progressivnoi obshchestvennosti*, p. 230.

32. Troitskii, *Bezumstvo khrabrykh*, p. 63.

33. P.A. Zaionchkovskii, *Krizis samoderzhaviia na rubezhe 1870–80–kh gg.* (Moscow, 1964), pp. 400–410.

34. Richard Pipes, *Russia under the Old Regime* (New York, 1974), pp. 311–12, 307.

35. See P.A. Zaionchkovskii, *Rossiiskoe samoderzhavie v kontse XIX stoletiia* (Moscow, 1970), pp. 234–61; and Theodore Taranovskii, "The Aborted Counter-Reform: The Murav'ev Commission and the Judicial Statutes of 1864," *Jahrbücher für Geschichte Osteuropas* 29, No. 2 (1981), pp. 161–84.

Chapter 6: Russia's Economy and Finances after the Emancipation of the Serfs

1. Quoted in Stepanov, "Mikhail Khristoforovich Reitern," p. 152.

2. Fedorov, ed., *Istoriia Rossii. XIX–nachalo XX v.*, p. 295.

3. Ibid., p. 285.

4. Gatrell, "The Meaning of the Great Reforms in Russian Economic History," p. 90.

5. A.N. Engel'gardt, *Iz derevni* (Moscow, 1987), p. 587.

6. Fedorov, ed., *Istoriia Rossii. XIX–nachalo XX v.*, p. 294.

7. Engel'gardt, *Iz derevni*, pp. 476–77.

8. Ibid., p. 475.

9. Kornilov, *Kurs istorii Rossii*, pp. 281–82.

10. Gatrell, "The Meaning of the Great Reforms in Russian Economic History," p. 89.

11. Stepanov, "Mikhail Khristoforovich Reitern," pp. 152, 150.

12. W. Bruce Lincoln, "The Problem of *Glasnost'* in Mid-Nineteenth-Century Russian Politics," *European Studies Review* 11, No. 2 (1981), p. 173.

13. A.V. Golovnin, "Zapiski dlia nemnogikh," *Voprosy istorii*, No. 11 (1997), pp. 86–87, 97–98.

14. See David Christian, "A Neglected Great Reform: The Abolition of Tax Farming in Russia," in *Russia's Great Reforms*, ed. Eklof, Bushnell, and Zakharova, pp. 102–14.

15. *Istoriia Rossii. XIX–nachalo XX v.*, p. 304; Gatrell, "The Meaning of the Great Reforms in Russian Economic History," p. 98.

16. On the income-tax problem, see Chernukha, *Vnutrenniaia politika tsarizma*, pp. 199– 243.

17. See V.G. Chernukha, *Krest'ianskii vopros v pravitel'stvennoi politike Rossii (60–70 gg. XIX v.)* (Leningrad, 1971).

18. Alfred J. Rieber, "Interest-Group Politics in the Era of the Great Reforms," in *Russia's Great Reforms*, ed. Eklof, Bushnell, and Zakharova, pp. 58–83.

19. A.N. Kulomzin and V.G. Reitern-Nol'ken, *M.Kh. Reitern. Biograficheskii ocherk. S prilozheniem iz posmertnykh zapisok M.Kh. Reiterna* (St. Petersburg, 1910), pp. 64–138.

20. Gatrell, "The Meaning of the Great Reforms in Russian Economic History," p. 99.

21. Fedorov, ed., *Istoriia Rossii. XIX–nachalo XX v.*, p. 302.

22. L.E. Shepelev, *Aktsionernye kompanii v Rossii* (Leningrad, 1973), pp. 84–85, 111–21. On corporate law and patterns of corporate entrepreneurship, see also Thomas C. Owen, *The Corporation Under Russian Law, 1800–1917* (New York, 1991); and Owen, *Russian Corporate Capitalism from Peter the Great to Perestroika* (New York, 1995).

23. Quoted in Samuel H. Baron, *Plekhanov: The Father of Russian Marxism* (Stanford, CA, 1963), p. 108.

24. S.L. Frank, "Iz razmyshlenii o russkoi revoliutsii" (1923), *Novyi mir*, No. 4 (1990), p. 219.

25. Kulomzin and Reitern-Nol'ken, *M.Kh. Reitern*, pp. 160–67.

26. Ibid., pp. 138–57.

27. See Thomas C. Owen, *Dilemmas of Russian Capitalism: Fedor Chizhov and Corporate Enterprise in the Railroad Age* (Cambridge, MA, 2005).

Chapter 7: The Opposition Movement in Post-Reform Russia: From "Thaw" to Regicide

1. Editorial in the newspaper *Moskovskie vedomosti*, March 1, 1882. Quoted in Troitskii, *Bezumstvo khrabrykh*, p. 171.

2. Kornilov, *Obshchestvennoe dvizhenie*, p. 20.

3. A. Kimbell [Alan Kimball], "Russkoe grazhdanskoe obshchestvo i politicheskii krizis v epokhu Velikikh reform. 1859–1863," in *Velikie reformy v Rossii. 1856–1874*, pp. 260–82; and Adele Lindenmeyr, "The Rise of Voluntary Associations during the Great Reforms: The Case of Charity," in *Russia's Great Reforms*, ed. Eklof, Bushnell, and Zakharova, pp. 264–79.

4. N.A. Berdiaev, "Russkaia ideia," repr. in *O Rossii i russkoi filosofskoi kul'ture: filosofy russkogo posleoktiabr'skogo zarubezh'ia*, ed. E.M. Chekharin, comp. M.A. Maslin (Moscow, 1990), p. 64.

5. Quoted in Kornilov, *Obshchestvennoe dvizhenie*, p. 123.

6. See Golovnin, "Zapiski dlia nemnogikh," *Voprosy istorii* (1996), No. 1, pp. 75–95; No. 2, pp. 102–21; No. 4, pp. 94–111; No. 5–6, pp. 118–40; No. 9, pp. 91–112; No. 10, pp. 80–99; and (1997), No. 1, pp. 98–119; No. 2, pp. 96–114; No. 3, pp. 76–100; No. 4, pp. 68–88; No. 5, pp. 95–123; No. 6, pp. 68–84; No. 7, pp. 100–20; No. 8, pp. 57–73; No. 9, pp. 114–34; No. 10, pp. 68–87; No. 11, pp. 79–101.

7. See Samuel D. Kassow, "The University Statute of 1863," in *Russia's Great Reforms*, ed. Eklof, Bushnell, and Zakharova, pp. 247–63; R.G. Eimontova, *Russkie universitety na grani dvukh epokh: ot Rossii krepostnoi k Rossii kapitalisticheskoi*

(Moscow, 1985); and Eimontova, *Russkie universitety na putiakh reform. Shestidesiatye gody XIX v.* (Moscow, 1993).

8. *Khrestomatiia po istorii SSSR, 1861–1917* (Moscow, 1990), pp. 112–17.

9. Ibid., pp. 117–19.

10. Z. Lenskii, "Pol'skoe vosstanie 1863 g.," in *Istoriia Rossii v XIX v.*, 2:271–324; and Kornilov, *Obshchestvennoe dvizhenie*, pp. 157–63. The course of the Polish uprising is reflected in detail in the pages of War Minister Dmitry Miliutin's memoirs. See D.A. Miliutin, *Vospominaniia, 1863–1864*, ed. L.G. Zakharova (Moscow, 2003).

11. Quoted in Svatikov, *Obshchestvennoe dvizhenie v Rossii*, p. 68.

12. See V.L. Stepanov, "Dmitrii Andreevich Tolstoi," in *Rossiiskie konservatory*, ed. Bokhanov et al., pp. 233–86.

13. On Tolstoi's policies, see Daniel Brower, *Training the Nihilists: Education and Radicalism in Tsarist Russia* (Ithaca, NY, 1975); and Allen Sinel, *The Classroom and the Chancellery: State Educational Reform in Russia under Count Dmitry Tolstoi* (Cambridge, 1973).

14. Pantin, Plimak, and Khoros, *Revoliutsionnaia traditsiia v Rossii*, p. 212.

15. Ibid., p. 229.

16. See Franco Venturi, *Roots of Revolution: A History of the Populist and Socialist Movements in Nineteenth Century Russia*, trans. Francis Haskell (New York, 1966).

17. Pantin, Plimak, and Khoros, *Revoliutsionnaia traditsiia v Rossii*, pp. 232–37.

18. *Khrestomatiia po istorii SSSR, 1861–1917*, p. 109.

19. Pantin, Plimak, and Khoros, *Revoliutsionnaia traditsiia v Rossii*, p. 243.

20. Ibid.

21. Ibid., p. 237.

22. Ibid., pp. 237–41.

23. See Daniel Field, "Peasants and Propagandists in the Russian Movement to the People of 1874," *Journal of Modern History* 59, No. 3 (1987), p. 438.

24. See E.L. Rudnitskaia, *Russkii blankizm. Petr Tkachev* (Moscow, 1992).

25. *Khrestomatiia po istorii SSSR, 1861–1917*, p. 110.

26. Troitskii, *Bezumstvo khrabrykh*, p. 80.

27. On the People's Will, see M.G. Sedov, *Geroicheskii period revoliutsionnogo narodnichestva* (Moscow, 1966), and S.S. Volk, *Narodnaia volia, 1879–1882* (Moscow, 1966). See also O.V. Budnitskii, *Istoriia terrorizma v Rossii v dokumentakh, biografiiakh, issledovaniiakh* (Rostov-on-Don, 1996); and Budnitskii, *Terrorizm v rossiiskom revoliutsionnom dvizhenii* (Moscw, 2000).

28. Pantin, Plimak, and Khoros, *Revoliutsionnaia traditsiia v Rossii*, p. 270.

29. Quoted in Zaionchkovskii, *Krizis samoderzhaviia*, p. 99.

30. Further waves of zemstvo petitions followed the political relaxation at the end of 1880 and the death of Alexander II. In all, thirteen zemstvo addresses containing political demands were submitted in 1878–81. See Zakharova, *Zemskaia kontrreforma*, pp. 32–41.

31. Quoted in Svatikov, *Obshchestvennoe dvizhenie v Rossii*, pp. 88–92.

32. On Loris-Melikov's political program and his plans for further development of the Great Reforms, see A.V. Mamonov, "Graf M.T. Loris-Melikov: k kharakteristike vzgliadov i gosudarstvennoi deiatel'nosti," *Otechestvennaia istoriia*, No. 5 (2001), pp. 32–50.

33. Quoted in Svatikov, *Obshchestvennoe dvizhenie v Rossii*, pp. 129–30.

34. On Pobedonostsev, see Robert F. Byrnes, *Pobedonostsev: His Life and Thought* (Bloomington, IN, 1968); A.Iu. Polunov, "Konstantin Petrovich Pobedonostsev—Man and Politician," *Russian Studies in History* 39, No. 4 (2001), pp. 8–32.

Chapter 8: Russia and the World, 1856–1900

1. A.M. Solov'eva, *Zheleznodorozhnyi transport Rossii vo vtoroi polovine XIX v.* (Moscow, 1975), pp. 97, 193–203, 225–26.

2. Ibid., pp. 118–46; and Solov'eva, *Promyshlennaia revoliutsiia v Rossii v XIX v.* (Moscow, 1990), pp. 173–92.

3. A.P. Shevyrev, *Russkii flot posle Krymskoi voiny: liberal'naia biurokratiia i morskie reformy* (Moscow, 1990), pp. 129–57; Jacob W. Kipp, "The Russian Navy and the Problem of Technological Transfer: Technological Backwardness and Military-Industrial Development, 1853–1876," in *Russia's Great Reforms*, ed. Eklof, Bushnell, and Zakharova, pp. 115–38; V.M. Khevrolina, ed., *Istoriia vneshnei politiki Rossii. Vtoraia polovina XIX v.* (Moscow, 1999), pp. 34, 42, 48.

4. John S. Bushnell, "Miliutin and the Balkan War: Military Reform vs. Military Performance," in *Russia's Great Reforms*, ed. Eklof, Bushnell, and Zakharova, pp. 139–58; and P.A. Zaionchkovskii, *Voennye reformy 1860–70-kh gg. v Rossii* (Moscow, 1952).

5. Khevrolina, ed., *Istoriia vneshnei politiki Rossii. Vtoraia polovina XIX v.*, p. 34.

6. Zakharova, "Aleksandr II," p. 204.

7. N.Ia. Danilevskii, *Rossiia i Evropa. Vzgliad na kul'turnye i politicheskie otnosheniia Slavianskogo mira k Germano-Romanskomu* (St. Petersburg, 1871), p. 61.

8. On Danilevsky, see Robert E. MacMaster, *Danilevsky, a Russian Totalitarian Philosopher* (Cambridge, MA, 1967); Edward C. Thaden, *Conservative Nationalism in Nineteenth-Century Russia* (Seattle, 1964), pp. 102–15.

9. On Pan-Slavism, see Michael Petrovich, *The Emergence of Russian Panslavism, 1856–1870* (Westport, CN, 1985). On the Slavic Congress and Ethnographic Exhibition, see Nataniel Nait [Nathaniel Knight], "Imperiia napokaz: vserossiiskaia etnograficheskaia vystavka 1867 g.," *Novoe literaturnoe obozrenie*, No. 51 (2001), pp. 111–31.

10. Pushkarev, *Rossiia 1801–1917*, pp. 551–58.

11. See N.N. Bolkhovitinov, *Russko-amerikanskie otnosheniia i prodazha Aliaski, 1834–1867* (Moscow, 1990).

12. Fedorov, ed., *Istoriia Rossii. XIX–nachalo XX v.*, p. 373.

13. See N.A. Khalfin, *Prisoedinenie Srednei Azii k Rossii (60–90-e gg. XIX v.)* (Moscow, 1965); and N.S. Kiniapina, M.M. Bliev, and V.V. Degoev, *Kavkaz i Sredniaia Aziia vo vneshnei politike Rossii. XVIII–80-e gg. XIX v.* (Moscow, 1994).

14. The relationship between economic and military and strategic motives for Russia's expansion in Central Asia remains a matter of debate. Richard Pierce gives priority to economic factors, Firuz Kazemzadeh to military considerations. See Richard A. Pierce, *Russian Central Asia, 1867–1917: A Study in Colonial Rule* (Berkeley, 1960), p. 13; and Firuz Kazemzadeh, *Russia and Britain in Persia, 1864–1914* (New Haven, 1968), p. 6. It should be noted that the new Central Asian possessions long remained unprofitable for Russia. From 1868 to 1880 the costs of annexing Central Asia were triple the revenue derived from it (Khevrolina, ed., *Istoriia vneshnei politiki Rossii. Vtoraia polovina XIX v.*, p. 130).

15. See Gerald Morgan, *Anglo-Russian Rivalry in Central Asia, 1810–1895* (London, 1981), pp. 10, 36–40, 213–14.

16. Khevrolina, ed., *Istoriia vneshnei politiki Rossii. Vtoraia polovina XIX v.*, pp. 95, 97.

17. P.A. Valuev, *Dnevnik P.A. Valueva, ministra vnutrennikh del*, 2 vols. (Moscow, 1961), 2:60–61.

18. Khevrolina, ed., *Istoriia vneshnei politiki Rossii. Vtoraia polovina XIX v.*, p. 113.

19. See Nathaniel Knight, "Grigor'ev in Orenburg, 1851–1862: Russian Orientalism in the Service of Empire?" *Slavic Review* 59, No. 1 (2000), pp. 74–100; and Robert Geraci, "Going Abroad or Going to Russia? Orthodox Missionaries in the Kazakh Steppe, 1881–1917," in *Of Religion and Empire*, ed. Geraci and Khodarkovsky, pp. 274–310.

20. Khevrolina, ed., *Istoriia vneshnei politiki Rossii. Vtoraia polovina XIX v.*, pp. 181–95.

21. See Bushnell, "Miliutin and the Balkan War."

22. A.J.P. Taylor, *The Struggle for Mastery in Europe, 1848–1918* (Oxford, 1954), p. 245.

23. Kornilov, *Obshchestvennoe dvizhenie*, p. 241. Alexander II personally ordered Aksakov banished from Moscow for his speech at a meeting of the Moscow Slavic Committee. See N.I. Tsimbaev, "Rech' I.S. Aksakova o Berlinskom kongresse i zakrytie Moskovskogo slavianskogo obshchestva," in *Rossiia i vostochnyi krizis 70–kh gg. XIX v. Sbornik statei*, ed. I.A. Fedosov (Moscow, 1981), pp. 184–93.

24. Alexander's toast is mentioned in, for example, S.D. Sheremetev, *Memuary grafa S.D. Sheremeteva*, 2 vols., ed. L.I. Shokhina (Moscow, 2004–5), 1:603, 669.

25. See *K.N. Leont'ev—pro et contra: lichnost' i tvorchestvo Konstantina Leont'eva v otsenke russkikh myslitelei i issledovatelei, 1891–1917 gg.: antologiia*, 2 vols. (St. Petersburg, 1995).

26. K.N. Leont'ev, *Vostok, Rossiia i slavianstvo*, 2 vols. (Moscow, 1885), 1:130, 132.

27. V.S. Solov'ev, "Russkaia ideia" (1888), *Sochineniia*, 2 vols. (Moscow, 1989), 2:238.

28. Quoted in Anan'ich, ed., *Vlast' i reformy*, p. 390.

29. Khevrolina, ed., *Istoriia vneshnei politiki Rossii. Vtoraia polovina XIX v.*, p. 277.

30. On the formation of the alliance, see A.Z. Manfred, *Obrazovanie russko-frantsuzskogo soiuza* (Moscow, 1975); and I.S. Rybachenok, *Soiuz s Frantsiei vo vneshnei politike Rossii v kontse XIX v.* (Moscow, 1993).

31. Quoted in S.S. Ol'denburg, *Tsarstvovanie imperatora Nikolaia II* (Moscow, 1992), p. 9.

Chapter 9: Under the Banner of Unshakable Autocracy

1. On Alexander III, see I.A. Murav'ev, ed., *Aleksandr Tretii. Vospominaniia. Dnevniki. Pis'ma* (St. Petersburg, 2001); O. Barkovets and A. Krylov-Tolstikovich, *Neizvestnyi imperator. Aleksandr III* (Moscow, 2003); A.N. Bokhanov, *Imperator Aleksandr III* (Moscow, 1998); A.L. Nalepin, ed., *Velikii kniaz' Aleksandr Aleksandrovich. Sbornik dokumentov* (Moscow, 2002); V.A. Tvardovskaia, "Aleksandr III," in *Rossiiskie samoderzhtsy*, ed. Bokhanov et al., pp. 215–306; and V.G. Chernukha, "Aleksandr III," *Voprosy istorii*, No. 11–12 (1992), pp. 46–64.

2. See Iu.V. Got'e, "K.P. Pobedonostsev i naslednik Aleksandr Aleksandrovich," *Sbornik Publichnoi biblioteki im. Lenina*, Vol. 2 (Moscow, 1928), pp. 107–34; repr. in *Konstantin Petrovich Pobedonostsev: pro et contra* (St. Petersburg, 1996), pp. 451–86.

3. On the political struggle in the spring of 1881, see Iu.V. Got'e, "Bor'ba pravitel'stvennykh gruppirovok i manifest 29 aprelia 1881 g.," *Istoricheskie zapiski*, Vol. 2 (Moscow, 1938), pp. 242–87; P.A. Zaionchkovskii, *Krizis samoderzhaviia*, pp.

301–78; Byrnes, *Pobedonostsev*, pp. 142–64; and A.V. Mamonov, "Graf M.T. Loris-Melikov: k kharakteristike vzgliadov i gosudarstvennoi deiatel'nosti," *Otechestvennaia istoriia*, No. 5 (2001), pp. 32–50.

4. E.A. Peretts, *Dnevnik gosudarstvennogo sekretaria E.A. Perettsa (1880–1883)* (Moscow and Leningrad, 1927), p. 38.

5. *Polnoe sobranie zakonov Rossiiskoi imperii. Sobranie tret'e*, 33 vols. (St. Petersburg, 1885–1916; hereafter *PSZ-3*), Vol. 1, No. 118.

6. See Zaionchkovskii, *Krizis samoderzhaviia*, pp. 413–19; and Zaionchkovskii, *Rossiiskoe samoderzhavie v kontse XIX stoletiia*, pp. 131–37. In Western historiography, see John Klier, *Imperial Russia's Jewish Question, 1855–1881* (Cambridge, 1995).

7. Quoted in Zaionchkovskii, *Krizis samoderzhaviia*, p. 452.

8. Ibid., pp. 460–65.

9. *Sobranie peredovykh statei "Moskovskikh vedomostei" za 1882 g.* (Moscow, 1901), p. 231.

10. See V.L. Stepanov, "Nikolai Khristianovich Bunge,"*Russian Studies in History* 35, No. 2 (1996), pp. 42–72. For a detailed account of Bunge's activities, see V.L. Stepanov, *N.Kh. Bunge. Sud'ba reformatora* (Moscow, 1998).

11. N.Kh. Bunge, "Zagrobnye zametki. Publikatsiia V.L. Stepanova," in *Reka vremen*, Vol. 1 (Moscow, 1995), p. 230.

12. Quoted in Stepanov, "Nikolai Khristianovich Bunge," p. 193.

13. Ibid., pp. 205–8.

14. V.L. Stepanov, "Ivan Alekseevich Vyshnegradskii," *Russian Studies in History* 35, No. 2 (1996), pp. 73–103.

15. The American historian Richard Robbins places the death toll from the famine and epidemic at 375,000 to 400,000. See Richard G. Robbins, Jr., *Famine in Russia, 1891–1892* (New York, 1975), p. 171.

16. *Pis'ma K.P. Pobedonostseva k Aleksandru III*, Vol. 2 (Moscow, 1926), pp. 169–70.

17. See A.Iu. Polunov, "Church, Regime, and Society in Russia (1880–1895)," *Russian Studies in History* 39, No. 4 (2001), pp. 33–53. For a more detailed study of Pobedonostsev's activities as supreme procurator, see A.Iu. Polunov, *Pod vlast'iu ober-prokurora. Gosudarstvo i tserkov' v epokhu Aleksandra III* (Moscow, 1996).

18. See A.Iu. Polunov, "The Orthodox Church in the Baltic Region and the Policies of Alexander III's Government," *Russian Studies in History* 39, No. 4 (2001), pp. 66–76; and Polunov, "The Religious Department and the Uniate Question, 1881–1894," ibid., pp. 77–85.

19. Zaionchkovskii, *Rossiiskoe samoderzhavie v kontse XIX stoletiia*, pp. 262–309.

20. G.I. Shchetinina, *Universitety v Rossii i ustav 1884 g.* (Moscow, 1976), pp. 81–145.

21. Quoted in Pushkarev, *Rossiia 1801–1917*, p. 300.

22. Heide W. Whelan, *Alexander III and the State Council: Bureaucracy and Counter-Reform in Late Imperial Russia* (New Brunswick, NJ, 1982).

23. *Sobranie peredovykh statei "Moskovskikh vedomostei" za 1884 g.* (Moscow, 1903), pp. 511–12.

24. Quoted in V.L. Stepanov, "Dmitrii Andreevich Tolstoi," p. 261.

25. *PSZ-3*, Vol. 5, No. 2882.

26. A.D. Pazukhin, "Sovremennoe sostoianie Rossii i soslovnyi vopros," *Russkii vestnik* 175 (January 1885), p. 53.

27. On Pazukhin's plan, see Zaionchkovskii, *Rossiiskoe samoderzhavie v kontse XIX stoletiia*; and Zakharova, *Zemskaia kontrreforma*.

28. See Zaionchkovskii, *Rossiiskoe samoderzhavie v kontse XIX stoletiia*, pp. 234–61.

29. Quoted in Zakharova, *Zemskaia kontrreforma*, p. 137.

30. Ibid., pp. 151–55.

31. Zaionchkovskii, *Rossiiskoe samoderzhavie v kontse XIX stoletiia*, pp. 411–28. See also V.A. Nardova, *Gorodskoe samoupravlenie v Rossii v 60–kh–nachale 90–kh gg. XIX v.* (Leningrad, 1984); and L.F. Pisar'kova, *Moskovskaia gorodskaia duma. 1863–1907* (Moscow, 1998).

Chapter 10: Nicholas II: A Policy of Contradictions

1. Quoted in S.S. Ol'denburg, *Tsarstvovanie imperatora Nikolaia II* (Moscow, 1992), p. 45.

2. In recent years, numerous Russian historians and journalists have turned their attention to Nicholas II. See A.N. Bokhanov, *Sumerki monarkhii* (Moscow, 1993); E. Radzinskii, *"Gospodi! . . . Spasi i usmiri Rossiiu!" Nikolai II: zhizn' i smert'* (Moscow, 1993); B.V. Anan'ich and R.Sh. Ganelin, "Nikolai II," *Voprosy istorii*, No. 2 (1993), pp. 58–74; and G. Ioffe, *Revoliutsiia i sud'ba Romanovykh* (Moscow, 1992).

3. F.A. Golovin, "Nikolai II," in *Nikolai Vtoroi. Vospominaniia. Dnevniki*, ed. B.V. Anan'ich and R.Sh. Ganelin (St. Petersburg, 1994), p. 81.

4. Quoted in Mironenko, ed., *Istoriia Otechestva: liudi, idei, resheniia*, p. 328.

5. Quoted in S.V. Kuleshov et al., *Nashe Otechestvo. Opyt politicheskoi istorii*, 2 vols. (Moscow, 1991), 1:201.

6. See L.G. Zakharova, "Krizis samoderzhaviia nakanune revoliutsii 1905 g.," *Voprosy istorii*, No. 8 (1972), pp. 119–37; Wortman, *Scenarios of Power*, Vol. 2, pp. 307–523.

7. Quoted in S.V. Kuleshov et al., *Politicheskaia istoriia. Rossiia—SSSR—Rossiiskaia Federatsiia*, Vol. 1 (Moscow, 1996), p. 394.

8. Fedorov, ed., *Istoriia Rossii. XIX–nachalo XX v.*, pp. 474–76.

9. V.S. Diakin, "Natsional'nyi vopros vo vnutrennei politike tsarizma (XIX v.)," *Voprosy istorii*, No. 9 (1995), pp. 130–42; and Edward C. Thaden, ed., *Russification in the Baltic Provinces and Finland, 1855–1914* (Princeton, 1981).

10. Quoted in Ol'denburg, *Tsarstvovanie imperatora Nikolaia II*, p. 142.

11. See A.P. Korelin, "S.Iu. Witte," in *Rossiia na rubezhe vekov: istoricheskie portrety*, comp. A.P. Korelin (Moscow, 1991), pp. 8–47; A.N. Bokhanov, "Sergei Iul'evich Witte," in *Rossiiskie reformatory*, ed. Korelin, pp. 221–58; and B.V. Anan'ich and R.Sh. Ganelin, *Sergei Iul'evich Witte i ego vremia* (St. Petersburg, 1999).

12. Quoted in Bokhanov, "Sergei Iul'evich Witte," pp. 231–32.

13. Quoted in Anan'ich, ed., *Vlast' i reformy*, p. 416.

14. Kuleshov et al., *Politicheskaia istoriia*, p. 409.

15. Fedorov, ed., *Istoriia Rossii. XIX–nachalo XX v.*, p. 468.

16. Quoted in Ol'denburg, *Tsarstvovanie imperatora Nikolaia II*, p. 160.

17. Fedorov, ed., *Istoriia Rossii. XIX–nachalo XX v.*, pp. 442–43; Bokhanov, "Sergei Iul'evich Witte," pp. 232–33; and Korelin, "S.Iu. Witte," p.19.

18. Pushkarev, *Rossiia 1801–1917*, p. 355.

19. Fedorov, ed., *Istoriia Rossii. XIX–nachalo XX v.*, pp. 440–60. On the development of finance capitalism in Russia, see V.I. Bovykin and Iu.A. Petrov, *Kommercheskie banki Rossiiskoi imperii* (Moscow, 1994).

20. V.S. Diakin, *Krizis samoderzhaviia v Rossii, 1895–1917 gg.* (Leningrad, 1984), p. 17.

21. Korelin, "S.Iu. Witte," pp. 22–23.

22. See M.S. Simonova, "Viacheslav Konstantinovich Plehve," in *Rossiiskie konservatory*, ed. Bokhanov et al., pp. 287–322; and Edward H. Judge, *Plehve: Repression and Reform in Imperial Russia, 1902–1904* (Syracuse, NY, 1983).

23. Quoted in Anan'ich, ed., *Vlast' i reformy*, pp. 440–41.

24. Quoted in Korelin, "S.Iu. Witte," pp. 18–19; see also Kuleshov et al., *Politicheskaia istoriia*, p. 419.

25. Ol'denburg, *Tsarstvovanie imperatora Nikolaia II*, p. 171. See also M.S. Simonova, *Krizis agrarnoi politiki tsarizma nakanune pervoi rossiiskoi revoliutsii* (Moscow, 1987).

26. Ol'denburg, *Tsarstvovanie imperatora Nikolaia II*, p. 174.

27. Korelin, "S.Iu. Witte," pp. 28–29.

28. Simonova, "Viacheslav Konstantinovich Plehve," pp. 311–12.

29. On the ideology of Asianism, see David Schimmelpenninck van der Oye, *Toward the Rising Sun: Russian Ideologies of Empire and the Path to War with Japan* (DeKalb, IL, 2001), pp. 42–60.

30. Ol'denburg, *Tsarstvovanie imperatora Nikolaia II*, pp. 105–6.

31. B.A. Romanov, *Ocherki diplomaticheskoi istorii russko-iaponskoi voiny, 1895–1907* (Moscow and Leningrad, 1955); and David M. McDonald, *United Government and Foreign Policy in Russia, 1900–1914* (Cambridge, MA, 1992).

Chapter 11: Opposition and Revolution

1. On the Russian liberal movement, see K.F. Shatsillo, *Russkii liberalizm nakanune revoliutsii 1905–1907 gg.* (Moscow, 1985); and V.V. Shelokhaev, *Liberal'naia model' pereustroistva Rossii* (Moscow, 1996).

2. See V. Ia. Laverychev, " 'Beseda' i tendentsii k konsolidatsii konservativnykh sil v Rossii kontsa XIX–nachala XX v.," *Otechestvennaia istoriia*, No. 3 (1994), pp. 43–55.

3. On the student movement, see G.I. Shchetina, *Studenchestvo i revoliutsionnoe dvizhenie v Rossii, posledniaia chetvert' XIX v.* (Moscow, 1987).

4. Hans Rogger, *Russia in the Age of Modernisation and Revolution, 1881–1917* (London, 1983), pp. 182–207.

5. Quoted in George Fischer, *Russian Liberalism: From Gentry to Intelligentsia* (Cambridge, MA, 1958), pp. 169–70. See also Richard Pipes, *Struve, Liberal on the Left, 1870–1905* (Cambridge, MA, 1970), and Pipes, *Struve, Liberal on the Right, 1905–1944* (Cambridge, MA, 1980).

6. K.F. Shatsillo, "Nikolai II: reformy ili revoliutsiia," in *Istoriia Otechestva: liudi, idei, resheniia*, p. 345.

7. Quoted in Ol'denburg, *Tsarstvovanie imperatora Nikolaia II*, pp. 228–29.

8. Quoted in Anan'ich, ed., *Vlast' i reformy*, p. 468.

9. Ibid., p. 472; Shatsillo, "Nikolai II: reformy ili revoliutsiia," p. 347.

10. Anan'ich, ed., *Vlast' i reformy*, p. 404.

11. Korelin, "S.Iu. Witte," p. 21.

12. S.V. Tiutiukin, "Fenomen massovykh sotsial'nykh dvizhenii," in Kuleshov et al., *Politicheskaia istoriia*, pp. 612–15.

13. Fedorov, ed., *Istoriia Rossii. XIX–nachalo XX v.*, p. 520.

14. S.V. Tiutiukin, "G.V. Plekhanov," in *Rossiia na rubezhe vekov*, comp. Korelin, pp. 233–80.

15. Quoted in Pushkarev, *Rossiia 1801–1917*, p. 308.

16. N.A. Berdiaev, *Istoki i smysl russkogo kommunizma* (repr. Moscow, 1990), p. 89.

17. V.V. Shelokhaev, *Politicheskaia istoriia Rossii v partiiakh i litsakh* (Moscow, 1993), pp. 26–46.

18. D.A. Kolesnichenko, "V.M. Chernov," in *Rossiia na rubezhe vekov*, comp. Korelin, pp. 296–334.

19. See K.V. Gusev, *Rytsari terrora* (Moscow, 1992).

20. See Robert Service, *Lenin—A Biography* (Cambridge, MA, 2000).

21. See Dimitry Pospielovsky, *Russian Police Trade Unionism: Experiment or Provocation?* (London, 1971); and Jeremiah Schneiderman, *Sergei Zubatov and Revolutionary Marxism: The Struggle for the Working Class in Tsarist Russia* (Ithaca, NY, 1976).

22. On the revolution, see Teodor Shanin, *Russia, 1905–1907: Revolution as a Moment of Truth* (New Haven, 1986); Abraham Ascher, *The Revolution of 1905*, 2 vols. (Stanford, 1988–92).

23. Fedorov, *Istoriia Rossii. XIX–nachalo XX v.*, pp. 526–28.

24. On the contention within governmental circles on the eve of the revolution and in the first months after it began, see R.Sh. Ganelin, *Rossiiskoe samoderzhavie v 1905 godu. Reformy i revoliutsiia* (St. Petersburg, 1991).

25. On the consequences of the decree of April 17, 1905, see Metropolitan Evlogy (Georgievsky), *Put' moei zhizni* (Paris, 1947).

26. Kappeler, *The Russian Empire*, pp. 328–41.

27. On the terror in 1905–7, see Pushkarev, *Rossiia 1801–1917*, pp. 398–99; and Anna Geifman, *Thou Shalt Kill: Revolutionary Terrorism in Russia, 1894–1917* (Princeton, NJ, 1993).

Chapter 12: On the Eve of Great Changes

1. Marc Szeftel, *The Russian Constitution of April 23, 1906: Political Institutions of the Duma Monarchy* (Brussels, 1976).

2. V.A. Demin, *Gosudarstvennaia Duma Rossii (1906–1917): mekhanizm funktsionirovaniia* (Moscow, 1996); and A.F. Smirnov, *Gosudarstvennaia Duma Rossiiskoi imperii, 1906–1917. Istoriko-pravovoi ocherk* (Moscow, 1998).

3. Fedorov, ed., *Istoriia Rossii. XIX–nachalo XX v.*, p. 533.

4. Anan'ich, ed., *Vlast' i reformy*, p. 532.

5. Quoted in Pushkarev, *Rossiia 1801–1917*, p. 393.

6. On the composition and activities of the First State Duma, see Fedorov, ed., *Istoriia Rossii. XIX–nachalo XX v.*, pp. 543–46; Pushkarev, *Rossiia 1801–1917*, pp. 393–405; and Terence Emmons, *The Formation of Political Parties and the First National Elections in Russia* (Cambridge, MA, 1983).

7. Quoted in Pushkarev, *Rossiia 1801–1917*, p. 394.

8. Ol'denburg, *Tsarstvovanie Imperatora Nikolaia II*, p. 323.

9. Ibid., p. 353.

10. D. Meisi [David Macey], "Zemel'naia reforma i politicheskie peremeny: fenomen Stolypina," *Voprosy istorii*, No. 4 (1993), p. 12. See also David Macey, *Government and Peasant in Russia, 1861–1906: The Prehistory of the Stolypin Reform* (DeKalb, IL, 1987).

11. See A.P. Korelin, "Petr Arkad'evich Stolypin," in *Rossiiskie reformatory*, ed.

Korelin, pp. 259– 305; P.N. Zyrianov, "Petr Arkad'evich Stolypin," in *Rossiia na rubezhe vekov*, comp. Korelin, pp. 48–78; A.Ia. Avrekh, *Stolypin i sud'by reform v Rossii* (Moscow, 1991); Peter Waldron, *Between Two Revolutions: Stolypin and the Politics of Renewal in Russia* (DeKalb, IL, 1998); Abraham Ascher, *Stolypin: The Search for Stability in Late Imperial Russia* (Stanford, 2001); and Alexandra Korros, *A Reluctant Parliament: Stolypin, Nationalism, and the Politics of the Russian Imperial State Council, 1906–1911* (Lanham, MD, 2002).

12. Fedorov, ed., *Istoriia Rossii. XIX–nachalo XX v.*, p. 553.

13. From Stolypin's speech to the Second State Duma, May 10, 1907, quoted in Ol'denburg, *Tsarstvovanie imperatora Nikolaia II*, p. 349.

14. Quoted in Korelin, "Petr Arkad'evich Stolypin," p. 274.

15. Fedorov, ed., *Istoriia Rossii. XIX–nachalo XX v.*, p. 554.

16. Pushkarev, *Rossiia 1801–1917*, pp. 423–33.

17. *Vekhi (Landmarks): A Collection of Articles on the Russian Intelligentsia*, trans. and ed. Marshall S. Shatz and Judith E. Zimmerman (Armonk, NY, 1994); and M.A. Kolerov, *Ne mir, no mech. Russkaia religiozno-filosofskaia pechat' ot "Problem idealizma" do "Vekh." 1902–1909* (St. Petersburg, 1996).

18. Shelokhaev, *Politicheskaia istoriia Rossii*, pp. 108–28.

19. Quoted in ibid., p. 114.

20. Quoted in ibid., p. 111.

21. Quoted in Korelin, "Petr Arkad'evich Stolypin," pp. 266, 284.

22. Quoted in Ol'denburg, *Tsarstvovanie Imperatora Nikolaia II*, p. 383.

23. Quoted in Pushkarev, *Rossiia 1801–1917*, p. 418.

24. A.S. Orlov, A.Iu. Polunov, and Iu.Ia. Tereshchenko, *Osnovy kursa istorii Rossii*, (Moscow, 2003), p. 382.

25. Ibid., p. 383; Pushkarev, *Rossiia 1801–1917*, p. 422.

26. Orlov, Polunov, and Tereshchenko, *Osnovy kursa istorii Rossii*, p. 383.

27. From Stolypin's interview in the newspaper *Volga* (Saratov), October 1909, quoted in Ol'denburg, *Tsarstvovanie imperatora Nikolaia II*, p. 410.

28. Meisi, "Zemel'naia reforma i politicheskie peremeny," p. 13.

29. See Shelokhaev, *Politicheskaia istoriia Rossii*, pp. 129–49; S.A. Stepanov, *Chernaia sotnia v Rossii, 1905–1914* (Moscow, 1992); and Walter Laqueur, *Black Hundred: The Rise of the Extreme Right in Russia* (New York, 1993), part 1.

30. Anan'ich and Ganelin, eds., *Nikolai vtoroi*, p. 198.

31. See Avrekh, *Stolypin i sud'ba reform v Rossii*, pp. 212–33.

32. Orlov, Polunov, and Tereshchenko, *Osnovy kursa istorii Rossii*, p. 386.

33. Quoted in A.N. Bokhanov, "A.I. Guchkov," in *Rossiia na rubezhe vekov*, comp. Korelin, p. 100.

Conclusion

1. On the diplomacy of the pre–World War I period, see D.C.B. Lieven, *Russia and the Origins of the First World War* (New York, 1983); and O.R. Airapetov, ed., *Posledniaia voina imperatorskoi Rossii. Sbornik statei* (Moscow, 2002).

2. Quoted in Ol'denburg, *Tsarstvovanie Imperatora Nikolaia II*, p. 381.

3. On military operations in World War I, see Norman Stone, *The Eastern Front, 1914–1917* (London, 1975); and A.M. Zaionchkovskii, *Pervaia mirovaia voina* (St. Petersburg, 2002).

4. Pushkarev, *Rossiia 1801–1917*, pp. 575–76; and Orlov, Polunov, and Tereshchenko, *Osnovy kursa istorii Rossii*, p. 390.

5. On economic and social affairs and the governmental crisis during the war years, see M.F. Florinskii, *Krizis gosudarstvennogo upravleniia v Rossii v gody pervoi mirovoi voiny* (Leningrad, 1988).

6. Pushkarev, *Rossiia 1801–1917*, p. 592.

7. On the activities of these organizations, see F.A. Gaida, *Liberal'naia oppozitsiia na putiakh k vlasti (1914–vesna 1917 g.)* (Moscow, 2003); and Lewis Siegelbaum, *The Politics of Industrial Mobilization in Russia, 1915–17: A Study of the War-Industries Committees* (New York, 1983).

8. See A.Ia. Avrekh, *Tsarizm nakanune sverzheniia* (Moscow, 1989).

9. Gaida, *Liberal'naia oppozitsiia*, pp. 101–54.

10. On Rasputin, see A.N. Bokhanov, *Rasputin: anatomiia mifa* (Moscow, 2000); and Edvard Radzinsky, *The Rasputin File*, trans. Judson Rosengrant (New York, 2000).

11. On the fate of the imperial family, see Iu.A. Buranov and V.M. Khrustalev, *Romanovy. Gibel' dinastii* (Moscow, 2000); and Mark Steinberg and Vladimir Khrustalev, *The Fall of the Romanovs* (New Haven, 1997). On contemporary Russian historiography on the Romanov dynasty, see A.Iu. Polunov, "Romanovy: mezhdu istoriei i ideologiei," in *Istoricheskie issledovaniia v Rossii: tendentsii poslednikh let*, ed. G.A. Bordiugov (Moscow, 1996), pp. 83–99.

12. Holland Hunter and Janusz M. Szyrmer, *Faulty Foundations: Soviet Economic Policies, 1928–1940* (Princeton, 1992). See also Mikhail Heller and Aleksandr Nekrich, *Utopia in Power: The History of the Soviet Union from 1917 to the Present* (New York, 1986), chaps. 7, 10.

Index

Nobility
bureaucratic restraint on, 23
in bureaucracy, 42–43
in conservative opposition, 235–236
counter-reform and, 186
education of, 66
Europeanization of, 16, 17
on juries, 120
Mongol invasion and, 6
Paul I's restrictions on, 19
in peasant reform planning, 96, 103–105
privileges of, 15–16, 17, 158
resistance to peasant reform, 34
service obligations of, 11–12, 15
Le Nord, 95
Northern Star, 94
Notes of the Fatherland, 59
Novgorod, 9
Novosiltsev, Nikolai, 21, 32

O

Obolensky, Dmitry, 118
Obolensky, Evgeny, 94, 98
Octobrists, 227, 230, 237, 243
Odoevsky, Vladimir, 56
"Official Nationality," 52–53, 59, 62, 72
Ogarev, Nikolai, 55
Okhrana, 218
Openness policy, 130
Opium wars, 163
Oprichnina lands, 8
Orlov, Aleksei, 85–86, 103
Orlov, Mikhail, 29, 86
Orthodox Church
Alexander III's policy on, 182–183
Alexander I's policy on, 35
Chaadaev on, 57
on enlightenment, 61–62
in Holy Land churches dispute, 83
in Kievan Rus, 4
Manifesto of October 17, 1905, 221
missionary activities of, 183
under Peter the Great, 15
in Turkish Empire, 72
Ottoman Empire. *See* Turkey
Ovsiannikov, S.T., 120

P

Panin, Viktor, 105
Passport system, 128, 132
Patriarchy, 182, 187, 200, 214

Paul I, 19
Pavlovna, Elena, 95
Pazukhin, Aleksandr, 186, 187, 188
Peace (arbitration) court, 118–119, 187
Peace of Paris of 1853, 85, 93, 160
Peasant Land Bank, 178, 231, 232
Peasant reform
under Alexander I, 21, 23, 27, 33
Alexander II's commitment to, 92
in Baltic region, 23, 33
cost of, 107
Crimean War defeat and, 86, 87, 89
in Decembrist program, 36–37
early stages of, 94
economic factor in, 93–94
emancipation proclamation, 105
impact on agriculture, 107–108
impact on economic development,
125–132
landed emancipation, 97–101
landowner opposition to, 23, 33–34
liberal historiography on, 90
negative features of, 106–107, 126–127
under Nicholas II, 200, 201–203, 222,
230–232, 234, 249
peasant factor in, 90, 92–93, 97
planning process, 95–105
preservation of commune in, 108–109
public opinion on, 105
Radishchev's call for, 16–17, 27
Soviet historiography on, 89–90
Westernizers' view of, 60–61
Peasants
allotments, 47–48, 107, 108
appanage, 97
counter-reform policy and, 181–182,
186–187, 188
courts, 108, 121, 126, 127, 187
crop yields, 127
on juries, 120
kulaks, 127
labor payments by, 126–127
land demands of, 225, 230–232
landholdings, 107, 126
in military, 93, 108
patriarchy preservation policy, 182, 187,
200
Populists' campaign among, 147–149
potato riots, 48
redemption payments of, 107, 126, 178,
222, 231

ABOUT THE AUTHOR

Alexander Polunov received his undergraduate and graduate training in history at Moscow State University, where he is now an associate professor in the School of Public Administration. He has been a visiting scholar at several academic institutions, including the Harriman Institute of Columbia University, the Kennan Institute for Advanced Russian Studies, Maison des sciences de l'homme in Paris, and Humboldt University in Berlin. He is the author of a monograph on the relationship between the tsarist government and the Russian Orthodox Church during the reign of Emperor Alexander III (1996).

ABOUT THE EDITORS

Thomas C. Owen has published four monographs on the social and economic history of the Russian Empire. His most recent book is *Dilemmas of Russian Capitalism: Fedor Chizhov and Corporate Enterprise in the Railroad Age* (Harvard University Press, 2005).

Larissa Zakharova, professor of history at Moscow State University, is the leading historian of the Great Reforms and their consequences. She has collaborated with American scholars in the writing and editing of three books: *Russia's Great Reforms* (Indiana University Press, 1994), *Reform in Modern Russian History: Progress or Cycle?* (Cambridge University Press, 1995), and *The Emperors and Empresses of Russia: Rediscovering the Romanovs* (M.E. Sharpe, 1996).

ABOUT THE TRANSLATOR

Marshall S. Shatz is Professor of History emeritus at the University of Massachusetts at Boston. His special interest is Russian intellectual history. He is the author of *Soviet Dissent in Historical Perspective* (Cambridge University Press, 1980), and *Jan Waclaw Machajski: A Radical Critic of the Russian Intelligentsia* (University of Pittsburgh Press, 1989). He translated and edited Michael Bakunin's *Statism and Anarchy* and V.O. Kliuchevsky's *A Course in Russian History: The Time of Catherine the Great* (M.E. Sharpe, 1997), and co-translated (with Judith E. Zimmerman) *Vekhi (Landmarks)* (M.E. Sharpe, 1994).

Printed in Great Britain
by Amazon

72764234R00173